The Theory and Practice of
Mental Health Consultation

THE THEORY AND PRACTICE OF MENTAL HEALTH CONSULTATION

Gerald Caplan

BASIC BOOKS, INC., PUBLISHERS

NEW YORK | LONDON

Second Printing

© 1970 by Basic Books, Inc.

Library of Congress Catalog Card Number: 77-103089

SBN 465-08450-8

Manufactured in the United States of America

Designed by Sophie Adler

I dedicate this book to the memory of my father, David Caplan. His rabbinical training and his warm interest in people enabled him to give wise counsel to many who were perplexed.

Foreword

STANLEY F. YOLLES, M.D.,
Director National Institute of Mental Health

The concept of a national mental health program—in which support from the federal government could supplement efforts of voluntary citizen's organizations, private foundations, treatment facilities, and the states—was first recognized by Congress with the passage of the Mental Health Act of 1946. Adoption of the statute made possible the initial organization of the National Institute of Mental Health. Through the NIMH, federal support of mental health programs has provided for the simultaneous development of mental health research, the training of mental health manpower, and the support of state and local programs to improve mental health services and resources.

In addition to establishing the NIMH, the Mental Health Act also authorized grants-in-aid to the states as an incentive to them to increase state support of mental health services. At that time, however, the public had not begun to accept the idea that a mentally ill person could be treated and his illness controlled outside a mental hospital.

During World War II, military medicine advanced the knowledge and use of a variety of short-term therapies; this experience provided a basis for further development of the concepts and practice of community psychiatry, even before the discovery and widespread use of psychoactive drugs.

Then, as treatment techniques improved in the 1950's and the use of psychoactive drugs demonstrated that mental illnesses in many cases could be controlled and alleviated, public attitudes began to change. There was a growing demand for additional public funds to provide better treatment for the mentally ill.

In 1955 the Health Amendments Act was adopted to provide funds to states to support demonstration projects in mental health services. These programs, although sharply limited, contributed to the development of community-based mental health services. However, the major congressional contribution in 1955 to the establishment of a national mental health program was the adoption of a resolution that made possible the organization of the Joint Commission on Mental Illness and Health to conduct the first nationwide survey and analysis of the extent of mental illness in the United States.

The Joint Commission published its final report, *Action for Mental Health,* in 1961. Its findings established the foundation upon which the national mental health program and the community mental health centers program are being developed.

To implement the Commission's findings Congress in 1963 adopted the Community Mental Health Centers Act, authorizing the appropriation of federal funds to support from one third to two thirds of the cost of constructing community mental health centers when applicants for federal grants qualified for federal support under terms of the statute.

In approving this legislation, however, Congress did much more than to appropriate federal funds to aid the development of a mental health services program. The intent of the statute was to locate the new mental health centers within the communities where patients and their families lived, rather than in the isolated and remote mental hospitals which had been the traditional locus of treatment of the mentally ill for more than a century.

As instructed by Congress, the Secretary of Health, Education, and Welfare established guidelines and regulations under which communities within the states could become eligible for federal construction grants to be administered by the National Institute of Mental Health. These regulations, in addition to establishing administrative procedures, translated new concepts into public policy.

The boundaries and composition of a community—in terms of the delivery of mental health services—were defined and drawn to serve the needs of people, rather than the traditions of geographical boundaries, political jurisdictions, and existing mental health facilities.

Of equal or greater importance was the establishment of the range of services required of each community mental health center. Five service components were established as "essential": inpatient services, partial hospitalization, outpatient services, emergency services, and consultation and education services.

With the inclusion of consultation and education services as essential under eligibility regulations of the Mental Health Centers Act, provision of preventive services became mandatory for the first time in a publicly supported mental health program.

As the events of the intervening years attest, the adoption of preventive services as a stated public policy not only added a new dimension to the mental health program; it set a new direction for all health programs in the United States. The Mental Health Centers Act brought prevention as a positive force (in contrast to a negation of illness) into the mental health service program; and with the adoption of the comprehensive health planning legislation of 1967, the federal government emphasized its intent to support community-based, comprehensive health care, to be developed in ways pioneered by mental health volunteers and professionals.

In those early months of planning community mental health services, it became increasingly apparent that a mental health program could not meet the needs of the people unless it worked to prevent mental illness and improve the mental health of populations as well as of individuals.

What was needed was for other helping professionals in the schools, the courts, the churches, and the social and welfare agencies within each community to have available to them the mental health consultation and education services they needed, in adapting what they considered to be their own primary functions in the community to the mental health needs of those people who came to them first for help in solving their problems.

As an objective, the notion of mental health consultation was founded on a degree of experience. Mental health professionals were accustomed to the concept of consultation, but in actual practice, consultations usually occurred when a nonpsychiatric physician consulted with a psychiatrist, or when a social worker, in search of referrals for a client, consulted with social workers in another health or welfare agency. The clergy—found by the Joint Commission to be the initial source to which many people turned for help in times of emotional crisis—was aware of the growing need for consultation, but not generally knowledgeable about resources available within the community.

For mental health professionals who staffed the first community mental health centers, the need to establish viable consultation services in the community became almost immediately evident once a center became operational. The mental health center staffs, in each community, set out to provide indirect help for the mentally ill by working with and, hopefully, influencing other "helping persons" in the community.

In *Theory and Practice of Mental Health Consultation,* Gerald Caplan presents the development of mental health consultation in the community setting. As Caplan states, this kind of consultation has developed "not as planning based on theory, but as a pragmatic reaction to demands." He describes the volume as a "current crystallization of work in progress."

No review of this volume can serve as a substitute for the book itself. As one of the first psychiatrists to teach and to practice community psychiatry, Caplan has a continuing, day-to-day professional involvement in the provision of mental health *treatment* services as they progress toward *preventive* services and—ideally—toward the provision of the entire range of *human* services which, of necessity, must be developed in modern American communities within the next ten years.

As he points out, mental health consultation is a way of communicating, not a new profession. It provides a way for a small number of mental health professionals to exert a widespread influence if those professionals understand consultation as the development of the shared concepts of the mental health center staff, projected toward immediate and distant goals, and based on the continuing process of collecting information about the community.

Caplan's definition of mental health consultation as a component of community mental health services is precise. His discussions of method are specific and expressly relevant to the practice of community psychiatry today. The chapter on training of mental health consultants is unique in the literature and of incalculable value to the professions.

In his introductory chapter, Caplan states as his aim that the whole area of interprofessional activity will become part of the *formal* lore of the mental health professions. He defines "interprofessional activity" in its broadest community sense and in so doing challenges the mental health professions to widen both their interests and their skills.

With Caplan, I am convinced that there is need for a process of progressive refinement of methodology in mental health consultation. Furthermore, there is an overriding need for the initiation of "evaluative studies of mental health consultation that will be frankly exploratory and that will aim for improvement of evaluation technology."

While such studies are being initiated, however, Caplan comments that he favors perseverance as mental health mediators between the community institution and the disadvantaged consumer. In this book, he provides the mental health professions with a map, a compass, and a vehicle with which mental health consultation services can arrive at their immediate objectives.

Preface

This book has been harder to write and has taken longer than any-thing else I have written. The first chapter was begun in 1963 and I finished the last chapter six months ago. Nor am I completely satisfied with the product—it is uneven in quality and it is not complete. There are several reasons for this. I think I know more about consultation than about other aspects of community psychiatry and, therefore, I am more aware of the vastness of my ignorance. My ideas and skills have been constantly developing, so that as soon as I have committed them to paper, I realize that other points should be added. Many of the topics are so involved that some chapters should really be books; they could easily become so if I included more case examples to illustrate my con-cepts and to define the provisos that in my own mind modify the princi-ples I put forward.

This is particularly true in regard to the chapter on consultee-centered administrative consultation. This and other parts of the book are written as though consultee organizations are stable institutions, but in our society many community agencies are in a state of tumultuous change—their structure, mission, administration, and staff are constantly in flux. This means that a consultant who operates solely along the lines I pro-pose in this book is likely to be ineffective. By the time he has pains-takingly built up his relationships, mapped the structure of the organiza-tion, and defined and delimited his role, his consultees may be on the point of leaving, and the newcomers will alter everything in an attempt to escape the fate of their predecessors. Moreover, organizations such as many of those that have recently emerged in the antipoverty and model cities fields are often staffed by people who have not had the opportunity for the systematic acquisition of traditional skills, which, in any case, might not be effective in these settings. Although these workers may ask a consultant to help them to struggle with the overwhelming difficulties they encounter, what they really need is not someone who will increase their capacity to do what they already know, but someone who will assist them to acquire new skills and who will meanwhile plug gaps by temporarily taking over essential tasks in supervision, planning, administration, and even line operations, until the staff can learn to accomplish these functions by themselves. They ask for a consultant, but they need someone who will combine consultation with straight-forward teaching, supervision, and collaboration—someone who will "pitch in and get his hands dirty." In another publication, I have recently discussed some of the issues involved in this kind of work in the Job Corps setting.[1]

This is an extreme example of the fact that, in practice, consultants will often be involved in situations that are less simple than those described in this book. I have found it very difficult to isolate issues and to define them with enough clarity to derive and communicate basic principles of technique without "purifying" them to the point of unreality. I hope that my readers will take this difficulty in exposition into account when they try to implement my ideas in real life. My book is intended as a general guide rather than as a "cook book" of exact prescriptions for action.

This book is the second of the trilogy I envisaged in my preface to *Principles of Preventive Psychiatry*.[2] The third volume will be devoted to problems of community practice in the mental health field. It will deal with issues such as those I have briefly discussed in Chapters 3 and 14. About some of them (Chapter 3), we already have a considerable body of information and experience, which merely awaits detailed formulation. The other topics represent a vast area, largely unexplored by mental health workers, and this is where I hope to work during the next few years.

ACKNOWLEDGMENTS

Many colleagues have actively contributed to the work upon which this book has been based, and it is a pleasure to acknowledge the help given to me by the following:

Jona M. Rosenfeld, Shlomit Hock, Frances Ackerman, and the other colleagues who worked with me at the Lasker Mental Hygiene and Child Guidance Center of Hadassah in Jerusalem from 1949 to 1952. Erich Lindemann, Elizabeth B. Lindemann, Donald C. Klein, and my other colleagues at the Wellesley Human Relations Service, 1952 to 1956. My fellow workers on the staff of the Harvard School of Public Health Family Guidance Center at Whittier Street, Boston, during the period 1955–1960, many of whom subsequently continued their mental health consultation studies within the framework of the Division of Mental Health of Harvard School of Public Health until 1964 and, after that, at the Laboratory of Community Psychiatry, Department of Psychiatry, Harvard Medical School. Among these I am particularly indebted to Charlotte E. Owens and Louisa P. Howe. Miss Owens was the coordinator and senior supervisor of our mental health consultation service. Dr. Howe was responsible for organizing the data collection and analysis in our evaluation study. Most of the tables in Chapter 12 were compiled by her. Hanna R. Fonseca and Marlene Hindley helped me prepare the bibliography. The Commonwealth Fund provided the financing for our consultation researches at Whittier Street, and our subsequent budget has been largely defrayed by the National Institute of Mental Health, Grants #MH 03442 and #MH 09214. A grant from the W. Clement and Jessie V. Stone Foundation has helped me complete the writing of this book, and to them and our other sponsors I wish to express my most sincere appreciation.

GERALD CAPLAN

Cambridge
November 1969

NOTES

1. Gerald Caplan, Lee B. Macht, and Arlene B. Wolf, *Manual for Mental Health Professionals Participating in the Job Corps Program.* (Washington, D.C.: Office of Economic Opportunity, May 1969), Document #JCH 330–A.
2. Gerald Caplan, *Principles of Preventive Psychiatry* (New York: Basic Books, 1964).

Contents

1   Introduction   3

2   Definition of Mental Health Consultation   19

3   Developing a Consultation Program in a Community   35

4   Building Relationships with a Consultee Institution   48

5   Building the Relationship with the Consultee   80

6   Client-Centered Case Consultation   109

7   Consultee-Centered Case Consultation   125

8   Techniques of Theme Interference Reduction   151

9   An Example of Consultee-Centered Case Consultation   191

10 Program-Centered Administrative Consultation   223

11 Consultee-Centered Administrative Consultation   265

12 Evaluation   294

13 Training in Mental Health Consultation   330

14 Mental Health Consultation and Community Action   353

    BIBLIOGRAPHY   382

    INDEX   395

The Theory and Practice of
Mental Health Consultation

[1]

Introduction

An outstanding challenge which today faces mental health specialists is connected with our realization that the number of actual or potential mentally disordered persons in the population exceeds our current capacity for direct remedial action. It is so large that we have little hope, even in the distant future, of being able to master the situation by significantly adding to our ranks through increased recruitment and training of specialized workers. The manpower pool from which we draw mental health specialists is already being drained to its maximum capacity. The growth of population in this country will inevitably lead to an increase in the numbers of the mentally ill, while at the same time our continued technological process entails increasing demands for other scientific and technical workers who will necessarily be drawn from the same manpower pool.[1]

We must conclude that in the future, possibly more than in the present, a considerable proportion of the mentally disordered will be dealt with by professional and nonprofessional persons who will have no specialized training in psychiatry and its allied disciplines. This opinion is to be considered in the light of the findings of a number of recent researches,[2] which show that only 10 to 20 per cent of those persons in the community who can be broadly categorized as mentally disordered are being dealt with by a psychiatric agency or have any direct contact with a mental health specialist.

Until about ten years ago most psychiatrists interested themselves solely in those persons who by a variety of chances entered the confines of their offices, clinics, or hospitals; and the fate of other community members was only dimly perceived to be a significant area of responsibility for mental health specialists. In recent years, however, the isolation of the psychiatrists from the community, partly imposed by the exclusion of some along with their psychotic patients in distant mental hospitals, and partly preferred by others because of the restriction of their focus to the intrapersonal depth-psychological aspects of their neurotic patients, has been rapidly breaking down. The mental hospitals are being brought closer and "opened up," psychiatric clinics and inpatient departments are appearing in general hospitals, and more and more psychiatrists are working in a variety of specialized mental health units which are being added to those community agencies in the health, welfare, and educational fields that have always maintained close contact with their surrounding populations.

This development has been accelerated by the changes in public policies heralded by President Kennedy's 1963 message to Congress on mental health and mental retardation, and by the consequent federal legislation, P. L. 88–164, the Community Mental Health Centers Act of 1963. By the end of 1970 about five hundred community mental health centers will have been funded by the National Institute of Mental Health, and it is projected that two thousand centers will be funded by 1980.* In all these centers, and in many others financed by state government and by voluntary and private funds, mental health consultation provided by psychiatrists, psychologists, psychiatric social workers, and psychiatric nurses to community caregivers is one of the obligatory basic services. This has resulted in a vast increase in the regular contacts of mental health specialists with members of other professions.

Within this changing professional situation, the psychiatrist and his mental health specialist colleagues are now becoming increasingly concerned about the fact that they are seeing only a minority of the cases which their professions have been specially designed to handle. The remainder are for better or for worse being dealt with by such community caregivers as general practitioners, lawyers, clergymen, teachers, welfare workers, nurses, and policemen.

The significance of this is not restricted to the regretful realization that we mental health specialists are not making as big a contribution to the welfare of our mentally disordered fellow citizens as we might ideally wish, in consequence of the realistic limitations of our professional numbers. It also includes a concern that those mentally disordered whom we do not see may not merely be missing the specialist therapies that we might have offered them but that the ministrations of our professional colleagues who lack specialized training in our subject may sometimes be doing them more harm than good. The same applies to an even greater degree in those numerous other cases in which the disordered

* Memo from the Director, NIMH, December 1968, fact sheet, Public Health Service, Health Services and Mental Health Administration, National Institute of Mental Health, Chevy Chase, Maryland.

person is dealt with entirely by his family, friends, and neighbors and is unable to obtain professional help of any kind.

It may be that this fear of harm is exaggerated. In fact, we have little scientific evidence to prove that mental health specialists and psychiatric clinics and hospitals are more helpful to the mentally disordered than other professionals and nonprofessionals. Indeed, we have reason to believe that the ubiquitous picture of the withdrawn and deteriorated chronic psychotic has been the result mainly of his incarceration and isolation in our mental hospitals, and not of his underlying illness. Psychiatry has, however, begun to learn from the mistakes of its past; and as a structured professional group we do have a developing culture and a ready means of communication within our own ranks so that we may improve on the basis of such findings. Moreover, we have reason to believe that isolation and interpersonal deprivation are not confined to the back wards of mental hospitals. They may occur "spontaneously" also in the general community, especially in metropolitan areas, and they may occur in general hospitals, nursing homes, child care institutions, and prisons, in all of which there are inmates who are actually or potentially mentally disordered.

It appears that although interpersonal influences may be only part of a multifactorial complex of pathogenic forces, biological, psychosocial, and sociocultural, which lead to mental disorder, they are probably significant in almost every case of established disorder in molding its course and in determining its outcome. This is most dramatically shown in the chronic psychotics who are the products of mental hospital back wards, but it can also be seen in many lesser instances, some of which are of a positive nature. For example, we have reason to believe that involvement in productive personal interaction retards the development of social incapacity in aged or arteriosclerotic persons; that brain damaged or congenitally retarded children can be significantly helped to improve their functioning by appropriate interpersonal stimulation; and that soldiers with battle neuroses can be rapidly rehabilitated if they are kept in their units and given appropriate social support.

Such thinking leads mental health specialists to interest themselves in what goes on in the interactions between the mentally disordered and those persons to whom they turn for help, or who intervene in their lives because of disorders of behavior. Since the numbers involved do not permit the mental health specialist to intervene directly with more than a minority of the disordered, the obvious alternative is to see whether he can help the latter indirectly by exerting an influence on the helping persons.

In fact, contacts between mental health specialists and other caregiving professionals and nonprofessional helping persons in the community have been rapidly increasing over the past twenty years. This has been partly because the psychiatrists are now more visible and more accessible than they were when they were shut off in their distant mental hospitals or in their psychoanalytic offices. It is partly due to the general education of the professional and lay public in mental health matters as a consequence of the earlier mental hygiene and child guidance movements and of our current push toward community psychiatry.[3] This has undoubtedly stimulated the expectation among many caregiving professionals that psychiatrists and other mental health specialists may be able to help them deal with the ever-present problems of handling their mentally disordered clients. It has also influenced community leaders to provide the financial resources to pay for such help from public funds.

Some mental health specialists have entertained greater ambitions than that of helping nonspecialist colleagues in the more effective management of the mentally disordered. They have attempted to use this type of interaction in order *to prevent* mental disorders in clients of the caregiving professionals. They have based this approach on the assumption that some mental disorders may be the result of an unhealthy adjustment to life's hazards, and upon the belief that caregiving professionals, such as doctors, nurses, and clergymen, who minister to persons during life crises, have the power to influence their clients to choose effective responses to their difficulties which will in turn increase their resistance to future mental disorder. They have therefore tried to help these colleagues learn how to be active agents for the promotion of positive crisis coping.[4]

These, and various other factors, have led to a great increase in the interactions between mental health specialists and community caregiving professionals over the past few years; but what, if any, mental health benefit has accrued to the population is hard to determine. The specialized knowledge of the mental health professions was traditionally developed to clarify issues that were relevant within their professional frameworks. The formulations about mental health and mental disorders and about the causes and manifestations of human behavior, as well as the techniques for remedying disorders defined as psychiatric, were developed in relation to the specialized roles and institutions in which the psychiatrists and their clinical colleagues worked. How many of these formulations and therapeutic techniques are applicable within the work situations of other professions and are in consonance with their different professional subcultures is hard to say. This difficulty is compounded by the fact that by the time a mental health clinician has completed his professional training and has internalized the values and conceptual patterns of his specialty he usually comes to feel that his ways of thinking and talking are "natural." He forgets how much time and effort it took him to learn to abstract from external and internal reality the artificially defined perceptions of his professional group, and he imagines that his ideas are generally applicable. He is therefore usually unaware that in his contacts with members of another profession there is the danger that by influencing them to accept his way of looking at things he may upset their systematic ordering of knowledge and behavior and may hamper their professional effectiveness.

Be that as it may, it is likely that some mental health specialists have sometimes helped members of other professions care for their mentally disordered clients and even engage in preventive work. At other times they have probably failed to achieve any significant goal. Other mental health specialists may not have done as well. Unfortunately, not only the content of the communications but also the details of the interactive process—that is, how the communications are made—are left to the informal predilection and natural style of each specialist. They have not been defined and regularized as a formal professional activity with defined goals, methods, and techniques. There has been no way of recording, comparing, and evaluating what different people have done, or of knowing why a particular specialist appears to have succeeded in one situation and not in another.

This book is one attempt to improve this state of affairs. Its contribution lies in defining as consultation one type of activity that commonly takes place when mental health specialists interact with caregiving professionals, and in differentiating these operations from other forms of professional interaction. Not only are the boundaries and goals of consultation defined, but its techniques are also described and categorized so that they can be taught and learned and so that they can be recorded, evaluated, and improved. In other words, an attempt is being made to formalize and professionalize certain aspects of the functioning of the mental health specialist that have till now been largely informal. These aspects are becoming an increasingly important part of his operations—quantitatively, because they are engaging a greater proportion of his time; and qualitatively, because they may afford him the opportunity to deal indirectly through the intermediation of other professionals and nonprofessional caregivers with that large group of actual and potential mentally disordered persons which his profession will probably never be able to handle by direct contact.

It is important to emphasize that in singling out one type of professional interaction, consultation, for special treatment in this book, I have no intention of belittling the importance of other types of interaction, such as education, collaboration, and coordination. It is hoped that these will in the future also be carefully defined, described, and evaluated, so that this whole area of interprofessional activity will become part of the formal lore of the mental health professions.

BACKGROUND

My interest in mental health consultation was stimulated as far back as 1949 when I was working at the Lasker Mental Hygiene and Child Guidance Center of Hadassah in Jerusalem, Israel. Part of our duties included the supervision of the mental health of about sixteen thousand new-immigrant children in the Youth Aliyah organization. These children, aged fourteen to eighteen, were cared for in over a hundred residential institutions, mainly situated in the communal settlements up and down the country and staffed by nonprofessional child care workers and educators. We had a small team of psychologists and social workers; and with these we were expected to diagnose and treat those children who were emotionally disturbed but whose condition was not so bad that they had to be removed from the regular educational setting. We rapidly discovered that this was an impossible task if we operated along traditional lines of accepting referrals and carrying out diagnostic investigations on individual children. During our first year we had about a thousand referrals, and however fast we worked we could never keep up with the demand, because the children stayed in the organization only two or three years; and the incoming population of children, separated from their parents and confronting the stresses and challenges of adapting to a complex new culture, was heavily weighted with emotional disturbance. We had to deploy most of our staff on the tasks of diagnosis and report writing, and we did not have the time to do anything therapeutically constructive for more than a tiny proportion of the children we saw.

Transportation difficulties in Israel at the time were such that it was sometimes more feasible to send a staff member out to an institution to investigate a batch of referrals than to bring the children in to one of our central clinics. Since we could not provide psychotherapy for the disturbed children, our psychologists began informally to discuss with the staff of the institution possibilities of local management that might reduce the pressure on the children or support them in working through their problems themselves. Little by little, the demands of the instructors and housemothers forced us to increase the amount of time we spent talking to them about the children we were seeing. We discovered that in many instances children were referred who did not appear to be mentally ill. The problem seemed rather that they were getting on the adults' nerves.

We found that many instructors and institutions appeared to have special difficulties with children of certain types. Thus, although the population of immigrant children was fairly randomly distributed among the different institutions and did not appear to vary much in its composition from one to another, we began to notice that one institution was continually referring bedwetters, while another was referring children with learning difficulties, and a third was plagued by aggressive children. If we asked the staff of the first institution whether they had children with learning or aggression problems, the typical reply was "Of course! How could one expect that children who have been brought up in the slums of Casablanca and have never been to school would not have difficulty adjusting to sitting on a school bench at the age of fifteen and would not let off steam by occasional violent outbursts?" Similarly, if we asked the staff of the other institutions whether any of their children wet the bed, we were told that this was a normal and predictable reaction of children made miserable by separation from their parents and families.

These were some of the experiences that influenced us to change fundamentally our ways of working. Apart from exceptional cases, we began to deploy our staff in what we then called "counseling" the instructors instead of investigating and reporting on the children. We concentrated on an instructor's perception of his pupil and tried to help him deal with the child's problem as he saw it. We altered the balance of our operations and began to spend most of our time in discussing, not the diagnostic classification of the child, but the various management possibilities that were available to the instructor.

A number of interesting findings began to emerge. We discovered that in many cases an instructor would be at his wit's end with a child and seemed to have developed an unduly narrow perspective on action alternatives. After a sympathetic and objective discussion, his range of alternatives seemed to widen, and he improved his chance of finding something that would work. Second, we were impressed by gross disorders of perception of the children revealed in the reports of many of their instructors. We began to talk of their "stereotyped perceptions" and to see as an important goal of our counseling the undoing or dissipating of these stereotypes. This proved relatively easy to accomplish by means of a discussion in which the psychologist introduced his own observations of the child as a human being in difficulties rather than as a "problem child." The dissipation of the instructor's stereotype of the child usually led to a dramatic change in the instructor's attitude and a consequent improvement in his management of the case.

The third significant finding was that some of the instructors who called upon us for help seemed quite upset themselves. They had become intensely emotionally involved with a problem child, and the stereotyping and narrowing of focus appeared to be symptoms of an emotional crisis in the instructor. He ascribed this to the child's behavior and his own inability to cope with it: but at times it appeared to us to be also related to other difficulties in the instructor's personal life or in the social system of his institution. At first our workers felt rather uncomfortable in these situations; but soon we found that our best results seemed to occur in those cases in which the instructors were most upset. In fact, we began to develop a system of priorities for consultation that was geared to choosing cases in which the instructors seemed to be in the most intense crisis. In this way we felt we could use our limited staff to best advantage.

In looking back on this early work, it is of interest to note that we did not choose to deal with the personal involvement of the instructors by techniques of uncovering psychotherapy which would have confronted them with the fact that they were displacing onto the child problems in themselves and their institution and then would have helped them work directly on these problems. This approach might have come most naturally to a psychoanalytic psychiatrist, but it was prevented in my own case by several factors. First, we were at that time engaged on some interesting research in the well-baby clinics of Jerusalem. We are trying to prevent emotional disorder in infants by identifying and remedying disorders of the mother-infant relationship. We were developing methods of focused casework, whereby we "unlinked" the mother's personal disturbance from its displacement onto her new baby. Our idea was that this might be accomplished in a few therapeutic sessions if we kept the focus of our interviews on material connected with the mother-child relationship and prevented the discussions from veering over into an examination of the mother's nonmaternal problems. We found that we could, in fact, do this by using the mother's perceptions of her baby and her feelings about it as the manifest content of our interviews.[5]

Our aim was to develop a method in which we could achieve the limited goal of preventing the mother's problems from invading her relationship with her new baby, or of reversing this process if it had already started, and of doing this in a short series of interviews. In this way, we could prevent the difficulty for the infants and not be forced to commit major staff resources to the protracted task of treating the neurotic problems of the mothers.

The counseling of instructors about their relationships with their pupils seemed to us very similar to this preventive work with mothers and babies, and we began to use a similar, carefully focused interviewing technique.

The second factor was that the directors of Youth Aliyah were watching our novel methods with some suspicion. They were paying for the treatment of the children under their care, and they were quite wary of our switch of focus to the instructors. They required continual assurance that the welfare of the children was our primary goal. Moreover, they had little administrative authority over the instructors, who were mainly volunteers from the communal settlements and were not employed directly by Youth Aliyah. The directors of that organization were therefore quite sensitive to anything that might interfere with the instructors' comfort and motivation to collaborate. They did not want us to upset the instructors by turning them into patients. In this connection, it is worthy of mention that after I left Israel, the staff of the Lasker Center gradually changed the emphasis in their counseling approach to the instructors and began more and more openly to focus directly on their personal problems and on the complications of social system issues in their institutions. This aroused increasing resistance, and eventually the whole counseling program fell into disrepute and was terminated.

I had one other reason for avoiding the uncovering approach in the counseling of the instructors, which seems rather strange in retrospect. My team was composed of the best psychologists and social workers I could recruit at that time in Israel; and most of these were talented and sensitive individuals, but on the whole they had not had much training in psychotherapy. I did not feel I could rely on them to manage the psychotherapeutic complications they would be likely to encounter if they used uncovering techniques. I felt it would be safer if they adopted an ego-supportive approach. Looking back, I believe this was a valid point; but nowadays I realize that the intricacies of mental health consultation technique make more, and not less, of a demand on psychotherapeutic sophistication and skill than traditional uncovering techniques. On the other hand, I still believe that with unskilled workers consultation is likely to do less harm than insight psychotherapy. The worst that will usually happen with unskilled consultation is that it will do no good.

Before leaving this brief discussion of our Israeli experience I want to emphasize one other issue. Because of the chance nature of the situation, we conducted most of our consultation in the institutions and not in our central offices. We rapidly discovered that this was most important. We could quickly pick up much more relevant information about the field of forces by actually going into the institutions. Also, the instructors felt more free to give an authentic account of their perceptions of the case on their home ground than they could have in the strange milieu of our clinical setting. I believe this aspect of our Israeli program has exerted an important formative influence on the style of operation of later mental health consultation programs.

In 1952 I came to Boston and began my work at Harvard School of Public Health, which continued till 1964, when I transferred to Harvard Medical School. During the first few years I collaborated closely with Erich Lindemann in his preventive psychiatry program at the Wellesley Human Relations Service. The work of Lindemann and his colleagues exerted a considerable influence on my thinking and on the pattern of development of what I began to call "mental health consultation" rather than "counseling," in order to differentiate it from the method of personal therapy developed by Carl Rogers.

By the time I joined them, Lindemann and his team had worked out a consultation method that was essentially the same as our Israeli counseling. Interestingly enough, they had also moved into this approach, not as a result of planning based on theory, but as a pragmatic reaction to the demands of their field. The Wellesley group had been interested in developing methods of observing and analyzing the behavior of children in the classroom situation as an objective way of screening a school population for disturbed children. Accordingly, their psychologists had obtained permission to sit at the back of the classrooms in the Wellesley schools and record the behavior of the students. After a short time the researchers began to be inconvenienced by the teachers' engaging them in conversation about their observations, before they felt they had anything scientifically valid to report. Nevertheless, as guests in the schools, they felt obliged to be polite to their hosts. Little by little, they discovered that these talks with the teachers seemed to have meaning in their own right. The teachers, on their side, found these informal chats of value in increasing their understanding of problem children.

Before long, what had originally been a side issue, and even an interference with the work of the researchers, became a formally recognized collaborative effort between the Wellesley School System and the Human Relations Service. Shortly after I arrived, a contract was signed to provide consultation on a systematic basis to the schoolteachers. This service continues to the present. I believe it is the oldest existing mental health consultation contract between a school system and an outside mental health agency.

To this day, the Wellesley consultation program bears the imprint of its origin, in that much use is made of classroom observation by the consultant as a basis for the discussions with the teachers. The Wellesley consultants have learned to rely on their own observation of the behavior of the problem child in the classroom in order to identify disordered perceptions in the teacher's story about her student. They also use the opportunity for joint observation of the child by themselves and the teachers to help the latter modify their unrealistic perceptions. This technique is similar to the "dissipation of the stereotype" that we worked out in Israel, which in turn was along the same lines as the "unlinking" technique of our focused casework in the Jerusalem well-baby clinics. Unfortunately, as we eventually discovered in Jerusalem, this "unlinking" of the mother's problems from the displacement onto the infant, although it lowers the tension in the mother-child relationship, rarely leads to stable benefit. The mother's basic problems are not improved by the "unlinking." She usually merely exchanges the displacement onto the infant for some other displacement within the family circle.

A similar process takes place if this technique is used in consultation; and nowadays "unlinking" is regarded by us as a major technical error, even though the consultee feels relieved and his current client may benefit. We will discuss this further in Chapter 7, at which time we will examine the ways we have developed in recent years with which to deal with the difficulty. The continuation of classroom observation at Wellesley as an expected and integral part of most consultations with schoolteachers, however, makes "unlinking" a particular hazard in that program.

There was a significant difference between the consultation with schoolteachers in Wellesley and the counseling of instructors in Israel, of which I was not conscious at the time, although it exerted an important influence on the development of our methodological thinking. The Wellesley schoolteachers were fellow professionals. The Youth Aliyah instructors were nonprofessionals. They were mostly volunteers from the general membership of the communal settlements. They usually had little, if any, training beyond that of a counselor in a youth movement. After a two-year "tour of operations" in the Youth Aliyah group, they returned to their work in agriculture or in some other aspect of the settlement economy. In many respects they resembled our present-day Peace Corps and Vista volunteers.

In those early years we did not pay much attention to analyzing the details of the consultant-consultee relationship; but in retrospect it seems hardly likely that a true coordinate relationship was possible between these nonprofessionals and the professional "experts" who were sent from our head office in Jerusalem to give a specialist's opinion on their students. To be sure, the specialists were not in fact very expert. They were about as youthful as the instructors, and they were very well aware of their own immaturity and lack of professional training. Moreover, interpersonal relationships in Israel in those early days of the state were, in general, egalitarian.

In any case, it may be significant that the emphasis on the nonhierarchical or coordinate relationship between consultant and consultee, which became a cornerstone of consultation theory and practice, came into focus only after consultation became a method used by one professional with another. Nowadays, it seems as though the wheel is turning full circle. There is much talk in mental health quarters of using nonprofessionals in local community mental health programs. It may not be long before psychiatrists will routinely be offering consultation to some of these indigenous caregivers. A situation similar to that in Youth Aliyah may thus develop, and it will be interesting to see what modifications in the technique of mental health consultation, as described in this book, will be necessitated by the differences between interprofessional and professional-nonprofessional relationships.

In 1954 I was asked to set up a mental health segment in the Field Training Unit of the Harvard School of Public Health at the Whittier Street Health Center of the City of Boston Health Department. This quickly led to the establishment of the Whittier Street Family Guidance Center, which continued its research and training operations until 1962, financed during its first five years by the Commonwealth Fund and later by the National Institute of Mental Health. During most of this period it was the locus of an intensive study of mental health consultation with public health nurses. The choice of this professional group as consultees was influenced by our interest in developing a collaborative relationship with public health workers as a focal point of our community mental health program at Harvard School of Public Health, and by the fact that at Whittier Street, and later in the extension of our program throughout the City Health Department, the nurses were the line workers who were most keen to collaborate with us. Working with public health nurses also had particular meaning in the light of the theoretical framework of preventive psychiatry that we were developing in cooperation with the Lindemann group at Wellesley. This emphasized the significance of periods of life crisis as turning points in psychological development, and the importance of the intervention of caregiving * professionals. Lindemann's studies of bereavement led him to work with clergymen in order to help them intervene preventively with the widowed so as to ensure their healthy traversal of their mourning crisis. In Wellesley, this approach was extended to collaboration between the mental health workers and the whole range of community professionals. Consultation with schoolteachers fitted neatly into this program.

Similarly, our consultation with public health nurses took on a primary prevention focus. These workers are in the front line in regard to contact with a particularly vulnerable lower socioeconomic class population, with whom they have close and continuing relationships. They visit their patients in their homes during such periods of life crisis as those occasioned by childbirth, especially the birth of premature or congenitally deformed babies; infectious disease, especially tuberculosis; and the disorders of old age. We began to see the role of our consultation program as providing support and guidance to the nurses so that in their everyday work with their patients they would promote healthy coping with life crises and thus reduce the risk of mental disorder in a widespread population.

For a period, our developing method was called "crisis consultation." Two crises were involved, the crisis in the client and the crisis in the consultee. As we gained more experience, we realized that many nurses came to us for consultation help with patients who were not currently in crisis but who presented management problems because of personality difficulties or frank mental disorder; and we began to realize the potential value of mental health consultation as a method of secondary and tertiary prevention of mental disorder.[6] We also discovered that only a small proportion of consultees were themselves in manifest crisis; and the refinement of our observations on this point led us to our formulations on "theme interference" in consultees—namely, idiosyncratic sensitivities which led to subjective interference with professional functioning and a range of possible degrees of psychological disequilibrium, of which a crisis or major upset was an extreme example.

The program at the Whittier Street Health Center, and later in the rest of the City of Boston Health Department, provided us with an excellent opportunity to work systematically on the development and refinement of our consultation method. Eventually, we set up a formal research project to evaluate the main technique that had emerged from

---

* Erich Lindemann uses the term "caretakers," but I prefer "caregivers" because it implies a less passive role for the recipient of care.

these explorations—"theme interference reduction." An account of this evaluative study is contained in Chapter 12.

The demands of this research exerted a circumscribing effort on our explorations of the consultation method during the period 1958–1962. All our efforts at Whittier Street were concentrated on individual consultation with public health nurses of the City of Boston Health Department; and eventually we restricted our practice to the one technique of theme interference reduction, which we were evaluating. Each professional category of consultees presents idiosyncratic problems. We rapidly became aware in Whittier Street of the difference between consulting with schoolteachers, with whom we had previously been accustomed to work, and offering consultation to public health nurses. These differences were linked with the different nature of the tasks and culture of the two professions, and especially with the different relationship of nurses and teachers with their supervisors.

A wider experience was also available to us through our link with the Division of Mental Hygiene of the Commonwealth of Massachusetts Department of Mental Health. This division was established as far back as 1922 by Douglas Thom in order to operate preventively oriented community clinics. They were originally called habit clinics by Thom, who felt that serious disorders in children could be prevented if their habits (or, in our modern terms, problem-solving and coping methods) could be improved. In 1952 Warren Vaughan, a psychiatrist from Lindemann's team in Wellesley, was appointed by Commissioner of Mental Health Jack Ewalt to direct the Division of Mental Hygiene. He embarked on a pioneering program of extending the Wellesley ideas throughout the state by opening a series of local community mental health centers which emphasized community organization, mental health education, and mental health consultation to caregiving professionals. In 1959 he was succeeded by Bellenden R. Hutcheson, and between them these two psychiatrists succeeded in raising the number of local community mental health centers in Massachusetts from nine to thirty-seven. Each of these centers was committed to a preventive approach and was administered in a partnership between the Division of Mental Hygiene and a local citizen voluntary association. Each center allotted a significant proportion of its staff time to mental health consultation in the schools, hospitals, courts, public health units, welfare departments, and child care institutions; as well as with clergymen, physicians, lawyers, policemen, and other professionals in the community. In 1968 Massachusetts adopted a new community-oriented legislative program, and the child-focused clinics began to be integrated into local comprehensive community mental health services.

Since 1954 I have been a senior consultant to this program and have been responsible for training the Division of Mental Hygiene staff who operate as mental health consultants out of the local centers. Over the years many of the senior staff of these centers—psychiatrists, psychologists, social workers, and nurses—passed through the two-year sequence of weekly seminars that I organized for them at Harvard School of Public Health. The first six months of these seminars were spent in my communicating to these field workers the current thinking on the theory and practice of mental health consultation developed by our Whittier Street group of researchers. The following eighteen months were spent in discussing case examples brought in from their daily work by the seminar members. These seminars, therefore, contributed an immense volume of data on the applicability of ideas drawn from our research to the real-life situation of a community clinic, and also on the variety of patterns of consultation which are molded by the demands of different settings and professions.

The extensive range of themes discussed in these seminars has served to broaden the base of the present book, as has my own increasing experience as an administrative consultant in many parts of the United States and overseas. Since the termination in 1962 of our evaluative research program on theme interference reduction with public health nurses, and since we moved in 1964 from Harvard School of Public Health to an expanded teaching and research program in the Laboratory of Community Psychiatry of the Department of Psychiatry at Harvard Medical School, our consultation experience has considerably broadened and diversified. We have done much more group consultation, both with a case focus and an administrative focus; and we have offered consultation to school systems, the Job Corps, and other antipoverty programs, welfare agencies, public health units, religious organizations, rehabilitation agencies, army units, and general hospitals. Despite this range of experience, the consultation field is so vast that I cannot claim that my present ideas represent more than a preliminary attempt at delineating a significant part of it. This book is presented, not as a definitive statement, but as a current crystallization of work in progress. Its contents have been molded by all the collaborators I have mentioned, particularly my colleagues in Israel, at Wellesley, at Harvard School of Public Health, at Harvard Medical School, and in the Commonwealth of Massachusetts Department of Mental Health; and also by my readings about the work of such pioneers as Jules Coleman, James Maddux, and Irving Berlin, whose contributions together with those of consultants from a number of allied fields are listed in the bibliography appended to this book.

NOTES

1. G. W. Albee, *Mental Health Manpower Trends* (New York: Basic Books, 1959).

2. G. Gurin, J. Veroff, and S. Feld, *Americans View Their Mental Health* (New York: Basic Books, 1960); L. Srole, T. S. Langner, and S. T. Michael *et al., Mental Health in the Metropolis,* Vol. I (New York: McGraw-Hill, 1962); W. J. Ryan, "Distress in the City," Summary Report of the Boston Mental Health Survey, 1960–1962, published in pamphlet by the Massachusetts Association for Mental Health in conjunction with United Community Services of Boston.

3. G. Caplan and R. Caplan, "Development of Community Psychiatry Concepts." Chapter 45 of A. M. Freedman and H. I. Kaplan (eds.), *Comprehensive Textbook of Psychiatry* (Baltimore: Williams and Wilkins, 1967), I, 1499–1520.

4. G. Caplan, *Principles of Preventive Psychiatry* (New York: Basic Books, 1964).

5. G. Caplan, "A Public Health Approach to Child Psychiatry," *Mental Hygiene, 35,* 235, April 1951.

6. For a full discussion of this, see G. Caplan, *Principles of Preventive Psychiatry.*

[2]

Definition of Mental Health Consultation

The term "consultation" is used in many different ways. By some it is applied to almost any professional activity carried out by a specialist— in England the professional office of a specialist physician is known as his "consulting room," and when he is interviewing or treating a patient, his secretary says "he is in consultation." Others use the term to denote specialized professional activity between two persons in regard to a third—thus two physicians "consult" about a patient, or a physician "consults" with a mother about her child. Some restrict the term to professional activity carried out by a highly trained person—a "consultant" —but without delimiting the activity or differentiating "consultation" from other functions of the "consultant."

In this book the term "consultation" is used in a quite restricted sense to denote a process of interaction between two professional persons— the consultant, who is a specialist, and the consultee, who invokes the consultant's help in regard to a current work problem with which he is having some difficulty and which he has decided is within the other's area of specialized competence. The work problem involves the management or treatment of one or more clients * of the consultee, or the planning or implementation of a program to cater to such clients.

The definition of consultation is further restricted to that type of professional interaction in which the consultant accepts no direct responsibility for implementing remedial action for the client, and in which professional responsibility for the client remains with the consultee just as

* The term "client" is used to denote the lay person who is the focus of the consultee's professional operations, such as a teacher's student, a nurse or physician's patient, a clergyman's congregant or a lawyer's client.

much as it did before he asked the consultant for help. The consultant may offer helpful clarifications, diagnostic formulations, or advice on treatment; but the consultee will be free to accept or reject all or part of this help. In other words, the consultant exercises no administrative or coercive authority over the consultee; and unless the latter completely implements his prescriptions, the consultant is not to be held liable for the outcome in respect to the client.

Another essential aspect of this type of consultation is that the consultant engages in the activity not only in order to help the consultee with his current work problem in relation to a specific client or program but also in order to add to the consultee's knowledge and to lessen areas of misunderstanding, so that he may be able in the future to deal more effectively on his own with this category of problem. It is this educational aspect of consultation that makes it a community method, since its goal is to spread the application of the specialist's knowledge through the future operations of those who have consulted him in relation to current problems.

The above definition applies not only to a single consultant dealing with one consultee but equally to one consultant and a group of consultees, or a group of consultants and a single consultee or group of consultees.

In defining consultation in this narrow way there is no implication that this is the "correct" usage of the term and that other authorities are "wrong" in their different use of it; but, on the contrary, there is the intention to recognize that confusion exists because so many workers legitimately use the term in so many different ways, and the desire to single out one among the various activities of a specialist for particular study and evaluation.

What has been written so far refers to consultation as a generic form of specialized professional activity. By the term "mental health consultation" we designate the use of this method as part of a community program for the promotion of mental health and for the prevention, treatment, and rehabilitation of mental disorders. In this case, the consultants are those with a specialized knowledge of the issues involved—psychiatrists, psychologists, psychiatric social workers, social scientists, mental health nurses, and psychiatric nurses. The consultees are drawn from the ranks of those caregiving professionals, who, as mentioned previously, play a major role in preventing or treating mental disorders but who customarily have no specialized training in psychiatry and its allied disciplines. They include family doctors, pediatricians, and other medical specialists such as obstetricians, internists, and surgeons, hospital and public health nurses, teachers, clergymen, lawyers, welfare workers, probation officers, and policemen. Although the primary role of each of the professionals does not relate to the mentally disordered, each of them may at times encounter a mentally disordered person among his clients. He may also encounter work problems which result from idiosyncrasies of behavior in a client that overtax his knowledge of psychology, and to understand which he may seek help and guidance from a mental health consultant. In addition, he may be interested in the implications of his routine professional operations in regard to his effect on the future mental health of his clients, and he may ask for guidance regarding his role in the prevention of mental disorders and in the promotion of mental health.

Mental health consultation is a method that has special merit from a logistic point of view in a community program, since it provides an opportunity for a relatively small number of consultants to exert a widespread effect through the intermediation of a large group of consultees, each of whom is in contact with many clients. In order to be effective along these lines the amount of time devoted by a consultant to helping a consultee deal with the mental health problems of a current case must be relatively short, and there must be a maximum educational carryover to the consultee's work with other cases.

DIFFERENTIATION OF CONSULTATION FROM OTHER SPECIALIZED METHODS

A mental health specialist who is formally or informally designated a "consultant" may engage in many types of professional activity which resemble each other to some extent in regard to goals, methods, and techniques and which are all based upon his fundamental knowledge of human motivation and human relations. These include supervision, education, psychotherapy, casework, counseling, administrative inspection, negotiation, liaison, collaboration, coordination, and mediation. We will achieve a higher level of professional functioning when the specialist is able to differentiate these various activities and employ each of them consistently in relation to his current assignment, his professional goals, and his understanding of the demands of each situation.

In order to highlight the specific characteristics of consultation it may be useful to emphasize the differences between it and some of these other activities, such as supervision, education, psychotherapy, and collaboration.

The main characteristics of supervision which differentiate it from consultation are that the supervisor is usually a senior member of the same professional specialty as the supervisee, whereas a consultant is usually of a different specialty from the consultee. The supervisor has some administrative responsibility for the work of the supervisee and is the representative of the agency in which both work and whose task it is to safeguard the quality of care for the agency's clients, with special reference to the fact that supervisees have limited experience and are still not fully independent professionals. In contrast, the consultant usually comes into the agency or institution from outside and is not a member of its regular staff. He bears no administrative responsibility for the quality of the consultee's work or for the care of the clients.

Supervision is a continuous ongoing process, and the supervisor's responsibilities include inspection of the supervisee's work and the initiation of discussion regarding those aspects which do not appear satisfactory. Consultation is initiated by the consultee or by the consultee's supervisor, and it usually takes place in an *ad hoc* pattern as an interaction or short series of interactions arising in relation to a current work difficulty, and terminating when this has been dealt with. The continuing relationship between a consultee and a consultant is not consolidated by regular meetings but provides a potential link that is activated in the future when help may be sought for a fresh work problem.

A supervisor has a higher position in the power hierarchy of the institution than his supervisee and can enforce decisions upon the latter. There is no power differential between consultant and consultee. The latter is free to accept or reject any message or prescription. The only difference in status derives from the authority of ideas—the extra competence of the consultant in his own specialty is explicitly or implicitly recognized by the consultee when he invokes consultation help. On the other hand, the consultant should reciprocally respect the consultee in his own professional specialty in which the consultant is not expert; for example, a consultant psychiatrist arouses the respect of the consultee teacher because of his specialist knowledge of interpersonal relations, and in turn the psychiatrist respects the teacher's special competence in pedagogy. This is a coordinate relationship as contrasted with the superior-subordinate relationship of supervision.

One type of supervision resembles consultation, and that is supervision of a special skill or technique which is usually part of a staff in-service training program—for example, a psychiatrist supervising psychologists doing psychotherapy in a mental hospital or psychiatric clinic. In some such instances the supervisor may not be a member of the full-time staff of the institution. He may be hired on a sessional basis purely as a supervisor. As a staff worker rather than a line worker he has very little administrative authority over his supervisee. His function may be regarded as being primarily to foster the professional development of his supervisee, and he may not be responsible for inspecting the quality of care of the patient. This may be somebody else's responsibility. Variations of such a role shade off to become almost indistinguishable from consultation; but close inspection may reveal an unstated or unexercised authority differential and administrative responsibility for the treatment of the client, which will be the essential difference between the two forms of interprofessional functioning.

Supervision of a skill or tutoring is one form of education. It is used not only in in-service training programs but widely in programs of professional training. In this context the supervisor, or tutor, is clearly seen as a teacher and the supervisee as the student. How do these and other educational situations differ from consultation? Since the latter has been defined as *help* plus *education,* there is clearly some overlap. The difference between consultation and most other types of education lies mainly, as with supervision, in the special coordinate facultative relationship between consultee and consultant as contrasted with the hierarchical obligatory relationship between student and teacher. A student may be free to enroll or not to enroll for a course, but once he has done so he undertakes to pay attention to the teacher, to do his exercises, and to carry out the precepts of his teacher. This contrasts with consultation, in which the consultee is continually free to come and go and to accept or reject.

Another difference is that in most education the teacher has some clear idea of the content of what he intends to impart to the student, whether this be factual knowledge or a range of skills or attitudes. This content may be imparted in various ways, systematic and less systematic. In contrast, the consultant usually has no preconceived idea of a content area he wishes to impart to his consultee. It is true that, like the teacher, he does have the goal of increasing the insight, sensitivity, or skill of the consultee and also, perhaps, of evaluating the extent to which he has succeeded in this; but his responsibility does not include an appraisal of the functioning of the consultee in regard to problems with which the latter has not invoked help; and he takes it for granted that his efforts will remain focused only on segments of the consultee's functioning.

Teachers who conduct problem-centered case seminars come closest to consultation, but even they are not entirely nondirective as regards topic; and although they base themselves upon material of current interest presented by a seminar member, they guide the discussions into such channels as will eventually cover the content area they are trying to teach. Associated with the need to impart a predetermined set of concepts or skills is the fact that most education is organized in the form of courses with a set structure, or in the form of continuous exposure of the students to the influence of the teachers for a period of time, limited by contract. In contrast, consultation may be invoked from time to time on an indefinite basis.

It is envisaged that however proficient a consultee may become in handling certain categories of work problem, he will always be liable in the future to be faced by unusual situations or cases that he may not understand or know how to handle, and in which he may be helped by consulting an expert. A professional worker should ideally continue learning all his life, and from this point of view there should be no end to education. But defining education in a somewhat narrower sense as specific activity to promote a high level of competence, the need for it should be reduced as a professional man becomes more competent and capable of high level independent operation. Experience shows that, in contrast, the need for consultation and its value may rise with increasing competence of the consultee. A public health nurse who has become quite sophisticated in regard to the mental health dimensions of her work is more likely to ask for, and profit from, mental health consultation than a nurse who does not have the insight and skill to identify the psychological complications of her cases.

The effectiveness of a professional worker, such as a physician, a nurse, or a schoolteacher, who is dealing with the mental health problems of a client, is likely to be influenced by subjective factors. Long-standing personality difficulties, personal or cultural prejudices or sensitivities, and current emotional upsets in the professional worker may distort his perceptions of his client and his remedial efforts. Some mental health authorities have suggested that this expectable complication should be dealt with by providing opportunities for psychotherapeutic help to such workers—usually in the form of group psychotherapy that focuses upon those personality problems which are most intrusive into the work field.

Mental health consultation deals with this problem in another way, and it is important to differentiate this technique from techniques of psychotherapy. Psychotherapy is here defined as a treatment procedure undertaken by a physician or other healing person in order to cure or relieve the symptoms of a mental disorder in someone who conceives of himself as a patient. An essential aspect of the role of "patient" is that the person seeks diagnosis and treatment because he is aware of personal pain or discomfort that he defines as an "illness." In entering into a relationship with the therapist he agrees to an infringement of his customary privacy, sometimes in bodily matters, such as undressing for a physical examination or allowing his bodily fluids to be taken for investigation, and invariably in the psychological sphere—for example, talking about thoughts, memories, and feelings which are usually hidden from others.

The recognition that this relationship gives the therapist special power over the patient has led to a system of controls over the professional conduct of therapists; and patients rely upon these when they invest their trust in a physician or other psychotherapist. In contrast, a consultee usually has no awareness of personal disorder other than his anxiety and frustration regarding his client. He may sometimes be aware of his own psychological problems and their intrusion into the work field, but he is asking for consultation about the work difficulty and expects his own privacy to be respected. The consultant takes care not to intrude upon this privacy, and he does not direct the discussion into an appraisal of the present or past personal life of the consultee or, in some types of consultation described in this book, even of the feelings of the consultee about his work. The consultant implicitly takes it for granted that, like himself, the consultee has personal feelings and psychological complications, but in the consultation discussions the explicit content upon which interest is focused is the problem of the client and the professional task of dealing with this. Instead of the hierarchial doctor-patient relationship, there is the coordinate relationship of two professional colleagues working together on a case, and personal matters are equally excluded by both.

This does not mean that the consultant is unaware of the emotional reactions of the consultee, and that he is blind to distortions of perception or of professional behavior resulting from them. In certain types of consultation, which will be discussed in detail in this book, he is particularly sensitive to these issues; but he deals with them nonverbally and by the way in which he chooses to discuss relevant aspects of the client's case, never by uncovering the consultee's private problems or by interpreting the connection between these and the professional difficulty.

In certain instances a consultee may wish to discuss his personal problems, either because he sees their relevance in the professional setting or because he develops a feeling of trust and respect for the consultant and wishes to take advantage of the relationship with a mental health expert to try to get help for himself. This request is invariably refused by the consultant. If it were accepted, the relationship would change from that of two colleagues on the same plane to the superior-subordinate doctor-patient relationship characteristic of psychotherapy.

Another difference between consultation and psychotherapy, even when the latter is invoked because of work problems, is that the primary goal of consultation is increased effectiveness in the work setting, whereas the primary goal of psychotherapy is cure for the patient. This may result in lowering his productivity, which might previously have been kept at too high a level for his personal comfort, or it may result in his leaving that job altogether.

A source of confusion in differentiating consultation and psychotherapy lies in the term "therapeutic" or "psychotherapeutic." Effective consultation will be helpful not only to the client but also to the consultee. The negative reactions of anxiety, frustration, shame, and guilt, which may have been provoked by the work impasse, will give way to feelings of gratification, confidence, and happiness. In certain cases, in which the work problem was linked with a personal problem in the consultee, his experience of success in handling this issue in his dealings with the client may have a reflexive meaning for his own life; and what was previously a topic that provoked insecurity may henceforward be handled in a confident, effective manner. In all these cases a secondary result of the consultation may be an increased state of psychological well-being in the consultee, and this may amount to a very real personality growth and development. The consultation may then clearly be said to have had a "psychotherapeutic" effect on the consultee.

It is well to realize that not only psychotherapy but many other experiences, too, may have a "psychotherapeutic" effect on a person. These include, in addition to consultation, education, religious conversion, specific life experiences such as life crises, and beneficial human relationships such as friendships and love relationships.

Another activity in which mental health and other specialists commonly engage is collaboration. By this term we designate the functioning of a specialist who is called in by another professional worker to help deal with a specialized problem arising in the condition of the latter's client. The specialist is invited not merely to enlarge his colleague's understanding of the case and to advise on action but also to take part in implementing the action plan. The responsibility for the client is shared between the two colleagues, each of whom is expected by the other and by the client to carry out the treatment procedures that are appropriate to his professional role. These treatment procedures may be carried out concurrently; for example, a psychiatrist may treat a patient by weekly psychotherapy sessions and the family doctor may also be seeing the patient during the same period to prescribe drugs or physiotherapy in order to handle the physical component of the case. The treatment may be carried out in successive phases; for example, the psychiatrist may take the patient into the hospital for three weeks for milieu therapy or for a course of electroshock and then send him back to the care of the family doctor. In such cases it is not uncommon for each colleague to maintain a continuing contact with the client during the phase when the other is carrying the main responsibility for treatment; for example, the family doctor may visit his patient once or twice while the latter is in the hospital under the care of his colleague, and the psychiatrist may arrange to see the patient for follow-up psychotherapeutic sessions after the main responsibility has been returned to the family doctor.

There are important differences between this pattern of professional interaction and consultation. In collaboration, the specialist determines his behavior primarily in relation to his assessment of the needs of the client, for whom he accepts direct responsibility. Whenever he has any doubt about the capacity of his colleague, he must undertake the treatment procedure himself, since it is his job to see that the client gets the best possible care. This will mean that any interest the specialist may have in promoting the professional advancement of his colleague will be a subsidiary aspect of the situation. Whenever necessary, the specialist will have to take over the entire management of the case, and most of his time and energy will be devoted to this, so that he will have less time for helping his colleague add to his knowledge and skill. Moreover, although the specialist may communicate to his colleague what procedures he is carrying out, these may be of a specialized nature and of no direct applicability to the work of the colleague. In consultation, on the other hand, much of the attention of the consultant is focused on the professional needs and capacities of the consultee, because the latter is entirely responsible for implementing the treatment plan. This means that the consultant must ensure that what he advises is in line with the consultee's capacities. It also means that since the consultee is himself carrying out the treatment, he is more likely to learn from the process how to handle such situations more effectively in the future.

If the specialist is so inclined, he may try to introduce a consultation element into collaboration in respect to the advice and guidance he offers his colleague about the latter's share of the treatment plan; but he does not have as promising a field for this as he does in pure consultation, because collaboration often involves a superordinate-subordinate relationship, in which the specialist is the "senior partner." The reason for this is that although responsibility for outcome is shared, the specialist usually carries the primary responsibility and the authority for determining the treatment plan. If his colleague does not accept the specialist's opinion, his recourse is either to withdraw or to change to another specialist. Under these circumstances, the specialist exercises some coercive power over his colleague, and in our culture this usually inhibits, or at least delays, learning. The ideas put forward by the specialist are seen as "his" ideas and may be accepted more or less readily as such. Only gradually are they likely to become part of the colleague's "own" system of thinking. In consultation, on the other hand, the consultee is under no compulsion to accept the consultant's ideas. This freedom means that he can take as his own anything that makes sense to him; and he therefore has the opportunity to become more sophisticated by discovering for himself previously unthought-of complexities without having to work through the tensions, however minor, of his relationship with an authority figure.

SUMMARY OF CHARACTERISTICS OF MENTAL HEALTH CONSULTATION

Let us now review and amplify our preceding discussion by briefly summarizing the characteristics of mental health consultation as we are defining it in this book.

1. Mental health consultation is a method for use between two professionals in respect to a lay client or a program for such clients.

2. The consultee's work problem must be defined by him as being in the mental health area—relating to (a) mental disorder or personality idiosyncrasies of the client, (b) promotion of mental health in the client, (c) interpersonal aspects of the work situation. The consultant must have expert knowledge in these areas.

3. The consultant has no administrative responsibility for the consultee's work, or professional responsibility for the outcome of the client's case. He is under no compulsion to modify the consultee's conduct of the case.

4. The consultee is under no compulsion to accept the consultant's ideas or suggestions.

5. The basic relationship between the two is coordinate. There is no built-in hierarchical authority tension. This is a situation that in our culture potentiates the influence of ideas. The freedom of the consultee to

accept or reject what the consultant says enables him to take quickly as his own any ideas that appeal to him in his current situation.

6. The coordinate relationship is fostered by the consultant's usually being a member of another profession and coming briefly into the consultee's institution from the outside.

7. It is further supported by the fact that consultation is usually given as a short series of interviews—two or three, on the average—which take place intermittently in response to the consultee's awareness of current need for help with a work problem. The relationship in individual consultation is not maintained and dependency fostered by continuing contact. In group consultation there may be regular meetings, but dependency is reduced by peer support.

8. Consultation is expected to continue indefinitely. Consultees can be expected to encounter unusual work problems throughout their careers. Increasing competence and sophistication of consultees in their own profession increase the likelihood of their recognizing mental health complications and asking for consultation.

9. A consultant has no predetermined body of information that he intends to impart to a particular consultee. He responds only to the segment of the consultee's problems which the latter exposes in the current work difficulty. The consultant does not seek to remedy other areas of inadequacy in the consultee. He expects other issues to be raised in future consultations.

10. The twin goals of consultation are to help the consultee improve his handling or understanding of the current work difficulty and through this to increase his capacity to master future problems of a similar type.

11. The aim is to improve the consultee's job performance and not his sense of well-being. It is envisaged, however, that since the two are linked, a consultee's feelings of personal worth will probably be increased by a successful consultation, as will also his capacity to deal in a reality-based socially acceptable way with certain of his life difficulties. In other words, a successful consultation may have the secondary effect of being therapeutic to the consultee.

12. Consultation does not focus overtly on personal problems and feelings of the consultee. It respects his privacy. The consultant does not allow the discussion of personal and private material in the consultation interview.

13. This does not mean that the consultant does not pay attention to the feelings of the consultee. He is particularly sensitive to these and to the disturbance of task functioning produced by personal problems. He deals with personal problems, however, in a special way, such as by dis-

cussing them in the form in which the consultee has displaced them onto the client's case and the work setting.

14. Consultation is usually only one of the professional functions of a specialist, even if he is formally entitled "consultant." He should utilize the consultation method only when it is appropriate in the situation. At other times he will make use of different methods. It may sometimes occur that the demands of a situation will cause him to put aside his consultation in the middle. For instance, if he gets information during a consultation interview that leads him to judge that the consultee's actions are seriously endangering the client, such as by not preventing suicide or not leading toward investigation and treatment for a dangerous psychosis, he should set aside his consultant role and revert to his basic role as a psychiatrist, psychologist, or social worker. He will then give advice or take action that he does not allow the consultee the freedom to reject. This destroys the coordinate relationship and interrupts the consultation contact in favor of a higher goal. Such dramatic occasions have been rare in my experience, but consultants must constantly keep the possibility in mind as a realization of the realistic limits of this method.

15. Finally, it is worth emphasizing that mental health consultation is a method of communication between a mental health specialist and other professionals. It does not denote a new profession—merely a special way in which existing professionals may operate. The process of this operation has been refined and analyzed and can be systematically taught and learned. The content of the consultation communication will naturally vary in accordance with the specialized knowledge and experience of the consultant. Thus, although psychiatrists, psychologists, psychiatric social workers, and psychiatric nurses should use the same techniques of consultation with a particular consultee, the content of their specialized remarks about the case of the client will differ. The consultant must have specialized knowledge about the topic on which the consultee needs help; and the professional training and experience of the consultant will determine the detailed nature and form of this knowledge.

TYPES OF MENTAL HEALTH CONSULTATION

A mental health consultant has no absolutely predetermined ground to cover in his contacts with his consultees. His job calls for him to react to their temporary feelings of need for help with current problems in their work field. These may involve the difficulties of a line worker in handling a particular client, or the problems of a group of administrators in developing or improving a program for part or all of the organization. The consultant must therefore be prepared for relatively unexpected shifts of focus both in regard to the content and scope of consultation problems and in regard to the identity and position of his consultees within the organizational structure of their institution.

Since this setting rarely provides him with the clear set of mutual expectations for defining his role to which he has become accustomed in his traditional work as a teacher, psychotherapist, clinical psychologist, or agency caseworker, he must develop a conceptual map that he carries within him into the sphere of consultation operations so that he can quickly choose an appropriate pattern in his responses to the demands of the situation.

This conceptual map must indicate the limits of his professional domain. Although his role may not be obviously prestructured, he is not in fact free to do anything that comes into his head or to respond completely to all requests from would-be consultees. He is constrained by the policies of his own agency, which, for instance, permit his participation in the work of the consultee institution only to the extent that by contributing to the solution of a current problem he may improve the operations of the organization in preventing disability or defect due to mental disorder in the community. These policies probably do not allow him to spend his time on problems of the consultee institution that have no clear connection with the mental health of the community. He is also constrained by the policies of the consultee institution that restrict him to working with certain members of its staff in such a way as to promote their accomplishment of its mission and to avoid upsetting its accepted patterns of communication and authority. His intervention is not likely to be welcomed if, at the invitation of an individual consultee, he takes sides in informal power struggles among the staff or if he suddenly disrupts the orderly processes of decision making that have been developed by the administrators of the institution.

In addition to his need to be aware of these constraints upon the limits of his consultation operations, the consultant is helped by a classification system which allows him to categorize each situation in such a way that he may know in general how it may be expected to unfold and what the most promising methods of dealing with it are likely to be. There are many useful ways of classifying mental health consultation for this purpose. I have found the following typology of value. It is a fourfold classification based upon two major divisions: (a) between a primary focus of the consultant on a case problem as contrasted with an administrative problem dealing with the program or policies of the institution, and (b) between a primary interest of the consultant in giving a specialized opinion and recommendation for solution of the work difficulty versus attempting to improve the problem-solving capacity of the consultees and leaving them to work out their own way of solving it.

In practice, a consultation situation will often not fall neatly into one of these four categories but will be of a mixed type. The details of the mixture may alter over time as the interactions of consultant and consultee change in relation to the unfolding of the situation. But if the consultant continually assesses the type of process in which he is involved and maintains an awareness of the relative loading of its different classificatory elements, he will find it easier to choose an effective general pattern of response.

The four consultation types are:

A–1. Client-Centered Case Consultation

The consultee's work difficulty relates to the management of a particular case or group of cases. The consultant helps by bringing his specialized knowledge and skills to bear in making an expert assessment of the nature of the client's problem and in recommending how the consultee should deal with the case. The primary goal of the consultation is for the consultant to communicate to the consultee how this client can be helped. A subsidiary goal is that the consultee may use his experience with this case to improve his knowledge and skills, so that he will be better able in the future to handle, on his own, comparable problems in this and similar clients. This is the traditional type of specialist consultation of medical practice, as when a general practitioner asks for an expert opinion on diagnosis and treatment from a cardiologist, when one of his patients is suffering from a complicated heart condition that he does not feel competent to handle satisfactorily on his own.

A–2. Consultee-Centered Case Consultation

Here, too, the consultee's work problem relates to the management of a particular client and he invokes the consultant's help in order to improve his handling of the case. In this type of consultation the consultant focuses his main attention on trying to understand the nature of the consultee's difficulty with the case and in trying to help him remedy this. The consultee's difficulty may be due to lack of knowledge about the type of problem presented by the client, lack of skill in making use of such knowledge in order to answer the question, lack of self-confidence so that he is uncertain in utilizing his knowledge and skills, or lack of professional objectivity due to the interference of subjective emotional complications with his perceptual and planning operations.

The primary goal of the consultant is to help the consultee remedy whichever of these shortcomings he judges to be present. The consultant may assist the consultee to increase his knowledge or skills, he may support and reassure him in increasing his self-confidence, and in the fourth category he may help him increase his professional objectivity so as to reduce the distortions in his perception and judgment of the client's condition. It is hoped that the improvement in professional functioning will enable the consultee to solve the problems of the client, and that this improvement will be maintained in relation to future clients with similar difficulties. The aim of this type of consultation is frankly to educate the consultee, using his problems with the current client as a lever and a learning opportunity; and the expertness of the consultant is focused on this task rather than, as in client-centered case consultation, on the diagnosis of the client and the developing of a specialist prescription for his treatment.

B–1. Program-Centered Administrative Consultation

The work problem is in the area of planning and administration— how to develop a new program or to improve an existing one. The consultant helps by using his knowledge of administration and social systems, as well as his expert knowledge and experience of mental health theory and practice and of program development in other institutions, in order to collect and analyze data about the points at issue. On the basis of this he suggests short-term and long-term solutions for the administrative questions of the consultee organization. As with category A–1, his primary goal is to prescribe an effective course of action in planning the program. He hopes that a side effect will be that the consultees will learn something from his analysis and recommendations that they can use, on their own, in dealing with future administrative problems of a similar type.

B–2. Consultee-Centered Administrative Consultation

This is the analogue of category A–2, but with a focus on problems of programming and organization instead of on dealing with a particular client. Here, too, the primary concern of the consultant is not the collection and analysis of administrative data relating to the mission of the institution but the elucidation and remedying among the consultees of difficulties and shortcomings that interfere with their grappling with their tasks of program development and organization.

In addition to lack of knowledge, skills, self-confidence, and objectivity in individuals, the problem of the consultees may be the result of group difficulties—poor leadership, authority problems, lack of role complementarity, communication blocks, and the like. The consultant's primary goal is to understand and help remedy these; and his hope is that his successful accomplishment of this task will enable the consultees to develop and implement effective plans, on their own, to accomplish the mission of their organization.

[3]

Developing a Consultation
Program in a Community

Mental health consultation, as one of the essential ingredients of an organized program of community mental health, must articulate in a planned way with its other elements in forming a body of methods and techniques that are designed to fulfill the overall mission of promoting the mental health of the population and reducing community rates of mental disorder. A mental health consultant in this setting is not an independent practitioner who responds to *ad hoc* invitations by other professionals to help them by using skills he happens to possess. He is one of the emissaries of his organization, who operates in the field as part of a carefully conceived institutional plan to deal with a community problem.

In planning a consultation program the following considerations are therefore relevant:

ESTABLISHMENT OF BASIC PHILOSOPHY AND MISSION

The overall mission of the mental health agency is primarily derived from the mandate it receives from the community. Its domain is officially defined by federal, state, county, or local government, or by formal decisions taken by voluntary associations and planning councils. This mandate is accepted by its governing body, which is either a part of the administrative structure of the executive branch of government or is a local incorporated board of directors. In any case, it is able to accept legal responsibility for such tasks as collecting and disbursing funds, renting premises, and hiring staff, and directing the other operations de-

35

signed to fulfill its mission. The latter includes reporting back to its sponsors on the use of funds and on the degree to which assigned goals have been achieved.

In the United States, the mission of a particular mental health agency is very much molded by public opinion, which mirrors the spirit of the times and which is expressed through current legislation, governmental administrative practices, and the policies of voluntary civic organizations. The feelings of need of the local community are communicated to the governing body of the agency and to its professional staff along these channels by its elected or appointed representatives, and also by direct communication of individuals and special interest groups, such as parents of retarded or emotionally ill children. A factor of increasing importance during the 1960's has been the influence upon the mission and style of operations of community agencies of "consumers" in the health and welfare field, namely the population which is supposed to be served. This is related to a significant change in the philosophy of civic and legislative leaders, who are becoming alert to the delivery of services to populations in need of them, rather than, as in the past, restricting themselves to the establishment of institutions and agencies to which appropriate clients may be admitted. This in turn is related to an increasing militancy in making their wishes known and participating in planning on the part of the deprived segments of the population, such as minority groups and the poverty-stricken inhabitants of metropolitan slums. This participation of the consumers is linked with civil rights, urban development, and antipoverty legislation.

The third factor that is significant in determining the mission of a mental health agency is the point of view and the professional knowledge and skills of its staff. These are to some extent determined by the attitudes of the governing board, which selects the director and possibly ratifies the appointment of other staff whom he recruits. An important aspect of appointing the director is for him and the board to explore whether or not their views about the mission of the agency are compatible. The need for consonance of views between the two does not end when the appointment decision has been taken. Throughout the period of his service, the director must pay particular attention to his sources of sanction, and must carefully define the extent to which the agency's mission is molded by the board and the public. Their mission is also influenced by the special interests and competence of himself and his staff, which in turn are modified by current ideologies within their professional reference groups.

How much leadership and initiative the professional staff should exercise in persuading its governing board to bring the agency's mission into line with current professional ideology is a complicated question. If the staff exercises too powerful a voice in this matter, there is always the danger of deviating too far from the will of the population and its leaders. On the other hand, it is its obligation to communicate adequately to its board the results of professional research, so that the representatives of the consumers and of the providers of resources may base their policy decisions on as wide as possible a fund of information about realistic possibilities of accomplishment. They must take account of the size and skills of the staff, their knowledge of latest scientific and technical experience, and their information about innovative thinking in other places.

This is a far cry from the oversimplified view held by some mental health professionals that, once appointed, it is up to them to mold the mission of their agency according to their own interests and skills; and then to "sell" their ideas to their governing body so as to secure its concurrence and support.

The dynamic interplay of all these factors leads to fundamental decisions, which are continually being modified, about the overall goals of the mental health agency, and about the relative priority of these in the light of the most pressing needs of the population, the supply of resources, the availability of other services in the community with which the efforts of the agency can be coordinated, and, most important, the value systems of the leaders. These decisions will determine, for instance, which subpopulations at special risk should have highest priority —for example, expectant mothers, young children, widows, old people in urban relocation areas, or socially deprived black slum children. The decisions will determine the ratio of staff time to be spent in the treatment of different categories of the mentally ill, as opposed to prevention of mental disorders or promotion of mental health. They will determine the degree of responsibility to be undertaken by the agency in dealing with cases within its own walls as compared with helping other institutions and professionals in the community to improve their handling of the mental health dimension of their work. By such decisions, the agency will divide its staff services between intramural and extramural activities; and in the latter category will develop an appropriate balance among such activities as education of community professionals, collaboration, public information and public relations, liaison, casefinding, and consultation. This in turn will affect recruitment and in-service training policies, so that the agency will be able to provide those technical services, such as mental health consultation, which are needed to fulfill its mission.

Two further points are worthy of emphasis. First, an essential aspect of the leadership role of the agency director is the continual redefinition of the mission of his organization, which must be kept in focus by his staff as the superordinate set of goals of all their efforts. Second, the mission must be understood in terms of solving problems of mental health and mental disorder of the population by using whatever people and methods seem best fitted for this, and not in terms of categorical services, or methods and techniques. The task of the agency should be to treat and rehabilitate mentally ill people, or to prevent mental disorder. It should not be seen as the provision of analytic psychotherapy, or casework, or mental health consultation. The latter approach leads inevitably to undue emphasis on role definition and restrictive specialization practices, and on bureaucratic procedures and hierarchies; on recruiting "good" cases to cater to the needs of particular methods and team members; and on rejecting or avoiding "unsuitable" cases that are not appropriate grist for the mill.

DEVELOPING A CONCEPTUAL FRAMEWORK

A fundamental task for the professional staff of the mental health agency is the development of an overall map of the goals that are involved in its mission and of the concepts that can be used to guide its achievement. The coordination of activities of staff members can be managed in two main ways. One approach, derived from traditional bureaucratic administrative practice, is to draw up a rational organization chart and to parcel out the tasks among various officeholders, each of whom has a defined role that articulates with those of occupiers of neighboring positions in the system. The effects of personal idiosyncrasies and shortcomings that may upset the system are minimized by the development of procedure manuals and a body of normative oral traditions that can be communicated to newcomers. This system works reasonably well in dealing with known problems in a relatively stable environment.

In recent years, a different approach has been developed, which places less reliance on the organization chart and the procedure manuals, although these must always be used to some extent, especially in a large organization, so as to formalize lines of authority and communication and to minimize arbitrary personal action. This new approach develops shared concepts among members of staff and a common view of immediate and distant goals, and then leaves it to individuals and groups to work out ways of pooling their energies on their own in order to achieve these goals. Coordination is ensured by shared values and theoretical models and by free communication and movement, rather than by restricting activities within contiguous role boundaries. Personal commitment to the current task is promoted because each member of staff has to use his own initiative and creativity to determine his contribution to the common goal; and he has to reach out actively to others whose help he needs in solving his work problems. This is a particularly appropriate way of dealing with the novel difficulties that develop in a rapidly changing environment, because it increases the potential for innovation, since each problem is dealt with in its own right rather than by a preplanned routine.

The crucial question, beyond that of establishment of consensus about the mission of the agency, is the development of an appropriate set of conceptual models to provide different members of staff with common guidelines and language with which to analyze and plan their operations. In my recent book, *Principles of Preventive Psychiatry*,[1] I have described such a set of conceptual models for community mental health that have proved valuable in developing population-focused programs for the prevention and control of mental disorders. Examination of these will reveal that mental health consultation is one of the methods which may be used by the staff of a community mental health agency in facilitating the operations of other professionals in promoting mental health and reducing the incidence of mental disorders (primary prevention); in shortening the period of disability of mental disorders by early recognition and prompt and effective treatment (secondary prevention); and in reducing the rate of residual defect following mental disorder in the population (tertiary prevention). The amount of staff time to be devoted to mental health consultation in contrast to other methods, the decision as to which staff members should act as consultants, and the choice of professionals and caregiving agencies in the community who will be provided with mental health consultation services will be determined by judging which current problems must be attacked, in what order, and with what intensity, so as most effectively and efficiently to carry out the defined mission of the program. This demands not a detailed blueprint of operations but a continuing process of collecting information about the community, and a succession of planning judgments about salient and practicable goals and about ways of achieving them through individual and joint staff action. This must be followed by evaluation of results, both in terms of cost and in regard to their contribution to the fulfillment of the mission.

SUCCESSIVE EXPLORATIONS OF COMMUNITY TO ESTABLISH GOALS

Two aspects of goal are significant—salience and feasibility.

Salience

1. Goals can be rank ordered in regard to their importance in satisfying current feelings of need in the community. The needs themselves will be felt with different degrees of urgency; and they will be felt by smaller or larger sections of the population, both consumers and civic leaders. In judging the salience of a goal, all these issues must be taken into account, including the fact that although it may be natural to oil the wheel that squeaks loudest, a bearing which is quietly rusting away may finally bring the machine to a halt. Ways must therefore be found of increasing the flow of information from just those people who may be in greatest need but whose plight may be hidden because of inadequate communication due to lack of skill, low access to communication channels, or cultural blocks. Also, it is not only the conscious awareness of need by the individuals concerned that is important, although the significance of this should not be underestimated, but a prediction of the consequences to the mental health picture of the community if the need is not satisfied by the agency. This involves a judgment as to whether the affected group will handle its problems by individual action or by utilizing other community resources if the mental health agency does not help it.

2. Salience of a goal is to be judged not only in regard to the need of those involved but also in relation to how significant it may be for achieving the mission of the program as set forth in its conceptual framework. For instance, the continuing need for help felt by a chronically dependent individual or group may be salient in its own right, but it may be judged less significant for achieving the mission of the program than that of other sufferers whose current crisis provides a leverage point for expanding the helping potential of the agency, or than that of key groups, highly visible or influential in their community, who, if helped, may act as an example or a catalyst to many others. Similarly, the choice of salient target groups must contribute to the overall balance of the program. For example, the different levels of prevention are likely to be differentially weighted in accordance with the agency's current mandate. This point was illustrated by the different emphasis in the recommendations of the Joint Commission's report and the Kennedy mes-

sage on the relative amounts of attention given to programs of primary prevention for a wide range of mental disorders versus secondary and tertiary prevention of the psychoses. The salience of feelings of need for help by widows having difficulties in adjusting to the death of their husbands, and the possibility of using staff time in offering consultation to clergymen and undertakers to assist them to satisfy this need, will be judged quite differently in accordance with which of these points of view dominates the philosophy of the mental health program.

The Joint Commission on Mental Illness and Health recommended that we should place our main emphasis on the treatment of psychotic patients in improved mental hospitals and questioned the validity of using scarce community resources on primary prevention.[2] An agency operating in line with this philosophy would devote little, if any, time to helping widows who were not currently ill. The Kennedy message, on the other hand, urged a change from our traditional focus on erecting institutions, for which appropriate patients are recruited, to the assumption of responsibility for identifying and satisfying the salient mental health needs of the population and to concentrating resources on preventing healthy people from becoming sick.[3] An agency identified with this philosophy would probably deploy significant resources in such programs as helping widows to adjust in a healthy way to the consequences of their bereavement, so as to reduce the number who would eventually break down psychiatrically.

3. It must be recognized that a judgment on the salience of a goal is relatively arbitrary, involving, as it does, a complicated tangle of factors. It is particularly susceptible to influence by the spirit and value system of the times and by fashions in professional style. These will, in turn, reflect both long-term and short-term historical trends. For instance, despite all the available evidence that mental disorder was most pressing among the poor and was so widespread as to overburden all efforts at direct professional action, it was not till the 1960's that it became fashionable within the framework of the antipoverty campaign to focus specialized mental health attention on metropolitan slums, and to do so with a self-help approach whereby the professionals were seen as the stimulators and supporters of preventive and remedial action by the poor themselves.

Feasibility

Discussions in regard to choice or priorities of goals also involve judgments on their feasibility. Resources are too limited to be dissipated in futile efforts to achieve currently unattainable ends. Practicability depends, of course, on whether effective methods are available and on the number and skill of staff. In addition, this judgment depends on a prediction about the chances of changing target individuals, groups, and institutions. Their rigidity and their current openness to outside influences of different types must thus be assessed. Here again, crisis concepts are important. Systems are more susceptible to change and more open to outside influence during periods of disequilibrium. At such times, an agency mobilized and ready to move in, if invited, with a concrete offer of help is likely to produce a far greater effect than would be possible during more stable times. On the other hand, individuals and institutions, whatever their level of equilibrium, differ in their receptivity to modification; and this must be taken into account in deciding where to work.

For example, urban unrest during the last few years, and the widespread realization of the key role of the police in triggering or in controlling civic disorder, have led to the judgment among many mental health workers that the city police force is an institution that ranks high on the local mental health salience scale. On the other hand, in many places the value systems and traditions of the police are dissonant with those of the mental health specialists, and there has been a history of poor relationships between the two groups. Moreover, the police force may have been so much the target of public criticism that it may have built up a rigid pattern of defenses against pressure to change. It might therefore be ranked quite low on the feasibility scale, and attempts by mental health workers to develop education and consultation programs for the police would be likely to fail.

Current events may, however, modify its feasibility. There may be a change of mayor, and the new man may force a shakeup of his police force. The police commissioner may reach retirement age, and a new director may be appointed from outside the area who may embark on a policy of reform and professionalization. Because of such changes, the police force might now be judged more amenable to influence by mental health workers, and in fact its administrative officers might even be eager to secure their help in furthering their own policies of educating their men and improving their understanding and relationships with the community.

It goes without saying that all change infringes on the rights or comfort of somebody and consequently is likely to provoke opposition. Mental health planners and organizers must therefore be continually alert to the probable ripple effects of changes that satisfy the felt needs of certain people and fit in with their own agency mission and professional concepts. What will be the inevitable opposition? Whose comfort will be upset? Whose rights will be threatened? Can this damage be overcome or minimized? Will the cost of the side effects be worth the central achievement? The answers to some of these questions can never be known in advance. But unless the questions are seriously asked, and there is reasonable assurance that the answers will be generally satisfactory, a judgment on feasibility must remain uncertain.

An important safeguard is to make every judgment contingent on continuing feedback about unexpected opposition and undesirable side effects, and to allot some resources to checks and balances and to mechanisms for modifying the ongoing program in the light of local conditions. However small the agency, this means creating maximum decentralization, so that as many decisions as possible are made by the man in the field, who is in the best position to understand the idiosyncratic details of the local situation and to assess the immediate reactions of those affected by the program.

EXPLORATIONS IN THE COMMUNITY

The development and molding of a mental health program according to the above considerations depend upon a continuing system of collecting and analyzing information that is based on the principle of refining our picture of the community by successive approximations. The following are some of the major approaches:

1. A cumulative history should be kept of the economic, political, and sociocultural life of the community, with particular reference to problems in the health, education, corrections, and welfare fields, and to the institutions and services that have been developed to deal with them. Especially important is information about the network of governmental, voluntary, and private community agencies; how the latter relate to each other; how they have worked out their domains; and what information, services, and clients are exchanged among them. Also significant is information about the power and communication systems of the community, and how these have changed over time in relation to developments in the other fields. A cumulative list of the caregiving professionals should be kept and, insofar as this is possible, a list of the unofficial caregivers —the influential people who informally offer support and guidance to others in need of help.

2. A series of maps and tables should be developed indicating the main demographic and ecological indices of the community. Particularly

important are data on movements of ethnic and racial subgroups in and out of different parts of the community; and these should be related to economic, political, and religious shiftings in the population.

3. Cumulative statistics should be kept on the adaptive casualties of the population, not merely routine physical morbidity and mental disorder indices, such as admissions and discharges to hospitals and outpatient clinics, and visits to physicians, but also as much information as is available in the general public health, education, corrections, labor, and welfare fields. These might include records of police blotters; court appearances, especially juveniles; alcoholism and drug addiction; unemployment figures; divorces; deaths, especially by suicide and homicide; and welfare rolls. Some of this information will be easily and cheaply obtained. Other items may require building collaborative relationships with official and voluntary community agencies. In some localities, a central record system in the health, education, and welfare fields is being developed with the aid of electronic data storage and retrieval devices. The information is collected by all relevant agencies and is pooled and processed to help each of the collaborating programs.

4. Registers should be developed of populations at special risk because of increased prevalence of indices of adaptive casualties, or because of poor living conditions or life experiences which involve deprivations that would be expected to be harmful, such as recently widowed or orphaned individuals, school dropouts, solitary old people with multiple physical disabilities, and children of psychotic mothers.

5. A cumulative register should be developed of those caregiving agencies and individuals who are potentially most strategic or usually most helpful to these high risk populations.

CHOOSING TARGET INSTITUTIONS
FOR A CONSULTATION PROGRAM

The best approach for a community mental health program is to focus for a relatively short period on each one of a series of agencies and institutions, each of which appears to offer the most rewarding avenue for action in light of all the previously mentioned factors. This demands a pragmatic approach. Opportunities that happen to present themselves should be grasped if they promise possibilities of achieving salient and feasible goals in line with the program's mission and the knowledge of the community. This is better than operating according to a systematic blueprint, because time and effort will be saved if the leverage of intercurrent crises in individuals and agencies is fully exploited. Community mental health workers should be alert to building relationships with any appropriate agency by offering help at a time of felt need.

In order to spread the results of mental health intervention throughout the community, ripple effects are important. Wherever possible, one should choose to work with highly visible agencies, so that information about the mental health program will be widely disseminated, and with those caregivers who occupy key positions in the community service network, so that improved procedures have a better chance of being copied by others. Obviously, institutions that reach large numbers of high risk clients are to be preferred. A pragmatic approach does not mean inactivity—even alert inactivity. Agencies with which one would eventually like to develop a mental health consultation program because they rate high on the previously discussed scales can be involved in minor types of collaboration that promote enough contact to begin forming relationships. For instance, they can be approached for information about their areas of community life, or they can be involved in simple studies that may yield results of value to them as well as to the mental health agency. Such contacts should not unduly burden either side; and since the expenditure of time for the mental health workers will be minimal, they will be able to contact a wide pool of agencies from which ripe targets may eventually emerge.

PROMOTING INITIAL CONTACTS

The fundamental principle is to create proximity and establish the reputation of being trustworthy, competent, and eager to help without infringing on the rights of other agencies or endangering their programs.

The firmest basis for initial contact is the offer of collaborative service for those clients of the agency whom its staff wishes to refer for psychiatric diagnosis or therapy. Such referrals should be accepted on a demonstration basis. The mental health workers should understand that their operations are being carefully observed to assess their willingness and capacity to collaborate with the other agency and to help its clients. It is particularly important, therefore, to take a referred case without delay and to accept it even though it might be an "unsuitable" or troublesome case. In fact, it has usually been carefully chosen, whether by conscious or unconscious design, precisely as a test case to establish the *bona fides* of the mental health workers. If the latter realize that the case is being used as a means of exploratory communication, they are less likely to treat it solely on its own merits and to deal with it in a routine traditional style that includes walling it off from scrutiny by the other community workers.

The rights of the patient to confidentiality and competent diagnosis and treatment can be safeguarded even while relationships with the other agency are being built. This means, however, sending an immediate written diagnostic and dispositional report and subsequent information on the progress of treatment or management to the other agency in language that its staff can readily understand. These reports should also provide opportunities for mental health workers to visit the community agency to discuss the case with as many of its staff as possible, thus initiating personal relationships and beginning to build a picture of its social system and culture. During these visits guidance can be offered on the current management of the client if he continues with the agency. For instance, classroom management of a child patient can be discussed with his teachers, principal, and guidance counselor in the school which referred him. Further visits to deepen these initial relationships can be made to gather information about the child's school progress and to report on the developments in his therapy. Once again, there need be no breach in confidentiality, because these developments need be discussed only in the most general terms. This is usually the level at which the educators wish to learn about the case anyway; they are rarely interested in its deeper dynamics, contrary to the stereotyped fantasy of many mental health workers. During these discussions the mental health worker has an opportunity to establish his trustworthiness and his expert competence. He can also talk, in passing, about some of the other services of the mental health program which the staff of the other community agency may someday wish to utilize.

Wherever possible, a single worker should be assigned to a particular target institution, so that he can build a personal knowledge of its social system and of its staff. He may act in liaison to communicate with both staffs about referred cases; and eventually he may be asked informally, and later formally, to lead discussions or seminars about mental health in other institutions, to collaborate in the joint management of cases with mental health problems, and finally to act as a mental health consultant.

DISTRIBUTION OF EFFORTS AMONG
COMMUNITY AGENCIES

The progress of consultation relationships with community agencies should be monitored. Stabilized and set patterns should on the whole be avoided. The program should be intensified or reduced with particular agencies so that it spreads increasingly from those which are most feasible to those which are most salient.

When indicated, regular consultation contact with one agency should be terminated and the workers transferred to a new one, leaving the communication channels open with the old agency for *ad hoc* "consultation on request." The hazard of dealing just with old friends because of habit or ease should be avoided. Eventually, a consultant may become so integrated within the structure of a consultee agency that he ceases to be effective. He may identify so much with its culture that he can no longer penetrate its blind spots and biases, and he may be so highly regarded that its workers may not wish to upset him with its less savory problems. Even if the results of the monitoring indicate the need for a long-term continuing consultation program with a community institution, such as a school system or a particular school, it may often be advisable to rotate consultants so that they do not spend more than two or three years in one place.

NOTES

1. G. Caplan, *Principles of Preventive Psychiatry* (New York: Basic Books, 1964).
2. Joint Commission on Mental Illness and Health, *Action for Mental Health* (final report; New York: Basic Books, 1961).
3. J. F. Kennedy, "Message from the President of the United States Relative to Mental Illness and Mental Retardation," February 5, 1963, 88th Congress, First Session, House of Representatives, Document No. 58.

[4]

Building Relationships with a Consultee Institution

INTRODUCTION

In preparing the ground for a consultation program in a caregiving institution, the consultant must go through a complicated and sometimes lengthy operation of building up relationships. His entry into the potential consultee insitution may result from a planning decision that he and his colleagues have made in line with the considerations discussed in the previous chapter. It may be a response to a formal invitation by the authorities of the institution, who are aware of certain needs that they believe the consultant agency may be able to satisfy. The consultant's entry may also be in response to an informal contact, such as a request for *ad hoc* help with a case by a subordinate member of the institution's staff, who has not necessarily obtained explicit sanction from his superiors for this. The first contact may be a visit by the consultant to obtain information about a case that has been referred to his clinic for diagnosis and treatment; and in that instance, too, he may be in touch with line workers or those in intermediate positions of authority in one of the subsidiary units of the institution.

As soon as the consultant decides that he is engaged on a process of preparing the ground for a potential program of mental health consultation, there are certain issues to which he must pay attention so that his relationship building may pursue an orderly course.

48

ELEMENTS IN BUILDING A RELATIONSHIP

1. First, he must be aware that in interactions with the staff of the institution both he and they are to be regarded as emissaries of their respective agencies, rather than as operating only as individual professional workers. This means that he must consciously shape his own actions in line with the policies of his agency, and must keep its staff informed of the progress of his operations, so that they may have an adequate opportunity to guide him and to articulate their work with his. He must also realize that the actions of the workers of the consultee institution are being similarly molded by their colleagues; and he must take into account that they are probably reporting back to their superiors and peers on what transpires in their interactions with him.

2. The second essential element is for the consultant to realize the importance of making personal contact with the authority figures of the consultee institution as soon after his initial entry as possible, no matter how or at what level he came into the system. The purpose of this contact is to obtain sanction for his exploratory and negotiatory operations in the institution. This is particularly important if he was called in informally to deal with a case by a subordinate member of staff. He should inform the latter that he wishes to introduce himself to the director of the institution. He can deal with any embarrassment of the staff worker by saying something like, "In our agency we have a rule that we must always make a call on the director of any institution that we enter, in order to introduce ourselves, tell him about our agency, discuss our purpose in his institution, and get his formal permission to remain in his domain." This type of formulation relieves the staff worker of the responsibility for making the introduction. This may be of some importance if, as not infrequently happens, this worker does not have easy access to the director. Often, the staff member who first reaches out for help to a mental health agency is marginal or deviant in his own social system. He does not find it as easy as more central staff to get help and support with his problems inside his own system and therefore may more actively search for outside assistance. He is a useful bridge in bringing the consultant in, but the latter must beware lest he become too closely identified with the marginal person and be perceived by the other staff of the institution as also deviant and therefore to be similarly walled off and kept out of its central communication network.

This may be prevented if the consultant makes rapid contact with the director of the institution and through him with other key members of its staff.

3. The latter point leads us to the third fundamental issue. The mental health worker must, as quickly as possible, explore the organizational pattern and social system of the institution in order to elucidate its authority and communication networks. He must take care lest he get a distorted view by relying too much on information given by the individual or group that called him in; and, wherever possible, he should aim to corroborate all the information they give him with stories of additional informants.

In these preliminary explorations, the mental health worker is trying to learn enough about the mission and goals of the institution and about the values and traditions of its workers to determine the nature of their salient problems and to ascertain whether he might help to solve these by making a contribution that might at the same time fulfill the mission of his own agency. Insofar as this is possible, he will foster the building of relationships of mutual trust and respect that may form a basis for such collaboration. He will get to know the staff of the institution and help the staff to get to know him and to understand the nature of the expert assistance he is able to offer in regard to the mental health dimension of their job. He will also communicate his readiness and availability to work with them in pursuit of mutual or compatible goals.

This process may focus on joint work with a mentally disordered client, who has been referred to his agency for diagnosis and treatment; or, such a case may provide an opportunity for a wider ranging discussion about the policies and problems of the two institutions and about the interests and values of their staffs with reference to possibilities of collaboration in pursuit of superordinate goals—that is, goals of value to each, which cannot be achieved alone but only by a pooling of resources and a joining of efforts.

In such discussions it is important for the mental health worker to realize for himself, and to communicate to the other professionals, that he is not being purely altruistic in offering to help them with their problems, but that he, too, has an axe to grind in this process. He cannot achieve his own professional goals of community-wide improvement in mental health and reduction in the incidence and prevalence of mental disorder in his population unless the other caregiving professionals in the community obtain an improved understanding of the mental health dimension of their work and utilize this in their everyday operations. He therefore needs the opportunity of their involving him in working with them on demonstration cases in order to deepen their understanding of this aspect of their roles. He stands to gain as much out of this interaction as they do; and he is not just being kindhearted in offering them his help on their cases. Such a message sets the stage for the kind of coordinate relationship of mutual involvement and interdependence which is the foundation for the kind of consultation advocated in this book.

While this exploration is being carried out, the mental health worker is trying to achieve two other goals. He is building channels of communication to key members of staff of the institution, and with them he is developing a common verbal and nonverbal language.

BUILDING CHANNELS OF COMMUNICATION

The development of communication channels involves finding key members of the communication network who have easy access to significant groups of line workers and also to the authority system, and then building relationships of trust and respect with them so that they will act as communication bridges between the consultant and the staff of the institution. In certain cases, the director of the institution will himself nominate such people—for example, the head guidance counselor and the nurse in a high school—and will ask the consultant to communicate with the system through them. In many cases the mental health worker will have to identify such people himself and to work out the terms of the arrangements whereby messages are transferred to and from the rest of the staff. Occasionally the director of the institution will himself act as the communication bridge. Since he is a busy man, this may mean that he wishes to exercise special surveillance over the operations of the consultant. On the other hand, this pattern has the advantage that through his office the consultant has potential access to the total institution, whereas most other communication bridges are likely to cover parts of the system less adequately than others.

The dissemination of messages is not an uncomplicated process. The communication link person is a gatekeeper as well as a message-exchange point. In the case of the director of the institution, the surveillance aspect is obvious. He needs to satisfy himself that the operations of the mental health worker are conducive to the welfare of the institution before he will allow messages to pass freely. Until he is satisfied, he is likely to be highly selective in deciding what types of messages and communications are to be allowed. At the beginning, he may permit only requests for consultation from senior and trustworthy staff who are able to defend themselves and the good name of the institution against any possible harmful effects of this "newfangled" psychological approach—the so-called "Horatio-at-the-bridge approach." Alternatively, he may promote requests for consultation from the weakest and most expendable members of staff and watch to see if the mental health worker damages them—the so-called "human canon-fodder approach." In any case, he will allow the communication channels to become free both in regard to content and destination of messages only insofar as he convinces himself that the mental health worker is both trustworthy and effective. At the stage at which he hands the matter over to his secretary as a routine mechanical operation involving transfer of messages between the mental health worker and anyone on his staff, the consultant may congratulate himself that he has established top sanction within the institution.

When the director deputizes somebody else to act as communicator-gatekeeper, added complications are often involved. The person chosen is usually someone whose role domain is bordered by, or overlaps, that of the world-be consultant, such as the head guidance counselor or psychologist of a school, or the chief supervisor of a public health nursing unit. These people not only safeguard the general interests of the institution but they are particularly sensitive to the implications of a possible new program of mental health consultation for their own vested interests in the organization. Until they are satisfied that their own status and work will not be endangered by the mental health worker, they are likely to be restrictive in regard to the messages they transmit. Often they will not permit direct interaction between the would-be consultant and the line workers but will themselves act as intermediaries; for example, the guidance counselor will collect from the teachers all the information about a problem child and will himself discuss the case with the consultant. Such a situation may be quite frustrating to the mental health specialist. He will do well, however, to realize that he must try to satisfy the gatekeeper that his fears of being superseded are unfounded, so that eventually this defensive obstructionism can be laid aside as unnecessary. He should avoid early attempts to bypass the communication block by finding alternative channels along which to communicate with the classroom teachers; and he should not complain to the school principal and demand a less obstructive gatekeeper. Bypassing the obstacle will leave it actively operating at his rear, which may be hazardous, as it usually is also in military operations. The guidance counselor's suspicions and insecurities will be aggravated by this maneuver, and he will probably find ways of making a nuisance of himself. He is usually a senior staff member of the institution and probably has many friends in positions of influence.

The second approach, via the principal, may not succeed because he probably intended the guidance counselor to act as a specially vigilant gatekeeper. If not, and if he authorizes the bypassing of the latter, the situation may develop along the lines already discussed, unless the reputation that the mental health worker has managed to build up in the institution is clearly so positive, and the behavior of the guidance counselor so irrational and out of line with the felt needs of the rest of the staff, that a clear and explicit administrative decision by the principal to bypass the obstructionist will arouse the wholehearted support of all of them. This is unlikely unless the consultant has been working for a considerable time in the institution, during which period he has painstakingly been building up his equity in terms of the effectiveness and lack of threat of his interventions.

The best way of dealing with the problem of an obstructive gatekeeper is for the consultant to work patiently with him, and with whomever he will allow to have limited access to the mental health worker, until suspicions and insecurity have had a chance to die down.

In those instances when the director of the institution gives the mental health worker *carte blanche* in choosing his own channels of communication to the staff, the consultant will do well not to deal with this as a purely mechanical matter, which can be solved by means of the notice board in the staff common room, or by notes left in staff pigeonholes, but to search out the natural communication link people and gatekeepers in the system and use these as message carriers—for example, the supervisors in a public health nursing agency. If and when these people suggest simple channels through secretaries or notice boards, the mental health worker can feel confident that he has dealt with the major obstacles to communication and can settle down to a routine.

OBSTACLES TO COMMUNICATION

There are two types of obstacles to free communication, apart from the language barrier that I will discuss in a moment. The first is connected with realistic conflicts of interest between the mental health worker and some or all of the staff of the institution, so that they feel obliged to reduce his operations by interfering with his data collection or his messages. The second involves distorted perceptions and irrational expectations that make him appear dangerous, even though in reality he intends to be helpful.

Conflicts of Interest

Conflicts of interest between the consultant and members of the problem-solving staff of the consultee institution can easily occur, and the would-be consultant should always be on the alert to identify them and not fall into the trap of considering all opposition to his operations to be manifestations of irrational resistance. In a school, for example, it is likely that a variety of ways of dealing with problems of mental health and mental disorder among the students have developed over the years, and that in this connection various staff members have been allotted functions that have become part of their professional domains. These will probably include the principal, the educational supervisors, the school physician, the school nurse, the truant officer, the guidance counselors, the remedial reading and arithmetic staff, and possibly a school psychologist and a school social worker. Each of these workers will have his part to play; and each may feel, with some justification, that a mental health consultant may trespass on his preserves, and at least may oblige him to change his ways of operating. It may well be that the consultant may fulfill functions that none of them is equipped to undertake, and that he may help them to do better and more easily what they were already doing before he came. But unless the consultant finds out what each has been doing and carefully defines his own role so as not to overlap their domains, and unless he succeeds in communicating this clearly to them, it is likely that some of them will overtly or covertly oppose his entry into their system. If he comes in with the sanction of higher authorities, such as the superintendent of schools or the school board, overt opposition may not be feasible. In that case, they will covertly obstruct him as an intruder who is threatening their interests. Hidden opposition of this type should not be mistaken for unconsciously energized acting-out behavior. It must be dealt with by negotiation and not by manipulation or interpretation.

Distortions of Perception and Expectation

The second type of opposition is more familiar to mental health specialists because it is similar to what they regularly encounter in resistance to casework or psychotherapy. It is likely that the staff's perceptions of the would-be consultant will be colored by a variety of anxiety-provoking fantasies, and these will block and distort communication with him.

Some of the distortions of perception and expectation will be cultural; that is, they will be shared by most of the staff group of the institution and will be based on the ideologies they hold in common. Examples are the fearful perceptions of a mental health specialist as a "mind reader," who will lay bare one's forbidden thoughts; as a therapist, who will uncover one's psychological weaknesses and treat one as a dependent patient; as a psychoanalyst, who will weaken defenses and advocate sexual and aggressive license; and as a judge, who will condemn one and make one lose face because of one's professional and personal mistakes or inefficiencies. A common fantasy is that a mental health specialist will make one talk about unmentionable topics and lift the lid off Pandora's box, and thus drive one insane.

To these specific mental health fantasies are likely to be added stereotyped expectations associated with strangers, who may blunder about inside the institution and open up channels of communication that should remain closed; or who may discover the skeletons in the closet and communicate this information to critics in the outside community. If the consultant enters the system with the sanction of a higher authority, such as the superintendent of schools, he may be perceived as the latter's agent or as his spy.

If the consultant comes from an agency with which the institution has had previous dealings, he is likely to inherit past difficulties that may have been involved in their relationship. Institutional "memories" are long. It is important for the consultant to investigate the history of transactions between his agency and the institution as far back as possible. In one case a consultant, who was at a loss to understand the prolonged suspicion that greeted all his efforts to establish his trustworthiness in a public health nursing unit, eventually discovered that fifteen years earlier a director of his agency had been extremely rude and critical toward the public health nurses. Since that time, an attitude of deep suspicion of his agency had become part of the traditions and ideology of the nursing unit. The image he had inherited was that, despite his initial placatory behavior, he would eventually deliver a devastating attack on the nurses, just as his predecessor had done in the past.

The investigation of the past relationships of consultant and consultee institutions should be carried out before the consultant's initial visit. He should find out as much as possible by talking to the members of staff —particularly the old-timers—in his own organization, and he should be alert to memories of previous contacts that had been interrupted, especially in an atmosphere of conflict. This information should, wherever possible, be supplemented by his reading old case reports and combing the correspondence files to see whether his agency's written records throw light on the social structure and culture of the target institution, with reference to its traditions of dealing with the mental health problems of clients, and also on the vicissitudes of its transactions with his own organization.

Personal characteristics of the consultant may also stimulate stereotyped distortions of perception and expectation. A Jewish consultant in a Catholic agency was initially perceived as a person who would be likely to ride roughshod over the religious sensitivities of his consultees, advocate contraceptives and abortion, and attack their belief in God and in the discipline of their church.

In dealings with particular consultees, these culturally based stereotypes are, of course, likely to be compounded by individual transference distortions. Since a consultant often comes into an institution during periods of heightened tension and group and individual unrest, precipitated by mental health crises in its clientele and by the difficulties of handling them, the normal defensive structure of individuals may be weakened. This catalyzes a quicker and more regressive transference to a newcomer than would usually be expected. Mental health specialists, whose experience of transference has been confined to psychotherapy, especially with neurotic patients, are likely to be surprised by the rapid appearance of significant transference manifestations in initial consultation situations. They may either dismiss the evidence of their senses or wrongly ascribe these reactions to psychopathology in the institution staff.

DISSIPATING DISTORTIONS OF PERCEPTION AND EXPECTATION

An essential part of the task of a consultant is to explore these irrational perceptual stereotypes and to counteract their effects. He learns about them from behavioral cues and by being sensitive to the inner meaning of the words and actions of the institution staff, particularly in their defensive maneuvers in regard to him. He should allow the staff full freedom to manipulate him and to ascribe the roles to him that reveal their stereotyped fears, their testing out to confirm their suspicions, and also their ways of warding him off. As soon as he has identified these, he should take steps to dissipate the distortions of perception and expectation and to replace them by providing the consultees with opportunities to see him in his true colors.

The most important thing is to interact with as many people as possible in the institution, so that they can have personal experience of him and not feed their fantasies from the distorted reports of others. As soon as he can, he should make the rounds of all the staff. In this connection he is often helped by being invited to give a lecture or to explain the work of his agency at a staff meeting. He should always accept such an invitation, despite his possible doubts of the value of effective communication to a group of strangers by means of a rather formal lecture or report. Valid though this point of view may be, such a situation provides the mental health specialist with an invaluable opportunity to show himself publicly in his true colors to the institution staff. Whatever the topic of his lecture, he should try to include in it, often in the form of asides or by indirect allusions, messages designed to counteract those fantasies that he has reason to believe are coloring their perceptions of him. Thus, he can mention popular misconceptions about psychoanalysts, establish his belief in the importance of impulse control, clarify his attitudes of respect for colleagues of other professions, and emphasize the importance of a nonjudgmental approach and of confidentiality.

The Jewish consultant, referred to previously, used such a lecture to tell his Catholic audience that he respected people of other religions, that it was important, from the point of view of mental health, to support religious adherence and, for example, to respect the strictures of the church against contraceptives. He also reported the findings of a research project concerning the pathogenic influence on mother-child relationships of failed attempts at abortion by expectant mothers, whose religion condemned abortion as akin to murder.

The main method whereby these stereotypes are dissipated is by repeated personal interaction between the consultant and the staff of the institution—particularly key staff who act as the opinion molders of their fellows. These interactions have a variety of manifest contents, such as discussion of cases, exploration of the operations of each other's institution, negotiation of a collaborative agreement, and definition of domain boundaries. Whatever the manifest content, the consultant must constantly be alert to the latent content, which includes the institution staff members' repeated testing out to validate their fearful stereotypes and his equally repeated invalidation of these stereotypes by the direct and indirect messages of his verbal and nonverbal behavior.

For instance, when the consultant in the public health nursing unit learned about his predecessor of fifteen years earlier, he repeatedly sought opportunities in which the nurses might expect him to show signs of expressed or suppressed criticism of their performance, and in each case he demonstrated his nonjudgmental and respectful approach. He also demonstrated similar attitudes when discussing the work of other professionals in the community and the behavior of characters in case histories that were discussed with him. In many different ways he communicated over and over again to the public health nurses, "You can trust me to be consistently respectful of other people, especially those with less power and authority than I, because I am sensitive to the basic importance of human dignity, even though I do come from the same agency as the man who insulted and shamed your colleagues years ago."

During the period when the mental health specialist's image is being actively explored by the staff of the institution, he should be alert to their testing him out through the media of the cases they refer, the situations with which they confront him, and the questions they ask. He should take into account that practically every one of these is a test case, with a latent content involving some question about his attitudes and ideology as well as a manifest content related to the reality predicament in the current work situation. The consultant should try to identify these latent content questions and then answer them, while at the same time he is talking sensibly in relation to the manifest content level.

Particularly significant are jokes, banter, and witticisms of the staff on the subject of mental health and psychiatrists. These are important ways of manifesting and releasing tension, but they are also opportunities for the consultant to communicate meaningful messages that will dissipate distorting fantasies.

Banter such as "Have you brought your couch today?" or "I'm glad you've come—I am being driven crazy by these kids—I need treatment myself" or "Watch your tongue, Phyllis, the head shrinker is listening to you" should never be allowed to slip past without a corrective response. The latter should follow suit with regard to the brand of humor of the provocation; for example, "When I come here I leave my couch at home" or "We all feel at the end of our rope at times—it's a good thing we are sane enough to stand plenty of punishment" or "I had better watch out myself in front of so astute an observer—it's a good thing mind reading only works on the stage."

Testing out of the consultant in relation to individual transference distortions goes on indefinitely in the consultation relationship, but at the institution level it usually dies down as the consultant establishes his reputation as a person worthy of trust and respect, and as he gradually works his way through the initial suspicions and fearful fantasies with which he is greeted.

AROUSAL OF TRUST AND RESPECT

For the consultant to be perceived as trustworthy, the staff must be convinced that he is in general sympathy with the goals of their program and that he will not endanger their ways of working and their personal status. He must establish himself as honest, reliable, and consistent. He must also satisfy them that he will maintain confidentiality both inside and outside the institution, and that he will not utilize the information he obtains about them to do them any harm.

In order to arouse the respect of the staff, the consultant must make them feel that in his field he has expert knowledge that is directly applicable to some of their work problems; that he can understand these problems from their point of view; and that he is willing and able to make his knowledge and skill available to them in a readily assimilatable form, in order to help them overcome their difficulties. He is expected to be aware of and understanding of their psychological sensitivities, and to assist them in their predicaments without overburdening them. Particularly important is the requirement that he should be able to communicate with them at their own level, and that his messages not be academic but focus specifically on the practical issues that are important to them.

By and large, the consultant arouses the respect of the consultees by his reactions to the cases and work predicaments they ask him about. His principal mode of communication is not by stating his assessment of the situations or by giving advice, although when appropriate he may do both, but by the questions he poses about the material. These do not take the form of an interrogation of the consultee. Instead, the consultant sits beside the consultee, as it were, and engages in a joint pondering about the complexities of the problem. His contribution mainly takes the form of widening and deepening the focus of discussion by suggesting new avenues for collecting information, new possibilities for understanding the motivations and reactions of the characters in the case history, and new ways in which the situation might be handled.

DISTORTIONS OF THE CONSULTANT

The dissipation of perceptual stereotypes is not only a problem for the consultee. It is important also for the consultant. He too may suffer from preconceptions and culturally based distortions of perception and expectation in regard to the consultees, especially in relation to a new institution or a new consultee profession of which he has had no previous professional experience but about which he has heard from others or experienced himself in the past in a nonprofessional role. For instance, a consultant who has never before worked in a school system may have preconceptions about schoolteachers and school principals that are based upon his own previous experience in school years before, when he was a student. In like manner, a consultant who has not previously worked with clergymen may have difficulty in relating freely and realistically to religious leaders, especially those high up in the hierarchy. The same may apply to consulting with senior army officers. A consultant may not only have problems with high status consultees toward whom in a non-consultant role he may have developed attitudes of dependency (and sometimes rebelliousness), but he may also have difficulty in realizing the professional worth of consultees or professions of lower status than his own. It is not uncommon for psychiatrists to begin working with public health nurses, sanitarians, or public welfare officials with some feelings of condescension. These often do not manifest themselves in an overt conscious form but can be inferred by the surprise with which the consultant reports about the intelligent ways in which his consultees deal with their problems. This belittling of the other profession is a major obstacle to effective consultation. Apart from anything else, it is likely to be picked up by the consultees, who are very sensitive to the consultant's underlying feelings and attitudes toward them.

Consultants must constantly scrutinize themselves for such evidences of prejudice or stereotypes, and must try to overcome them in the same way in which they deal with this in their consultees—namely, by honestly trying to get to know the consultees through repeated interaction and observation.

Consultants, like consultees, are also apt to have their perceptions distorted by individual transference reactions. Since the consultant is more likely than the consultees to be undisturbed emotionally by work or social system problems of the consultee institution, he is less likely to suffer transference distortions because of the specific work situation. On the other hand, he too has a private life and is a member of staff of an agency, and in both areas intercurrent upsets may occur and may affect his emotional equilibrium. He must pay special attention to the effects of such matters on his professional balance, and must be particularly alert to a possible consonance between a private crisis, in which he happens currently to be involved, and the predicaments discussed with him by his consultees. It is not at all unusual for a crisis in a client to link with a current upset in a consultee and also with a disequilibrium in the consultant.

DEVELOPING A COMMON VERBAL AND NONVERBAL LANGUAGE

The removal of distortions of perception between consultant and consultees provides an opportunity for free communication but for the latter to be effective the two sides must share a common language. It is not enough for the consultant to avoid the technical jargon of his mental health specialty in talking with his consultees. He must realize that he has to make a special effort to learn the relatively private and idiosyncratic modes of communication of the consultee institution. These relate not only to vocabulary but also to such nonverbal behavior as gestures, comfort distance between people, punctuality, degree of interpersonal formality, signs of deference and respect, and ways of making appointments.

The consultant must constantly search for feedback from his consultees to validate that they have understood his messages, and he must check to see that he has understood their verbal and nonverbal communications. In the beginning he will often be surprised at the divergences in meaning that he will uncover by this cross checking. If he omits it, he will undoubtedly run into difficulties.

GROUND RULES FOR COLLABORATION

Associated with the task of developing a joint language is the need continually to work out and maintain consensus on the ground rules for collaboration. The nature of the consultant's operations in the institution and of the problems he is dealing with will change over time, as may the identity of the staff who ask him for help and the legitimate reasons for them to invoke his services. At each stage the consultant should ensure that his current role is clearly defined and that the institution staff knows what kinds of situation are appropriate to discuss with him and what they may expect from the collaboration. These ground rules should include a clear awareness of the source of sanction for this joint activity and also of the latter's limits—that is, who is or is not allowed to contact the consultant, where, at what time, for how long, how often, through which channels, and for what purpose. What can the consultant be expected to do, and what must he or will he not do?

SUCCESSIVE STAGES OF SPECIALIST ROLE

At the beginning of his contacts with an institution, the consultant may be a relatively unknown and unsanctioned visitor, whose operations are confined to helping a single staff member with a particular client, whom the specialist may observe or examine in order to make a diagnosis, prescribe treatment, or refer to another agency. In effect, he may be seen as a link with his own clinic, to which he will be expected to refer patients who need investigation or therapy.

At a later stage, the consultant may have received permission from the director of the institution to explore possibilities for more extensive collaboration. He may be invited to meet with staff members to increase their knowledge of mental health matters by giving them a lecture, leading a discussion, or directing a seminar. During such interactions he will learn about their work problems and the common difficulties they encounter in their clients, and they will discover whether his expert knowledge is relevant to their concerns and whether he is willing and able to assist them with the problems they feel to be important. He is seen mainly as a visiting expert, whose role is that of staff educator.

At that point the mental health specialist may be invited in, on an occasional or a regular basis, to talk with individuals or groups of the staff about problem clients. He will be expected to screen these and either to refer them to his clinic for investigation and treatment or suggest disposition to an outside agency, or else he may be expected to offer advice on appropriate management within the consultee institution. By now, he is seen as a consultant offering client-centered case consultation. He may also be expected to act as a collaborator in certain cases, and to treat some of the clients himself, either during his visits to the institution or back in his own clinic. He is, in addition, likely to be asked to carry back messages about clients who are being treated in his clinic and to provide reports from his colleagues to the institution staff about the progress of these cases.

At this stage, his role may have a variety of segments—liaison, staff educator, screener and diagnostician of clients, collaborator in treating clients of the institution, and client-centered case consultant. As he continues with his work in the institution, these role segments may continue and may be supplemented by additional elements, or he may give up certain functions as he takes on others. For instance, as he moves more into a consultant role, he may no longer personally take on as patients the clients of that institution, who may be dealt with by his colleagues back at the clinic; or reports on the progress of patients in therapy may be made directly by his colleagues without his intermediation.

At about that stage, it may become obvious to the director and staff of the consultee institution that they can receive adequate help if they discuss their cases with the consultant rather than asking him to examine each client who is a source of difficulty; and that this conserves time and allows the consultant to assist them with more cases. This usually leads to a move from client-centered to consultee-centered case consultation. Eventually, the administrators of the institution develop enough trust and respect for the consultant to invite his advice on policy and program development, and he is asked to give program-centered and, later, consultee-centered administrative consultation.

This succession of phases may take a varying amount of time to unfold. It is usually a lengthy process. The process may not develop beyond a particular phase because of the complications of the situation in a consultee institution or because of the talents and interests of the consultant. It is important that the mental health worker be fully aware of the phase that the process has reached, and that he ensure that, in addition, this be made explicit to the staffs of his clinic and of the consultee institution by the negotiation and renegotiation of a series of agreements or contracts governing his operations as they develop over time.

THE CONSULTATION CONTRACT

It has become customary to use the term "consultation contract" for the agreement between the consultant and consultees about their complementary roles. This term has the disadvantage of implying the existence of a legal document, which is rarely the case; but it does emphasize an issue of importance, namely that there has to be negotiation between consultant and consultees that leads to a formal or informal agreement, involving sanctioned mutual behavior and some sort of exchange of goods or services. The use of the term also emphasizes the need not only for the initial negotiation of an agreement but also for renegotiations to change the terms of the agreement, when the situation of the two parties alters with the passage of time.

Obtaining Sanction

Initial sanction for the entry of the consultant into the consultee institution is obtained from the director or one of his representatives. This has already been mentioned. As the consultant develops his successive roles he must take care to obtain sanction for his operations also from people in the intermediate layers of the authority hierarchy of the institution down to and including the line workers with whom he will be working. For instance, in a school in which he will be working with classroom teachers to help with problem children, he should clarify what he will be doing, not only with the principal, but also with the vice-principal and the educational supervisors, as well as with the teachers' group. All these people must understand the nature of his activities and agree in general with his goals and methods. If he misses people in any of the layers, he is likely to run into difficulty, because they may undermine his program overtly or covertly. Of particular importance is the sanction of the middle management or supervisory group. They are usually in a position to exert a great deal of influence on the line workers, and their support is essential in the development of a smoothly running program.

Obtaining sanction is essentially a simple matter, once the consultant has explicitly recognized that he needs to do it. Usually all that is necessary, in addition to his general activities in arousing trust and respect, is for him to go from one person or group to another in the system, as he learns about their needs and works out what he is able and willing to do to satisfy them, and explore with them whether what he has in mind seems sensible to them. He also elicits their reactions and suggestions for modification, so that he, in effect, gives them a hand in molding his program to suit their perceptions of their work problems and of the ways in which he can be most helpful. What emerges then is a joint plan, or rather a series of successive modifications of the joint plan, as he discusses it with the various workers and authority figures concerned. Eventually, when the details of the plan have been worked out, all the relevant people have been involved and know about them. They have all had an opportunity to modify them and therefore have a personal commitment to supporting the plan.

It is clear that this type of careful layered working through may be time consuming. It should not be hurried. The consultant should allow time for the people in different positions in the institution to consider the implications of his operations for their own work, and to think out ways in which he can best help them or their peers and subordinates in the social system without interfering too much with their traditional ways of managing their affairs. The introduction of a new person into a system invariably involves some disruption. This cautious approach minimizes the latter and provides an opportunity for the integration of the consultant's efforts into the existing problem-solving system of the institution.

Content of the Contract

In addition to its sanction for his operations in general, the contract must specify what those operations must be and also must spell out or imply the details of that exchange between the two parties which is the basis for all contracts.

In the early stages of the consultant's work in an institution, both sides may have only vague ideas about these issues. The contract at that time will mirror this by stating that the mental health specialist and the staff of the institution are engaging in explorations to see whether they can work out mutually acceptable goals and methods of collaboration. Such a contract may not be in writing or be formalized but may be implicit in the discussions between the would-be consultant and the potential consultees. I have found it advantageous, even in these early stages, to make this type of agreement explicit, and to emphasize that I expect the exploratory phase to lead to concrete findings that will eventually be included in a new agreement between the parties concerned.

As a result of my experience, I have also come to the conclusion that as early as possible, and certainly as soon as clear details of complementary roles begin to emerge, it is advantageous to begin formulating the contract in writing. This does not have to be a formal document. Usually it takes the form of an exchange of letters. The written word is an excellent way of revealing misunderstandings, which may be obscured in verbal discussions. It is important that these be corrected as early as possible in order to arrive at true consensus.

These letters should specify how often and for how long the consultant will visit; how potential consultees will communicate with him; the type of cases that it is appropriate to discuss with him; the kind of consultation to be involved (that is, case consultation and/or administrative consultation, client-centered and/or consultee-centered); what help he will offer (that is, advice, referral, collaboration or not, enlargement of the consultee's understanding, etc.); and the nature and limits of confidentiality. The contract should also specify what the consultant will *not* do—for example, psychotherapy for personal problems of consultees, discussion of intrastaff problems such as relationships of line workers and supervisors, intervention in staff conflicts, etc. It should also specify in what way the consultant and his agency will benefit from the program —for example, the amount and type of payment; or if no direct payment is involved, the professional rewards, such as the contribution of the consultee group to the achievement of the consultant's mission of promoting mental health or reducing the incidence of mental disorder in the population for whose well-being he has some responsibility.

Renegotiation of Sanction and Content of Contract

It is clear from what has already been said that the negotiation of the initial contract takes the form of a series of steps involving a number of successive approximations to an eventual stable agreement between the parties concerned. It is important to emphasize that this agreement may not be very stable but should be expected to change with the passage of time and because of various types of alteration in the situation both of the consultant and the consultee agencies and of the community in which they operate.

The term "consultation contract" may obscure this, because most legal contracts usually have greater stability and can be relied upon not to change for long periods, even though it is recognized that occasionally they may need review and modification.

Consultants should always write into the contract a clause dealing with systematic review and revision—for example, that the parties should meet once a year to evaluate the consultation program and suggest improvements in the terms of the agreement.

In addition, the consultant should be alert to the need to conduct such a review when unexpected changes take place in the policies of his own organization or in the program or personnel of the consultee institution. It is particularly important to initiate such a review if there is a change in any of the key posts of the consultee institution which may affect the sanction of the consultation program—for example, a change of school principal or a change of nursing supervisor in a public health agency. On such occasions, it is rarely wise to rely on the new officeholder's being adequately briefed about the program by his predecessor and, more significant, on his being in full agreement with the terms of a contract, in the gradual formulation of which he was not involved. Instead, the consultant should realize that he must start almost from the beginning to negotiate sanction with the new man and to involve him in a major review and possibly a detailed reformulation of the content of the contract. The goal of this is that the new man should feel that this is a program which he has had a chance to mold and to which he can wholeheartedly commit himself, rather than somebody else's project that he has inherited.

Sanction Maintenance

In addition to these systematic and situationally determined renegotiations of the contract with those members of staff of the consultee institution who are directly involved with the program, the consultant must also ensure that significant figures of power and influence higher up in the system of which the institution is part, or in positions of influence in the community, are continually kept informed of his operations and are stimulated to support him. These people are usually very busy and the consultant should not annoy them by intruding unduly on their time; but every once in a while he should seize an appropriate opportunity to send them a copy of a short report about the consultation program or to visit them for an informal chat about his work, so that they may keep abreast of his progress and have a chance to make explicit their support. This should lead to such a situation, for instance, that when the local superintendent of schools, or the chairman of the board of education, is at a banquet and the lady sitting next to him tells him that she has heard disquieting reports that a psychologist from the local community mental health center is carrying out some kind of mysterious investigation on the mental health of students, he can immediately and comfortably reply that he knows all about the program and there is nothing mysterious about it —that in fact the psychologist's visits are part of an excellent modern program to promote the mental health of children by providing specialist support to teachers and school principals, and that he is very proud of it. An effective superintendent of schools would probably make this kind of response in any case, but the consultant should ensure that he has visited him sufficiently recently and has kept him well enough informed of the developments in his program that the superintendent feels quite confident that all is well and does not need to check up on the program immediately when he gets to the office next day.

COMMON METHODOLOGICAL ISSUES

The following methodological issues are frequently encountered by consultants engaged in building relationships in consultee institutions:

Ensuring Adequate Communication of the Contract to Consultees

The consultant can rarely rely on the communication network of the consultee institution to convey undistorted messages about the details of the contract to all members of its staff. He should therefore take every opportunity to clarify and confirm the essential points himself, particularly those which are emotionally complicated. This means that he should gladly accept all opportunities offered to him to talk to groups of the staff, and, whatever the topic of the meeting, mention the points he has in mind as supplements or asides to his scheduled remarks. He should also repeat them over and over again whenever he is talking to individual staff members. For instance, he should repeatedly tell them that consultation deals only with work difficulties and never with private personal issues of the consultee, that the consultation discussions are confidential, that he will not carry messages or in any other way intervene or take sides in differences of opinion among staff members, and (if the contract includes consultee-centered consultation) that the help the staff can expect from him will lead to enlarging and deepening their understanding of the psychological aspects of their clients so that they and their supervisors can develop more effective ways of handling their work problems.

Dealing with Status Problems

The goal of relationship building is to achieve a coordinate or non-hierarchical relationship with the consultees, so that they will not be forced or feel coerced to accept what the consultant says just because he says it. Since they will be free to accept or reject, they will quickly and without dependency tensions be able to take as their own any ideas that make sense to them within the framework of their own conceptual and value systems. This desirable situation is achieved by the consultant's behaving in a noncoercive and respectful way and by various techniques that will be discussed in the next chapter. But the development of such a coordinate relationship will be obstructed if in fact the consultee has very low status in the consultee organization while the consultant is a senior member of staff of the consulting agency—for instance, if the psychiatric director of the community mental health program offers consultation to a junior nurse's aide or a student teacher. When this happens, the consultant must take special steps in the consultation interaction to "divest himself of rank."

This is particularly difficult if the consultant and consultee are respectively senior and junior members of the same profession. When this is the case, it is very hard for the consultee not to see the consultant as a role model and to feel compelled to do whatever he says, despite being admonished to feel free to reject any part of the consultant's statements.

The best way of handling this problem is to avoid it, by taking care to appoint a consultant who is of a different profession from the majority of staff members of the consultee institution.

Another common status difficulty which complicates the task of relationship building and contract negotiation arises when the would-be consultant is of obviously lower status than the authority figures in the consultee institution—for instance, when a junior social worker attempts to negotiate a contract with the superintendent of schools. A useful way of dealing with this is for a senior member of the consultant organization to open the negotiations with the authority figure and, after the initial phases, for him to introduce the junior staff member as his personal representative, upon whom, as it were, he confers his own power and status. In dealing with a large organization, it may be necessary for negotiations to be carried out at a variety of levels in the consultee hierarchy by representatives of the consonant levels of the consultant ladder of rank. In an army mental hygiene service, for instance, the psychiatric director, who is a major, will negotiate with the general commanding the camp; the social worker, who is a lieutenant, will negotiate with the captain who commands a unit; and the enlisted man social work technician will negotiate with the noncommissioned officers of a company. After the initial contacts, it may be possible for some of the negotiation to be delegated to lower status representatives, but there are obvious limits to this—the general is not likely to take kindly to negotiating a consultation contract with an enlisted man. Although the army is an extreme example, this principle also holds in less hierarchical settings. There must be a culturally acceptable consonance between the rank of parties to a negotiation in order to allow relatively free communication.

Resistance to Consultation as a Publicly Visible Sign of Professional Inadequacy

In many potential consultee institutions the development of a consultation program is hindered by the attitude that when a staff worker asks for consultation this is an admission of professional incompetence. This would be the case especially with regard to consultee-centered consultation. The way this problem has often been successfully overcome is for the consultant to emphasize that consultation deals with cases in which the *problems of clients* are complicated, unclear, and confusing, rather than using the formulation that consultation seeks to help *consultees* who are confused about their clients.

The first formulation allows the consultant to educate the staff of the consultee institution to the realization that for them to recognize clients whose problems are particularly complex demands professional sophistication in mental health matters. This makes the identification of a case as appropriate for consultation a sign of professional merit, instead of inadequacy.

This message must be directed by the consultant to the power and influence figures of the institution, particularly the supervisory group. If they accept the formulation and its associated value judgment, they will set the pattern for the rest of the staff.

Avoidance of Undue Dependency among Consultees

This is, of course, largely a matter that is determined by the transactions between the consultant and individual consultees, and it will be dealt with at this level in the next chapter. It does, however, have an institutional aspect. The consultant can make his task with individual consultees much easier if he handles appropriately his relationship with the staff as a whole.

In order to arouse their respect and their expectation that they will be helped if they consult him when they encounter a mental health difficulty in their work, he must establish himself as an expert in the field of mental health. But he must be careful to define his expertise as a circumscribed matter, and to make it clear to all concerned that outside his own field he is a layman who is perfectly comfortable about confessing his ignorance and uncertainty and in asking others for clarification and guidance. In particular, he must not be bashful in communicating his lack of knowledge regarding the professional fields of his consultees, and he should sincerely ask them to educate him in regard to the realities of their professional work. He should encourage the consultee group to be active also in teaching him to understand their work problems as they see them, and the range of ways they have developed for conceptualizing and dealing with them. In other words, he must help them see that the role of consultee is an active one, and that in large measure they will be responsible for making optimal use of what he brings to them.

In fact, this is basically true, because the fundamental difference between the operations of a mental health specialist dealing directly with his own patient and as a consultant dealing indirectly with a client through the intermediation of a consultee is his ability to understand the consultee's point of view and potential for action with the client. The consultant must be a student of the social system and the role problems of the consultee, and his best teachers will be the consultees themselves.

Identifying and Managing the Specific Problems Relating to the Professional Culture of the Consultees

I have already emphasized that it is a fundamental part of the role of the consultant to build up as rapidly as possible a picture of the social system and culture of the consultee institution, as well as of the individual and group characteristics of its staff. He will be aided in doing this if he learns the idiosyncratic features of the subcultures of different categories of community agencies and consultee professions. If, for instance, he builds up a body of information about public health units, schools, churches of different denominations, and welfare agencies, and if he learns the special characteristics of each class of agency and its professionals, he will more rapidly know what to look for and how to be prepared to act when he first visits a new institution of that type.

As an example of such professional and institutional idiosyncrasies, we can take public health nursing units, many of which seem to have the following characteristics:

1. Public health nurses are usually overburdened—they have bigger case loads than can easily be managed. This is often related to their low status in health departments, such that whenever there is an overall budget cutback, their establishment tends to get reduced. Moreover, there is an overall shortage of nurses, which also applies to the public health field. Because of this situation, public health nurses are particularly sensitive to being given extra burdens, which not infrequently happens when people higher in the public health authority system react to new ideas and add new functions to the agency without being able to supplement its resources. Consultants must therefore be very careful not to add to the nurses' burdens, such as by asking unnecessarily for return visits to patients, for time-consuming studies in connection with consultation sessions, or for more or longer consultation interviews than is absolutely essential. Group sessions are expensive in staff time and should be arranged only when it appears that they will have more value to the nurses than individual interviews. Consultation should be clearly seen by all concerned as a way of lightening rather than increasing the work load.

2. Associated with this work burden is the common finding that public health nurses are meticulous about time. They have to be in order to keep up with the pressure of work. The consultant should be as careful to appear on time to his appointments as he is in his psychotherapy schedule, which is geared to the "fifty-minute hour." He should be particularly careful to end interviews, and especially group meetings, exactly on time.

3. Public health nurses can easily evade work difficulties associated with their clients. They can be too busy to visit a troublesome patient, or they can knock softly on the door and leave when it is not immediately opened. This is in contrast to an elementary schoolteacher, who is forced to deal every day of the school year with a problem child in her class. Because of this, consultants must be especially careful to build and maintain the correct intensity of consultation relationship with public health nurses so that they will be motivated to return to discuss difficult cases. All intermediate sessions in a consultation sequence should end

with the consultant's arranging an appointment for the next interview. He usually cannot afford to leave this up to the consultee, as he often can with a teacher.

4. Many public health nursing problems involve patients in apparently irremediable life situations—members of chronically deprived groups, with low intelligence, no instrumental or social skills, broken families, problems simultaneously in health, economic, legal, educational, social, and welfare fields, etc. When the consultee expresses feeling of hopelessness, this may seem to the consultant to be only reasonable. Optimism on the part of the consultant may appear the approach of a Pollyanna. And yet, as a consultant gains more familiarity with the work of experienced public health nurses, he discovers that they often do manage to make an effective contribution in these cases—not in remedying the total situation, but in dealing with their relatively narrow but nevertheless significant health segment, and in mobilizing other sources of community support and assistance. This work may be impeded in a general way by cultural prejudices relating to race, patterns of sexual behavior, cleanliness and order in the home, or style of child rearing. But most experienced nurses manage reasonably well to help most of their patients within the traditional framework that has gradually been worked out by their profession over many years of empirical trial and error in their field. Most of them are able to maintain their professional poise and to make their contribution effectively in their everyday practice in situations that are likely to appall members of the mental health professions, who are not accustomed to working in such a field. Incidentally, these same nurses would probably be demoralized if they were faced by the everyday problems of a mental hospital ward, to which our profession has become accustomed and which we have learned to master.

It is only the occasional cases that upset a public health nurse. If she is well trained and experienced and has absorbed the lore of her profession, it is likely that these upsetting cases are caused, not by the inherent difficulties of the client's situation that are common to most of her cases, but by some personal sensitivity of her own or by some lack of support in the system of her public health unit. If the consultant does not deal with this sensitivity but reassures the consultee about the case or disentangles her perceptions of the client from her own problems, her handling of this case will improve, but she will go on repeating this difficulty with other clients, unconsciously selected from her large case load. If the consultant is successful in his efforts to help her overcome the specific area of her sensitivity in the work field, this process will lessen and eventually stop, and the public health nurse will be able to deal more or less helpfully and with professional empathy and objectivity with this type of case, as with her others.

In my experience, I have found that it takes a mental health consultant some time when he first starts to work with public health nurses to believe the evidence of his senses in this regard, and to overcome his initial agreement with his consultee that the case she presents is indeed hopeless because of the dramatic impact of the client's multitudinous problems.

5. Because of the multiproblem character of many of her cases, because despite her generalist professional tradition the approach of the public health nurse is to refer cases to specialized agencies, and because most of her clients are already in contact with numerous community agencies, the problem of communication with other institutions in neighboring fields and of coordination of professional effort looms large in her work. This is a problem to the solution of which mental health consultation can make little contribution. True, an expert consultant, especially a social worker, may have a much better knowledge of the network of community agencies and how to energize them and communicate with them than does a public health nurse; but the communication of such information by means of individual sessions directed by highly paid mental health specialists who are in short supply is not a practical proposition. Insofar as failure of the public health nurses to communicate adequately with other agencies may be the result of a devalued professional self concept with attendant defensiveness, it may improve as a side effect of consultation, which raises both confidence and sense of responsibility. Apart from this, the approach to the problem should clearly be not consultation but systematic education, preferably with groups of supervisors, who will then each in turn pass on the knowledge and skill to their supervisees.

Consultants should be alert to issues of common concern such as this in their experience with the nurses, and when they are identified the consultants should deal with them by initiating or advising other methods of remedy than consultation.

6. A factor that is partly responsible for aggravating the above problem, but that also has meaning in its own right, is that a special characteristic of public health nursing units at the present time is the high mobility of nurses, and the entry into the field of many young, poorly trained, and inexperienced professionals. In any year it is likely that one third to one half of the staff of a unit will change. Many of the newcomers will be girls just out of hospital nursing schools, who may have had scanty training in public health. There may be a few old-timers in the

unit, but the majority of staff may be nurses with under two years of service in the agency. The young girls may leave within a year because of marriage or pregnancy, or to explore other avenues of professional and personal fulfillment.

This poses a problem to the consultant who is eager to make a lasting contribution to the unit. From this standpoint it may be a relative waste of his time for him to spend it in individual consultation with nurses, whose service will be so fleeting and whose needs may be basically related to a lack of knowledge and skill that is more efficiently dealt with by systematic education in groups and by individual supervision. On the other hand, his contribution via consultation to individuals will have a carryover, through modifying the values and traditions of the social system of the agency. His effect on individuals will, as it were, reverberate in the group, and thus in turn influence new nurses as they appear.

A consultant in a public health nursing unit must not mechanically appear once a week to provide individual consultation to those who request it, as for instance he might validly do in an institution with a more stable population of workers, such as a school. He must constantly guide his operations in order to achieve an optimal balance between individual and group consultation and other methods, such as education of public health nurses and their supervisors.

7. This raises the question of the place of group consultation for public health nurses. The advantages are clear—the consultant's communications are received not only by the transients but also by the more stable members; the supervisor, who is usually one of the most stable persons in the unit, as well as the key person in spreading messages to others, can be present; the peer group support strengthens each of the nurses vis-à-vis the consultant and facilitates a nonhierarchical relationship; nurses can benefit from the emotional and cognitive contributions of others "in the same boat"; more experienced nurses can contribute information about the realities and possibilities of the nursing role that may be relatively unknown to the consultant; inexperienced nurses can direct attention to problems that may be obscured among their seniors by the defenses and blind spots caused by prolonged frustration and resignation; cultural stereotypes and prejudices can more easily be identified and possibly handled; and common theme distortions, due to shared social system problems interfering with work, can be dealt with as group problems.

On the other hand, group meetings are expensive in terms of scarce nursing time, and individual theme interference may be harder and sometimes even hazardous to deal with in a group, in which the consultant does not have as much control over the content of discussion as in an individual interview. Moreover, the problems of an individual may not be a salient issue for others in the group, and these others may be essentially wasting their time as passive bystanders or even as interested observers, while the consultant is dealing with the problems of somebody else.

8. A point worthy of mention is connected with the low status of nurses in the public health hierarchy. They may not be the lowest, but they are in fact quite low "on the totem pole"; and in order to maintain their professional equilibrium they have therefore had to work out ways of resisting pressure from the higher levels of the power hierarchy, who may try to force them to take on all kinds of new responsibilities as the changeable winds of fashion blow. Public health is in general an authoritarian setting, connected with its history as an agent of community control over hazards and nuisances in the social as well as physical environment. Public health nurses are therefore trained to adopt a disciplined compliance with orders from above. The result has been the development of a subtle informal type of passive or hidden resistance to pressure and a cultural suspiciousness of promises of support and extra resources to be given in return for supplementary or new duties.

All this makes for particular difficulties in consultation. First, it is hard for a consultant who is probably a member of a higher status profession, such as psychiatry, to overcome informally in the consultation inverview the formal authority differential between himself and the nurse, and to establish their relationship as nonhierarchical. Second, he must expect prolonged testing out to determine his *bona fides,* and particularly whether he or his agency intends to continue with this help, or whether they will make promises of support that will suddenly be withdrawn. Third, the consultant must never underestimate the need to obtain the full sanction of the line nurses as a group. Because of their low status in an authoritarian setting and their superficially disciplined behavior, he may make the mistake of thinking that as long as their superiors have sanctioned his operations the staff nurses will comply. They will, of course, do so on the surface. If, however, they are not themselves convinced of his trustworthiness and potential for helpfulness, he will soon find that his efforts are blandly and effectively vitiated by a whole variety of hidden obstructions, ranging from missed appointments for all kinds of apparently authentic reasons, to patients who suddenly vanish into thin air, to banal time-wasting requests for "nonconsultation," and to a progressive dwindling of the number of consultees until he has nothing at all to do on his visits to the unit.

9. The last, but far from the least, idiosyncratic aspect of consultation with public health nurses is connected with the role of the supervisor and her traditional relationships with her line nurses. Consultants who for the first time begin to work in public health nursing units often run into difficulties with the supervisors, and they may ascribe these to personality disorders in the latter. I have been impressed over the years by the number of well-trained clinicians among my student consultants who initially report to me that the nursing supervisor in their unit is paranoid or obsessional. Sometimes this may be true, although the evidence adduced for this diagnosis is usually not appropriate. More often, what the inexperienced consultant is picking up is not behavior caused by personality disorder but characteristic role-prescribed behavior of a supervisor which is in keeping with the realities of the public health nursing mission and traditions. For instance, a characteristic feature of the role of a public health nurse is that, in contrast to a hospital nurse, she is operating far from medical supervision. She has to make many decisions involving judgments of complicated health issues in her patients, who may not have been seriously investigated by a physician for a long time. The tradition of nursing is that nurses carry out a doctor's instructions, and that a physician is professionally responsible for what she does. This is also true in public health. The medical director of the department carries the ultimate responsibility. Moreover, as a public employee he is very visible, and his responsibility is governed not only by professional ethics but also by law. Add this to the previously mentioned historical tradition of authoritarian control, and one begins to understand the dilemma of public health nursing, in which a large number of low-status generalists, many of them young girls just out of school, are operating far from base in a complicated and technically difficult field, which may be politically quite sensitive in relation to the possibility of complaints against officials, who may have been appointed by rival party leaders.

One way that has been worked out to deal with this is to control the operations of the public health nurses through a corps of experienced supervisors. In theory, this stable and dependable group is the link between the health officers and the distant field. This has led to the situation that in many health departments the supervisor is the person held responsible for all action with patients; and the public health nurses of varying experience, who come and go, are regarded not as independently responsible professionals but as her agents. She is supposed to know all the patients in her population and to control their treatment in line with the orders of the health officers. She does this through the operations of her nurses, for whose every movement she is held personally responsible.

Of course, in practice, the number of contacts with patients is too great for a supervisor to be able to master them; but nevertheless if anything goes wrong with a patient, it is not the nurse but the supervisor who is held accountable. And this naturally increases her need for surveillance and control over her group of supervisees, as well as her sensitivity to any factor that potentially interferes with this aspect of her duties.

Consultation of the kind described in this book is a prime example of such a factor. Traditionally, consultants in public health nursing, such as specialists in nutrition or orthopedic nursing or physiotherapy, do not see consultees except in the presence of the supervisor, who can hear what they suggest to improve the treatment of the cases in her sphere of responsibility, and who can also use the consultation session to extend or deepen her knowledge of the behavior of her supervisees. Any difference of opinion between her and the consultant can be dealt with directly in this face-to-face confrontation. This style of consultation reduces the possibility that inevitable tensions between her supervisees and herself will be complicated by their appealing for support to an outsider.

In contrast, our style of mental health consultation usually demands a private and confidential relationship with the nurses, from which their supervisor is specifically excluded. This places a cognitive and emotional strain on the system, and the focus of this burden is upon the supervisor.

In addition to all this, the supervisor acts as a gatekeeper in the system to make sure the consultant is safe for her supervisees—but in this regard, her role does not differ significantly from that of gatekeepers in other institutions, such as schools, to which I have referred earlier in this chapter.

A consultant who has learned about these constraints within which a public health nursing supervisor operates will be especially careful in his dealings with her, and will develop ways of operating that allow him to fulfill his consultation goals without endangering the precarious balance of her control over her supervisees. If his style of consultation involves recommendations on nursing action, he will arrange for the supervisor to be present during the session or during a formal summing-up conference about the case with himself and his consultee. If she is excluded from the consultation, he must be meticulous not to say anything that his consultee can interpret as advice on action; and he must restrict himself to adding to the consultee's knowledge, understanding, or freedom to operate, while leaving the action plan to be worked out by the consultee in collaboration with her supervisor. He must also be on the alert to forestall or interrupt any attempt by his consultees to drive a wedge between him and their supervisor or to play off one against the other—for instance, by manipulating him to support them in conflicts they may have with her.

He must spend time at each visit interacting personally with the supervisor to give her a chance to get to know him as a trustworthy and effective individual. He must also learn to talk freely with her, even about cases that he has discussed in consultation, without leaking any confidential information about the behavior of his consultees.

10. Because of the formal style of operation of many public health nursing services, it is useful for the consultants to collaborate with the nursing administrators in developing a written statement of their consultation policies and procedures that is communicated to all members of their staff. This statement is an expression of the administration's view of the consultation contract and provides the formal framework that molds the expectations of the nurses in regard to their relationships with the mental health consultants. The following is a good example of such a policy statement that was developed by a city visiting nurse association:

MENTAL HEALTH CONSULTATION

Mental health consultants are regularly assigned for service to each nursing unit. These consultants may be psychiatrists, psychologists, social workers, or mental health-psychiatric nurses. They visit each nursing unit at weekly or bi-weekly intervals. A rule of thumb is that any situation, family, or patient that a nurse wishes to discuss in relation to aspects of mental health or mental illness will be appropriate for consultation. Mainly, this consultation will be conducted on an individual nurse-consultant basis. For example, a nurse might wish to clarify her understanding about the meaning of symptoms she observes in a patient and by exploring certain aspects of the situation with the mental health consultant, her approach to the problem may be eased. During this discussion, the consultant will not make any direct suggestions for her choice of nursing action. If the nurse needs to reach a decision regarding what she should do in relation to these possible choices or alternatives, her supervisor would guide her according to customary agency policy.

The content of all discussion with the mental health consultant will be geared to work discussion, and not to the feeling of the nurse or her own life experiences. It is taken for granted that the nurse naturally is concerned about certain perplexing or unclear aspects of a family or patient situation and the consultation discussion will be limited to this area. The nurse's own feelings or personal life experiences, important as these may be, will be considered inappropriate for consultation discussion. Neither will it be considered appropriate for the discussion to consist of analyzing any possible reasons for differences of opinion between staff nurses or disagreements that might exist between a staff nurse and her supervisor.

When a nurse desires to meet with a consultant, she should request her supervisor to schedule such a consultation session. The supervisor should know which patients or families are to be discussed, but the details of the consultation between the nurse and the consultant are to be completely confidential and need not be shared with the supervisor, since there will be no recommendations for nursing action.

If a common group of problems appear to be present in a district and the supervisor and nurses desire a small or large group meeting in order to discuss these with the consultant, the supervisor can request this and make such arrangements. These problems also would, of course, concern the work situation with patients or families and not personal problems or intrastaff situations.

Any suggestions for improvement of the consultation service are always encouraged, and may be given directly to the consultant or indirectly through the supervisor to the consultant.

[5]

Building the Relationship with the Consultee

INTRODUCTION

Whatever the type of consultation, the effect of the consultant's intervention is mediated by the relationship between the consultee and himself. This must be a relationship of mutual trust and respect, so that what each expresses has importance and significance for the other. The consultee must be open to the cognitive and affective influence of the consultant, but at the same time he must feel sufficiently independent to accept only those aspects of the consultant's ideas about the case that fit in with his own needs and with his subjective impressions of the realities of his current professional situation.

The ideal consultation relationship is one of *coordinate interdependence,* in which each side both gives to and takes from the other. The consultee must educate the consultant to understand as much as possible about his work setting and about the complications of his role vis-à-vis the client. He must also help the consultant pinpoint the special difficulties of the case, so that he can usefully plan his consultation intervention. The consultee must then work out a new approach to the client based upon selected aspects of the consultant's formulations. The role of consultee certainly includes dependence on the consultant. The latter gives him emotional support and cognitive guidance through enlarging and deepening his understanding of mental health issues and through clarifying previously unperceived patterns in the dynamics of the case. In this process the consultant brings to bear expert knowledge not normally available to the consultee. But the dependent role of the consultee is fulfilled mainly by an active process of drawing what is needed from the consultant and not by merely passively receiving what the latter offers.

The consultant, on his side, is striving to understand the realities of the consultee's present professional situation and its problems. Even in client-centered case consultation, in which his major focus will be upon elucidating the intricacies and implications of the client's case, he knows that his eventual formulations and recommendations will be of value only insofar as they are acceptable and feasible to the consultee. In consultee-centered consultation, his dependence on the consultee, who is the arbiter of the action outcome, is even more obvious. As a consultant, his expertness only improves the situation to the extent that it serves the current needs and capabilities of the consultee. However much the consultant may know about the culture of the institution and the consultee profession, as well as about the personality and history of the consultee and about the details of the client's case, he will never be able to formulate a contribution to the consultee's knowledge and skill that is *exactly* consonant with the latter's needs and capacities and those of his social system. Nor can he absolutely ensure that this formulation will be used as he intends it. If he were to have coercive power over the consultee he could force him to accept the formulation, but apart from his not being certain that his ideas are entirely appropriate, such coercion would most probably mean that the suggestions would remain a foreign element in the consultee's thinking and would take a long time to be integrated, or perhaps would be rejected as soon as the consultant left the scene.

This mixture of mutual dependence, accompanied by the need for activity on both sides, ideally demands that consultant and consultee develop a professional partnership in which each makes his own contribution to the elucidation of the client's case and how to deal with it. Each relies on the other for supplementation, both in bringing special knowledge to bear (whether about the mental health implications of the client's case or about the opportunities and constraints of the consultee's role), and also in the mutual emotional support of working together to achieve a superordinate goal.

In our culture, consultees usually have little difficulty in realizing their dependence on consultants for emotional support and for contributions of expert knowledge and skill. They find it harder to understand the demand the consultation situation makes on them for activity in teaching the consultant to understand their professional predicament and role complications. On the other hand, consultants readily perceive the need to provide support and guidance but find it difficult to realize the extent of their real dependence on the consultees, not only for essential information about the professional role of the consultee and for the mediation of action outcome for the client, but also to achieve the consultant's fundamental community mental health goals of population-focused prevention. The latter demands the type of chain reaction that mental health consultation is designed to produce by the continuation of its effects after the termination of the current case through the integration of new knowledge and skills within the future functioning of the consultees. Consultants who do not realize this do not see that there is an existential basis for the coordinate relationship in consultation. In actuality, the nonhierarchical approach is not just an idealistic technical device—it is demanded by the realities of the situation.

GETTING TO KNOW THE CONSULTEE

Before the consultant can promote the building of a relationship with the consultee, the two professionals must get to know each other. The consultant must therefore arrange opportunities for contact between them. This can be accomplished in two main ways: (a) by establishing "spontaneous" proximity and (b) by scheduling formal interviews.

Establishing Proximity

This may be engineered by means of social gatherings, such as by accepting an invitation to coffee with the group of public health nurses on the occasion of a visit to a public health unit, or by sitting around chatting in the staff common room or in the cafeteria in a school. It may also be achieved as a side effect of some formal activity, such as in a group discussion following a lecture, or in "hanging around" after the lecture is over.

The essential point is for the consultant to bring himself within talking distance of the consultee in a setting where it is socially acceptable for them to talk informally with each other without significant commitment on either side. In this situation, the consultant should behave in such a way as to appear approachable, and should perhaps initiate the contact with some informal bridge comments about the weather or questions about the institution.

Scheduling Meetings

On a number of occasions we have found it valuable to arrange with a public health nurse supervisor or school principal for a series of scheduled interviews with members of their staff in systematic rotation. These interviews are set up quite explicitly so that the potential consultees may get to know the consultant and so that he should learn something about the clientele of the institution. It is often important to keep the focus off the work of the consultees, in order to reassure them that it is the problems posed by their clients and not their own personal methods of working which the consultant wishes to investigate.

In some cases, nurses or teachers may be reluctant to spend time alone in a room with a consultant, whom initially they may misperceive as a dangerous figure or as someone who has nothing valuable to offer them. It is just such potential consultees who probably have most to gain from scheduled interviews. These interviews, therefore, should, if possible, not be arranged on a voluntary basis. It does not matter if the potential consultee is urged into the room unwillingly by his supervisor or administrative superior. The essential issue is for the consultant to prove during the course of the interview that he is a friendly person, who is interested in the mission of the agency in dealing with the problems of its clients, who is worthy of trust and respect, and who is not dangerous. The latter point has been dealt with in the previous chapter; it involves demonstrating to the potential consultee that the consultant is not seductive or critical, will not attack defenses, and will not uncover weakness or unacceptable thoughts.

In such interviews, as well as in the informal contacts, the consultant should set the stage for the building of coordinate relationships by talking spontaneously and frankly about himself and his institution, about the goals and methods of his own work, and about his reasons for being in the consultee institution. He should freely discuss the current stage of the consultation contract; or if this is still in its preliminary phases, he should spell these out. Also, without "protesting too much," he should take an appropriate opportunity to mention some of the main things that will not be included in his operations, such as diagnosis and psychotherapy of the staff, intervening in intrastaff tensions and conflicts, and leaking confidential information between levels of the institutional hierarchical structure.

The procedure adopted by a consultant in getting to know his potential consultees in a particular institution will be chosen in relation to his understanding of its culture. The consultant must act in ways that conform with local usage. The best way of finding out what would be expectable and acceptable is to discuss the matter with the gatekeepers, such as the principal in a school or the supervisors in a public health nursing unit. The consultant should be flexible and fit in with their suggestions and arrangements. He may quickly learn from such a discussion that the gatekeeping person does not yet sanction free contact with subordinate staff. He will then focus upon reducing the ambivalence of the gatekeeper until the necessary sanction is obtained to allow formal contact with potential consultees. While this process is developing, he may also move along informal lines of establishing proximity with the latter, if he has meanwhile obtained the necessary sanction from the appropriate level of the authority system for free movement within the life space of the institution, such as permission to enter the staff common room or cafeteria. It is important that in these situations his presence should be acceptable, and that he not be perceived as an intruder or uninvited guest.

FUNDAMENTAL ISSUES IN RELATIONSHIP BUILDING

The following are the main points that consultants should bear in mind in building the consultation relationship:

Relationship Building Is a Directed Process

In psychotherapy, the therapeutic relationship often develops spontaneously—that is, without the active direction of the therapist. It is usually conceived that transference emerges from the unconscious of the patient and, as it were, is invested in the therapist, who presents himself as a new object partially to replace some of the former ones. Although many psychoanalysts emphasize the importance of actively working to build up a therapeutic alliance with those aspects of the observing ego of their patients that are most closely related to reality, the emphasis in uncovering types of psychotherapy and in psychoanalysis is on a nondirective approach. This is less so in supportive and manipulative psychotherapy.

In mental health consultation, the techniques we have developed are an interesting amalgam of the uncovering and supportive approach. On the one hand, they are quite directive. The consultant must accept the responsibility for actively fostering the building up of the optimal type of relationship between his consultee and himself; and here, as in other aspects of the method, he must decide what content to permit in their discussions and what issues he must prevent from being verbalized, or inhibit if they do emerge. On the other hand, within the constraints to which he adheres and which are sanctioned by the consultation contract, he fosters the freest possible expression by the consultee of the latter's perceptions and expectations of the client. He uses these expressions, both verbal and nonverbal, as projective material whose inner meaning he must interpret to himself in order to understand the unconscious aspect of the consultee's predicament; and this understanding is the basis for his every intervention.

In contrast to the techniques of uncovering types of psychotherapy, which seek to promote the insight of the patient into the nature of the subjective basis for his perceptions and the personal sources of his distortions, the consultant seeks to support and maintain the defensive displacement of the consultee's problems onto the story he tells about the client. The psychotherapist, therefore, often confronts the patient with evidences of distortion in his story and forces him to try to understand his feelings about the issues, and the source of these feelings in his current or past experience. The consultant, on the other hand, studiously avoids raising any question about the authenticity of the consultee's perceptions of the client's case, and keeps the focus of their discussion on the client rather than upon those who are discussing him.

The analytic psychotherapist, and particularly the psychoanalyst, obtrudes the realities of his own personality as little as possible onto the attention of his patient. His goal is for the latter to have the maximum opportunity to transfer unconscious fantasies onto the new object, and only after this transference has taken place to question the authenticity of the situation, so that the true meaning of the expressed feelings may be understood. The consultant is eager to avoid regressive transference with its inevitable concomitant of infantile dependence. He therefore continually keeps his consultee aware of his presence and his role by actively expressing or implying what his thoughts and attitudes are about the case and about his collaborative endeavor with the consultee. His talkativeness is in marked contrast with the silence of the psychoanalyst.

A major problem in technique for the consultant is how to maintain enough verbal and nonverbal communication with the consultee during the early stages of a consultation so that the optimal relationship is fostered, while providing the opportunity for the consultee to speak freely about the case and assuring him that the consultant respects his ideas and is not trying to obtrude his own before he really knows what the problem is all about. Each consultant will handle this dilemma in his own characteristic way. I deal with it by means of a special type of interviewing technique.

I sit beside the consultee, actually or metaphorically, and I involve him in questioning the material he presents about the case. I do not allow the consultee to talk for more than a few minutes without interrupting him with questions. I avoid, under all circumstances, a situation in which I listen in relative silence while the consultee tells a long story about the client and then turns to me at the end and says, "What do you think about it and what should I do?" First, I probably will not know what he should do. Second, since I may not yet know what the elements in the story really mean to the consultee, I will not wish to say something the inner meaning of which to the consultee I will not know. Third, by then my silence will have allowed the consultee to develop doubts about my attitude to him, and when he asks, "What do you think?" he may mean "about me?" I prefer him to know the answer to that question without having to ask.

I have developed methods of interviewing so that my constant interruptions of the consultee's story are made tactfully and are not felt by him to be a hindrance and a frustration. On the contrary, the questions I ask are always such that they give him the chance to enrich his story by bringing in additional details about the client and his human predicament, and especially about the characteristics and relationships of the people involved.

My questioning never takes the form of a cross examination of the consultee. He does not feel that I am scrutinizing or testing his knowledge, actions, or attitudes. I accept and respect his current state of knowledge about the case. The purpose of my questions is to get as full a statement of this knowledge as possible, so that the two of us may try to understand the complications of the case and jointly wonder about possible patterns of forces and inner meanings in the client's life.

While asking these questions, which demonstrate my own expert knowledge by bringing into focus a wider and wider series of issues that may previously have been thought by the consultee to be irrelevant and therefore not worthy of his attention, I am also continually showing my respect for the consultee's powers of observation and for the privileged position of his profession in being able to get such significant data. I am careful to avoid questions that the consultee is likely not to be able to answer; and where I am in doubt I phrase questions in such a way that he does not lose face if he has not made the necessary observations. In fact, consultees usually have a wealth of detailed information about cases they present. This information has often not been collected systematically, or with the same system as that involved in a psychiatric investigation; but since the consultee is likely to be especially concerned about this case, he will have observed a great deal more than he himself believes to be relevant.

The net result of such an interview technique is that, as the consultation discussion progresses, the consultee's thinking about the case gradually becomes richer and more complicated, and at the same time he feels supported, because the consultant is working actively with him in a joint endeavor to make sense out of the confusing material. He feels that his confusion is shared by the consultant, and he is reassured that this lack of clarity is an expectable stage in solving the mysteries of the client's predicament.

Fostering the Consultee's Self-Respect

This side-by-side joint wrestling with the complexities of the case is the basis for an appropriate relationship between consultee and consultant. It provides the consultee with expert help and support, while emphasizing his own specialized role as the contributor of the important information upon which the understanding of the case is to be based. This fosters the professional and personal self-respect of the consultee, which may previously have been weakened by his feelings of confusion and helplessness about the case.

Another source of weakness in the consultee may be a feeling of loss of face associated with an open confession of professional failure by his asking for consultation help. This may have a personal basis in some unsolved problems of dependency in the consultee. It often is complicated by the culture of the consultee institution. In some agencies competent professionals are expected to deal with work problems on their own. Asking for help is a sign of inadequacy. This may be part of the informal value system and in contradiction to official policy enunciated by top management that was responsible for hiring the consultant. In contrast, the consultant may be perceived by the line workers as being useful only to new and inexperienced professionals.

One way of handling this has been referred to in the last chapter, namely communicating to the staff that consultation is to be invoked whenever they encounter a complicated or confusing *situation,* in order to help them clarify it, rather than to help them with their own confusions. This type of formulation is often successful and leads to a situation in which it becomes a mark of professional merit and sophistication for a worker to identify a case situation as being complicated enough to merit consultation.

The explicit focus of the consultant on the client and his case, rather than upon the consultee and his handling of the case, is in line with this approach.

Another technique is for the consultant to make it clear to his consultees that their cases are intellectually taxing to him just as much as to them. A consultee must feel confident that the consultant is taking the case predicament seriously. There must be no question but that the case is a suitable issue for consultation. Consultees are sometimes fearful of making fools of themselves in wasting a consultant's time on a simple case and thus revealing the depths of their ignorance in mental health matters. From the point of view of relationship building, a consultant will be well advised not to demonstrate his specialist brilliance by snap diagnostic judgments and prescriptions. He may, indeed, hit the nail on the head as far as the client is concerned, but he may leave the consultee in a state of self-depreciation over his own inadequacies in not being able to recognize the obvious, or in a state of intimidation in the face of the omniscient expert—both of which are inimical to a future coordinate relationship.

If the consultee can be protected from loss of face, the more involved and upset he is about a case the quicker will he develop a meaningful relationship with the consultant. His increased tension and frustration at not being able to understand and act render him more open to the consultant's intervention, while at the same time the consultant's handling of the consultation situation prevents the development of continuing dependency and fosters the consultee's professional autonomy. The consultant makes his specialist skills available and acts, as it were, as a supplementary ego during the consultation while stimulating the ego strength of the consultee so that the consultee maintains and increases his own feeling of mastery both during and after the consultation contact.

Dealing with the Consultee's Anxiety

A consultant must differentiate two main types of anxiety in consultees: (a) about the case and (b) about the consultant.

Anxiety about the Case

This is what drives the consultee to ask for consultation. Especially in a first contact with a new consultee or with a consultee who has not yet developed a stable consultation relationship, the consultant must be careful not to reduce this anxiety too soon or the consultee will have no reason to continue the contact. It is particularly important not to lower anxiety about the case by techniques of reassurance. These not only reduce anxiety quickly (if they are successful) but coincidentally they attack the ego strength of the consultee as a mature adult and induce him to accept a childlike dependent role in relation to the consultant, who because of his high status and superior knowledge can assure the consultee that his fears are exaggerated or unfounded.

Instead of such reassurance, the consultant should deal with the consultee's anxiety about the case by means of the ego support of a joint examination of the facts and a sharing of concern. If the consultee feels that the consultant has truly understood the intricacies of the case and takes the situation seriously, and yet remains professionally calm even though concerned and sympathetic about the client's predicament, he will identify with these attitudes, and his own anxiety level and fear of disaster for the client will be reduced. This type of anxiety reduction will not interrupt the consultation, because it is the result of the consultee's growing relationship of trust and respect for the consultant, and this is what now holds them together.

There is one situation in which this approach may not work. If the consultee is so upset about the case that he becomes panicky, and the consultant fears that he may engage in impulsive activity, it may be necessary to use reassurance—at least to reduce the tension to bearable limits. An alternative is for the consultant to increase his own involvement in the case, by asking the consultee to report developments by telephone or by increasing the frequency of consultation sessions. The effect of this is not so much to reduce anxiety—in fact the consultant's actively demonstrating his own concern may appear to validate the consultee's fearful judgment—as to help the consultee to put up with it, through the consultant's sharing the responsibility for a possible unfortunate outcome.

It is worth emphasizing that there are limits to the consultant's support of the consultee in standing firm in a case despite anxiety regarding danger to the client. Sometimes this anxiety may be valid and there may indeed be danger in the case, even though the reason why the consultee is getting upset may be subjectively determined. Sometimes the consultant may decide that there is a significant hazard in the case apart from those aspects that are upsetting to the consultee. I have in mind actual danger to life, such as the possibility of suicide or homicide in the client, or a major psychosis that demands immediate attention.

Under these circumstances, the consultant must be guided by his fundamental responsibilities as a mental health specialist rather than by the niceties of consultation relationship-building technique. He must explain to the consultee that the information about the client in his judgment merits emergency action that must take precedence over the consultation contract; and he must, if necessary, personally intervene in order to ensure that the safety of the client and his family is safeguarded. If the consultee agrees with this formulation, the resulting action will be collaborative. If he disagrees, the consultant will be forced to take unilateral action. This may upset the consultation relationship, but it cannot be helped.

It is of interest that in my nearly twenty years of experience as a consultant and supervisor of consultants, involving thousands of cases, I can recall no more than four instances of this nature. It appears that in all social systems in which consultants are utilized, there are other formal and informal safety valves and control mechanisms, which identify and handle serious emergencies, so that they are not brought into the mental health consultation setting.

Anxiety about the Consultant

This acts in the opposite direction from anxiety about the case. It tends to prevent or to cut short contact between the consultee and the consultant and therefore should be actively combatted at every opportunity. This anxiety is usually shared by many potential consultees in the early stages of contact between a consultant and their agency. As he becomes better known and his reputation as a trustworthy and competent specialist becomes established, the anxieties about him on the part of individual consultees are reduced. New members of staff may, however, need to discover for themselves, rather than be assured by the old-timers, that he is safe and dependable.

The two sources of anxiety about the consultant are the quasi-realistic expectation that he will uncover their work deficiencies and shame or blame them, or make them dependent on him, and such irrational fantasies as have already been discussed in the previous chapter—that he will read their minds and reveal guilty secrets, that he will attack their defenses, or that he will drive them insane.

Both types of expectation must be invalidated by the consultant's behaving toward the consultee in such a way as to refute them. He must be prepared for constant testing out in the early stages of the relationship and must beware of saying anything that can be interpreted by the consultee as a sign that he is judging the quality of the latter's work. For example, I have found it advisable not to compliment consultees on good work they may have done on the case, because although this may be ego supportive, it also carries the implication that I am indeed making a judgment about the consultee's work performance. On this occasion I made a positive appraisal, but the consultee may be left with the worry that I have made negative judgments about other aspects of his work, which I am tactfully concealing or perhaps reserving for future communication.

It is important to be entirely nonjudgmental and to make this very obvious, particularly in instances in which the consultee appears to be especially fearful. In such situations the consultee will often bait a trap by mentioning examples of obvious ineffectual professional behavior, in order to draw the consultant's fire. The response should be a clear reaction, not in terms of the consultee's behavior, but with an explicit focus on the client. An exaggerated example of this from my own experience was an old public health nurse who, in orienting me to the low-income neighborhood in which she had worked for years, told me that she constantly carried around a "bottle of vitriol" that she was prepared to spray in the face of the first man who tried to rape her in a dark passageway of one of the housing projects. I had no way of telling whether she was in earnest or was pulling my leg, but I reacted by seriously considering society's problem in helping anomic chronically deprived people improve their impulse control, and then suggested that I would be interested in discussing details of a case example, if not of attempted rape, at least of some lesser antisocial behavior among her patients, so that we could better understand some of the complicated factors involved.

Fear of the consultant will usually be easy to detect from the consultee's manner in interacting with the consultant. It will often be manifested, not by verbal and nonverbal signs of overt anxiety in the consultant's presence, but by the elaborate preparation of the case report or by the consultee's asking for consultation on a case in which there is no significant problem, or in which he ostentatiously demonstrates his sophistication in mental health matters and his knowledge of psychological terminology. In such instances of obvious or hidden anxiety, the consultant's first goal is not to understand the intricacies of the case or to assess the nature of possible theme interference but to understand and handle the consultee's anxieties about him. This must be done without making the issue explicit. A psychotherapist in such a situation might well openly refer to the anxiety and might talk with his patient about possible causes. A consultant must understand in his own mind the nature of the fear from the implications of the consultee's behavior and then invalidate the distorted perception or expectation by his remarks about the client that reveal to the consultee the consultant's basic attitudes of friendly sympathy and personal respect for people.

For example, a young public health nurse brought as her first consultation case a teen-age patient who was continually being cowed, overawed, and browbeaten by her father, a successful drugstore operator, who had worked his way up from a deprived background and who was driving his daughter beyond her capacities. The nurse presented the story very tentatively and kept repeating to the consultant, who was a senior psychiatrist, that she was not sure of the facts, that she had not had time to work the case up properly, and that if he wished she would go back and get further information, etc. The consultant realized that both the content and manner of presentation were evidence of the nurse's fear of him, and he was very careful to show his respect for her privileged status as a professional, who had access to a wealth of information from her field contacts that psychiatrists only rarely can obtain in office visits. He gave her the opportunity to demonstrate to him and to herself the richness of her observations. By his aligning himself with her in confronting the problem of her patient, he was able to show her that she already had so much data that it would probably take them at least one or more consultation sessions to digest it, whether or not she collected further information from follow-up visits to the drugstore. In talking about the teen-age patient, he raised the possibility that although the father might indeed be pushing her beyond her capacities, some of the daughter's perceptions of him might be the result of her feelings of uncertainty about her own identity and consequent underassessment of her own worth.

The Consultant as Role Model

In the highly charged atmosphere of the consultation setting, especially when the consultee is upset by a work impasse, the consultant not only actively takes on a supplementary ego role but passively—by his mere presence as a trusted and respected person—is likely to be accepted by the consultee as an auxiliary superego and ego-ideal figure. In other words, his attitudes are likely to be incorporated in regard to the consultee's self-assessment and to his personal prescriptions for his own behavior.

Insofar as the consultant maintains a friendly, respectful, nonjudgmental attitude in the face of the consultee's statements about his management of the case, the latter's feelings of personal failure and self-condemnation or shame are likely to be relieved, with a consequent increase in freedom from undue constraint in thought and action.

As far as his operation as an ego-ideal or role model is concerned, it is important for the consultant to bear this in mind as he discusses the case and demonstrates to the consultee his attitudes about the client and his own mode of professional operation. These are likely to be introjected by the consultee.

The consultant must consciously try to keep his own overt reactions in consonance with the style with which he would like the consultee to identify. He must avoid role identity distortion by taking care to keep his own specialized professional thinking in the background. For instance, although the case may arouse his psychiatric interest in relation to its depth psychological or diagnostic implications, he should discuss it only at the level of general human relationships or on the plane that he knows to be of direct relevance to the professional style of his consultee. In the previous example of the teen-age girl and her pharmacist father, for instance, there was evidence that incestuous fantasies were being stimulated both in father and daughter; and from a psychopathological point of view it might have been fascinating to explore this further, as well as to assess the degree of narcissism in the girl's personality in relation to her early experience with her mother. The consultant had consciously to set aside this specialized psychiatric line of inquiry, as not being relevant to the current level of the public health nurse's concerns and to her professional role.

As role models, there are three aspects of functioning, which probably are common and acceptable to all caregiving professions and which mental health consultants should try to demonstrate in their reactions to the cases presented by their consultees: (a) empathy, (b) tolerance of feelings, and (c) the conviction that with enough information all human behavior is understandable.

1. By empathy, I mean the capacity to look objectively at the realities of the client and the people with whom he is related, and at the same time to have some subjective experience of their feelings—as it were, to resonate with them at the feeling level and thus share their experience even at a distance.

2. By tolerance of feelings, I refer to the consultant's demonstration that he is not unbalanced psychologically through his free expression of feeling in regard to the *dramatis personae* of the case. I do not mean that he uncovers feelings related to his own private life. On the contrary, he demonstrates his human affective resonance with the client while maintaining the boundaries of his own privacy. By example he encourages the consultee to do the same. I will discuss this further later in this chapter in connection with the avoidance of psychotherapy.

3. The third point is particularly important. I believe that much of the upset felt by consultees is linked with their fear of irrationality in their clients, which probably, in turn, is related to their anxiety about their own irrational impulses. A fundamental message of consultation is that if one spends enough time and collects enough information, one can eventually discover the patterns of forces in the case and then understand the attitudes and behavior of the people involved as logical manifestations of their interacting motivations and goal-oriented strivings, however strange they may initially appear.

Clarification of Consultation Contract

In initial sessions with a new consultee a consultant should informally discuss the main points of the consultation contract. In my experience, this issue must be dealt with repeatedly in order to make sure that consultees really understand it, especially if the contract calls for consultee-centered consultation and this is an innovation in their institution. The communication should be made piecemeal, as may appear appropriate during the session, rather than as a pat little "lecture."

Maintaining Confidentiality

One more message must be conveyed explicitly and repeatedly in these early contacts, namely that the consultant undertakes to preserve the confidentiality of material communicated to him by the consultee. In particular, he promises not to tell the consultee's superiors anything about the consultee's handling of the case, even though he may be expected to discuss the problems of the client also with them.

The development of trust between consultee and consultant will to a large extent depend upon the way in which the consultant fulfills this promise. This is not the relatively simple matter it is to preserve confidentiality with a psychotherapy patient. The particular problem is that in institutions with a technical or administrative supervisory system, the supervisors are likely to be very interested in the consultant's views on the case, and often also on his judgment of the consultee. In negotiating the consultation contract, the consultant can relatively easily obtain administrative sanction for not making reports on his consultees to their supervisors, but he cannot sidestep the predicament of talking with them about their clients. A supervisor can legitimately request formal or informal consultation regarding a client whose case is being handled by one of her supervisees.

Moreover, it is important for the consultant to build and maintain a good working relationship with the supervisory group, who are the gatekeepers who exercise major control over the flow of consultees. Such a relationship necessitates regular interaction—most consultants find it advisable to meet, if only briefly, with the supervisors at the beginning and end of every visit to the consultee institution. It is therefore almost inevitable that during such interactions there will be some discussion of those clients who are currently a source of concern to the staff.

This complication should be discussed with consultees, and they should be assured that in a discussion with a supervisor the consultant will talk only about the client, basing his remarks upon information likely to be already known to the supervisor, and never about the way in which the consultee is dealing with the case.

Many consultees will not trust the consultant in the early stages of their relationship, and will test his sincerity by finding out afterward what he told the supervisor. If he is meticulous in keeping his promise, they will eventually realize this; and he will soon develop a reputation for trustworthiness that will make it easier for him to build relationships with new consultees in that institution.

In the early stages, the consultant should be alert to signs of suspiciousness in his consultees and should then repeat his promises of confidentiality. He should also watch for the typical testing-out maneuver of the consultee's trying to involve him in a discussion about the supervisor or about other staff members. This should always be immediately interrupted; and the consultant should lead the discussion back to the client, or if necessary remind the consultee of the basic agreement not to discuss colleagues. Occasionally, it may even be advisable to say something like "I can no more discuss your supervisor with you than I can discuss you with her."

The confidentiality of the consultation interviews is most likely to be endangered if the consultant has not succeeded in building good relationships with the supervisors, especially in a public health nursing agency where the supervisors realistically feel the need for a good deal of control over their supervisees. If a supervisor does not trust the consultant not to trespass on her domain and suspects that he may side with her supervisee against her, or may give action directives that run counter to agency policies as interpreted by the supervisor, she may lie in wait and interrogate the consultee about the content of the interview as soon as the consultant has left the building.

Consultation confidentiality is one-sided. The consultant binds himself not to divulge what transpired. The consultee is not similarly bound, and must be free to use whatever went on in the consultation session in whatever way she sees fit. Moreover, the consultant is not in a position to interfere between a supervisor and her supervisee, and to tell the former what questions she may or may not ask the consultee.

The upshot of all this is that even though the consultant will not talk, the nurse can have no confidence that what she tells him can be kept secret from her supervisor. This introduces a constraint that prevents the nurse from freely sharing with the consultant her perceptions and expectations about her cases, which is an essential prerequisite for the kind of consultee-centered consultation described in this book.

One way of handling this problem is for the consultant to redouble his efforts to develop a better relationship with the supervisor, and to convince her that he respects her domain prerogatives. Another way, which has in my experience proved successful, is to raise the issue as a technical problem in meetings with the group of supervisors. Without divulging the identity of the supervisor causing the trouble, and sometimes without even discussing it as an actual problem in this public health nursing division but as one that has happened in the past and must therefore be prevented in this program, the supervisors can be shown how important it is for them to allow their nurses to keep to themselves the details of what they say to the consultant about their management of their cases. The result of such discussions has been that the supervisors as a reference group then constrain each of their members to avoid such inadvertent interference with the confidentiality of the consultation interviews.

Since a public health nursing division is a fairly small social system with well-developed channels of informal communication, it often happens that such a discussion in the supervisor's group becomes known throughout the agency, and this further improves the reputation of the consultant as a trustworthy person.

"One-Downsmanship"

This negative variation on the well-known Potterism is not an elegant term, but it expresses graphically an important issue in consultation relationship building. Consultees, whether as a testing-out maneuver to validate the consultant's assertion of his coordinate status or because they wish to express their sincere feeling of inferiority to him, will often manipulate the consultation situation so as to demonstrate their lower status or to maneuver the consultant into showing his superiority. Common examples are the expression of undue deference to the consultant's opinions, inviting him to make the next appointment at a time inconvenient to the consultee, or offering to accept unaccustomed burdens in collecting additional information about the case.

Since the cornerstone of the consultation relationship is the coordinate interdependence of the two participants, which means not only that the consultant has no coercive power over the consultee but also that the latter retains full professional authority, dignity, and responsibility in dealing with the client, even though he invokes the consultant's expert assistance in clarifying the complexities of the case, it is essential that the consultant not acquiesce in this one-downsmanship manipulation by the consultee.

The consultant must be alert to such a possibility, and whenever he identifies it he should counter in similar manner. For example, he should answer deference by deference—both in his tone of voice and in his attention to the opinions and comfort of the consultee; he should make it clear that he recognizes that the consultee is a busy man and that the next appointment must be at a time that suits his convenience; and he must emphasize that the purpose of consultation is to lighten the load on the consultee and not to increase it, so it is not appropriate for the consultee to collect information over and above that which is readily available during his ordinary work on the case.

If there is a major formal status differential in the consultant's favor, he must himself make use of one-downsmanship in order to set the consultee at ease and emphasize that in this setting they are meeting each other on an equal footing.

Avoidance of Psychotherapy

Assumption by the consultee of the role of a psychotherapeutic patient in relation to the consultant is a particular and especially difficult type of one-downsmanship. Sometimes the consultee may slide into this maneuver in so subtle a way that it may initially escape the consultant's attention, until he suddenly discovers that he is involved in a clearly hierarchical relationship. One common example of this occurs when the consultee in a most natural manner begins to talk of his feelings of anxiety about the client and then about his feelings of inadequacy, frustration, shame, or hopelessness about his conduct of the case. If the consultant's response is the equally natural expression of his understanding and sympathy for the consultee, this may appear to be merely an ego-supportive maneuver. Certainly it is a response that would come easily to a caseworker, or a psychotherapist, or even to a nonprofessional friend. Unfortunately, this is a response that negates the coordinate nature of the relationship, because at that moment one party is expressing emotional disturbance and is communicating this inferiority to the other, who is exhibiting emotional stability and is expressing sympathy and encouragement. This means that from his position of superior strength the consultant is providing emotional supplies to the consultee and nurturantly catering to his dependent needs.

In a relationship of a patient and his psychotherapist this hierarchical situation is completely appropriate. The therapeutic contract permits and even encourages the patient to express emotional disturbance and irrational thoughts, and demands that the therapist maintain psychological balance and rationality. In their encounter they agree that both should focus on the personal needs of only one—the patient. Whatever the personal needs of the therapist, he is expected to be able to keep them under control. Their relationship is based upon this superiority of the therapist, which is the guarantee to the patient that it is safe for him temporarily to lay down his defenses against irrationality and to confront his own weakness.

In consultation, on the other hand, both parties must be on an equal footing. This situation will be strained if the consultee is in fact psychologically upset by his impasse with the case. If, however, he is allowed to save face by not having to express his upset openly, the subjective disturbance can remain a private matter, which, like many other private problems, can be kept apart from his professional operations and need not significantly affect them. In particular it will not interfere with his relationship with the consultant.

Before describing how the consultant may handle this type of issue, I will discuss some of the reasons why a consultant should avoid psychotherapy, apart from its interference with the nonhierarchical relationship of the consultation setting.

In this discussion I use the term "psychotherapy" to denote an explicit professional method whereby a therapist, who is a physician or other recognized healing person, treats a patient, who feels or is felt by others to be psychologically sick, with the goal of shortening or reducing his illness and returning him to healthy mental functioning. For our present purposes certain elements of the relationship between patient and psychotherapist are significant: (a) The patient is dependent on the therapist, and this dependency involves vulnerability. Society protects the patient by a code of ethics to which the therapist must adhere, under the surveillance of the law and also of his guild that recruits, selects, trains, and licenses him, and controls his actions. The patient feels free to place himself in the power of the therapist because he can rely on this societal surveillance and control. (b) The relationship of the patient and therapist is governed by a contract, either explicitly negotiated between them or covertly understood by both because of common usage in their culture. The patient asks to be cured of his illness and offers some form of payment. He also undertakes to adhere to the therapist's requirements both in the investigation and in the treatment process. The therapist offers to use his best diagnostic and therapeutic efforts. He also demands adherence by the patient to his professional demands, such as the open expression of feeling and thoughts, including those normally kept private, and despite the pain and embarrassment this might cause the patient. (c) It is expected that however positive the initial relationship between patient and therapist, negative features will eventually appear because of the invasion of the patient's privacy and because the therapist will influence the patient to confront aspects of his functioning that he was previously repressing or in some other way avoiding, and that are likely to upset him. Transference, which originally may be positive, will soon pass through negative phases. Resistance is an inevitable aspect of psychotherapy.

The contract between patient and therapist guarantees that they will continue meeting during these negative phases, and that they will have an opportunity to understand and deal with the resistances and negative transference as a fundamental feature of the treatment process.

In contrast, the consultation contract provides no sanction for invasion of the consultee's privacy, no societal guarantee to the consultee that the consultant will not make illicit use of knowledge about his weakness to harm him, and no assurance to the consultant that the consultee will continue to see him if resistance and negative transference are aroused. The consultant has no hold, as it were, on the consultee. The consultee, on the other hand, has no right to use the consultation setting to deal explicitly with his personal problems, because it has been established by the administrators of the institution for the purpose of helping him improve his professional handling of his clients and not to deal with private matters.

It may be that a consultee will develop a trusting relationship with a consultant and a deep respect for his psychological acumen as a result of their discussion of a client's case. He may then formally or informally ask the consultant to help him with one of his personal problems, possibly a problem which is similar to that of the client. If the consultant agrees, and turns the consultation interview into a psychotherapeutic session, both parties will be misusing "company time." It may be thought that this infraction of the rules is not significant, since it is inherently a situation in which good is being done. But the consultant must realize that if he breaks the rules on this occasion, the consultee may later fear that the consultant will deviate from the contract in other areas, such as in reporting on him to his superiors. Moreover, the consultant will not be able to give the consultee effective treatment for his problem, because he will not be able to use his ordinary diagnostic or psychotherapeutic techniques in the absence of a proper therapeutic contract. The superficial counseling, which is all that is likely to be possible, probably will not do enough good to offset the upset in the coordinate nature of the consultation relationship. This may not matter if the consultation on the current case has already been satisfactorily concluded, but it is likely to color their ongoing relationship and prevent future consultations. Almost inevitably, the consultee will leave the session with unresolved feelings of personal dependency on the consultant, and this will weaken rather than strengthen his feelings of professional autonomy, especially if he sees a link between unsolved problems in his private life and work difficulties.

As important as all these issues that relate to the functioning of this one consultee are the possible implications of the consultant's deviation from the consultation contract in respect to his ongoing work in the consultee institution as a whole. Consultants must remember that the rules of confidentiality in regard to the content of the consultation interview apply to them and not to their consultees. The latter cannot be forced to keep this material secret. They will possibly talk to some of their friends in the agency about what went on. They may not go into detail about their private life, and the communication may sound as innocent as "I had such a good session with Dr. Smith today. He is really a very kind and wise man. He was a great help to me in dealing with a problem I am having with my old mother." In the relatively closed social system of a consultee institution, in which outsiders, especially interesting outsiders like mental health consultants, are a welcome subject for gossip, the implications of such an innocent remark will be rapidly disseminated. Potential consultees, who are aware of problems in their own personal life—and who isn't?—may then become afraid of asking for consultation, lest the consultant in their case, too, breach the barrier between the professional and the private spheres. The incident will be taken as proof that the mental health specialist, despite all his protestations to the contrary, is really interested in making the staff into patients and not treating them as colleagues.

TECHNIQUES OF AVOIDING PSYCHOTHERAPY

1. The best way of handling this problem is to prevent it. The danger is greatest in individual consultee-centered case consultation, especially those cases involving theme interference in which a personal problem of the consultee has been displaced onto the job situation. The consultation techniques to be used in dealing with this will be discussed in Chapters 7, 8, and 9. At this point I will focus on one aspect, how the consultant handles the consultee's feelings, because this has implications for counteracting the natural tendency of this type of consultation to slide into psychotherapy.

In other types of individual consultation and in group consultation it is relatively simple for the consultant to help his consultee express his feelings about the case and to realize that such feelings as anxiety, shame, guilt, and anger are a natural reaction in a mature professional who is struggling to assist a distressed client, with whom he empathizes. The consultee's emotional upset is the more expectable because if he is involved with and committed to aiding his client, the case impasse that occasioned the consultation is likely to make him feel frustrated. As mentioned previously, the consultant can help his consultee express his feelings and increase his tolerance for them by talking about his own similar reactions in such cases. In group consultation, the legitimization of such expression can be validated by other members of the group. The consultant's main task is to demonstrate that a professional can freely discuss his feelings about a case without talking about his private life, even if associations to personal matters are possibly stimulated in his consciousness by the details of the client's predicament. In group consultation the ground rules support this by explicitly excluding all mention of private material.

In individual consultee-centered case consultation, on the other hand, group support is missing, and the influence of the consultant's example may not be sufficient to counteract the pressure of the emergent personal problem of the consultee. This is rendered more likely because of the privacy and confidentiality of the setting, the image of the consultant as a clinician with whom it is natural to share personal feelings, and the development of a consultation relationship of trust and respect.

Experience with many consultees suffering from theme interference has demonstrated that there is an expectable chain of associations, which, if not interrupted, leads from verbalization of feelings about the client to talking about private matters. This chain of associations starts with the consultee's reported perceptions of the client, and continues to his feelings about the difficulties of the case, to his feelings about personally significant details of the case, to memories of similar feelings about this whole category of problem, to memories of similar feelings about examples of this problem category in his own life, to details of his current personal problems that are similar, and then to links with significant personal problems of his past life, followed by the explicit or implicit request for the consultant's counsel. It is precisely this chain of associations that therapists try to energize when they focus discussion on a patient's feelings about an incident in an objectively told story. Their goal is to stimulate the emergence into consciousness of the underlying present and past problems. The consultant's goal, on the other hand, is to avoid this process, and to keep the consultation discussion focused on the apparently external and personally unrelated story of the client's life.

Accordingly, the consultant in individual theme-interference cases should never ask the consultee how he feels about the case or about any of the incidents described. All questions should be phrased in such a way as to elicit an objective answer, for example, "What went on?" "What kind of woman was the mother?" "What did the baby look like?" Questions like "What did you think went on?" "What was your impression of the mother?" should, if possible, be avoided, because they may lead the consultee to a discussion of his personal reaction. Questions like "How did you feel about the mother?" or "What were your feelings about the way the mother handled the baby?" should be avoided.

If the consultee spontaneously begins to talk about his feelings, the consultant should as soon as possible interrupt and divert the discussion to some aspect of the client, usually by asking a question to elicit further facts or making a comment about the case. As previously mentioned, the consultant should not talk about the consultee's feelings, even supportively.

On occasion the consultee manages to verbalize strong feelings about the case, often of a negative nature such as disappointment, shame, anger, guilt, or frustration, before the consultant can stop him. If he is clearly upset, it might be felt as a personal rebuff if the consultant were to ignore this expression entirely in his response. In such a situation, I have found it valuable to let the consultee know that I have heard his cry of pain, while at the same time emphasizing by my response that I do not regard it as a sign of weakness but the natural human reaction of a respected colleague with whom I am having a task-oriented professional discussion. I do this by a brief comment that refers to the frequency with which sensitive professionals have a subjective affective resonance as they empathize with their clients, and I put myself in the same boat so that we get back onto the same level in continuing to discuss the case. An example of the kind of comment I might make to a consultee who voices hopelessness about the case is "I know from experience how you must feel. *We* professionals often react strongly to cases like this. It is just this empathy with the client that assures him that we care about his predicament. Let us once more try to understand how this man sees his problem. What makes him feel so hopeless?" In this example, apart from my one-downsmanship response, I am implying that our emotional reaction is a source of strength in our conduct of the case, which is likely to be perceived as such by the client, and that it need not impede our continued joint attempt to unravel the complexities of the case. Also, I deal with the hopelessness of the consultee by directing the discussion not toward him but toward the possible displacement object of the client.

2. Discussion of the client is the safety zone of consultation. Whenever a consultation interview threatens to get out of hand because the consultee begins to discuss his personal feelings, incidents from his private life, details of his relationships with his peers or administrative superiors, or problems of the social system of his agency in which he is trying to get the consultant to intervene despite the terms of the consultation contract, the consultant should try to get back as soon and as smoothly as possible to a discussion of the client's situation. Experienced consultants use this as an almost reflex safety device, whenever they get into interviewing difficulties. As long as they are talking about the client's predicament, the consultant can be sure that he is within the sanctioned terms of his contract and that he can have the breathing space to consider how to react to the conscious or unconscious manipulations of his consultee.

3. If a consultee is obviously tense and upset, the consultant should be especially careful not to allow him to gain control over the interview by embarking on a long and rapid monologue. This should be dealt with by means of frequent interruptions by questions to clarify the facts of the case, and by the consultant's beginning as soon as possible to offer some conceptual framework that might suggest how the different elements are linked or what factors seem to be particularly significant.

4. The consultant should beware of generalizations by the consultee —for example, the initiation of discussion of a general topic, such as enuretic children, rebellious adolescents, or engaged couples. This is especially so if the consultant suspects any personal link with the general category, such as if the consultee is a married women with children who might be wetting the bed, or is a young nurse who might be involved in disciplinary conflicts with her supervisor, or is a woman who has just got engaged. Even without such hints, the consultant should be concerned lest discussion of a categorical problem might be a conscious or unconscious device to raise with him an issue that is relevant to the private life of the consultee. As soon as the discussion gets properly under way, there is little to stop the consultee's suddenly saying, "All this has special meaning to me because I, too, have this problem." When that happens the consultant will have no case to which to retreat for safety and will have to deal with the predicament by refusing to continue the discussion on the basis of the terms of the consultation contract, which is awkward and almost certainly will mean loss of face to the consultee and a blow to the relationship.

This matter should be dealt with preventively by ensuring that early on in every consultation the discussion be focused on the details of a specific client and his family or social situation. Whenever the consultee makes a generalization about categorical issues, the consultant should respond by asking how this relates to the case under discussion, and should then continue the analysis of the case in relation to the idiosyncratic elements of this client's predicament. In this way he supports and strengthens the element of displacement and prevents the consultee's thinking about—or talking about—his personal problems.

5. If the consultee manages to elude the consultant's preventive efforts and does begin to talk about his private life, this should be tactfully but quickly interrupted; and then after a suitable supportive bridge comment that affirms the consultant's continued respect for the consultee despite his confession, and possibly some form of one-downsmanship to re-establish the nonhierarchical nature of the relationship, the consultant should, as usual, get the focus back onto the client. For instance, during a discussion of an enuretic child a teacher said to the consultant, "I feel especially upset about Johnny because for years now I have been plagued with this bed-wetting problem with my own son." The response of the consultant was not "I am sorry to hear that. What form does the bed-wetting take with your boy?" but "I am sure your own experience will have made you especially sensitive to the feelings of Johnny and his mother. How do you think Mrs. Brown has dealt with the problem of other people's knowing about Johnny? Has she felt a sense of personal failure and as though others condemn her as a poor mother?" At some stage it might be possible to say something like "It is sometimes a good thing for our clients that *we* professional people are also human and have problems, so that we can more sympathetically understand theirs."

The consultant in such instances must try to convey the implication that most of us professionals have personal problems but that usually we can keep them confined to our private lives, so that they need not intrude into the work sphere; and that often we can capitalize on our past or present private turmoil in our professional operations, because of increased ability to empathize and to understand the intimate details of similar psychosocial predicaments in our clients.

6. How should a consultant handle explicit requests for psychotherapy or for a referral to a therapist? It is noteworthy that experienced consultants, who operate along the lines already discussed, rarely encounter direct requests for psychotherapy among their consultees. The latter quickly learned by implication that such requests would not be appropriate in this setting. If they are legitimately seeking a psychotherapist, they do so along other channels in their private life such as by talking with their personal physician, their clergyman, or with their family or trusted friends. An environment in which there is sufficient sophistica-

tion in mental health matters to be conducive to the establishment of a mental health consultation program in the agency system is likely also to have recognized provisions for individual diagnosis and therapy for emotional disorders. In isolated rural areas this may occasionally not be true, and under such circumstances the mental health consultant may be the only available specialist counselor whose advice can be sought in such a matter. In that case, the consultant must make the explicit judgment as to whether to offer this help despite its threat to his consultation program.

The more usual situation is that the consultee asks for advice as to whether or how to get personal therapy either as a testing-out way of validating the consultant's promise that he will not act as a diagnostician and psychotherapist for the staff of the consultee institution, or as a more or less conscious and deliberate deviation from the consultation contract under the pressure of personal problems stimulated by or manifested in the consultation case.

If in the first of these instances the consultant accepts the testing-out gambit, and either offers clinical service or gives the consultee the name of a psychotherapist, the result is likely to be unfortunate both for the future relationship with that consultee and, when the news gets around, with other members of staff of the institution. I have already discussed the negative consequences of the second instance. How then should the consultant deal with this predicament when it arises?

The important thing for such a consultant to realize is that, except in the excessively rare emergencies of an acutely psychotic consultee who is a potential danger to himself or others, there is no realistic reason for the consultant to deal with this matter. He can say something like "It is true that I am a psychiatrist, but in this setting I have been hired as a mental health consultant to work with you and other staff to improve our service to the institution's clients. I cannot give you valid advice about private matters, because in order to do so we would have to discuss your personal affairs so that I can satisfy myself that you do indeed need psychiatric attention. After all, most of us have various problems of life adjustment and psychological complications, but very few people need to see a psychiatrist. If we spent our time in my giving you a screening or diagnostic interview, this would not be what you and I are being paid for here. If I give you an appointment to come and see me in the clinic, this will complicate our future consultation work, because the relationship between a psychiatrist and a patient is very different from that between us two operating as colleagues working together on consultation cases. I am proud that you have enough trust in my judgment to ask for my counsel in this matter, but I suggest that under the circumstances it would be better for you to talk about this with your own doctor or with some other person whom you trust and respect." Of course, the words actually used here, as in other examples in this book, must be what come naturally to the consultant as he interacts at that moment with his particular consultee. The verbal formula is not important—it is the meaning of the message that counts.

7. In this last example the consultant may be forced to mention the terms of the consultation contract. This should be done lightly and tactfully, because it is a form of coercion; and even though its terms apply as much to the consultant as to the consultee, it will usually be seen by the latter as implying the use of force by the consultant to prevent the consultee from satisfying his needs. This necessarily destroys the essential element of the coordinate relationship between them.

If all the consultant's efforts to allow the consultee to save face, and to realize that both parties are involved in a situation that is ordered by the consultee institution and its responsibilities for its client population, do not achieve the hoped-for results, he will be forced to invoke the terms of the consultation contract as an explicit sanction. This will probably be a major blow to his future working relationship with that consultee, but the action will safeguard his relationship with the other consultees in the institution. In some cases, despite his initial frustration, it may also reassure that consultee about the consultant's steadfast and nonpunitive adherence to the contract; and he may decide in the future to return for consultation on the consultant's terms and to build a coordinate relationship with him.

Ending the Initial Session

Unlike most other interprofessional operations, in which both sides have a clear initial expectation of the likelihood and approximate number of future contacts, consultation presents a situation of ambiguity. In his communications to potential consultees during the process of negotiating the consultation contract, the consultant talks in terms of one to four sessions as being the expectable number that will be needed to deal with most cases. But when a consultee comes for the initial session in his first few cases, neither party can be sure whether these cases will require more than a single session. Before a firm relationship between the two has been established, there will be a tendency for consultees to want to interrupt or to postpone the second contact, because anxiety about the case will probably have been reduced by the consultant's ego-supportive maneuvers and yet the relationship may not yet have become sufficiently strong to bring the consultee back against the pressure of the centrifugal forces of his yet unallayed anxieties about the consultant.

It is therefore unwise for the consultant to end an initial session by saying, "Whenever you feel like it, please come and see me again for further discussion of this case." Apart from other considerations this is inadvisable because the consultee may wrongly interpret the statement as meaning that the consultant does not really want to go on talking about the case, which must somehow have been unsuitable, and yet is too polite to say so openly—an example of the formula "Don't call us, we will call you when we have an opening!"

If the consultant has clear indications that he will complete the consultation in the one session, there is no problem. If, as is more usual, especially with a new consultee, he feels halfway through that at least one more session is needed, both to continue exploring and building the relationship and also to deal with the case consultation itself, he should begin to prepare for the ending of this session in terms of ensuring the second meeting. Experienced consultants do not leave this to a sudden decision and effort in the last few minutes of the interview. Instead, they begin about halfway through the session to make remarks about how complicated the case seems, how much material there is to try to understand, how interesting are the patterns that are beginning to emerge. Having laid this groundwork, it emerges as perfectly natural, and almost not worth mentioning at the end, that a second session is essential in order to continue the process of clarification. The consultee should by then have no doubt that the consultant is deeply involved in the case. The consultee should also not feel any pressure from the consultant to collect more data before the next session, although he himself may wish to return to the client so as to get more information about particular issues.

The consultant should not try to pull together the discussion at the end of the first session but should leave it in an interrupted state with many obviously unanswered questions. He should avoid summarizing formulations because they may lead (a) to premature closure, which will reduce the likelihood of the consultee's return, and which may be wrong because of lack of information; (b) undue lowering of consultee anxiety about the case because they imply that it is already solved; (c) unlinking, in cases of theme interference, because the consultant still has no clear idea about the patterned way in which the consultee's subjective problems are distorting his perceptions and expectations of the client (this technical problem will be fully discussed in Chapter 7); and (d) breaking the displacement by allowing the consultee to leave the session with an awareness of the general outlines of the case such that on his own he will see its implications for his personal problems, a process that the consultant might have been able to prevent if it had begun to happen during a consultation discussion.

[6]

Client-Centered
Case Consultation

INTRODUCTION

Client-centered case consultation is the most familiar type of consultation practiced by mental health specialists. A consultee has difficulty in dealing with the mental health aspects of one of his clients and calls in a specialist to investigate the case and to advise on the nature of the difficulties and on what the consultee should do about them. Usually the specialist personally examines the client, makes a diagnosis, and writes a report with recommendations for disposition and management. The consultee translates appropriate aspects of the recommendations into a plan that he feels to be feasible in his setting and then takes action.

The primary goal of this type of consultation is to develop a plan that will help the client in question. A subsidiary, but not unimportant, goal is that the consultee should learn something from the encounter with the consultant that will increase his ability to handle this category of case better on his own in the future. The secondary educational goal is limited because it is envisaged that the client's difficulties are of an unusual nature, and probably future clients of the same type will also need to be seen by a specialist. Also, the amount of interaction between consultant and consultee is minimal—most of the consultant's time is spent with the client—so there is little opportunity for education of the consultee.

Consultants who place greater emphasis upon the educational goal of client-centered case consultation will try to increase the proportion of their consulting time spent with the consultee. Some consultants do this by collecting all or most of their information about the client from the consultee, rather than from a personal investigation of the client. The more they do this, the closer their operations get to consultee-centered case consultation. This may not be without hazard, however, because in the latter type of consultation there is no expectation that the consultant will provide an expert diagnostic assessment of the client. He is required only to add to the consultee's understanding of certain aspects of the case. In client-centered case consultation, on the other hand, the consultant is specifically asked to diagnose the client and give the consultee a treatment prescription. It is essential that the diagnosis and prescription be correct. This depends upon the consultant's obtaining accurate information about the client, which in turn usually means that he must investigate the latter himself. He can rarely rely upon a consultee to provide him with an undistorted view of a client with whom the consultee is having difficulty, and the diagnostic investigation often requires specialized data collection in the form of psychiatric or casework interviews or psychological testing.

A consultant who has worked with particular consultees on many cases may come to rely on certain types of information they can give him and may feel less need for validating these data by his own investigations. He may also be able, as it were, to triangulate by collecting information from two or three informants in the consultee institution, either in separate contacts or in a group consultation—for example, with three or four teachers and the nurse in a high school, all of whom are involved with the same student. In this way he can explore for consonance or discrepancies in their stories and begin to build up a valid picture of the client. This will reduce his need for personal contact with the latter, but since he has to take responsibility for a diagnostic assessment, he will be wise to see the client for at least a short time himself.

In some types of client-centered case consultation the consultant is not required to commit himself to a diagnostic judgment but only to a screening assessment; and in these situations there may be no need for him to see the client. For instance, in some school systems a committee consisting of guidance personnel, a school psychologist, a social worker, a nurse, and some of the educators meets regularly to review problem cases in order to decide on plans for special education or guidance within the school or on referral of the children to specialized outside agencies, such as a child guidance clinic, a hospital, or a social agency, for further investigation and treatment. A psychiatrist may be called in to offer consultation to this group, either occasionally in relation to an unusually difficult case, or on a regular basis to review routine problems. In this kind of situation the consultant may feel comfortable in giving his opinion on the basis of the documents and the accounts of the individuals present, without needing to see the children himself.

In cases in which the consultant spends little or no time with the client, he will have a good opportunity to get to know the consultees and to assess the nature of their difficulties with the client and their capacity to understand his diagnostic formulations and to carry out his recommendations for disposition and management. In the more usual cases in which the consultant spends most of his time with the client and hardly sees the consultee at all, or communicates with him only by telephone or writing, the consultant must make a special effort to get to know the consultee and to learn how to communicate with him. The reason is that no matter how accurate the diagnostic formulation and how wise the prescriptions for disposition and management of the client, these will achieve little unless they are understandable, acceptable, and feasible to the consultee, who is the person responsible for implementation.

STEPS IN THE CONSULTATION PROCESS

Consultation Request

The request for consultation help may come directly to the consultant through personal contact, by telephone, in writing, or else indirectly through secretaries or other staff. It may take the form of a detailed account of the condition of the client, the difficulties in his management, and a specific set of questions about the nature of the problem and how the consultee should deal with it. If there is direct communication, either face to face or by telephone, the consultant can ask for supplementary information not only about the client's condition and history but also about the consultee's work situation and the feasible possibilities for referral and modifications in management. He can use this information to guide him in investigating the client, and more important, to enable him to make a written or verbal report which will satisfy the consultee's expectations, which will be communicated in language that he can understand, and which will be practicable within the context of the consultee's work setting and existing skills and resources.

If the consultation request comes in writing or through secretaries or other staff, it may occasionally contain the essential information about the client and the consultee, but often this is not so. It is common in medical practice for a consultation request to consist of a short note in a case record or on a slip of paper saying "Please see and advise" or

"Consultation requested on this case of enuresis." Especially if this is a new consultee, such laconic requests should be treated with caution. The professional person asking for help may use the term consultation, but this may mean something different to him from what it does to the mental health specialist. He may be having difficulty with the client and may wish the specialist to take over the case, either completely or partially. The apparent request for consultation may in fact be a referral. In that event he will be angry if the consultant sends the client back with a message about disposition and management, feeling that the specialist is dodging his responsibility. On the other hand, a message that seems like a referral may be intended as a request for consultation advice, and the physician or other professional who refers the case will be even more angry if the specialist does not return the client but takes him over as his own patient.

The best way of dealing with this is, wherever possible, to telephone or talk directly to the consultee and to clarify the specific nature of his request as well as to obtain further information about the client and the work situation. Even busy consultees will rarely resent such contacts by the consultant. Rather than perceiving these as unnecessary intrusions, they will probably interpret them as a sign that the consultant is interested in their work predicament and eager to be as helpful as possible. Such a verbal contact will also establish proximity for beginning to build the relationship which is the basis for all consultation, even the most client-centered.

Assessment of the Consultation Problem

It is already clear that in this type of consultation the consultant must assess two problems: (a) the nature of the client's difficulties and (b) the liabilities and resources of the consultee and his work situation in relation to this client.

Assessment of the Client

There is no need to dwell on the diagnostic assessment of the client, except to emphasize that the consultant must keep in mind the immediate purpose of his investigation and must plan his diagnostic strategy accordingly. The consultee will usually want a quick answer, and so the investigation should be as short as possible, consonant with the giving of a valid opinion. The consultant will usually have to answer two fundamental questions: Is the nature of the client's condition such that referral to a specialized professional or agency for further depth investigation or treatment is essential? Whether or not the client should be referred, what can the consultee do to help the client by modifying his ways of handling him within the consultee's usual work setting?

The answer to the first question usually demands the collection of enough information, by interviewing the client and possibly members of his family, so that a general diagnostic formulation can be made. A precise diagnosis is often not required, so that lengthy interviewing, diagnostic testing, and home visiting are not necessary. If they are, this should be done as a second stage—probably within the context of referral of the client by the consultee to a specialized mental health agency.

The answer to the second question demands not the usual kind of psychiatric diagnosis, based upon assessment of psychopathology with its implications for expert treatment by specialists, but an assessment of the client's current human predicament in terms of the practical and psychological tasks that confront him and his involvement with significant others—for example, his family and friends—and with the caregiving persons to whom he turns for help, such as the consultee and the other professionals of his community. Recommendations that may emerge from an assessment on this plane will deal with modifying the client's network of role expectations and associated positive reinforcements and negative sanctions; providing advice and guidance in regard to ways of dealing with current life problems; and giving emotional support to relieve anxiety, guilt, and depression and to help the client tolerate confusion and frustration and persevere in grappling with his difficulties.

In making this type of assessment, the consultant will interest himself in the details of the human predicament in which the client is currently involved, not as a set of precipitants or consequences of his psychopathological deviations, but as the central focus for the investigation. In the army setting, for example, as pointed out so vividly by Bushard,[1] the consultant would not focus so much on the investigation of the soldier's symptomatic picture; on his choice of obsessional, hysterical, or other defenses; and on the patterns of characterological weaknesses displayed. Instead, he would concentrate on the details of his difficulties in dealing with the demands of his duties, and on the nature of his relationships and patterns of communication with his peer group and superiors that are apparently not providing him with the supports and the identifications he needs in order to mold his commitment to his role. The consultant may, for instance, discover that some difference in culture, possibly linked with race, religion, or class, has initially interfered with free communication between the soldier and his peer group. This isolation may not have been significant until the soldier was burdened by the demand to perform some duty that strained his resources, or by some home problem such as the illness of a family member, or a conflict with his girlfriend. Lack of communication with his peer group and superiors would then mean not only an absence of support and guidance but that his preoccupation with his problem and consequent reduction in efficiency would not be understood and tolerated as a temporary phenomenon and might be greeted by negative sanctions and an increase in duty demands and burdens. Eventually, the soldier might try to escape by the delinquency of going A.W.O.L. or by developing symptoms that cause the others to perceive him as psychiatrically ill. Once he has cast himself into the delinquent or patient role, the expectations and reactions of the others in his unit move the focus of their and his attention from his real problems onto his deviant behavior. The consultant's purpose should be to reverse this process and to uncover information both about the soldier's predicament and about the blocks in his communications, so that the significant people around him may understand the nature of his human difficulties, may learn how to communicate with him, and may utilize their usual methods of support and guidance. Such an assessment, as is evident from this example, implies that the consultant should investigate not only the client but also his milieu, particularly his relationship with the consultee.

Assessment of the Consultee Setting

This brings us to the consultant's second area of assessment—the liabilities and resources of the consultee and his work situation in relation to the client—which is the essential other part of the consultation picture. A great deal of traditional client-centered case consultation is carried out in the specialist's office, as when a patient is referred by a general practitioner or a student by a schoolteacher to a psychiatrist for a consultant's opinion. In this situation of isolation, it is very difficult for the consultant to do any more than investigate the client. Information about the client's relationship with the consultee must mainly be based on the client's statements. If the consultee and his institution are not known to the consultant, he can only use his imagination or his general knowledge of the culture of such consultees to guess their relevant liabilities and resources. His recommendations are consequently likely to be less than ideal. The best procedure for the consultant is, instead, to do his work not in the isolation of his office but by entering the environment of the consultee, for instance, by seeing the student in the school, the patient on the medical or surgical ward or in the well-baby clinic, the soldier in his unit, and the disabled person in the vocational rehabilitation office. In many instances of offering client-centered case consultation to general practitioners it has even been possible for the psychiatrist to arrange to see the patient in the physician's office.[2]

There are many advantages in this method of working, such as the opportunity for relationship building and the ease of effectively communicating the consultant's opinion; but the main benefit is that the consultant can explore directly the links between client and consultee and also the details of the potential help the consultee has to offer.

The blockage of communication between client and consultee may not be due entirely to a deficiency in the client. It may be influenced by an inability of the consultee to hear or to understand what the client is trying to say. An important part of the consultant's task is to act as a communication bridge between the two, but in order to do so he must be able to assess both sides of the system.

In a well-baby clinic, for example, a psychiatrist was consulted by the pediatrician in regard to a Negro woman whose fifteen-month-old son was suffering from head banging, which appeared to be due to maternal neglect of the child. The consultant saw the woman in the well-baby clinic and found her to be suffering from feelings of deprivation and a mild reactive depression, which were interfering with her relationship with her child. After some initial difficulty in rapport, he was able to get through to her, and then she told him that the reason for her depression was her husband's departure from the home. He had lost his job as a meatpacker, about eight months previously, because of a fight he had had with the foreman after getting drunk. His drinking had then increased and he could not get another job. He began to stay out nights and she suspected that he was going with other women. She applied to welfare, and the worker told her that she would get Aid to Dependent Children (A.D.C.) if her husband formally left her. The couple decided that this would be the best plan, but the welfare worker made her take her husband to court, get a formal separation, and sue him for nonsupport of the child. The mother said that her husband was forced to run away altogether in order to avoid being jailed. The worry over the whole affair had made her depressed. She had nobody to whom she could turn because they had only recently come up from Mississippi, and all her relatives were back in the South.

The psychiatrist wondered to himself why this fairly characteristic and not uncommon story was not known to the workers in the well-baby clinic, who apparently perceived the case as one of maternal deprivation due to intellectual dullness in the mother. He was struck by the lack of rapport between the pediatrician and the woman, and also by the lack of communication between the well-baby clinic personnel and the workers in the welfare department.

He noticed that the pediatrician seemed particularly hurried in his dealings with the clinic patients, and in particular that he did not have much time to talk with the public health nurses. The latter seemed to know a fair amount about the patient's family problems, but they too felt that the woman was of low intelligence and they ascribed her neglect of the child to this factor. They had been angry for some time about the policy of the welfare workers in forcing mothers on A.D.C. to bring their husbands into court for nonsupport, and because of this anger they did not readily communicate with the social workers. The nurses were also angry at having to deal with so many Negroes from the South. They felt that the latter were a shiftless lot, who traveled North in order to have an easy life on welfare.

The pediatrician appeared to be a warm and kindly man. His hurry at the clinic seemed to be due to the pressure to get back to his middle-class private practice, and this was related to the low rate of remuneration for part-time employees of the city health department well-baby clinics. His lack of communication with the public health nurses was in part due to strained relations with their supervisor, who felt he was short-changing the clinic because he rushed in and out so quickly, and in part related to his low opinion of the nurses because of the poor quality of their written reports in the case records. Since he rarely discussed cases personally with the nurses, he had no realization of the richness of their information about many of his patients.

The mother's depression and its origins could have been adequately assessed by the psychiatrist even had he seen her in his own office. In order to obtain the other information he had to spend some time in the well-baby clinic, and it can be seen that this information was necessary in order to formulate a meaningful plan for dealing with the case. The alienation of the Negro mother from her baby was only part of a total picture of communication blocks—between the woman and her husband, between the woman and the pediatrician, between the pediatrician and the public health nurses, and between them and the welfare workers. Moreover, despite the sad realities of slum life and inadequate medical care and welfare services in an urban ghetto, there were many assets in the situation that might be mobilized in behalf of the woman and her baby—the warmth and interest of the pediatrician, the public health nurses' knowledge of local conditions and local resources, and the potential of using the welfare workers for constructive rather than destructive purposes by helping them to deal with this case more flexibly.

The consultant might have made a diagnosis of depression in the mother and a recommendation that she be referred to a psychiatric clinic for anti-depressant medication. A more significant consultation, however, would focus on building communication bridges among the participants, and on enabling the pediatrician to understand the woman's predicament and to find a way to mobilize the existing resources in his professional domain so as to help with her major life problem.

It may be instructive to compare the consultant's operations in this example with what he would have done if he had been using consultee-centered case consultation. In that case he would probably not have seen the Negro woman at all but would have spent all his time talking with the pediatrician about the patient. He would undoubtedly have noticed from the consultee's story that his view of the woman was unduly restricted and that he had not collected additional information from the public health nurses. Unless the nurses were also included among his consultee group, he would not have had access to the detailed information about the woman's marital history or about the influence of the A.D.C. workers. If the consultee group did include all the well-baby clinic workers he probably would have obtained most of the story in a single session, although he might not have been able to rule out an intellectual deficit in the patient, as he was in fact able to do from his own interview with her. He could, however, have been able to raise the question of the alternatives of mental retardation and depression, and to help the workers collect more information in order to differentiate the two. He would probably have been in a better position to understand the significance of the communication blocks and resistances in the pediatrician and the public health nurses, because he would have had more time to explore whether these were mainly produced by the culture and social system of the health unit or by personal idiosyncrasy of the individuals. This knowledge would probably have given him more leverage to remedy the situation than he had with a client-centered case consultation approach, in which his contact with his consultees was more time-limited and his intervention had to be shorter.

In actuality, in this example the communication blocks were mainly situational and were little influenced by the personal idiosyncrasies of the health workers. It was therefore possible for the consultant to ameliorate the pattern by means of a relatively short communication in the form of concrete and specific advice on case management. This would not have worked if the blocks had been rooted in deep prejudice or in theme interference. Had this been so, the theme interference reduction techniques of consultee-centered case consultation would have been essential. Such consultation probably would have had to continue over two or three sessions, in order for the consultant to obtain the necessary information, to build a relationship of sufficient intensity to provide enough leverage, and to plan and implement his consultant intervention of theme to interference reduction.

In contrast, the client-centered approach enabled the consultant to complete his main work in one session. Although he spent much of his time with the client, he did spend about thirty minutes in all with the pediatrician and the public health nurses, and this time was sufficient for him to collect the necessary information about their social system and about their involvement in the case, as well as to make his consultant intervention. The kind of information about the consultees and their work situation needed by a client-centered case consultant is usually rapidly obtained by observation of interactional cues and by fairly superficial, though sensitive, interviewing techniques. In this example, for instance, the consultant observed the hurried manner of the pediatrician and his lack of rapport with the Negro woman. He asked him a few questions about the patient and about the work situation in the clinic. Then he talked briefly to the nurses and their supervisor about the patient, the policies and practices of the welfare workers, and about the city's arrangements for staffing the well-baby clinics. All his questions dealt with facts about the system that could easily be discussed openly by the professionals concerned, and that required a minimum of interpretation of underlying motives by the consultant, whose main task was to fit his findings together into a meaningful pattern in order to form the basis for his intervention.

Of the thirty minutes of interaction with the pediatrician and the nurses, the consultant spent about twenty to twenty-five minutes on his assessment. During that time he not only elicited the facts of the situation but he also learned something about the style of communication of his consultees—particularly the pediatrician, to whom his consultation report would have to be delivered. This allowed him, as it were, to "tune in to the consultee's wavelength," so that he could communicate his appraisal of the case and his recommendations in such words and manner that they would be readily understandable and acceptable to the pediatrician.

The Consultation Report

In client-centered case consultation the consultant's intervention takes the form of a report—usually written in a letter or in the case record. Wherever possible, this written communication should be supplemented by a face-to-face discussion or by a telephone call, which affords the consultee the opportunity to clarify the consultant's meaning and allows the latter to make sure that his recommendations are understood and are feasible in the consultee's setting.

It is most important that the consultant's vocabulary be acceptable to the consultee. Psychiatric jargon is usually not appropriate. On the other hand, the consultee should not feel that the consultant is talking down to him, which might occur if the consultant uses oversimplified expressions when dealing with a sophisticated professional. The golden mean can only be found if the consultant gets to know the communication style of the consultee's profession and the personal patterns of communication of the particular consultee; and if he makes a determined effort to talk at the right level.

It is not only the choice of words that is significant but also the nature of the concepts that the consultant communicates. These must fit the culture of the consultee. For instance, a pediatrician or a general practitioner usually feels uncomfortable if a psychiatrist talks to him about pregenital sexuality, castration fears, latent homosexuality, or incestuous fantasies. Such topics are commonplace among mental health workers, but to many other professionals they are strange and distasteful or disturbing. They may be important issues in the specialist's own diagnostic formulations. However, since his report is not addressed to himself or to a mental health colleague but to a consultee of another profession, it should contain only material that can be utilized by its recipient.

The consultant's educational goal should not be to teach the consultee the specialized subject matter of psychiatry or psychology but to enable him to deepen his understanding of those aspects of his client's human nature that are within the usual purview of the consultee's profession. As implied in the previous section, the major content area of the report should be concerned with the current life predicament of the client, with his ineffectual efforts to cope which have led to the disturbance of functioning with which the consultee has to deal, and with the consultant's recommendations as to how the consultee may stimulate more effective coping and may call in additional human and material resources to aid the client in his efforts.

For instance, in the previous example of the Negro mother of the head-banging child, the consultant wrote the following report:

> I agree that the head banging is probably the result of the child's being deprived of his mother's care and affection. The mother is of normal intelligence but appears dull because she is suffering from a depression that appears to be a reaction to her present unsatisfactory life situation. She left

her family and friends in Mississippi when she came to Northville. Her husband lost his job eight months ago and has had no steady employment since then. He is separated from his wife. He has a problem with alcohol, the seriousness of which is hard to determine from the woman's story. She is on A.D.C. and in order to comply with local welfare policy, she took her husband to court for nonsupport. The woman now lives a lonely, isolated life and is grieving for her husband and for her family and friends. Because of her own feelings of deprivation she is not able to give adequate attention to her child.

I recommend that the well-baby clinic workers help the mother explore alternative avenues for dealing with her problems with her husband. The public health nurse, for instance, might contact the husband—the mother knows his address and sees him occasionally. I have the impression that it is the pressure of the court order that is the main factor in keeping them apart. It would be valuable if the man could be induced to come in for an interview with the pediatrician so as to involve the father in the responsibility for the care of his child. The main purpose of such an interview would be to offer him help with his alcohol and employment problems, through referral to the Public Employment Service Office in Northville and possibly to the Alcohol Clinic at Northville Hospital. The public health nurse might contact the welfare worker and explore other avenues than A.D.C. for supporting the family until the father gets back on his feet. The assistance of the neighborhood lawyer at the Oxford Multiservice Center might be needed to disentangle the legal aspects of the nonsupport situation.

From the mother's story, it seems that the trouble between her and her husband is not deep-seated. It was probably precipitated by his not being able to cope with the job at the meat-packing plant for which he was not fitted, and his finding escape in alcohol. If I am correct, superficial support and guidance by the public health nurse should be sufficient to help the couple get back together and readjust their marriage. If not, the social worker at the Alcohol Clinic should be able to help; and if this does not work out, I suggest a referral to the Oxford Family Service worker at the Multiservice Center. The mother's depression is not deep enough to warrant psychiatric treatment. I have every hope that it will lift as soon as her marital problems begin to clear up. If not, she may eventually need antidepressant medication.

I recommend that the pediatrician continue to see the mother and baby at regular intervals at the well-baby clinic in order to supervise the progress of the case and to coordinate the work of the other professionals through the efforts of the public health nurse. I will be interested in the outcome, and I would be pleased to see the woman again in about three months to see how she is doing and to make other suggestions should these be necessary. Please feel free to call on me before then if anything unexpected occurs.

This was a complicated case with many aspects that necessitated a lengthy report, but it will be noticed that all the consultant's statements are direct and to the point. There is no abstruse discussion of psycho-pathology—the consultant commits himself in clear language to the judgment that although the mother is depressed, she does not, at this time, need specialized psychiatric care but can continue under the supervision of the well-baby clinic. He also spells out concretely the various types of professional intervention needed and differentiates the tasks of the pediatrician and the public health nurse, as well as the need to call in other professionals and community agencies. Of considerable importance in this and many other complicated cases is the statement that the consultant offers to see the client again for a re-evaluation and invites the consultees to turn to him for further consultation help if things do not turn out as expected. This acceptance of a continuing interest in the case, and a sharing of responsibility for its outcome, is likely to be an important source of emotional as well as cognitive support to the consultees. They will feel more secure and will probably do a better job because they are assured of the psychiatrist's specialized backing. At the same time, he leaves no doubt in his report that they continue to be in charge of the case, and so he in no way weakens their feelings of professional autonomy and independence.

This report also offers a good example of a consultant's "bridge-building" role. His recommendations provide a concrete opportunity for building or rebuilding relationships between the client and her husband, the pediatrician and the public health nurses, the nurses and the welfare workers, and the well-baby clinic staff and several key neighborhood agencies. This psychiatrist happened to have firsthand knowledge of the local caregiving agencies. In instances in which this is not so, the consultant can often obtain this information from the consultees, who usually can name the appropriate agencies, even though they may not have thought of invoking their aid on the case in question.

Implementation of the Consultant's Recommendations

In line with our definition of consultation, the implementation of the consultant's recommendations is a matter for the consultee. Since he carries the responsibility for the case, it is his prerogative to accept or reject the consultant's suggestions. The latter should be of such a nature that if the consultee decides to accept them he should have the knowledge and skill to implement them with the resources immediately available in his agency.

Especially with a new consultee, the consultant may not feel confident that this ideal can be attained. For instance, in the case I have just described, considerable skill would be needed by the pediatrician and the public health nurse in order to motivate the husband to come to the well-baby clinic, to counsel the couple on their marital difficulties, to persuade the welfare workers to find an alternative to their standard A.D.C. approach; and to refer the couple to the other agencies as well as to interest the busy agency workers in the case. Is this not a tall order for the usual staff of a well-baby clinic? Actually the consultant had considerable experience with public health workers and had good reason to believe them capable of carrying out such a plan. Each consultant must learn for himself the limits of the capacities of his consultees. It is a measure of the insularity of most mental health clinicians that when they come out of their offices into community agencies, such as schools, courts, public health units, and welfare offices, they are surprised to find how skillful their non-mental health colleagues often are at handling interpersonal tasks that the specialists regard as complicated.

In spite of this, however, many consultees will require some assistance from the consultant in finding out how to go about implementing his recommendations. This is often an essential part of the consultant's contribution and is another reason why he should discuss his written recommendations verbally with the consultees.

In our case example, both the pediatrician and the public health nurse had a number of questions about how they should handle the case in conformity with the psychiatrist's suggestions. He was able to answer in quite specific terms many of these questions, such as how to approach the husband and what to say to the welfare workers. More important, he was able to present himself as a role model in regard to his expressed attitudes of empathy and understanding for this young couple from a rural background, caught up in a complex of forces beyond their comprehension and control, in a bewildering and frightening metropolis. In this way he once again acted as a bridge and paved the way for the clinic workers to see the tragic human qualities of this family, so that they might be better able to communicate empathically with them and also to interpret the case to the other professionals.

Follow-up

Whenever possible the consultant should end a consultation by arranging to obtain follow-up information, as in this example. This is important for two reasons—first, as a rough method of evaluation of the efficacy of the consultation. If the report on the client at the end of three to six months is favorable, this may not have been the result of the consultee's efforts or of the consultant's recommendations, but at least it is consonant with a good result. By discussing the progress of the case, the consultant may also learn more about the consultee's ways of working and how these appear to have been influenced by his own intervention, which may help him to improve his consultation recommendations in future cases. If the report turns out to be negative, the consultant can be more confident in accepting it as an evaluation of his consultation efforts. Since it emphasizes his lack of success, it provides him with a stimulus and a lever to review what he did and to try to identify errors in technique which he will remedy in the future. It is likely that the consultee, too, is disappointed with the result and perhaps also with the consultant. A review of the case will provide an opportunity for a discussion of how the consultee thinks the consultant might be more helpful to him, which the consultee would probably have been reluctant to initiate spontaneously. In the setting of a follow-up case review, both consultant and consultee can engage in an objective analysis of their joint endeavors without either side's engaging in recriminations but in a spirit of pooling ideas to improve their future efforts in behalf of clients.

Apart from this, the mere fact that the consultant shows his personal involvement in cases to the extent that he wishes to devote time and serious thought to follow-up investigations is likely to have a beneficial effect on the consultation relationship. It consolidates the continuing bond between the consultee and consultant, and it prepares the way for continuing discussion not only of the case in point but of other cases with which the consultee may be having difficulty. Our approach to consultation emphasizes the principle that the consultant should not take over from the consultee his professional responsibility for the client and thus diminish the consultee's autonomy and independence. This involves, however, the hazard that the consultee may perceive the consultant as someone who wishes not to involve himself and "get his own hands dirty" in cases but only to operate in the privileged position of a bystander and critic—a sort of kibitzer in a chess game. Despite all his attempts to paint an image of himself as a helpful colleague with a nonhierarchical approach, this may interfere with the development of an optimal consultation relationship. The consultee's awareness of the consultant's authentic interest in the cases, manifested in realistic terms by the consultant's zeal in following them up to determine their outcome, serves to counteract such a negative impression.

In this connection, it is important to emphasize that in the follow-up discussions the consultant should by his manner and by the form and wording of his questions leave no doubt in the consultee's mind that it is the fate of the client on which the consultant is focusing and not possible shortcomings in the consultee's operations. Insofar as the consultant may be interested in understanding how professional intervention may have modified the course of development in the client's life, he must be sure to convey the impression—which in fact should be his true feeling —that both he and the consultee are equally involved, each with his own assigned role and responsibility, the consultant for contributing the specialized evaluation of the problem and recommendations on how to deal with it, and the consultee for translating these recommendations into a feasible plan and taking direct action to implement it.

NOTES

1. Bruce L. Bushard, *The U.S. Army's Mental Hygiene Consultation Service. Symposium on Preventive and Social Psychiatry* (Washington, D.C.: U.S. Govt. Printing Office, 1957), pp. 431–445.
2. A. J. Brook, "An Experiment in General Practitioner–Psychiatrist Co-operation," *Journal of College of General Practitioners 13,* 27, 1967.

[7]

Consultee-Centered
Case Consultation

INTRODUCTION

In consultee-centered case consultation the consultant's primary focus is upon elucidating and remedying the shortcomings in the consultee's professional functioning that are responsible for his difficulties with the case about which he is seeking help. As usual in consultation, the content of the discussion is mainly restricted to clarifying the details of the client's situation so as to increase the consultee's cognitive grasp and emotional mastery of the issues involved in caring for him. This is likely to lead to an improvement in the consultee's professional planning and action, and hopefully to consequent improvement in the client. But in consultee-centered consultation, improvement in this client is a side effect, welcome though it may be, and the primary goal is to improve the consultee's capacity to function effectively in this category of case, in order to benefit many similar clients in the future. Because of this educational emphasis, the consultant uses the discussion of the current case situation, not basically in order to understand the client, but in order to understand and remedy the consultee's work difficulties, as manifested in this example. He therefore focuses his attention selectively on certain appropriate aspects of the case that provide evidence about the professional work problems of the consultee, rather than on investigating the condition of the client as a person in his own right.

The significant information in this kind of consultation, therefore, comes from the consultee's subjectively determined story about the client and not from the objective reality of the client's situation. Because of this, there is usually no need for the consultant to investigate the

125

client directly by seeing or interviewing him, and he can restrict his information to what the consultee says about the case.

Since the consultee is having cognitive, and often emotional, difficulties in dealing with this client, which are the factors impelling him to request consultation, it is likely that his description of the case will not be accurate. It may be one-sided, incomplete, or distorted. If the consultant does not examine the client himself, how can he determine the true situation and hence realize the nature of the discrepancies between this and the consultee's account, from which he can pinpoint the latter's shortcomings? The doubt raised by this question impels some consultants to collect independent objective information about clients discussed in consultee-centered case consultation. They usually do not conduct as exhaustive an investigation of the client as they would in client-centered case consultation, in which they are responsible for a substantive diagnosis and a detailed remedial prescription; but they do try to obtain some objective picture of the client, such as by classroom observation or by asking other observers to describe him, in order to compare this with the consultee's story. I do not feel this to be necessary, and I believe the majority of workers in this field agree with me. Our experience teaches us that if we listen carefully to the consultee's statements about his case, we can usually identify his biases, distortions, and areas of inadequate perception or planning from the internal consistency and inconsistency of his observations; from evidence of exaggeration, confusion, or stereotyping; and from signs of emotional overinvolvement or underinvolvement with one or more of the actors or situations in the client's drama.

This approach has one obvious drawback. Since the consultant's information is restricted to what the consultee *says,* the consultant can never be certain how this is related to what the consultee *does.* The consultation can deal only with the consultee's *capacity* for professional action and not with his actual *behavior.* This is in keeping with the fact that usually the consultant is not a member of the same profession as the consultee and therefore would not be competent to judge or direct the details of the latter's technical operations, or for that matter to perceive the "objective reality" of the client in conformity with the cognitive and experiential framework of the consultee's professional subculture. This point emphasizes the differentiation of consultee-centered case consultation from case supervision. The goals of consultation are limited to remedying certain defects in the already acquired professional knowledge and skills of the consultee that become salient and visible in specific case situations. Supervision and other forms of professional education have the goal of systematic positive enhancement of knowledge and skills. Supervision also has the goal of protecting the clients of the program and must therefore have access to information from which valid judgments can be made about the professional worker's behavior and its effect on his client.

Once again, it is important to realize that consultation has a restricted, though significant, function in a professional program. We must understand the use of consultation as one element of a range of "staff" and "line" operations.

TYPES OF CONSULTEE-CENTERED CASE CONSULTATION

I have found it valuable to differentiate four types of consultee-centered case consultation, related to the four common reasons for the work difficulties that underlie the need for consultation. These are: (a) lack of knowledge, (b) lack of skill, (c) lack of self-confidence, and (d) lack of professional objectivity.

Lack of Knowledge

The consultee's inability to handle the case may be due to his lack of knowledge about the psychosocial factors involved in such situations or he may not see the relevance of theoretical concepts he learned at school to the realities of this client's problems. Courses in psychology, psychopathology, and community mental health have in the past often been inadequate in training schools for such professions as nursing, teaching, medicine, and the law. They are improving, but older practitioners may have some shortcomings in these subjects, and recent graduates may not have learned how to utilize generalized abstract concepts in analyzing particular case situations. Certain topics, such as crisis theory, which are of great importance in appreciating the significance of the common predicaments of everyday life, are even today rarely part of the curriculum in professional training, nor are other essential subjects such as drug addiction, alcoholism, suicide, and mental retardation. However much time and effort may be devoted to these subjects in professional training schools, advances take place in the field that may not be adequately covered by continuing education and in-service training. Moreover, curriculum content in all these educational programs must necessarily be of a relatively superficial general nature to allow scope for the acquisition of the main body of traditional knowledge of the profession. It is inevitable that from time to time the professional worker will be confronted by problems that demand specialized knowledge that neither he nor his supervisors possess or can be expected to acquire in any systematic course.

When the consultant recognizes that the difficulties of his consultee are due to such lack of knowledge about mental health, he can obviously remedy the situation by imparting the missing information. In doing so, he should, as indicated earlier in this book, avoid disturbing the role identity of the consultee.

In a well-organized professional institution or program there will be little need for consultee-centered case consultation occasioned by lack of knowledge. Recruitment and selection will ensure that workers are well trained. The level of their knowledge will be continually upgraded and kept in consonance with job demands by supervision and in-service training programs. Only occasionally will an unusual case overtax these systems and lead to a demand for consultation. If a mental health consultant encounters more than a few instances of this type he should, in addition to dealing with each case on its own merits, take steps to draw to the attention of the appropriate authorities the need to supplement their routine supervisory or in-service training efforts. The mental health specialist may himself take a part in this by providing didactic seminars for supervisors or for line workers. The former are more appropriate, because they lead to a wider spread in communicating the new information and ensure a more lasting effect, because the supervisors are likely to continue working for the organization longer than the line workers. There is also less danger of the consultant's disturbing the role identity of stable senior professionals than of juniors who might identify with him as a role model. In addition, when the specialist filters his knowledge to the line workers through the supervisory group, the latter will translate his ideas and concepts into the acceptable professional and institutional communication modes of that setting.

My reason for emphasizing the need for the consultant to be alert to the need for an educational input into the system when he is confronted by more than a few consultation cases of this type is that consultee-centered case consultation is an expensive form of interprofessional operation, especially on an individual basis. It repeatedly takes up the time of a highly trained specialist to disseminate information that could be imparted just as effectively and much more cheaply by straightforward group educational methods.

In the absence of an adequate supervisory or in-service training program in a consultee institution, the consultant should use group consultation in dealing with frequently occurring work difficulties due to lack of knowledge. According to the changing demands of the situation he can modify his method so as to turn certain sessions into more or less systematic didactic seminars when he comes across areas of ignorance that are common to the majority of the group, while exploiting their motivation to learn because of the relevance of the issues involved in the material that emerges from the current cases presented by one or more of the consultees.

Lack of Skill

In certain cases, the consultant may judge that the consultee's work difficulty is due not to his lack of understanding of the psychosocial issues in the client's situation but to lack of skill in finding a solution to the problem, either by means of his own direct efforts or by invoking the help of other professionals or community agencies. The consultant, accordingly, will attempt to help the consultee improve his skills. Since methods and techniques are even more idiosyncratically related to professional culture than is basic theoretical knowledge, all the safeguards against disturbing the role image of consultees, mentioned in the previous section, must be re-emphasized here. In particular, the consultant must avoid giving straightforward prescriptions for action, unless he has a wide and intimate knowledge of the range of normative behavior in the consultee profession and in the particular consultee institution. Even then, he should not prescribe an answer to the questions in the case but put forward a range of alternative ways of handling the problem, which he has learned to value from previous experience of what workers have used in that institution. This is complicated by the fact that the consultee may have unsuccessfully tried many or all of these methods before finally giving up and asking for consultant help. Rather than listening to the problems presented by the case and then suggesting alternative solutions, the consultant might be better advised to carry out a joint appraisal with the consultee of how he has already tried to deal with them, and by means of this discussion attempt to enlarge the consultee's understanding of the factors that may have contributed to the intransigence of the case, which may reveal additional options for action. This is a tricky situation because the consultation can easily slide into a supervisory-type session, with the consultee's expecting the consultant to criticize or praise his efforts and to pass judgment on his professional functioning.

Whenever a consultee institution has a functioning supervisory system, I try to steer clear of this kind of consultation intervention by suggesting to the consultee that he subsequently seek help from his supervisor, or by inviting the supervisor in to the consultation interview and shifting from my central consultant role to that of a specialist resource person, while the supervisor takes over the primary task of helping the consultee begin to work out appropriate methods and techniques. In any event, skill development is not a matter that can be dealt with in one or two interviews but demands continued practice and then reflection about what seemed to work and what seemed to fail, a process that is greatly helped by the support and example of a role model, namely a supervisor. The function of a mental health consultant in this process is first to identify from the cases presented to him that one or more of the workers have inadequate skills, and then to energize the supervisory or in-service training system, as well as offering his expert help in improving the latter in the mental health area. Logistically, the most effective role for the mental health specialist is to act as a resource person to the supervisory group, to help them work out the most effective ways of upgrading the skills of their consultees.

I am not advocating that when a consultant discovers that a consultee is having difficulties in a case because of lack of skill he should forthwith terminate the session by referral to the supervisor. Such action would clearly exert a deleterious effect on his consultation relationship with the line workers, even though it was sincerely meant to avoid infringement on the domain of the supervisors as well as to prevent waste of scarce and expensive consultation time. What I am suggesting is that once the consultant decides that he is dealing with a consultation case of this type, he should focus his efforts for the remainder of that interview on gaining a deeper understanding of the nature of the consultee's skill difficulties, adding to the latter's understanding of the issues involved, and supporting him in exploring how he might go about improving his skills within the established framework of his institution.

In consultee organizations that do not have an active system of supervision—for example, a diocese in which the parish priests are relatively independent—a mental health consultant may be the only person available to help consultees improve their skills. Here again, he should try to operate on a group basis rather than on an individual basis. Not only is this logistically sound in spreading the effect of his specialist efforts, it also allows him to restrict himself to the role of a resource person, while supporting members of the group in sharing with each other methodological ideas that they have developed within the social framework and culture of their own profession. For instance, in dealing with a case of alcoholism presented to the consultation group by a clergyman, the consultant can contribute specialist information about the difficulties likely to be encountered in dealing with the alcoholic's wife, who may be unconsciously driving him to continue drinking. The consultant leaves to the group the question of how a clergyman could best exploit the potentials of his role and the influence of his congregation in dealing with her. The consultant could also bring home to the group the realistic assets and constraints of the available medical clinics, self-help groups, and community mental health facilities that they might try to involve in their action planning, while encouraging individual group members to recount the success or failure of their differing attempts to secure specialized community help in similar cases among their own congregants. Almost invariably the methods and techniques recommended by the group members will not be the same as, or will be subtly different from, those that the consultant might have suggested—unless he was reporting what other clergymen of that denomination had told him in the past.

Lack of Self-Confidence

Occasionally the consultee's confusion and uncertainty about a case may be caused by generalized lack of confidence, related to such factors as ill health, old age, or inexperience. The consultant's role is then to provide nonspecific ego support and to smooth the consultee's path to other supportive figures in the consultee organization. If the consultant finds widespread lack of self-confidence among certain classes of workers in the institution—for example, new nurses in a public health unit or new teachers in a school—the chances are that there is some inadequacy in the supervisory or administrative system, so that the newcomers are not being properly directed and supported by their organization. If the consultant can stimulate an improvement in this situation he should do so. If not, he might organize a few group "consultation" sessions, which would be mainly geared to providing an opportunity for peer support among those in the same boat, as well as communicating to the group the solicitude and support of their administrative authorities for their inevitable temporary initial problems of adjustment.

Lack of Objectivity

In a well-organized institution or agency in which there is an effective personnel system, good administrative control, and a well-developed supervisory network, most cases that present themselves for consultee-centered case consultation fall into this fourth category. The consultee's difficulty with his client is caused by defective judgment based upon a lack of professional objectivity and a loss of normal "professional distance." The consultee, as it were, gets either too close or too distant from one or more actors in the client's life drama, so that he is not able to perceive them accurately enough to carry out his task. Another way of describing the situation is that personal subjective factors in the consultee invade his role functioning, distort his perceptions, and cloud his judgment, so that in this current case he behaves less effectively than is usual for him and thus is not able to utilize his existing knowledge and skills. By the time he comes for consultation, this situation is usually aggravated by his feelings of confusion and frustration engendered by the impasse in the case and by a greater or lesser feeling of professional failure and consequent lowering of self-esteem, all of which add to his loss of professional poise.

Of all types of consultation this is the one that most taxes the coordinate relationship of consultant and consultee; because if the consultee's loss of poise is openly mentioned or discussed, it emphasizes an objective discrepancy between him and the consultant, who is relaxed and apparently in perfect control of his personal life in the professional setting. It is therefore important for the consultant to deal with the relevant issues by discussing them in relation to some actor in the client's drama, to himself, to some other example, or to a fictitious displacement object in an anecdote or parable. The goal of such a "displaced" discussion is to help the consultee regain, without loss of face, his professional poise and objectivity, both in connection with the presenting case with which he has become subjectively involved and also, implicitly, in connection with the sensitive issue of his personal life or professional functioning of which this case is an example.

There is a vast range of possible causes for lack of professional objectivity, including inadequate professional training and idiosyncratic personality factors, such as low intelligence, poor judgment, insensitivity, and poor motivation. The consultation setting, however, exerts a filtering effect; and in practice most cases are found to fall into five overlapping categories: (a) direct personal involvement, (b) simple identification, (c) transference, (d) characterological distortions, (e) and theme interference.

Direct Personal Involvement

The consultee's lack of professional objectivity is due to his deviating from the professional role relationship with the client and replacing this to a greater or lesser degree by a direct personal relationship. Examples are the physician who falls in love with a patient, the teacher who builds a maternal relationship with one of her pupils, or the white nurse who reacts to a black patient primarily on the basis of racial prejudice.

In some of these cases the worker is conscious of the deviation from his professional role, and this conflict may be more or less stably re-solved at the expense of a variable amount of guilt—for instance, the clergyman who seduces and has an illicit affair with a congregant, or the psychoanalyst who falls in love with a patient and interrupts the analysis in order to get married. Such cases are not likely to come to consulta-tion, although less extreme ones may not uncommonly fall into the do-main of the supervisor, part of whose duty it is to protect clients from being exploited by being made objects for the satisfaction of the per-sonal needs of their supervisees.

In other cases, the worker is more or less unconscious of what is hap-pening and may not realize the nature of his personal involvement, or he may consciously suppress or deny his awareness of it because of guilt and shame. Such cases not uncommonly come for consultation and are, of course, quite common in supervision and in professional training situ-ations, in which a directed effort is made to help young practitioners learn to control the expression of their personal needs in the work set-ting and to develop a professional identity that provides them with other goals which they can satisfy by restricting themselves to dealing with the personal needs of their clients. This is mainly accomplished, in addition to the usual ways of inculcating the traditional value system of the pro-fession, by exposing the neophyte to a senior who acts as a role model and who demonstrates by his words and actions feasible ways of operat-ing in conformity with the professional ideology. The neophyte can iden-tify with these ways and can eventually incorporate them as his own. For instance, a noted professor of psychiatry was in the habit of helping psychiatric residents learn to admit, accept, and control their feelings of sexual arousal while dealing with attractive patients of the opposite sex by telling them that one of the methods he often used in alerting himself to a possible diagnosis of hysterical character disorder in a young woman was by noticing that while talking to her he got an unexpected erection. Even though she was not being obviously seductive, and al-though he did not find her personally attractive, his erection told him that he was unconsciously picking up sexualizing stimuli that she was emitting. By talking openly and without embarrassment about his own incongruous bodily reactions, and by showing how he could exploit these to achieve professional goals for the benefit of his patient, he was communicating to his students not only a useful piece of diagnostic tech-nique but also an important message about effective ways to resolve con-flicts between personal and professional needs.

In consultation, direct personal involvement with the client by the consultee can be identified from a variety of verbal and nonverbal cues in the consultee's story and behavior. The consultant's intervention is directed to influencing the consultee to replace the satisfaction of his personal need by the satisfaction of professional goal achievement. This may be accomplished, without loss of face for the consultee, through discussing the client's problems in the same area, namely his conflict between getting direct personal satisfaction from the consultee versus getting the consultee's help in dealing with his problems so that he can satisfy his personal needs in normal life situations. The following report by a psychiatric consultant to a school system illustrates how this can be done:

The consultee in this case is a female guidance counselor in a junior high school. She is about forty years of age, unmarried, decidedly overweight, and living with her elderly parents. She is regarded by her colleagues as competent and frequently quite effective in her work but as a rather odd person who can make people uncomfortable in social exchange.

The particular case in question involved a thirteen-year-old boy, whose parents were divorced and who had recently come to live with his aunt and uncle. Almost from the beginning the boy had been perceived as a problem at home, around the discipline area. He would not obey his aunt and uncle, nor would he conform to most of their expectations about proper activities and limits for an adolescent boy. While bright enough he had also become something of a discipline problem at school and his grades were suffering accordingly. The guidance counselor further reported that the teachers in the school for the most part "didn't understand him" and that while he was reasonably popular with the students at school, in her view he was "really a very lonely boy." All this foregoing description was presented in a calm professional manner with no evidence of undue emotional participation or sensitivity on the part of the guidance counselor. After some further discussion of this kind, and some attempt to explore the possible meanings of the statement that the boy was really a very lonely boy, it seemed that the case did not involve any significant lack of objectivity and so the consultant discussed it with the guidance counselor from the point of view of increasing her knowledge and offering some general remarks about the needs of adolescents and the effects of divorce of parents upon the developing adolescent personality. The guidance counselor seemed satisfied with this and the session was terminated.

A week later the guidance counselor called requesting another appointment, and when the consultant arrived at the school he was presented with the problem of this same boy once again. Essentially the picture was presented as previously, but there was a repeat on the theme of the lonely boy who nevertheless was popular with the students. This second time around there was a note of extra intensity in this remark, evidenced by a heightening in color, a speeding of the speech rate, and several occasional deep intakes of breath that almost amounted to sighs. Acting on these cues, I proceeded to ask the guidance counselor for further description of the boy. This time she said that his popularity was not general with the students but seemed to be focused primarily among the girls in the school. She then added, "He's actually a very, very good-looking boy. He's quite tall for his age, very handsome, and very well developed for a thirteen-year-old." This last sentence was delivered with further intensification of autonomic indicators of emotion while the facial expressions remained controlled and calm. In this same way the guidance counselor went on to say that the youngster comes in to see her very often and that he wants to talk about himself. She indicated that the boy has discussed his feelings concerning living with his aunt and uncle and that she herself has been trying "to help him plan for his future. He's a bright boy and he needs to work out his plans and his feelings so he can go on to get an education."

It was apparent here that the guidance counselor was rather intensely involved with this youngster at several levels, some of which from the point of view of her professional role function could serve as appropriate motivators but others of which were obviously too intense and were bound to produce difficulties in her professional relationship with the boy. Her emphasis upon the youngster's physical attractiveness was repeated several different times in different ways, and it is clear that this was a major factor in drawing her to him. It was at this point that I also realized that in several of my past consultations with this guidance counselor, cases with similar features had been presented although the degree of involvement was far less intense than in the present one. The technical problem then was to find a way of indicating to the guidance counselor that the degree of closeness which had developed between herself and the boy had its negative qualities in terms of interfering with the possibility of giving him the kind of professional and objective guidance help he needed. Since it was obvious that this could not be done through referring to the teacher's own feelings about the boy, the situation had to be reversed and the message transmitted exclusively through talking about the boy's reactions. Fortunately, this case gave ample opportunity to do this.

The intervention was formulated after further discussion stimulated by the consultant around the fact that the boy showed a real desire and need to come in for extended conversations with the guidance counselor. When this had been clearly established, I then said to her that it was apparent that this was a youngster who for reasons that were obvious in his past history was a lonely boy, that he did need guidance, and that it was quite possible that the guidance counselor could perform a real service for him. I then added that there was one caution to be observed. Because of his loneliness and because of some of the special areas of sensitivity in a young adolescent, he could easily form much too close an attachment to the guidance counselor and become much too dependent upon her for direction and for companionship. The need was to find a way to let him know that interest in him was high, that he was accepted, but that she, the guidance counselor, felt sure he could also achieve satisfactory emotionally close relationships with others of his own age and with a wide variety of adults. As actually delivered, my message was formulated in a fairly casual confidential tone to the effect that "You and I both know how kids around this age, especially if they've had separations from people who are important to them, can attach themselves to friendly teachers, almost seeing them as people to make up for things they've lost in the past and the things they haven't had out of life. We don't have to be put off by this but just recognize it for what it is, and make it clear to the youngster what he can reasonably expect to get from us and what is beyond reasonable expectation." The emotional atmosphere in which this was delivered is best described as quite *entre nous* and was therefore participated in with some pleasure by this particular individual. She went on to describe several instances in the past in which youngsters have behaved in just this manner unless she found it necessary to gently let them know "I wasn't their mother."

A brief outcome observation was available in this instance since upon subsequent consultation about other cases this one was brought up with the information that the youngster still came in from time to time, and was receiving counseling, but that he had "taken the hint pretty well and isn't quite so involved with me now." This last, I feel, is pretty good confirmation that a cognitive statement about the client was also received in a meaningful emotional sense, since it had a lot to say about the emotional participation of the consultee in her relationship with this youngster.

Another consultation technique in cases of direct personal involvement is for the consultant to use himself as a role model. Since he is probably of a different discipline from his consultee, he presents himself as a model of a "generalized professional," much as the psychiatrist did with the guidance counselor in the previous example when he developed what he called the *"entre nous"* atmosphere—that is, "We two professionals are talking together about this lay client." Having set the stage in some such manner, the consultant talks about the client in such a way as to demonstrate his own professional attitudes of sympathetic empathy coupled with distance. In cases in which personally or culturally based racial or religious prejudice interferes with the consultee's capacity to come close to the client, the consultant provides a model of a professional who is able to bridge a cultural gap and, by making a special effort, to succeed in penetrating to the idiosyncratic humanity of the client. If necessary, he can emphasize the special personal difficulty involved for the professional and recount some anecdote of his own experience of laboriously dissipating his stereotyped perceptions and expectations of members of a strange culture. In this way, similar to the method used by the professor of psychiatry in teaching his residents, the consultant can reduce the distance between himself and his consultee, and emphasize their coordinate human difficulties in gaining professional mastery over obtrusive personal feelings and biases.

Simple Identification

It is not uncommon for a consultee's work difficulties to be due to his identifying rather than empathizing with the client or with one of the actors in the client's life situation. This identification may be part of a general transference reaction, in which he may be reading into the pattern of the client's drama some aspect of his own life. I will discuss this in the next section. The identification may also be a relatively isolated feature, which I call "simple" identification. The consultee does not interpret or misinterpret the client's situation or manipulate it to conform to a significant pattern from his own current or past life but perceives it as something idiosyncratic to the client. On the other hand, his judgment of the situation is disturbed because he identifies with one of the actors in the drama and takes sides in the conflict.

Usually, the identification is fairly easy for the consultant to identify, because it is energized by some obvious similarity between the identification object and the consultee—for example, they may be of the same age, sex, ethnic group, or profession, or have some obvious characteristic in common such as obesity, a stammer, being recently married, having a nagging mother, or having recently had surgery. The identification is usually also indicated by the consultee's describing the object in very positive and sympathetic terms, while adopting a partisan condemning attitude to other actors in the client's drama who are characteristically perceived in stereotyped derogatory terms. For instance, a young unmarried nurse with an Irish name requested consultation in regard to an adolescent female Irish patient, who was convalescing after tuberculosis. The nurse was obviously quite angry with the patient's parents, whom she described as overbearing and depriving. She was particularly incensed that they would not allow their daughter to go out on dates, and she felt that their hostile overprotectiveness was interfering with the patient's social development. As the nurse's story unfolded, and as the consultant explored the reasons she adduced for her opinions, it became clear that her negative judgment about the parents was not based upon significant evidence but upon her too freely accepting as valid the patient's querulous complaints and not realizing that the girl's attitude toward her parents was highly ambivalent. Moreover, the nurse had not listened seriously to what the parents had said, having quickly made up her mind that they were not telling the truth in order to hide their harsh treatment of their daughter.

In a case such as this, the task of the consultant is to act as a role model with whom the consultee can identify, and to demonstrate an empathic approach to all the relevant actors in the client's life situation. In the case in point, the consultant involved the consultee in a joint examination of the details of the patient's behavior and verbalizations, and in a discussion of how one could infer her probable mixed feelings about her parents and her desires and insecurities about going out again into social situations after returning from the relative isolation of a sanatorium. The discussion also focused on evidence indicating the difficulties of the parents, who had still not recovered from the shock of their daughter's tuberculosis, that had special significance in Irish culture, and who were confused about how to handle the vicissitudes of the girl's adolescent development. By using the leverage of the consultation relationship, the consultant influenced the consultee to look at the case afresh from the same distance and with the same empathic solicitude as his own. By the end of the first consultation session, the nurse was beginning to weaken her identification with the patient. During the second consultation interview she was able to utilize her existing knowledge of parent-child relationships during adolescence and of the psychosocial complications of tuberculosis to gain a balanced understanding of the case. She was then able to make some home visits and confirm to her own satisfaction the validity of the interpretations of the evidence that she and the consultant had developed, and to work out ways of helping the girl and her parents grapple with their problems. It was this personal experience of dealing with the patient and her parents as people with their own idiosyncratic identities that confirmed to the nurse, as much if not more than the words and attitudes of the consultant, that the girl was separate from her, and that one needed to collect data and then self-consciously go through a procedure of analyzing it before one could understand how she felt, instead of jumping to the conclusion that one knew it intuitively almost as though the patient were an extension of oneself.

Transference

Every psychoanalyst knows how frequent it is for his patients to transfer feelings and attitudes from past key relationships and fantasies not only onto him in the treatment context but onto many other objects in their current life situations, including colleagues and superiors at work and also clients or customers with whom they have continuing contacts. This occurs, not only among patients who are quite sick, but also among the fairly healthy analysands in training analysis. It is therefore not surprising to find that professionals not infrequently encounter difficulties with their clients because of transference distortions of their relationships with them. In contrast to the "simple identifications" I have just discussed, these difficulties arise from the consultee's imposing onto the client's case a pattern of roles that derives from his own previous life experience or fantasies. This leads to a preordained set of attitudes, stereotyped perceptions and expectations, and fixed judgments on the part of the consultee in relation to the actors in the client's life situation; and it blocks an objective appraisal of the actual issues in the case. It also prepares the ground for the consultee to act out his own fantasies through the medium of the case instead of planning and implementing rational professional action based upon an objective analysis of the needs of the client.

Usually, such transference distortions are held in check by reality testing, and in most mental health professionals they are usually temporary phenomena. This is aided by the culturally supported separation of professional and private life that directly buttresses the reality testing and control functions of the mature ego, as well as being introjected into the ego-ideal and superego. In the less than ideal situations of everyday experience, however, professional workers include people with varying degrees of mature ego development and strength. This is manifested, among other ways, in a variable propensity for transference and acting out in the work setting. This problem, although usually not defined in such terminology, is a significant issue for administrators and supervisors, who maintain surveillance over their subordinates and ensure that they control their irrational impulses. In certain cases the supervisors single out for special attention workers whom they characterize as "immature," "unstable," or "overly dependent," and whose recurrent weakened ego functioning they buttress with appropriate emotional supplies or management controls. For instance, a public health nursing supervisor reported to a group of her colleagues at a seminar on supervisory techniques that one of her staff nurses had experienced an emotionally deprived childhood, having been orphaned early in life and brought up in residential institutions. The supervisor said that this nurse had recurrent difficulties with older people, both on the staff and among her patients. She would rapidly build up an overly dependent relationship with them, which was particularly incongruous with patients or with the parents of patients. She would then badger the parent figures for attention and then, when this led inevitably to frustration, she would turn against them and accuse them of all kinds of wrongdoing.

The supervisor reported that this nurse was most effective with children, and that she was particularly successful in working in a hostel for crippled children that was within her district, although she had to be carefully watched lest she slip into her typical pattern in relating to the housemother.

The supervisor dealt with this nurse on the one hand by trying to steer her toward working with young people rather than with potential parent figures, and on the other hand by giving her extra supervision and emotional support whenever she noticed her beginning to get emotionally embroiled with an older person.

It is the repetitiveness and stereotyped nature of the transference pattern that make such individuals recognizable to their supervisors, and these cases often do not come for consultation. In the absence of adequate supervision, or if the disorder of functioning is not so obvious, workers with such problems do request consultation.

For example, a schoolteacher requested consultation about Jean, a girl in her fifth grade class who had recently become a disciplinary problem. She described the girl as being immature and given to temper tantrums that were precipitated by emotional scenes in which she obstinately refused to do what she was told. The consultant noted that the teacher talked about her pupil with barely concealed hostility. She was especially upset by Jean's immature and "whining" behavior, and about the fact that she seemed "to imagine she could get away with murder," by which the teacher meant that the child felt she had a privileged position and did not have to conform to the rules of the class. In discussing the case, the teacher said how surprised she had been to find this girl so immature because she distinctly remembered having no trouble at all with Jean's sister, who had been in her class three years earlier. At that time she had got to know the parents and had thought they were a well-balanced couple who took good care of their children. When she began to have trouble with Jean, she had talked with her mother, and it became "abundantly clear" that Jean had a "privileged position in the household" and was the pampered child who was always preferred, especially in comparison with her older sister. There appeared "to be constant fights between the two sisters, and invariably Jean would be protected by the mother and the other sister punished."

The consultant noted that the teacher discussed certain aspects of the case in a quite stereotyped way, as though her statements were quotations —for instance, the remark about the "abundantly clear" evidence that Jean had "a privileged position." At such times she spoke with particular intensity. Moreover, as the consultant tried to get the teacher to give the evidence on which she based such assertions as those concerning the sibling rivalry and Jean's privileged position, it appeared that this was very flimsy. The pattern of Jean's family drama seemed preformed in the teacher's mind, and in fact so did her perception of Jean's behavior. Other information that the teacher gave about Jean, in response to the consultant's questions, did not conform to the main picture she was painting of her. The child's behavior with her classmates seemed trouble-free and her record in previous grades was good. There was no indication of any current family or other environmental predicament that might have precipitated a sudden change in Jean's behavior. She had not been a problem at the beginning of the present school year; and in fact when the parents had come for their routine interviews with teachers just before Christmas, the teacher had given the mother a good report about her daughter. It had been on that occasion that she had realized for the first time that Jean was the younger sister of the child she had taught three years earlier. Jean's family name was quite a common one, and the two sisters did not resemble each other. She remembered her surprise at meeting the mother again, and she was even more surprised that after the Christmas vacation Jean had begun to deteriorate so rapidly.

By this time, the nature of the difficulty began to clarify in the consultant's mind. In addition to the evidence in the current case he remembered that this teacher had consulted him earlier in the year about another girl in her class, who was suffering from a learning disorder, and in that case too the child had been described as somebody else's younger sister; but this had not appeared important to the consultant, and he had dealt with the case by a somewhat didactic discussion about the nature and causes of learning disorders. That case had not improved but had been "resolved" by the child's being taken from the class because the family suddenly moved to another part of town.

The consultant did not know anything about the teacher's personal life, but he hazarded a guess to himself that she probably had a younger sister with whom she had been involved in unresolved conflicts similar in pattern to those she was now imposing on the case of Jean. In this regard it appeared particularly significant that Jean became a problem to the teacher only after she discovered that she was "a younger sister." It also seemed that Jean's poor behavior occurred only in class with that teacher and was apparently a reaction to the teacher's method of handling her.

The consultant dealt with this case in two ways. First he involved the teacher in a discussion of details of Jean's behavior in the classroom, in an attempt to influence the teacher to observe her more closely as a person in her own right, rather than as a stereotyped "younger sister." This appeared to have only a limited effect. Second, the consultant discussed the teacher's relationship to Jean, as it were, in reverse. He pointed out that her behavior had regressed following the teacher's interview with her mother before Christmas, during which they had discussed her older sister. He put forward the hypothesis that after this interview the mother had told Jean that the teacher had been very fond of the older sister and remembered her quite vividly, and had possibly told her that the teacher hoped Jean would be as successful a student. The consultant then involved the teacher in a discussion of what this might have meant to Jean, and the nature of the conflict that might have been set up in her mind, so that she now might imagine that the teacher was continually comparing her with her older sister. The teacher, in this discussion, began to identify with the consultant, reversing roles and empathically imagining how Jean felt as a younger sister, and how she was casting the teacher into a stereotyped role as either the older sister or the mother figure. The consultant then posed the management problem as being for the teacher to work out ways of convincing Jean that her teacher was not a representative of her family constellation, and that Jean was a person in her own right and not just a "younger sister."

During the second consultation session, the teacher quite suddenly made a switch in her patterned perceptions of Jean and began to talk about her as a child struggling to overcome in the classroom her misperceptions of her teacher. She then began to plan various alternative ways of dealing with her so that Jean might discover that her teacher was neither a mother figure nor an older sister figure but somebody who was trying to educate her and to help her achieve increasing maturity.

During the remainder of the school year this teacher asked for consultation about two other cases, neither one of which was a "younger sister." She gave follow-up reports on Jean, whose behavior disorder had apparently completely resolved within three to four weeks following the second consultation discussion about her problems.

Characterological Distortions of Perception and Behavior

Overt disturbances of work performance due to enduring psychiatric disorders in workers are usually dealt with and kept in check by administrative and supervisory controls. It is not uncommon, however, for covert or minor disturbances to evade the scrutiny of the controlling authorities in the organization and then to appear in consultation. For example, a consultant saw a female teacher who invoked his help with a ten-year-old boy whom she described as continually masturbating in her class. He was falling behind in his work and often sat with a withdrawn and dreamy expression on his face. She was sure he was masturbating because he often sat with his hands in his trouser pockets. She also talked about another boy in the same class who was always bothering the girls, one of whom complained that he tried to look up her skirts as she was coming down the staircase.

Further discussion revealed that several other children in the class were apparently also engaging in "harmful sexual behavior." In no case did the consultant find evidence in the teacher's stories to substantiate anything other than normal expectable behavior in children of that age. Moreover, the teacher gave her reports with obvious vicarious satisfaction, and her own behavior during the interview was rather seductive—she was wearing a short skirt, and she kept crossing and uncrossing her legs and drawing attention to them by ostentatiously and ineffectually trying to cover her knees with her skirt. Her handshake was warm and clinging, she spoke in a husky low voice, and she fluttered her eyelashes —like a sexy model in a TV commercial.

Many consultants would be cautious or even pessimistic about the likelihood of success in such a case of apparently long-standing character-ological disturbance. How could two or three sessions of consultation, even if repeated several times in connection with successive cases of "sexual behavior," produce any amelioration of this teacher's classroom performance? In order to improve her professional functioning would it not be necessary to help her solve her underlying Oedipal conflicts by means of deep psychotherapy or even psychoanalysis? And yet with all her apparent emotional conflicts, this girl was successfully holding down a job; and although her colleagues and superiors felt she was a bit strange and at times irritating, they believed her to be a reasonably steady worker. Her educational results with most of her students were not obviously worse than those of her colleagues. Clearly, despite her emotional problems, she did have sufficient control over herself most of the time to maintain a reasonable degree of task orientation. Although she behaved seductively to the consultant, this was within socially acceptable bounds.

The consultant attempted to handle the case by supporting the teacher's defenses and lowering her anxiety. He discussed each of the children about whom she complained, from the point of view of increasing her intellectual understanding of the nature of their behavior; and, although he had difficulty in keeping a straight face, he reassured her most earnestly that for a ten-year-old boy to play absent-mindedly with his genitals while daydreaming in class, or for him to engage in mild sexual horseplay with a not unwilling girl of the same age, was not unusual or abnormal. He also demonstrated by his manner toward her that he was not upset by her seductive behavior and yet was not impelled by it to deviate from his task-oriented approach to the professional problems she was posing. He was cool and maintained a proper distance, and yet he showed that he was most interested in her work difficulties and willing to spend three interviews seriously discussing them. At the end of the three sessions the teacher reported that the "masturbating boy" was much improved—in fact, she now talked about him with much empathy as a little boy whom she was helping by special tutorial attention to capitalize on his literary interests and talents, rather than being forced into the boredom of going at the slow pace of the rest of the class. Whether there had in fact been some objective change in the boy's behavior, or whether her report was in the nature of a "transference cure," the consultant was not able to determine.

During the remainder of the school year this teacher requested consultation about other cases of the same type. Each time the consultant used a similar approach with apparently identical results. He had the impression that although he was certainly producing no significant change in the personality pattern of the teacher, he was helping her maintain or regain her professional composure in the face of disequilibrating factors about which he had no knowledge, and which every now and again would threaten to disturb her work performance.

Such relatively nonspecific help in controlling transference in the work setting by opposing regression, increasing professional distance from clients, relieving negative or inhibiting feelings, such as of anxiety or anger, and supporting defenses, such as intellectualization, can often be better accomplished in group than in individual consultation. As long as the ground rules of the group discussions are clearly defined to exclude the analysis of personal problems of the participants, the consultant can stimulate consensual peer validation of the norms of behavior, both of clients and professionals. The group setting provides for more distance between consultant and consultees and lessens the intensity of transference to him, or at least provides him with more options in managing it. It also provides individual members with the continuing support of their peers in relieving their anxieties and in controlling their own fantasies and impulses so as to shore up their weaknesses in these areas.

Theme Interference

Whereas major transference reactions regularly invade the work setting mostly in disturbed individuals or in organizations lacking adequate administrative controls and supervisory supports, many years of experience in mental health consultation have taught me that minor transference reactions of a special type occasionally complicate professional functioning in most people, whatever their state of mental health. However healthy the workers, and however well organized their institutions, it is not uncommon for unsolved present or past personal problems to be displaced onto task situations and for this to produce temporary ineffectuality and loss of emotional stability in dealing with a segment of the work field. The signs of this process are not difficult to identify. A professional who is usually quite effective and emotionally balanced suddenly encounters a work situation that seems inexplicably confusing and upsetting. If his supervisors or peers see what is happening they do not quite understand it, because they know that usually he is able to handle such a problem with his existing knowledge and skills. On this occasion, however, something seems to be blocking him, and he seems unaccountably sensitive to some aspect of the case. This sensitivity is obscured by the fact that the case impasse naturally leads to the professional's increasing concern and frustration, so that it is difficult to know whether he is upset by the recalcitrance of his client and his situation or by some sensitizing trigger in the case or in his own life. In fact, it not infrequently happens that the worker is simultaneously upset not only by the case, with which he is having professional difficulties, but also by some social system disequilibrium in his institution or between it and its surrounding community, and also by some problems in his private life. One sometimes gets the impression of a series of interlocking upsets in the client, in the professional, in the organization, and in the community. And yet as far as the consultee is concerned, all his worry is focused on his difficulties in trying to handle the upsetting complexities of a single problem case.

Prolonged study of these cases, some details of which are included in Chapter 12, has led to the following formulation: A conflict related to actual life experience or to fantasies in the consultee that has not been satisfactorily resolved is apt to persist in his preconscious or unconscious as an emotionally toned cognitive constellation which we call a "theme." (In this we follow the lead of psychologists like H. A. Murray who have utilized a similar concept—for example, in elaborating the Thematic Apperception Test.)

In the present situation, since the theme is a continuing representation of an unsolved problem or of an experienced defeat or important need frustration, it carries a negative emotional tone of rankling failure. It also has a repetition compulsion quality. This usually takes a syllogistic form, involving an inevitable link between two items or statements: Statement A denotes a particular situation or condition that was characteristic of the original unsolved problem. Statement B denotes the unpleasant outcome. The syllogism takes the form, "All A inevitably leads to B." The implication is that whenever the person finds himself involved in situation or condition A, he is fated to suffer B, and that this generalization applies universally—that is, everyone who is involved in A inevitably suffers B.

Normally, the theme is adequately repressed or otherwise defended against, or it is expressed through some stable symptom or inhibition. Sometimes, for a variety of possible reasons, there is an upset in this equilibrium and the theme may become salient and threaten to emerge into consciousness. This may then be defended against by the person's displacing the theme onto some consonant aspect of the work situation. In particular, it may be superimposed onto the actors in some client's life predicament, the pattern of which provides appropriate potential transference objects.

A series of cues in the case form a perceived gestalt that is equated by the professional worker with Statement A (the Initial Category). This arouses the expectation that the client, or other actor in the client's drama, who is involved in this statement will inevitably suffer the fate linked with Statement B (the Inevitable Outcome). For instance, if Statement A (Initial Category) is "A person who masturbates excessively" and Statement B (Inevitable Outcome) is "His nervous system will be damaged and his intelligence will be blunted," the syllogism takes the form *"All* people who masturbate excessively damage their nervous systems and blunt their intelligence." This theme may be a sequel to guilt-ridden conflicts over masturbation in the professional worker's childhood and adolescence, and represents a foreboding that one day in the future a punishing nemesis will inevitably strike.

When, for a variety of possible reasons, there is a disequilibrium in the defenses against this old conflict and the deeper fantasies that underlie it, the situation is ripe for the invoking of a defense by displacement onto some appropriate work situation. The consultee unconsciously selects a client from his case load, and from certain cues in his statements or behavior, fits him into the Initial Category of "a person who masturbates excessively." This then arouses the expectations that "his nervous system will inevitably be damaged and his intelligence blunted." The worker becomes very upset by this foreboding and begins to make a number of abortive attempts to prevent or stave off the expected doom—for example, in the case of a schoolchild who is not doing well in class, by applying increasing pressure on him to memorize lengthy passages of poetry in order to prevent deterioration in his memory, or by oversolicitous advice to his mother to make sure he does not stay up late lest lack of sleep hasten the nervous degeneration.

These remedial or preventive efforts are usually panicky and inconsistent, and a realization of their obvious ineffectiveness confirms the consultee's certainty that the expected doom cannot be prevented despite all his abortive struggles. Unconsciously, his consolation is that this time the catastrophe will occur to a client and not to himself. At a deeper level, there may also be the reassurance that he stage-managed and directed the whole drama by manipulating the actors to conform to his theme and so achieved some measure of mastery by this vicarious experience.

Sometimes, the cues in the client's story are objectively and accurately perceived. In our example, the child may indeed be masturbating excessively, as defined by himself, his parents, and his physician. Sometimes, the cues may be misperceived or misinterpreted in order, as it were, to force the client into the Initial Category so that he can be exploited as a displacement object for the theme. For instance, the child may be masturbating, but not more so than most; or cues may be grossly misinterpreted so that the client is stereotyped as fitting the Initial Category without reasonable evidence, such as if he suffers from acne and appears dreamy and seclusive, signs that are misinterpreted as bodily and behavioral concomitants of masturbation.

Whether or not the client objectively fits the Initial Category, once he has been, as it were, clicked into place in it, the case becomes a test case for the inevitability of the theme outcome. There is an absolute expectation of the specified nemesis. If this did not occur, or rather if it were perceived by the consultee not to occur, the syllogism of the theme would be invalidated—that is, not *all* cases in the Initial Category would have suffered the Inevitable Outcome. This is what, at some level, the consultee is trying over and over again to prove in order to reassure himself that there is some hope in his own case. The repetition compulsion, however, in his own superego, demands that each time the test case should indeed validate the inevitability of the punishment. This is ensured by his manipulation of the actors in the drama, and if this fails, by his misperceptions of what transpires, along the same lines as in traditional "fate neuroses," or repetitive acting-out patterns in hysterical character disorders.

A professional with such a theme interference is apt to have a succession of failure cases conforming to this pattern as long as his conflicts remain salient, or as long as he does not find other ways of defending against them or resolving them.

A mental health consultant may relieve such theme interference in two possible ways. Both are based upon his capacity to influence the perceptions and expectations of his consultee by the leverage of the consultation relationship. The first approach is to influence the consultee to change his perceptions of the client so as to remove him from the Initial Category. This could be done by helping him realize that his perceptions of the cues in the client's story were not accurate, or by influencing him to reinterpret the cues so that he concludes that the client does not in fact fit the Initial Category. For instance, in our case in point, the consultant might help the consultee to realize that acne, dreaminess, and introversion do not necessarily indicate excessive masturbation, and he might confirm this by pointing to evidence of schizoid tendencies not only in the boy but in other members of his family, as well as evidence of hereditary oiliness in their skins leading to familial acne and saborrhoeic dermatitis. In the event that the child, his parents, and even his physician have complained about excessive masturbation, the consultant will have a more difficult task, but he might shake their story by pointing out that they all came from a subculture that was strictly moralistic, especially about sexual matters, and that their outstanding sensitivity made them liable to exaggerate the degree of masturbation. In other words, although it was indeed likely that the boy did masturbate, it seemed that four or five times a week could hardly be defined as "excessive," compared with cases of boys of that age who are known to masturbate four or five times a day.

The effect of such intervention by the consultant, if it works, is to influence the consultee to give up his displacement onto this client, who is now no longer perceived by him as fitting the Initial Category. This therefore frees the client from the expected Inevitable Outcome, and the consultee's vicarious interest in him and panicky treatment of him are dissipated. This consultation maneuver is named "unlinking," because essentially it results in the unlinking of this client from the consultee's theme. The consequence is that the consultee can now relate to the client without distortion and can deal with him objectively, and with his customary professional understanding and skill.

Unfortunately, although the result may be salubrious for the client it is not so for the consultee and for some of the latter's other clients, because the theme has not been weakened by the consultation and may even have been strengthened. The consultee may unconsciously interpret the consultant's eagerness to prove that this client was not an example of the Initial Category as being due to his sharing the consultee's belief that all such cases have the expected bad outcome. Since the theme is left intact or strengthened and the displacement object has been unlinked, the consultee is likely to begin unconsciously searching immediately after the consultation for another appropriate object. If he has a sufficiently large case load, it will not be long before he discovers another "excessive masturbator," and once again the drama will be re-enacted.

Because of this, we regard "unlinking" to be a cardinal error in consultation technique, even though consultees often gain temporary relief from their tensions and the current client is quickly benefited.

The second consultation approach is for the consultant to accept, at least for discussion purposes, the consultee's categorization of his client as fitting into his Initial Category. The consultant, by this agreement, confirms the consultee's judgment that this is a *test case* for his theme. The consultant then proceeds to invalidate the syllogism by persuading the consultee to re-examine the evidence upon which he bases his certainty of the Inevitable Outcome, and influencing him to realize that although such an outcome is indeed one of the possibilities, there are several others, and in fact much of the evidence favors one or more of the latter. When the consultee's certainty about the inevitability of the bad outcome has thus been weakened, his tension begins to fall, and some of the interference of the theme begins to lessen. This may be sufficient for him to cease his panicky ineffectual tampering with his client; and, instead, he may be able to continue working with the case with some return to his normal effectiveness. His subsequent experience with the client then allows him to corroborate at firsthand that what he had expected as Inevitable Outcome did not in fact occur, or appear likely to occur, despite the fact that the client conformed to the Initial Category. Since the case had continued to be a test case, this one exception to the syllogism is sufficient to invalidate it and to weaken or dissipate the theme. Because the theme applies also to him, the invalidation of the syllogism for his client also has an effect of significantly reducing the consultee's tension regarding his own underlying conflict.

We name this method of consultation "theme interference reduction." If it is satisfactorily accomplished, it should lead not only to an immediate lowering of tension in the consultee, and a raising to normal of his objectivity about his current client, but also to a weakening of the theme, a consequent reduction in the pressure of its associated conflict, and a reduced compulsion to displace this and work it out repetitively on future clients.

Two final points are worthy of emphasis. First, although both the mechanism of theme interference and the consultation method of theme interference reduction have been discussed on a cognitive parameter, they clearly have a major affective component. Likewise, although the consultation method handles this material in an apparently superficial manner, what is being dealt with is not really superficial but is a surface derivative with depth psychological implications and leverage possibilities. Second, by accepting the consultee's displacement, and by dealing with the theme within his defensive framework, it may be invalidated without the loss of face, and the arousal of the major resistance, that would most likely occur if his defenses were undone and the consultee had to confront his underlying conflicts directly. Moreover, the consultant does not have to know the details of these conflicts in his consultee in order to invalidate the theme. He can operate quite effectively by dealing with the same projective material in the client's story that the consultee has chosen to act out his conflicts. He can rely on the fact that the objects and situations have been unconsciously chosen by the consultee to match his own previous life experience and fantasies; and as long as the consultant correctly identifies the salient patterns, he obtains, as it were, a direct leverage on his consultee's unconscious material and processes. This means that the consultant does not need to infringe on his consultee's private life and can successfully complete an invalidation of the theme without having to uncover the details of its personal implications for the consultee.

[8]

Techniques of Theme
Interference Reduction

There are three steps in the technique of theme interference reduction: (a) assessment of the theme, (b) the consultant's intervention, and (c) ending and follow-up.

ASSESSMENT OF THE THEME

The main questions to be answered in assessing the theme are: Is this consultation? Is this consultee-centered case consultation? Is the consultee's work difficulty caused by lack of objectivity? Is the lack of objectivity due to theme interference? What is the Initial Category? What is the expected Inevitable Outcome? With which actors in the client's drama does the consultee identify? These questions must be answered in an orderly process involving a sequential narrowing of the field of inquiry accompanied by an increasing magnification from a superficial to a deeper and deeper scrutiny of the details observed or inferred.

Preliminary Phases

The consultant must ask himself whether the approach to him is really for consultation proper, whether it is an episode in contract negotiation or relationship building, or whether it is really a request for collaboration or for help with referral of a difficult case. If he decides that it is the beginning of a consultation, he must decide, within the framework of the currently existing contract, whether it is to be dealt with as case consultation or administrative consultation, and if the former, whether it is to be client-centered or consultee-centered.

151

PHASE 1. *Superficial Scanning of a Wide Field*

In instances of consultee-centered case consultation, the consultant, even before he begins to deal with the case, must be preparing himself for what he might meet. He should continually keep himself up to date about currently salient issues inside the consultee organization and in its surrounding community that might have repercussions on his potential consultees. His purpose is to enter a consultation situation with an expectational set, so that he is prepared to respond quickly to the significance of what a consultee may bring to him. Often, the concern of an individual consultee, as mirrored in his story about his client, is consonant with an issue that has reverberations at successive levels of the interpenetrating systems and subsystems of his organization and of its community. For instance, the local newspaper was currently writing editorials about problems of law and order, and was particularly incensed about adolescent rebellion and delinquency that were seen to be getting out of control. Recent meetings of the Parent-Teacher Association had been focusing on demands that the school system teach good citizenship and conformity to community norms, while at the same time pressing with equal vehemence for improvements in curriculum and modernization of teaching methods to increase the capacity for creative thinking as well as the college entrance examination scores of the students in this middle-class population. In the particular high school that the consultant was about to visit, a new principal had recently been appointed—a young man with progressive ideas, who was reputed to be inconsistent in his dealing with disciplinary problems because he felt caught on the horns of the dilemma of impulse control versus freedom to develop innovative thinking among the students. The principal appeared to be passing these inconsistent demands on to his teachers, and was having problems in maintaining their morale and motivation. This was exacerbated by a clique of teachers who were rebelling against his authority and who were led by a senior teacher, who had been passed over for the post of principal. Recently there had been trouble at the school involving some teenagers who had been caught smoking marijuana. At a neighboring high school there had just been an insurrection of the students in opposition to new rules about clothing and haircuts. As the consultant was removing his coat in the cloakroom, he met the janitor, who greeted him with special emphasis and said he had probably been called in about Jackie Ormerod, who had attacked a fellow student with a knife the previous day, and who was a real "murderous ruffian" who would undoubtedly "come to a bad end." In fact, when the consultant met with his first consultee, the client did not turn out to be Jackie Ormerod; but it was not surprising to discover that the case did involve an adolescent who was having problems with impulse control, and that the teacher was particularly sensitive and ambivalent regarding his own role as a representative of the repressive "establishment."

In the above case, the consultant was tuned in to the consultation problem even before he entered the school building, and certainly before he sat down with his consultee. Such an expectational set should produce extra alertness so as to enable the consultant to give a quick answer to the question "Why is this consultee asking me for help with this particular case at this time?" The fact that it did not turn out that the consultant was asked for help with Jackie Ormerod should serve as a warning that this mental set should not act as a pair of blinkers in blinding him to less obvious aspects of the consultation that might be idiosyncratic to this particular consultee, and might not be in tune with the salient social system issues of the moment. In the case in point, the consultant must be alert both to the likelihood of a consultation focused on impulse control versus freedom to foster creativity and also to the need quickly to put this whole complex of expectations aside if he finds in the early stages of the interaction with his consultee that something else appears to be bothering him.

The incident with the janitor is of particular significance from the point of view of consultation technique. As the consultant walks through the building on his way to the consultation interview, he should be sensitive to the atmosphere in the corridors and offices, especially to apparently casual remarks and to the verbal and nonverbal cues involved in the way he is greeted. I have learned to ascribe special importance to the way I am received by the secretary of the principal in a school, or by the clerk in the front office of a public health unit. Such people usually have a considerable fund of informally obtained salient information, and their smiles, frowns, welcoming gestures, or attitudes of being too preoccupied to attend immediately to my business tell me a lot about my current standing in their organization and about the relative urgency and system-relevance of problems that will be discussed by individual consultees with me during that visit.

I also have learned to pay attention to whether a consultee seems to have come to see me because of his own initiative and volition or because he has been persuaded to come in, or even forced in, by his supervisor or administrative superior. In the latter case, I am alerted to the possibility that the problem may relate more to some lack of objectivity in the supervisor than in the consultee or that the consultee may be having some idiosyncratic problem that is not consonant with the salient concern of the rest of the organization.

Once I am in the room with my consultee, I focus all my attention on him, helped and hopefully not hindered by my preliminary scanning of the interpenetrating social systems of which he is a part. My first question to myself, after deciding that I am dealing with an instance of consultee-centered case consultation, is whether my consultee is having work difficulties that impel him to see me based on lack of knowledge, lack of skill, lack of self-confidence, or lack of objectivity. In answering this, I once again have a preliminary mental set that is based on my previous experience with this consultee and on my knowledge of the traditions and ways of working of his organization. For instance, I may know that in a particular public health nursing agency, recruitment and in-service training, coupled with effective supervision and a clear understanding of the role of consultation, makes it almost inevitable that any, except the newest nurses, will be coming to me because of lack of objectivity. My main evidence, however, comes from the consultee's manner and the way in which he tells the story of his client.

PHASE 2. *Microscopic Assessment of the Consultee's Behavior*

The consultant must first assess the degree and nature of the consultee's subjective involvement in the case. I find it a useful principle to judge all consultees at this stage to be suffering from theme interference unless I can rule this out. My reason is that theme interference will manifest itself by cognitive perplexities and emotional reactions that are found also in personal involvement, simple identification, transference, and characterological distortions, all of which may to some extent be present. Only if I am unable to identify a syllogistic theme with its definable Initial Category and Inevitable Outcome, calling for specific consultation intervention to break the link between the two, will I fall back on one of the simpler assessments, which then may appear appropriate. If I find no evidence of subjective involvement and of a lack of professional objectivity, I will by default, as it were, put the case into a residual category of lack of knowledge, lack of skill, or lack of self-confidence.

Evidence pointing to subjective involvement consists mainly of (a) affective responses of the consultee during the interview, and of (b) cognitive distortions, such as confusion, stereotyping, and judgments unrelated to the evidence.

AFFECTIVE RESPONSES The consultant must be alert to signs of segmental emotional upset in the consultee as he discusses the case. These have to be differentiated from signs of expectable emotional involvement in a professional worker who feels responsible for a difficult case and committed to finding a way out of a work impasse. It is only natural that a highly motivated worker should be emotionally aroused in this situation and should express anxiety and frustration about his inability to resolve the difficulty, and concern for the welfare of the client. The consultant must also take into account the temperament of the consultee that will influence the degree of his normal emotional arousal and expression in such a situation.

These nonspecific types of emotional arousal and upset must be differentiated from those that may be idiosyncratically related to a particular aspect of the client's situation or the work difficulty. Previous knowledge of the consultee and of the norms of behavior in his profession and institution will aid this differentiation, as will his reactions when he is asked to talk about other cases in his current practice, or about issues peripheral to the central topic of this case. The consultant is looking for a gradient of emotional arousal or upset that peaks in an idiosyncratically exaggerated way as the consultee talks about certain aspects of the consultation case.

Concern about the case must also be differentiated from anxiety about the consultant or the consultation setting, especially in new consultees or new programs in which experience has not yet demonstrated to the consultee that consultation leads to help and not to burden or condemnation, and involves no loss of face with peers and supervisors. Especially in such instances, and to a lesser extent also in others, the consultant must be alert to the consultee's trying to hide his feelings and to present a façade of relaxed poise. Consultants who are already skilled in psychotherapy, casework, or psychological interviewing will have no difficulty in identifying telltale discrepancies between tone of voice, verbal content, and relaxed facial expression on the one hand and strained posture, muscular tension, and unconscious tapping of feet or autonomic manifestations on the other; as well as between ostensible verbal content and a choice of words, some of which may carry more emotional loading or emphasis than might be necessary to convey the message.

When the consultant identifies some element or actor in the consultee's story about the client that seems linked with increased emotional tension in the consultee, he will be well advised to steer the interview temporarily away from this focus. He does this in order to ascertain whether there will be a fall in the consultee's tension and also to prevent the consultee from becoming too upset. The latter result would endanger his self-control and would make him lose face and also weaken the stability of a possible displacement—for instance, if the consultee were to get too upset he might himself realize the nature of his subjective involvement. After a while, the consultant should lead the interview back to the "hot" area and see whether as he approaches it the consultee again becomes upset. By getting the consultee to repeat his story from different points of departure, the consultant can pinpoint those aspects that are regularly associated with an increase in emotional arousal and can confirm his initial assumptions concerning issues or displacement objects with which the consultee is specifically emotionally involved.

Sometimes, evidence about emotional involvement may be derived from the consultee's report about his actions in the case. If these appear to be "beyond the call of duty," or obviously discrepant with his own usual behavior or the norms of his profession or institution, they will indicate that the consultee in this case may be influenced by an unusual affective component.

COGNITIVE RESPONSES The main evidence for theme interference comes from an assessment of the consultee's cognitive response to the client and his social network. Of particular significance is a segmental lack of clarity or a stereotyping in the consultee's report of his perceptions of particular actors or situations in the client's life drama. Global confusion about the case is not so significant, because it may be the result of lack of knowledge or unfamiliarity with that type of case, or inability to understand a complex situation. This should, however, be interpreted in the light of the consultee's usual level of understanding and what is expectable in that institution. More important is the consultant's finding that the consultee tells a clear and understandable story about the client, apart from certain aspects of the case. Sometimes, the consultee's patchy confusion is obvious; and sometimes, the consultant identifies it because he, himself, feels confused or unclear about particular actors or incidents and infers that this must have been brought about by the way in which the consultee told the story, even though the consultee was apparently giving a clear account of the case.

Lacunae in the consultee's case report are useful clues—for instance, a description of a family in which no mention is made of the husband or of one of the children. In such instances it is advisable for the consultant not to interrupt the consultee to ask for the missing information at that point, because this may endanger the consultee's defenses. Instead, the consultant should record the omission in his own mind, and later he should casually ask the consultee about it. Not unusually, he will then find evidence of confusion or stereotyping. Another possibility is that the consultee will say that he has no information on that point. If it seems appropriate, the consultant can then involve the consultee in a joint project of trying to imagine what the missing information might be, by saying, "I wonder what that husband is like." This may sometimes elicit a purely projective story from the consultee that may be most revealing of an important aspect of his theme interference—such as, "He is an unemployed Irish laborer. It is not surprising that he was not present when I visited. Such men usually do not spend much time at home with their wives, except to make them pregnant. I suppose he was out carousing with the boys."

The most characteristic and specific evidence in the cognitive response of the consultee is stereotyping. The consultee perceives some actor or situation in the client's drama, not on the basis of objective appraisal of the gestalt of sensory cues from the world of reality, but on the basis of a preformed image in his mind's eye, possibly stimulated by one or two sensory cues that are then incorporated into a complete pattern.

Stereotyping can be recognized by the following characteristics: (a) The outline of the perception is clearer and more consistent than life. It does not vary in response to changes in circumstances. (b) The perception has a heroic or villainous character that is larger than life. (c) The consultee perceives the actor in exaggerated, oversimplified, global terms —such as that he is all black or all white, all good or all bad. (d) The consultee uses emotionally toned or banal hackneyed words or clichés to express his perceptions. It is as though he were quoting from some widely accepted list of commonly used phrases, rather than using his own normal vocabulary. Examples of stereotypes derived from recordings of the statements of consultees that conform to these patterns are: "He is a poor, crippled creature." "She is a large, immobile, Buddha-like figure." "He is a typical, henpecked milquetoast." "This seven-year-old boy is a real ruffian." "She is a beautiful, intelligent, competent young woman." "She is sullen and dull and completely neglects the baby." "This is a defective baby and will probably never grow up."

When there are superficial indications, such as the above, that the consultee is perceiving some actor in the client's drama in stereotyped terms, the consultant should not directly question or cast doubt on the perceptions, but later in the interview he should ask the consultee to shed further light on this aspect of his story. This should elicit the evidence on which the consultee based his perceptions; and the consultant should investigate whether this was such as to be regarded as adequate in the consultee's professional subculture to substantiate previous statements. This exploration should be carried out with delicacy and care in order not to confront the consultee with incompatibilities in his story before the consultant has decided on his plan of intervention, for fear of unlinking the client from the Initial Category and destroying the test case.

Assessment of Initial Category

In exploring for a possible theme interference, the consultant must look for items in the consultee's story that symbolize or give expression to the two elements of the major premise of the syllogism, Initial Category and Inevitable Outcome.

In investigating the Initial Category, the consultant observes the consultee's behavior and listens to his story about the client in order to identify whether the consultee appears to be perceiving in the case a personally significant pattern. If he demonstrates stereotyping, this may be obvious, because the reason for the stereotyped misperception is likely to be that he is imposing a personally meaningful pattern onto the case. More difficult to identify are the instances in which the consultee's perceptions of the case are apparently in line with objective reality, or with what any other member of his profession would perceive under the existing circumstances, and yet seem to be given undue weight and to be reacted to by the consultee with exaggerated affect. It must be remembered that the fact that a perception is accurate does not rule out its being invested with fantasy. A good illustration of this is drawn from a psychoanalyst's reported vignette of the beginnings of an analytic session:

> Mr. Smith lay down on the couch and after an embarrassed pause said, "As I was following you into the office just now, I had the strange fantasy that I was taller than you and was looking down on your bald head!" I responded, "Since you are 6ft. 4in. tall and I am only 5ft. 7in. this observation is hardly surprising, but I understand what you mean when you say you have the *fantasy* of being taller than me. The analytic material of the past few sessions has been linked with your feeling toward me as you felt toward your father when you were a small child. What you are expressing today may be a repetition of wish-fulfilling fantasies you had as a toddler that you were or would one day be bigger and more powerful than your father, on whom you would then look down." Mr. Smith said he felt that was probably true, and proceeded to describe memories of walking around the house wearing his father's shoes and his hat, and flourishing his walking stick.

The essential aspect in defining the Initial Category lies therefore not in determining whether or not the consultee's perceptions of the client and his social network are objective, useful though this may be, but in delineating the emotionally toned concept that the case portrays for the consultee. It is also important to identify the situational cues in the case, which act, as it were, as hooks onto which the consultee hangs this concept. For example, a nurse talked with obvious fascination and some revulsion about a woman who had three illegitimate children, all from different fathers. This seemed to the consultant to be for her an emotionally significant aspect of the case. The consultant then wondered to himself whether the Initial Category was "a woman who has an illegitimate baby" or "a woman who has several illegitimate children," or some similar cognitive element. He therefore involved the nurse in a detailed discussion of her patient from various points of view, from which it gradually became clear that what was upsetting to the nurse was not just the fact of illegitimacy but her conclusion that this plus other details of the patient's life made it clear that the woman was promiscuous and was having frequent sexual intercourse with many men. The nurse reported that on two occasions during her visits to the home she had encountered strange "men callers"; and her tone of voice as she described them, as well as some of her allusive references to what they were "calling" for, indicated her suspicions that the sexual carryings on of her patient were not only illicit but probably perverted. From this, the consultant developed the assumption that the Initial Category was "a woman who is promiscuous and has repeated, and possibly perverted, sexual relations with many men." As will be seen later, it is important in theme interference reduction to assess the specific details of the categories, in order to use these in breaking the obligatory link between them, while supporting the consultee's use of the client's situation as a test case that validates or invalidates his personal theme.

In addition to identifying the cues in the client's current situation that form the principal elements of the perceptual gestalt which acts as the vehicle for the consultee's expression of the Initial Category, the consultant should also be on the alert to detect "preconditions" in the story, which add extra elements that are specifically meaningful for the consultee in his definition of this case as a test case. In our previous example, as the consultant explored the nurse's story about her patient, he discovered that she seemed to ascribe particular importance to certain aspects of the patient's early history. The nurse said that this woman had experienced a deprived childhood, that her father had been killed while she was a baby, and that her mother had been a "loose-living woman." The nurse's evidence for the latter assertion seemed particularly flimsy, and this alerted the consultant to the possibility that it was a purely projective statement. From this and other material, the consultant modified his formulation of the consultee's Initial Category to "a woman whose mother was immoral and who, because of being brought up by her, develops into a promiscuous woman, who has frequent sexual relations, probably perverted, with many men." The significance of such "preconditions" is that only clients who fit, or are perceived to fit, these as well as the other elements of the gestalt will constitute a test case that energizes the theme. Thus, a woman who has one or two illegitimate children, but shows no other evidence of promiscuity, might not stimulate a theme interference in this consultee. Likewise, a promiscuous woman whose mother was not immoral might escape the theme interference. Of course, if the consultee was in great need of a displacement object because of some current emotional disequilibrium in her private life that demanded an outlet by a defensive displacement, she would be apt to select a less than perfect case and fill in the missing details of the Initial Category from her imagination.

Assessing the Inevitable Outcome

Having identified the consultee's Initial Category, the consultant must search in the consultee's report of the case material for evidence about the Inevitable Outcome. He is helped in this by the realization that it always constitutes some form of doom or bad end, and also that it will be linked to the person who is the subject of the Initial Category or to one of his dependents. From the point of view of interviewing technique, the difference between this assessment and that used by a psychologist interpreting the projective material in a T.A.T. is that the latter is usually accomplished by reading a completed protocol. In consultation, on the other hand, the consultant must make his interpretations while he is taking an active part in a continuing discussion with the consultee about the case of the client, a discussion that must flow smoothly and make sense in its own right. In other words, the manifest content of the consultant's interventions must be appropriate for someone reacting sensibly and sympathetically to the consultee's story, and engaged in a joint appraisal of the significance to the client of the various aspects of his predicament.

Within this evolving context the consultant will try to identify whether the person named in the Initial Category is the one who is expected by the consultee to come to a bad end, or whether it is one of the dependents of this person; and to identify the exact details of the doom envisaged by the consultee. The consultant usually accomplished this in three phases. First, he develops a hypothesis that identifies the victim and the nature of the expected catastrophe in general terms. Then, he gets the consultee to repeat his story from various points of view in order to confirm this hypothesis. Last, he explores further in order to identify the specific details of the expected outcome.

Sometimes, the consultation interview reveals evidence about the Inevitable Outcome before the consultant has assessed the Initial Category, and in fact the latter can be identified by tracing back from the end result to what it was that led up to it. For instance, a teacher talked with considerable feeling about a child in her class who she felt was especially vulnerable to mental disorder and would probably end up in an "asylum." Further discussion revealed that her stereotyped expectation of doom for this child was linked to her perception of the child's mother as "an ineffectual woman with many children, who could not take proper care of them." Similarly, a clergyman discussed a man in his church who he apparently expected would progressively lose control and behave homosexually. It soon became obvious that he expected this bad outcome because the man had been raised in a fatherless family by a mother, a grandmother, and two aunts without any strong male figure to provide a masculine role model.

When such material is freely presented, the consultant can take note of it; but he should avoid exploring further to elicit details of the Inevitable Outcome, by probing questions or by stimulating the consultee to repeat aspects of his story, until he has satisfactorily assessed the Initial Category. The reason is that until the latter is accomplished the consultant is constantly in danger of bringing about unlinking as he discusses the case. For instance, in the case of the child of "the ineffectual mother with many children," the consultant might, while discussing the vulnerability of the pupil to mental disorder, inadvertently say something about the obvious strengths of the mother as a warm, protective, nurturing figure, despite all her burdens with a household full of children. This reality-based statement, if accepted by the consultee, would weaken the assignment of this mother to the Initial Category and might interrupt the consultation by unlinking this case from the syllogistic theme.

The third phase of assessing the Inevitable Outcome, namely the specification of the details of the doom fantasy, is of major importance. For example, in our previously discussed case of the promiscuous mother, the question in the consultant's mind was whether the bad outcome focused on the mother or on one or more of her children. To begin with, he obtained equivocal evidence. The nurse talked about possible gynecological troubles of the patient. She also was worried about signs of "degeneration" in two of the three children, one of whom had a kidney lesion and the other a harelip and signs of mental retardation. All the

162 | *The Theory and Practice of Mental Health Consultation*

family seemed destined for trouble! Further exploration revealed that the nurse's real preoccupation was with the children, whose current lesions were seen by her to be merely a portent of a much worse fate that was in store for them. With absolutely no evidence to base it on, the nurse said she felt the child with kidney trouble would very likely develop uremia and die; and a little later she hazarded the guess that the child with the harelip must have multiple congenital abnormalities of his central nervous system and would probably gradually degenerate. She also hinted that although the third child seemed superficially healthy, she was not at all sure that he was as well as he appeared. The consultant then explored to find the nurse's underlying assumptions in these expectations; and she revealed evidence of an irrational belief that this woman had damaged her sexual organs because of her promiscuity and perversion, and that this would be associated with prenatal damage to her children. Moreover, the nurse felt that the lack of adequate mothering that the mother had experienced in her childhood would inevitably affect her own maternal behavior, so that she would not take proper care of her crippled children in the home and would not obtain adequate medical treatment for them. She felt that this would hasten their bad end.

In the above case the damage to the mother's sexual organs was a "precondition" of the Inevitable Outcome in the same way in which the immoral grandmother had been a "precondition" of the Initial Category. The theme with its "preconditions" could now be formulated as "a woman brought up by an immoral mother (precondition) who is promiscuous and has repeated sexual intercourse with many men (Initial Category) will damage her sexual organs and will not take proper care of her children (precondition), who will consequently be born with constitutional defects and will inevitably degenerate and die from a variety of physical illnesses (Inevitable Outcome)."

As a final note on this case, the consultant recorded after his first interview, "After the nurse and I had come up to the office, at the end of the consultation interview, and she was putting on her coat, I said that this was certainly a complicated case and that I looked forward to continuing the discussion next week. She replied by saying, 'Just wait till next week—they may all be dead!' I looked surprised and she said, 'Oh, I was just kidding!'" Such a doorstep validation of a theme category is not rare, and reveals the way in which a primitive fantasy can maintain its existence in an otherwise rational professional worker.

Multiple Themes

The consultant's assessment problems are frequently complicated by the finding that there appear to be several themes displaced onto the case. These sometimes overlap—for instance, several Initial Categories have a common core, or the alternative Inevitable Outcomes may be similar. The reason is that the consultee may be suffering a disequilibrium in some aspect of his emotional life that is associated with a weakening of defenses against several unsolved conflicts relating to various levels of his psychological history and development. A number of these activated themes may be more or less adequately dealt with by displacement onto different aspects of a current professional case.

The consultant must try to tease these sets of categories apart in his assessment and must decide which is the most salient theme, or the most amenable to handling in connection with the current case, relying on opportunities presented by future consultations to deal later with the other themes. If these themes are not adequately dealt with in the current consultation, it is likely that when their salience rises they will interfere with the consultee's work with some other client and will be brought in for the consultant's attention.

A report by a consultant that illustrates this point, as well as many of the previously discussed aspects of assessment technique, is the following:

The patient being discussed is Mary Jones, an eighteen-year-old high school senior.

During our first meeting, Miss O'Reilly, a young staff nurse, presented the background to the case. She told me that in actuality she was asked to be of service to Mary's mother who was pregnant for the thirteenth time with her eleventh child. She said that because the mother had had so many children previously, the mother was not very concerned about the present pregnancy. However, she said the mother was very concerned about her oldest daughter Mary. Miss O'Reilly described Mary as being "attractive, young, and slender." She said that Mary's mother feels that Mary has "no direction." She said that the mother was concerned that Mary didn't know what she wanted to do career-wise, whether she wanted to go to college, etc. She said the mother was also concerned that Mary's present involvement with her boyfriend might result in marriage. Miss O'Reilly said that she reassured Mrs. Jones that these uncertainties were normal for an eighteen-year-old and that she would find direction in time. However, Miss O'Reilly said that what bothers her is Mary's "physical problems." Specifically, Miss O'Reilly was concerned about menstrual problems that Mary has had since age eleven. She said that during Mary's periods, she has severe headaches, backaches, and cramps that last three to four days and that often require her to remain home from school and work. Miss O'Reilly also reported that when Mary was fifteen, she fainted once following severe lower back pain, and that she was evaluated at the Adolescent Unit at Woolwich Hospital, where she was told that her menstrual cramps were "all in her head." Miss O'Reilly said that Mary now refuses to see a male doctor, that she wouldn't allow a rectal examination at the time that she was being evaluated at the Adolescent Unit, and that she continues to be overly modest, to which Miss O'Reilly said, "I can understand this." Miss O'Reilly felt that she could understand that Mary would not want to go back to a doctor to be told that it was all in her head.

Miss O'Reilly said she offered to call Whittington Women's Hospital for Mary, to see if a female gynecologist could be arranged for her; she said that Mary said she might be interested in going if such an arrangement could be made. At one point in the discussion of the history, Miss O'Reilly commented that she understood how Mary felt because "I myself had this problem."

It was at this point in the presentation that Miss O'Reilly said that she didn't know where to go from here.

Since Miss O'Reilly had related Mary's problems very closely to difficulties of her own, I chose to explore other areas with the consultee. I asked Miss O'Reilly about Mary's functioning in other areas—for example, around the house and at work. She reported that Mrs. Jones feels that Mary doesn't do much around the house and that her next oldest daughter does more. However, Mary is very responsible at work—i.e., at Woolwich Hospital where she works as a laboratory technician. She cited another area of Mrs. Jones's concern—namely, that Mary doesn't take care of her arthritis by taking aspirin and other medication when she has a flare-up. During this discussion, Miss O'Reilly offered the possible explanation that perhaps Mary was hostile to her mother for having so many children or that she might be embarrassed by her mother's being pregnant again.

I also asked Miss O'Reilly some general questions about other relationships in the family. I learned that Mary has a younger brother, aged fourteen, with rheumatic fever, to whom Miss O'Reilly feels that Mrs. Jones caters a great deal.

After I felt that other potential areas of importance had been explored, I returned to asking Miss O'Reilly what she thought Mrs. Jones was concerned about regarding Mary's irregular and difficult periods. (I found it very useful to ask Miss O'Reilly what she thought Mrs. Jones's concerns were as a way of getting at Miss O'Reilly's concerns about possible outcomes for Mary.) Miss O'Reilly said that Mrs. Jones didn't know what would happen to Mary and that this was what upset Mrs. Jones. She also said that Mrs. Jones was concerned that employers wouldn't let Mary go for three days every month because of her period. She also thought that Mrs. Jones might be concerned that her daughter might not be able to have children.

At this point, I thought that the major theme for Miss O'Reilly was that if Mary Jones did not have her periods straightened out now, she might not be able to have children in the future. I was reluctant to make an intervention on this theme at this point, because I thought that it might dissipate her tension too quickly. Instead, I focused on another theme which appeared to me at this point to be more tangential. This theme placed Mary in the category of being an unregimented, undirected young girl, who has trouble adjusting to regimentation in household regulations. The outcome of this category for Miss O'Reilly was that Mary might not be able to assume responsibility and work on her own when she graduates from high school. I pointed out to Miss O'Reilly that although Mary was as she described her, she was also able to do work when it was expected of her—for example, at Woolwich Hospital. This intervention was very brief. We agreed to meet next time to discuss this further.

In thinking over the case I felt that several possible themes might be operant at this time. I thought that Miss O'Reilly might feel that when a girl has irregular periods, she might not be able to get close sexually to a man. This might have the further outcome that the patient may not be able to get married, might not be able to have children, or might be a poor marriage partner, once married. I speculated whether the eventual victim of the outcome category might be not Mary but her future husband.

When I met with Miss O'Reilly again, I explored all of these potential themes by asking her what Mrs. Jones seemed to be concerned about. Miss O'Reilly felt that Mrs. Jones was not concerned about any of the above issues—i.e., she did not think that Mrs. Jones was worried that Mary wouldn't get married or that she wouldn't be able to enjoy sex, or that she wouldn't be able to have children. Miss O'Reilly thought that Mrs. Jones was concerned that no employer would put up with Mary's needing to miss work, or that Mary would become unhappy because she wouldn't be able to participate "in anything" and that Mary wouldn't be able to take care of herself during her periods, because she would be alone.

At this point, the theme seemed to be that a girl who has irregular periods, who needs to be taken care of at home in bed by her mother when she has these irregular periods, and who doesn't assume responsibility around the house, will be unhappy, alone, and rejected when she gets out into the world at large, because she has irregular periods. I pointed out to Miss O'Reilly that although Mary certainly does get people to take care of her whenever she can—for example, when she has irregular periods, when she has arthritis, etc.—when she does not have someone to take care of her—for example, at work—she does a responsible, capable job. I told her then that I thought that although Mary was this kind of person, if Mary was really uncomfortable about her periods when she was graduated from high school, she could, on her own, then be able to obtain the appropriate medical treatment for them. Miss O'Reilly then told me that Mrs. Jones was concerned that she might not be a good parent if she didn't prepare her daughter adequately for handling her periods on her own. She also said that she would talk to Mrs. Jones and explain to her that Mary could in her own time handle this problem herself. When Miss O'Reilly suggested this course of action for herself, I felt that the theme had been partially dealt with. Miss O'Reilly seemed considerably more relaxed at this point of the interview.

However, Miss O'Reilly again raised the question about what she should do, specifically, regarding the appointment at Whittington Hospital. I asked her what would happen if she did nothing, and she felt that Mary would also then do nothing, because she was too frightened of the gynecological examination. It seemed to me that a new theme was developing —namely, not that Mary was too dependent to take care of herself, but that she was too frightened to take care of herself. I asked Miss O'Reilly what she thought Mary was frightened of, and she went into great detail regarding the severe pain that might occur during a gynecological examination. It seemed then that the theme might be something like "a girl who has severe irregular periods will never be able to have a gynecological examination on her own because she must be so frightened of it." I suggested to Miss O'Reilly that a girl with severe periods like this might become less frightened in time as she came to understand more about what actually happened in a gynecological examination, and that although such an examination might be uncomfortable it was also bearable. Miss O'Reilly agreed that it was bearable and that maybe she might talk to Mary about the gynecological examination and what it entails. I then tied this in with the previous theme, saying that when Mary was finally in enough discomfort, and motivated enough, she would probably be able to seek out on her own the necessary treatment, once she knew that it was not a terribly painful experience. I suggested that it might take time for her to arrive at this position, when she might feel free to arrange for such an examination for herself, but that this was part of preparing oneself for adulthood. I pointed out that the mother seems to feel that she needs to prepare Mary for adulthood by taking over more responsibility for her, whereas in fact Mary would be better prepared for adulthood if the mother let Mary assume more responsibility for herself. Miss O'Reilly then suggested that she would call Whittington Hospital to see if it were possible to have a female gynecologist, but that she would then simply relay that information to Mary and leave it to her from there, giving her, of course, some supportive explanation of what happens in a gynecological examination.

I felt that both of these themes were partially dealt with but that probably I will be seeing other evidence of these concerns with Miss O'Reilly in the future.

CONSULTANT INTERVENTION

The goal of the consultant's intervention is to invalidate the obligatory link between the two categories that express the theme. The consultant accepts and supports the displacement of the theme onto the client's case and the definition of this case as a test case by concurring with the Initial Category in all its details that are personally meaningful to the consultee. The consultant then engages the consultee in a joint examination of the link between the Initial Category and the Outcome Category and helps the consultee realize that this outcome is not inevitable. Since the syllogism formulates the connection as invariable, if we can demonstrate that on even one occasion in an authentic test case that meets all the consultee's unconscious requirements the connection between the categories does not hold, we will dissipate or weaken the theme. This has direct implications for the consultee's expectations in the current case, but it also has meaning vis-à-vis the enduring unconscious constellation of thoughts and feelings in the consultee, so that a weakening of the theme lessens its likely interference with other cases and also reduces the tension of the consultee in relation to the relevant conflictive issues in his own life.

The invalidation of the stereotyped expectations of the consultee is not fundamentally an intellectual process, although the consultant carries it out in relation to the cognitive content of the syllogistic categories. The leverage to accomplish this comes from the consultation relationship, which makes the consultant an influential figure for the consultee whose words and behavior have a special meaning. Therefore, it is important for the consultant to make sure that he has fostered the building up of the appropriate affective relationship between the consultee and himself before he attempts to reduce the theme interference. When he is sure of this relationship, and after he has identified the details of the Initial Category and the Inevitable Outcome, the consultant then proceeds to weaken the link between them. There are four principal techniques from which the consultant can choose in accomplishing this goal: (a) verbal focus on the client, (b) verbal focus on an alternative object—the parable, (c) nonverbal focus on the client, and (d) nonverbal focus on the relationship.

Verbal Focus on the Client

This is the most usual technique and derives logically from the structure of the method. The consultant discusses the evidence bearing upon the consultee's prediction of the outcome by involving him in a joint examination of the facts of the case. The consultant demonstrates that although the Inevitable Outcome is one logical possibility, there are other possibilities too; and that the evidence indicates that one or more of these is more probable than the doom that the consultee envisages. It is important that this examination of the evidence be sufficiently detailed and the bad possibility sufficiently considered that the consultee cannot escape the confrontation with reality by imagining that the consultant is denying or evading the issues.

The consultant should take care not to communicate to the consultee his own formulation of the theme categories in abstract conceptual terms. If he does so, there is the risk that the consultee will become conscious of the immediate relevance of these abstract categories for his personal life. The unconscious displacement of his conflicts onto the client will be undone. Such direct confrontation with his own involvement is likely to arouse considerable anxiety and to stimulate immediate defensive maneuvers. The consultation relationship will probably not be sufficiently potent to handle this eventuality, nor will the amount of time available during consultation be sufficient to work through the resistance problems involved. In other words, for the consultant to state the theme in abstract terms entails the risk of turning the consultation into a psychotherapy session.

Because of this, the consultant should take care to focus all his statements on the idiosyncratic details of the client and his social situation. In this he relies on the fact that the consultee unconsciously chose this as his test case, and the significant details must have important links to derivatives of his unconscious conflicts. The reasoning is similar to that used by Felix Deutsch in conceptualizing his technique of associative anamnesis,[1] in which he emphasizes the importance of using a patient's own words as a way of stimulating emotionally toned associations that are unconsciously significant.

Here, as elsewhere in our style of consultation, the consultant strives to communicate in the same mode as that which the consultee uses to communicate with him. The consultee is expressing his ideas concerning the theme by implication, and the consultant follows suit. This is similar to the mode of communication used by a small child and a psychotherapist in play therapy. The child expresses his fantasies and fears through manipulating the toys. The therapist interprets to himself what this means and then intervenes in the game and modifies its progress in order to mold the child's fantasies to conform with reality and to calm his fears. Some child psychotherapists do not restrict themselves to communicating obliquely by the inner meanings of the play but make verbal formulations similar to the interpretations of adult uncovering types of psychotherapy. They "make the unconscious conscious." The latter style is obviously antithetical to our approach in consultation, because it gives up the benefits we derive from operating within the defensive framework of our consultee.

The following report by a consultant is an example of this type of theme interference reduction:

The nurse introduced this case by saying it had "given her the shock of her life." She went on to say that on the day before Thanksgiving, she had anticipated visiting several families living in a housing project but at the last moment felt somewhat "depressed" at the thought of having to face some of the problems she knew existed in these particular homes. She decided instead to visit a family which she thought of as possessing a nice, healthy, normal home. In this home the parents were people in their early thirties and were quite good-looking. In fact the nurse described the mother as "attractive enough to be a model." The shock involved finding this ideal family disrupted, with the wife having dyed her hair blond and informing the nurse that she was in the process of getting a divorce from her husband. Then followed a good deal of history, all of which was totally new to the nurse who had been seeing this family for a long time, concerning abusive behavior on the husband's part, drinking, unfaithfulness, etc. The element which disturbed the nurse the most was what she saw in the wife as a feeling that she was going to start her life over again. "Imagine that, with eight children and the oldest only fifteen!"

At this point the nurse was speaking with considerable intensity and rapidity and other autonomic indicators of emotional involvement. She jumped rather quickly to talking about numbers of divorced people she knew who seem very bitter toward their ex-spouses and implied that a number of these divorcees were leading sexually promiscuous lives. As the nurse talked on it became apparent that she saw an almost inevitable connection between the loss of a mate, either through divorce or through death, followed immediately by the woman involved losing control over her sexual impulses.

As the nurse continued to discuss this case, her degree of involvement became even more obvious, and she stated that she intended to increase the frequency of her visits to the family to see if she could be of any preventive help in this situation. However, at the same time, she expressed very little confidence about her ability to do anything effective, and she also gave real evidence that her professional objectivity in this situation was quite low as a consequence of the rather strong emotional overinvolvement on her part. Indeed in one sense there was a strong degree of fascinated overidentification on the part of the nurse with this attractive young divorcee who was now free to indulge her impulses. The extent to which real evidence of theme interference existed here was best seen when in response to my questioning about what the wife meant by the phrase "beginning a new life." I was told that she had not actually used these words but that it seemed to the nurse that this is what the woman was thinking about. "She is really quite beautiful and well, I guess what I'm saying is that she could get involved with someone quite easily."

Consultation approach to this situation involved first accepting as a real possibility the danger that the nurse verbalized. That is, I agreed with her that under these conditions and living in the project environment which the nurse described very graphically it certainly was one thing to consider in the future adjustment of this woman, but I then went on to say that there were a number of other possibilities that I could visualize also. I then used information which the nurse had given me about this woman to point up a number of very definite personality assets and strengths in her which might work toward some other kind of outcome also. The nurse agreed with this, saying that these things were listed as some of the reasons why she "admired this woman so much." I emphasized that it was still much too early to be able to say which way the thing might go but that I felt that we would not go too far wrong if we kept these alternatives open and on the table.

As I was about to leave after this initial consultation, and as so often happens in these situations, while I was walking out the door the nurse gave additional confirming evidence. She began to talk about a young and rather attractive student nurse who was currently in the unit, and to say that this student had been sharing with some of the nurses some of her current social experiences. "She's a very sweet and lovable girl, but I just wonder about the fact that she has an apartment of her own and is really having quite a gay and wide-open time for herself. She's been telling us something about her weekends and I must say that things have changed since I was a girl." This was said in a tone of voice that did not imply censure or moral indignation; rather, there was a wistful and sad quality present, conveying a definite sense of self-pity.

At the second consultation a week later, I got the nurse to talk further about her knowledge of this young potential divorcee; and as she spoke there came out a mixture of objectively positive information indicating many strong points in her basically healthy personality structure and, on the other hand, evidence of the nurse's identification with this woman, in terms of descriptions of her as having a "bright pleasant personality" and a number of competencies in many areas of life. After this had gone on for some time, I found the opportunity to try to formulate my message in a concise, meaningful way. I said that because of all we knew about Mrs. X., it seemed reasonable to consider the possibility that the situation here, despite the serious disruption in her life which had taken place, might not be so delicately balanced on a thin edge with real trouble looming on either side. I then added, "Besides, even if she did get involved with someone, you and I both know that this wouldn't be the end of the world either." I went on to say that both of us knew of many situations in which people have become involved with all sorts of difficulties and yet have managed to come out of them again and lead successful, responsible lives.

At a subsequent meeting a month or so later, the nurse mentioned this case briefly, describing now her efforts to be of assistance to the young mother in rearranging her life and making sure that the young children were properly cared for. Her manner was much more professional in discussing the case, and there was no intense interest in the details of the sexual and romantic aspects of this mother's life. I believe that the thing that happened here was a weakening of the unconscious automatic connection which the nurse tended to make between loss of a male figure who provided external controls over sexual impulses and the concomitant inevitable breakdown of the woman's own internal controls.

The above case illustrates an additional point of technique. The consultant "dosed" his intervention in accordance with his awareness of the consultee's level of identification and emotional arousal. He did not give a simple direct verbal message all in one speech. Instead, he made appropriate comments in the latter part of the first session, once he had defined the two categories for himself; and he continued to feed in this message in the following session, but always in relation to additional case material that he stimulated the consultee to produce. An experienced consultant learns that the most potent intervention is made when his consultee is within a range of moderate emotional involvement with the identification objects in the case and at an appropriate level of anxiety. Below this range the messages are ineffective; and when emotional upset is too high, the displacement is endangered and the messages might be taken personally. One consultant has formulated this aspect of technique as "maintaining the *caseness* of the theme."

Verbal Focus on an Alternative Object—The Parable

When the consultant feels that the displacement is endangered, for whatever reason, and the consultee is close to a conscious awareness of the link between the client and himself and consequently of his underlying conflicts, the consultant must find some way of discussing the theme at a greater distance. As long as he has correctly identified the syllogistic categories, he need not be overly concerned that greater distance will make the discussion merely an intellectual interchange, because he relies on the knowledge, or at least the assumption, that the formulated categories are derivatives of unconscious material relatively free from defensive distortion. His goal is, as it were, to talk directly to the consultee's unconscious within the safety of an acceptable defensive framework. This was available when the consultee unconsciously chose to avoid confronting the theme by displacing its core issues onto the client. As this displacement weakens, the consultant must attempt to provide a replacement.

In the previous case example, such a weakening of the displacement was seen in the final moments of the first session, when the consultee likened the patient to one of her colleagues who was "having quite a gay and wide-open time for herself." This type of statement is always a danger signal, and in this instance the next association continued the process of reversing the displacement, when the consultee began to talk explicitly about herself. True, she restricted herself to talking about how "things have changed since I was a girl," but her tone of voice revealed a mood of introspective self-pity, and it is easy to imagine that if the consultant had made a suitable response she could fairly easily have moved one step further and begun to talk, or at least to be conscious of, her own sexual pressures and lack of fulfillment, perhaps with regretful memories of past opportunities not grasped. In fact, the consultation session was just on the point of ending, which probably explains why the forbidden material was allowed to come so close to consciousness. The episode confirms the wisdom of that consultant in restricting himself to a partial intervention in that interview and leaving it till the following session to drive his message safely home.

By the following session, the consultee's emotional pressure had lessened enough for her to have restabilized her displacement onto her patient, and it was feasible for the consultant to continue with verbal communications focused on the current case. Had there been evidence of continuing or increased instability of the displacement, and had the consultee continued talking about her young colleague or about her own past or present life, the consultant would have had to leave the case and use a more distant object, onto whom he would hope the consultee might be influenced to displace her theme. The mechanism whereby this maneuver is accomplished is for the consultant to direct the discussion away from the current case onto one that is superficially as different as possible but that portrays the same two categories.

This method of communication has been used throughout history to convey emotionally potent messages with minimal arousal of resistance in the listeners. It has been much used by religious leaders seeking to convey ethical messages that are contrary to current values or that might arouse undue guilt and shame if communicated openly. I refer to the parable or fable. Traditionally, it consists of telling a story, obviously fanciful or apparently of an actual happening, the *dramatis personae* of which provide widely applicable identification objects. The behavior of the characters and the outcome of the story convey the message or moral. The mutative power of the communication lies in its providing the listeners with the opportunity to identify secretly and without loss of face with the characters, and thus vicariously experience the reward or punishment involved in their actions, while also allowing all to feel free not to identify and therefore not to feel pilloried or admonished. In effect, it uses a similar mode of communication to the consultation technique we have previously described, the difference being that the characters were invented by the parable maker and are public identification objects rather than being unconsciously chosen by the consultee as idiosyncratic objects. The other difference is that the themes built into the parable by the artist or religious leader are universal themes of depth psychological significance to many people, whereas the theme of the consultee is intensely meaningful only to him and is based on the inner details of his own previous experience and psychological development.

Both the parable of the religious leader and that of the consultant are works of art, and the artist's talent is an important factor in determining potency. Some consultants have more talent in the telling of the parables than others. Their productions have a more vivid and veridical impact and will often reduce a theme interference in a consultee who has lost his displacement onto the consultation case, whereas less talented consultants in such situations will produce some "sad and unconvincing story" that has no effect on the consultee.

Apart from its artistic element, the requirements of the consultation parable are simple to enumerate. Once the consultant has a clear idea of the Initial Category and the Inevitable Outcome, and feels that he can no longer use the consultation case to break the obligatory link between them, he invents an anecdote that portrays the theme and then discusses its details in order to show that the Inevitable Outcome is only one of the possibilities emerging from the Initial Category, and that in the fictitious case another outcome was in fact experienced. The consultant builds the elements of his anecdote from the details of the consultation case, but he chooses a setting as far removed as possible from the current one, and the characters in his story must be obviously very different in their superficial characteristics from the client and his social network, as well as from the consultee. In contrast to the parables of religion or literature that derive some of their potency from being obviously bizarre, unreal, and mythological, a consultation parable should ring true. Wherever possible, it should be based upon some real memory of the consultant, but he should change it and shape it so that it fits neatly into the mold of the theme. Each consultant will develop his own style of parable making. I rely on the fact that I have traveled a great deal and have worked in many lands. My settings and characters are drawn from Jerusalem, Alaska, Hawaii, Turkey, Norway, Ireland, and other places that are obviously a long way from the City Health Department in Boston or the Massachusetts Job Corps Camp where I happen to be doing my consultation. I also change the sex, age, race, and social class of my characters to be very different from the *dramatis personae* of my consultee's case.

The following report by a consultant with considerable talent for parable making illustrates this technique:

Mrs. Graham said the reason she wanted to talk to me today was because she was so mad about Children's Hospital. I waited for her to continue and then she said they still had not sent over any evaluation on the child who has repeated first grade twice. It is interesting that Mrs. Graham still does not give this child a name, but always calls the other child by his name, Bob. She again wanted to speak of these two children together but after saying that Bob was to be permitted to stay on at the school and repeat the first grade, she went on to say that the other child couldn't do this because they had a rule that a child could repeat a grade only twice.

She continued by saying she thought Children's Hospital had really let her down because she felt the mother was not being helped to face up to her child's lack of intellectual ability. I said that this was the child who seemed to be so lovable and had made such a good social adjustment. I was trying to separate out for Mrs. Graham again the lack of intellectual ability from the child's personality. I said that I remembered the case because I had been so impressed with how much the school and the parent had been able to do for this child to make him relate so well to people, and that this was so important for children with limited intellectual ability because they could really get along so well in the world if they knew how to get along with people. Mrs. Graham quite perceptibly straightened up a little bit and said that this was true. Then she said that when she had visited this home the last time, the little boy had said, "Come in, Mrs. Graham," and had asked her to sit down . . . and had given her such a sweet smile. She said that kids who were smarter might have stepped all over her and rushed past her and let her find her own way in the house. For the first time I could pick up a real feeling of sensitivity in Mrs. Graham to this child as a person, and I wondered if this accounted for the upsurge of anger at Children's Hospital, where she thinks they are not giving enough attention to and rather are brushing aside this child.

She went on to say that the mother had called and called and called and couldn't get an appointment. Now she says that the school will have to make some recommendation to this mother and she knows the mother is going to be disappointed and unprepared to make any plans for next year. Besides this, if the child is referred to a special class, he should be brought to the school so they can do tests, etc., this spring . . . so as to be ready for this fall. I listened to this and then I asked what facilities there were for special classes in this area. This was a lucky question, as Mrs. Graham immediately said this was another worry for her.

She said that she had visited the special class a couple of weeks ago to get an idea of what kind of teacher there was and so that she would know what she was letting this kid in for. Almost immediately I recognized this as something quite unusual for a nurse to do, and it points to a particular involvement with this child and his mother.

She then went on to say she was really worried about whether this would be the right place for this little child because all of the children in primary grades there were Mongoloids or very defective children. From this description, I could see that this was worrying Mrs. Graham as much as her anger at the hospital, and possibly there might be some blaming of the hospital because Mrs. Graham is feeling so guilty at putting this "sweet little kid" in with other children who are, to Mrs. Graham, grotesque and undesirable. At the back of my mind, I wondered if perhaps somewhere in Mrs. Graham's family there may be some history of mental retardation or brain damage. I remembered other cases from previous consultations which corroborated this. At one point she said, "I can really understand how the mother feels about sending the kid out of her home."

I thought I would make a try at reducing some of the anxiety about whether these children were really grotesque little monsters or not, so I said I had always had a very warm spot in my own heart for some of these kids because I had had a very close friend in California who had taught a class of children like this. Then I said that in hearing this friend's description of some of these children, and her ability to describe their personalities as very different, and their capabilities—restricted as they were —I had felt almost as if I had known some of these children myself. I said I recalled particularly her description of a child who had a gross hydrocephalic condition. In fact, it was quite unusual that this child should have been able to get around as he did because his head was so large that it made it difficult for him to really balance. (I was making this picture as vivid as I could so that it would have a grotesque element about it, because I wanted to make my message come through . . . that despite this grotesque appearance, this child's personality could shine through.) Then I said that the child had a way of coming over to my friend, and he would rub against her and rest his poor head against her shoulder as if he could get some balance from her. On the other hand, he could be quite naughty and she could also discipline him when he needed it. I put in this matter of disciplining because this is also a sensitive spot for Mrs. Graham and I was trying to bring in the control element here as applying to everyone, thinking that if these kids could be regarded as needing limits they might also be regarded as being human beings like the rest of us . . . at least in Mrs. Graham's perspective.

As I talked, Mrs. Graham started rubbing her eyes and I could see she was close to tears and really that this was quite moving for her. Mrs. Graham herself is a very gruff and sharp-speaking person, with quite a bit of rigidity . . . so that the softness coming through is quite striking when it appears.

I concluded by saying that actually our little friend in the present case might seem to be much out of place because his physical appearance and his personality and adjustment are so very good; again, I said this was a tribute to those who had been helping him but that, actually, these other children, too, could very well have some of the same attractive traits and as we got to know them we might not think this was too bad a placement at all for this little fellow. Mrs. Graham at once responded by saying very firmly that she certainly would see that something was done about this child and that she was going to make an appointment with the school principal the next day to see that some decision was made one way or another. I really feel that her feelings about the child came a little more into perspective through our discussion today.

I asked whether there had been any tests in the school itself which would give more to go on in suggesting such a placement. Mrs. Graham said he had had a number of tests and they were all zero. Here she indicated this not by saying the word but by holding up her hand and making the sign of a circle. Just in case Mrs. Graham might be feeling guilty because she might think it was terribly bad to think of this child as being retarded when he looked so normal, and that she might be wrong, I pointed out that the fact that he had made such a good adjustment to his playmates, to the teacher at school, and in his home would make the lack of intellectual proficiency stand out even more. I said this was really a very good diagnostic indication, because if we had been able to discover more in the way of poor relationships with his family, his parents, his teacher, or something in his actions pointing to his being depressed or perhaps acting out, then we might have considerable misgivings because we'd had, in all of our experiences, enough cases in which children who were disturbed were not able to achieve in school. I was really pleased with Mrs. Graham's next remark because I felt this showed a growth in her perception. She immediately said this child was quite different from Bob who is a disturbed child. In the beginning, Mrs. Graham had held very fast to the feeling that Bob was also retarded and she had denied right down the line that there could be anything at all that could be disturbing in the way he had been getting along with his parents . . . although she had told me of his feeling jealous toward a younger sibling. Mrs. Graham spent the rest of the session talking about Bob. . . .

SUMMARY

It seems clear in this session that Mrs. Graham has some personal involvement with this mentally retarded child and was really in a state of upset because she felt she might be pushing this child into a class situation of grotesque little monsters. I think Mrs. Graham has some horror of grossly mentally defective children or children who may have brain damage. She has real affection for this little boy because of his appealing personality, and she was unable to see that these other children in this class setting also have individual personalities. I have an idea that at the very beginning of this series of consultations, Mrs. Graham equated mental disturbance, emotional difficulties, and possibly other psychiatric difficulties with mental disturbances and probably grotesque deformities. I think this is probably why she was upset when the time came near to make some recommendation for placement. It was so unusual for a nurse to make a visit to a special class. This almost had an element of Mrs. Graham's going to the school to confirm her own fears rather than to find out if this would be a good placement. I think that at this time there has been some progress in Mrs. Graham's being able to separate out differences between lack of intellectual ability and intellectual ability that is interfered with because of emotional difficulties. There is still a great deal of denial about the role of parents in relation to disturbances in children.

The above report is an excerpt taken out of a series of interviews. The salient theme appears to be that individuals who have brain damage or are mentally retarded are apt to look grotesque and abnormal and they will be rejected by others as though they were beyond the human pale, so that eventually they will go down the drain. The Inevitable

Outcome has not yet been specifically defined by the consultant, but meanwhile in the previous session he had obviously been working on reducing the expectation that a diagnosis of mental retardation must inevitably carry the connotation of rejection because the sufferer would appear inhuman. At the beginning of the present consultation interview, the nurse's outspoken criticism of the Children's Hospital, which seemed like a displacement of a personal feeling, together with the other signs cited in the consultant's report, raised the suspicion that as the tension in the theme was being weakened by consultation, the need for the consultee to utilize a defensive displacement onto the client was lessening, and there was some danger that she was about to talk openly, or at least to think consciously, about her own feelings about the person in her own life who was the original object of her worries about retardation or brain damage. This stimulated the consultant to move the discussion away from the client to the anecdotal parable he invented on the spur of the moment, in order to continue the process of reducing the theme interference.

Particularly significant was the consultant's storytelling technique of painting so sensitive and appealing a picture of the fictitious defective that he brought tears to the eyes of the consultee, and then the artistic brainwave of including the segment about the teacher's having to discipline the child, which implied so graphically that a mentally retarded person was not to be regarded as so fragile and vulnerable as the nurse obviously regarded her own patient, but could be reacted to in many ways like a child of normal intelligence.

Nonverbal Focus on the Case

A potent technique of delivering to the consultee the message that he does not have to worry so much about the danger of the expected Inevitable Outcome is to do it not by symbolic communication through the use of words but by behavorial signs. The consultant discusses the outcome with an obvious lack of anxiety and talks in quite a relaxed manner, for instance, about continuing the discussion at the following consultation session. The consultant used this nonverbal approach to supplement his verbal communications in the previously cited case of the about-to-be-divorced woman who might lose control over her sexual impulses. He not only evinced lack of anxiety by postponing the completion of the discussion until the next session but also by saying that "we will have to wait and see how events unfold." The implication was clearly that he believed that the bad outcome envisaged by the consultee was rather unlikely.

This lack of tension and pressure for quick action by the consultant will have a theme reduction significance for the consultee only if he believes the consultant has a real understanding of the nature of the danger that the consultee perceives in the case. It is therefore essential that the consultant should have demonstrated his own involvement in elucidating the complexities of the case, and have indicated his awareness of both the Initial Category and the Inevitable Outcome. Only then will his lack of anxiety have an impact. Otherwise, the consultee will believe that the consultant's relaxed behavior means that he does not care about or does not understand what is likely to happen to the client.

In this as in other aspects of consultation, the consultant must be continually aware that he is a significant identification object for the consultee, and he should self-consciously make positive use of this.

Nonverbal Focus on the Consultation Relationship

The fact that the consultee has dealt with a personal problem through theme interference in his professional work indicates two things: first, he must be experiencing a current disequilibrium in a psychosocial conflict that previously must have been precariously resolved; and second, he must be prone to the use of displacement as a defense. Moreover, it is also likely that the displacement onto the client is of recent origin, and so it is apt not to be very stable.

It is therefore not surprising that a consultee with theme interference is often found to transfer his displacement fairly easily to other objects. These may include characters in a parable made up by the consultant. They also include the consultant himself, particularly when the emotional bond with him intensifies as the consultation relationship develops. The consultant should always be alert to the possibility of the consultee's acting out his theme in the consultation relationship by ascribing a particular role to the consultant and then playing a complementary role himself in a typical process of "acting out in the transference" that is so familiar to us in psychoanalytic treatment. When this happens, the consultant should be prepared to divine the inner significance of this charade in which he is being involved and, as with his discussion of the case, accept the Initial Category and then invalidate the expectation of the Inevitable Outcome. He should do this nonverbally, in contrast to the customary behavior of the psychoanalyst, who would deal with such an episode by interpreting it in words and bringing to the conscious awareness of his analysand not only the inner meaning of his actions in the "here-and-now" of the analytic session but the link between this and the bygone happenings or fantasies of "there-and-then."

Usually, the nonverbal invalidation of the expected outcome of the Initial Category in the behavioral sequences of the consultation interaction is carried out by the consultant concurrently with his dealing in identical manner with the same theme through his verbal and nonverbal reactions to the client's case. This may be rather complicated, because the consultant must be thinking simultaneously on a number of levels. He has to discuss with the consultee the manifest content of the case in a way that has meaning in its own right. He must be thinking of the latent content both of the consultee's statements and of his own about the client, and formulate his remarks accordingly. He must also be watching what his consultee is doing nonverbally in the transference and must himself be behaving in such a way as to convey an invalidating rather than a validating message about the theme outcome on that parameter. Talented consultants have a well-developed capacity for such simultaneous thinking and behaving on a number of planes, and of understanding the operation of wheels within wheels within wheels. The technical problem is made somewhat easier by the fact that the theme with its pair of inevitably linked categories is common to all the parameters, and once it has been identified the patterns on the different planes can be seen to conform to it.

An example of this technique was the following: A nurse brought a case for consultation that involved a young woman of Italian parentage who had just got married to a Bulgarian man. The husband, a truck driver, was described as a very powerful man, who was quite taciturn and drank heavily, although he was not an alcoholic. The wife was being followed by the nurse as a prenatal patient who had Rh negative blood. Although there was no evidence on which to base this, the nurse was quite worried that the husband would be unfaithful to his wife and would eventually leave her in the lurch, especially if she gave birth to a damaged baby. There was also the expectation that the wife would be belittled and exploited by the husband.

As the story about the couple unfolded, the consultant became aware that the nurse was beginning to behave toward him in a somewhat unusual manner. The nurse was rather small and mousy in appearance, and the consultant happened to be a rather tall and well-built man. They had previously had several consultations regarding other cases, in which a variety of themes had emerged and had been satisfactorily dealt with; and the consultation relationship had become fairly warm and relaxed, after an initial period of some tension and anxiety in the first of these cases—but not beyond the bounds of the expectable norms in that setting.

On this occasion, however, the consultant noticed that as she talked about her expectations that her patient would be browbeaten and eventually pushed aside by her powerful husband, the nurse began to act with increasing timidity toward him during the interview. She began to intersperse her remarks about the patient with deferential comments; and as the interview reached its close, she talked about how she didn't want to bother the consultant with the case, how busy he was, and how unnecessary he probably felt it was to continue to follow it.

The consultant by then had defined the theme to be "A weak and helpless woman who builds a link with a big powerful man and becomes dependent upon him will inevitably be exploited and belittled by him and will be cast aside when her needs increase and she becomes a nuisance to him." This theme was being portrayed both by the case and by the pattern of reciprocal roles that the consultee was manipulating in the consultation interaction. If the nurse could perceive the Bulgarian man being unfaithful to his wife and rejecting her when she developed Rh sensitization or gave birth to a jaundiced baby, she would validate her theme expectation. The same would happen if the powerful consultant were to push her around and if he were to express disinterest in her problems with this case, particularly as she followed it toward the zero hour of the fantasied family debacle.

The consultant dealt with the theme in two parallel ways. He involved the nurse over three interviews in a discussion of the facts of the case, during which he concurred with her perceptions of the power ratio between the huge, rough Bulgarian truck driver and his delicate Italian wife. He then involved the nurse in a discussion of the evidence in the case on the basis of which they might make a prediction of the likelihood that the man would infringe on his wife's rights and would leave her in the lurch in her hour of need. He admitted this as a possibility, particularly in view of the truck driver's frequent absences from home both because of his job and because he often went drinking with his pals. And yet there was plenty of evidence of the man's behaving most solicitously to his wife, going out of his way to drive her to the hospital for her blood tests, and making arrangements for his older sister to come and live with them at the time of the delivery, so that she could help the young mother with her first baby. From such signs, it appeared likely that the man was, in fact, preparing to support his wife in all possible ways as her time of crisis approached.

In addition to this verbal intervention focused on the case, the consultant also invalidated the link between Initial Category and Inevitable Outcome nonverbally by his reactions to the consultee's manipulations of the consultation interaction. First, he emphasized his own strength and potency by his forthright statements about the case, by a variety of allusions to his extensive experience in dealing with prenatal problems, and by reading up and then quoting to the nurse some recent research work on the psychosocial problems of Rh negative pregnancy. Then, he countered every manipulation of the consultee designed to get him to infringe on her rights by emphasizing his deference and respect for her professional expertness in providing public health nursing support for this young couple grappling with the problems of early marriage complicated by cultural dissonance and blood incompatibility. He took care to communicate his awareness that the nurse was as busy a professional as he was, and to arrange interviews to suit her convenience rather than his own. He did not direct the consultee's further data collection about the case but made it clear that he appreciated the new light she managed to throw on the case by her astute observations during her home visits. He expressed his own intense interest in the case, his initial perplexity about the possible outcome, and his keen desire for a second and third consultation interview—all their previous consultations had been completed in one or two interviews. At the end of the third interview he issued a warm invitation to the nurse to come back to see him if the patient's blood sensitivity titer should show a dangerous rise, or if her baby should turn out to be damaged. In all these ways he conveyed by his tone of voice, by his behavior and by his expressed attitudes toward the consultee and her patient, that he was using his power for their benefit and not to push them around, and that he would continue to offer his help as long as it was needed and would not reject them if their demands increased.

The effect of this dual approach on the consultee was quite striking. By the end of the second interview her tension died down; and instead of talking about the husband as a huge brute, she began to speak warmly and appreciatively of his efforts to support his wife, and of how she could help him by explaining the nature of the Rh problem. The nurse's manner toward the consultant changed at the same time. She reverted to her previous role of self-respectful collaboration, and she began to demonstrate autonomy and initiative in her handling of the case. After the woman gave birth three months later, the nurse reported to the consultant that all had gone well, that the baby was healthy, and that the marriage appeared stable and happy. From her description of the way in which she had supervised the family during the final somewhat anxious weeks of the pregnancy, when the blood sensitivity titer had shown a moderate rise, the consultant judged that the nurse had been operating at her customary level of skill and efficiency and had been a source of considerable support for the young couple.

ENDING

Once the consultant has completed his verbal and nonverbal intervention to break the link between the syllogistic categories, and a satisfactory result has been evidenced by a fall in the consultee's tension and a reversion to his customary level of empathy and professional objectivity, the consultant should terminate the sequence of interviews. He should step back and leave the consultee to continue dealing with the case on his own. It is important that the consultee should experience his subsequent success with the case as his own doing and not the result of the consultant's direction, so that he will not be able to evade the realization that he has personally mastered the previously impossible task.

To be sure, the client's predicament may be such that no perfect solution is possible; but when the consultee's theme interference has been reduced by the consultation interviews, he will be able to view the client objectively and to bring into operation his full professional range of knowledge and skills, which will undoubtedly be of significant help to the client. The main issue from the consultation point of view is not whether the consultee can solve all the client's problems but whether he can maintain close contact with him and be intimately involved in his predicament, so that the consultee can see for himself that the client has several options in managing his own fate and that the expectation of a single inevitable global nemesis was unfounded. If, in addition, the consultee realizes that he has played an active part in increasing the options and preventing the stereotyped bad outcome, he validates in experience the idea of mastery of the theme conflict that he discovered to be a theoretical possibility during the consultation discussions.

It is this personal experience with the client that confirms the consultant's messages, and this fulfills a similar function in consultation to the working-through phase of psychoanalysis that drives home to the analysand the insights initially stimulated by the analyst's mutative interpretation.

FOLLOW-UP

A successful theme interference reduction is usually completed in a series of between one and three interviews over a period of three or four weeks. The process as a whole may last several more weeks, as the consultee continues working with the client while he corroborates experientially the breaking of the link between the theme categories. If all goes well, the consultee should by then feel significantly less tension about the theme and should be able to deal with the client's case with his customary professional effectiveness. He should also have achieved freedom from the pressure of the underlying conflicts, so that the theme does not interfere with his objectivity in other similar cases, and perhaps with the conduct of his own life.

The result of the consultation is likely to be visible in two ways. First, there should be an obvious fall in tension in the consultee and an improvement in his professional objectivity, as evidenced by his way of talking about the client during the consultation interview. This occurs fairly quickly after the consultant has intervened to invalidate the consultee's expectations of inevitable doom in the case. Sometimes, if the consultant does not feel that the message has been adequately received and he prolongs the consultation over a further session, this behavioral and verbal change in the consultee may also be corroborated by his report of changes in his handling of the case and of consequent improvement in the client. But, as previously indicated, the consultant should usually have left the case by the time the consultee really engages himself with the client in line with his new capacity for perceiving him objectively. This means that the consultant should not be around to hear about such improvement.

It is therefore important to arrange for follow-up reports by the consultee after his tension has subsided and after his behavior in the case has stabilized. The consultant should handle his request for follow-up information somewhat lightly and delicately, so as not to raise doubts about the theme. The best way of accomplishing it is to terminate the series of sessions by saying that the consultant will be pleased to offer help as need arises with other cases and that on the occasion of future contacts he will be interested to learn what transpired with this client.

In Chapter 12 I discuss the problem of evaluation in this type of consultation and describe a systematic evaluation research project. At this point, I would only mention that a practicing consultant always needs some rough measure of his level of success with his ongoing cases, not only as a yardstick for his own self-respect, but also as a guide to the improvement of his professional operations. In addition to the evidence of immediate fall in tension and gain in the consultee's objectivity in response to the consultation intervention, there is a second source of evaluative data that the consultant may use. This depends on continuing contact between the consultee and the consultant which provides information that the theme is no longer interfering with the consultee's professional operations. The best evidence for this is if the consultee continues to request help in cases in which a similar theme interference is identified but if the degree of interference falls in successive cases, until eventually the consultee appears not to be disturbed by this theme and requests consultation only for cases with other themes. Such a gradual reduction of intensity of theme interference in successive cases is more persuasive evidence than a sudden disappearance of that particular theme from future consultations, and certainly than the fact that the consultee ceased asking for consultation on his cases. These situations may just as well be interpreted as signs of a major failure of consultation; the consultant may inadvertently have alerted the consultee to be conscious of the theme and of its significance for his personal life, so that when it emerges again in connection with other cases he consciously or unconsciously avoids the consultant in order to safeguard his vicarious use of the client in handling his own conflicts.

As usual, the most reliable evaluative evidence obtained by follow-up contact with the consultee is negative. If succeeding cases demonstrate the continuation of theme interference at the same level of intensity, the consultant can be confident that either he has not correctly identified the linked categories of the syllogism with a sufficient degree of specificity or that he has not adequately invalidated the consultee's expectations of the inevitable bad outcome. This should stimulate the consultant to renew his efforts and to modify his technique until he finds something that changes the situation. Such a practice is the most promising basis for improvement in consultation knowledge and skill.

THEME INTERFERENCE REDUCTION IN A GROUP

The techniques of theme interference reduction were developed for use in individual consultation. This was partly due to the historical accident that we accomplished most of this development as part of the evaluation research project to be described in Chapter 12. The design of this study demanded that our consultation be carried out with individuals and not with groups. Since that time, however, we have made a number of attempts to adapt the method to the group setting. Consultation in a group has obvious economic advantages in conserving scarce consultant time, as well as in offering peer support to render less likely the risk of sliding from the consultation into psychotherapy that usually taxes the skill of even the most experienced consultant.

The main obstacle in trying to use these techniques in a group is that the consultant, however skilled he may be in group dynamics, exerts less control over the content of discussions than he does in an individual interview. In particular, if the group members have any psychological sophistication, someone is likely to see through the defensive displacement of a consultee who has a theme interference. This may lead to one of the other participants' making an interpretation that lays bare the displacement—for example, by some such statement as "The emotional way you are talking about the reactions of this girl to her mother makes me suspect that you have a similar problem with your own mother!"

One method we have used to overcome this obstacle is to be meticulous in laying down the ground rules of the consultation group so as to outlaw any comments about the private life of participants. The consultant begins the group with a discussion of the differences between group psychotherapy and group consultation, and binds all participants to respect the boundaries of personal privacy as an essential condition for membership and for his willingness to lead the group. Nevertheless, it is difficult for the consultant to prevent interpretive comments by group members toward each other, especially in an emotionally exciting situation; and once an interpretation has been made, the leverage of our technique will be dissipated.

Another problem in trying to use the theme interference reduction method in a group is related to the idiosyncratic nature of theme interference. Group consultation has obvious merit when the work problem being discussed is being currently encountered by all or most members of the group. Occasionally, they may all share a theme interference; for example, a group of nursing supervisors may all be having a problem dealing with their nursing director in an authoritarian setting, and this may in part be related to personal tensions each may have had during adolescence in her relationship with her mother. It is the rare girl in our society who emerges from adolescence with a stable and completely resolved solution of her ambivalent feelings toward her mother. The consultant, in this situation, can focus on the pattern of role problems in the work setting, realizing that some of the tension is due to displacement from the precariously solved problems in the private life of the consultees.

More usually, however, one of the group presents a work impasse for group discussion that is linked to that consultee's individual experience, which may be unlike that of most other participants. Assuming that as he involves the group in an assessment of the problem, the consultant succeeds in preventing anyone from realizing and weakening the displacement, what is likely to be happening is that one consultee will be having effective consultation but the rest of the group will only be participant observers. For them, the discussion will be an educational rather than a consultation experience. This has some value, in increasing their cognitive grasp of the factors involved in an illustrative case, which may be not unlike many cases they may meet currently or in the future. But the specific emotional impact of theme interference reduction will be felt only by the consultee who is presenting the case and not by the others.

We are continuing to explore such issues, and eventually we may work out a better adaptation of theme interference reduction to the group setting. There are indications that what may emerge will be a focus on those work problems with clients that are caused by displacements of currently unsolved problems in the social system of the institution. Where the local culture or the consultation contract forbids the open discussion of these social system difficulties, it may be that techniques similar to those described in this chapter will be an effective method of helping a group of consultees master their predicament.

RATIONALE OF THEME INTERFERENCE REDUCTION

It would be superfluous to repeat here what I have already said about the mechanism of theme interference. I would like to supplement these views with a discussion of the rationale of the ameliorative process involved in reducing this theme interference. First, however, I wish to draw attention to the striking consonance of my views and those of Aaron T. Beck of Philadelphia, who has written two papers entitled. "Thinking and Depression" [2] that propose a novel approach to the understanding of the cognitive aspects of depressive psychosis. Beck suggests that instead of considering the ideational content of depressed patients to be a derivative of a primary affective disorder, it might be valuable to focus on the cognitive element in such illness and to consider the emotional reactions to be concomitants of this. He analyzes the manifest and latent thought content of a series of depressed patients and demonstrates the existence of regularly occurring cognitive patterns. In his analysis, he makes use of a term that he derives from Piaget.[3] He postulates an enduring component of cognitive organization and he names this a "cognitive schema." He likens this postulated cognitive element to those discussed by other authors, such as Rapaport's "conceptual tools," [4] Postman's "categories," [5] Bruner's "coding systems," [6] Sarbin's "modules," [7] and Harvey's "concepts." [8]

Beck's "schemas" are almost identical to our "themes." He conceives of them as relatively stable cognitive structures built up as a result of previous experience that channel thought processes. "When a particular set of stimuli impinge on the individual, a schema relevant to these stimuli is activated. The schema abstracts and molds the raw data into thoughts or cognitions . . . . In the formation of a cognition the schema provides the conceptual framework while the particular details are 'fitted in' by the external stimuli." [9] Beck postulates that schemas exist in varying degrees of complexity, including "fully developed syllogisms."

Beck then goes on to discuss how such schemas can be identified. They are not directly observed but must be inferred from the data obtained from a person's behavior and verbal content. In the case of depressed patients, the salient schemas have a characteristic content.

> Frequently the operation of a particular schema may be inferred from a recurrent unreasonable thought. A patient, for example, reported feeling anxious when a small poodle approached him. The thought preceding the anxiety was, "It's going to bite me." On further exploration, he realized that he consistently had a thought of this nature whenever a dog approached him—irrespective of how small, tame, or passive the animal might appear. In such cases, it is possible *to reconstruct the syllogism* * that appears to have been applied by the patient in reaching this conclusion. In the terminology of formal logic, the major premise (corresponding to the schema) would be: "All dogs that come near me will bite me." The minor premise, or special case, would be: "This object sniffing me is a dog." The conclusion, or application, would be: "The dog is going to bite me." . . .
>
> It is suggested that in this case the external configuration (the dog) evokes the schema (major premise), which abstracts the specific details of the situation (minor premise) and produces the cognition (conclusion). Even though the precise sequence may vary from the steps in formal logic, the derivation of the conclusion from the major premise (schema) appears to be essentially similar to that found in deductive reasoning. If the major premise is invalid, then the conclusion will be invalid even though the logical operations may be flawless. Consequently, by observing a recurrent erroneous conclusion, one can infer the content of the idiosyncratic schema. This has important implications for psychotherapy. . . .[10]

It will be noted that what I call the "situational cues" Beck calls the "external configuration" that his patient latches on to in evoking his schema. In the depressed patients studied by Beck, the schema always led to an automatic conclusion carrying the implication of personal failure and unworthiness, similar to the Inevitable Outcome of doom in our theme interference.

*My italics.

Beck derives a method of psychotherapy from his model of the cognitive schemas of his depressed patients which, like his basic framework, bears much similarity to our consultation method of theme interference reduction.

> The application of this conceptual model to psychotherapy consists, first, in an attempt to shift the patient's mode of judging himself and his world from an exclusively deductive to a more inductive process; i.e., to form his judgments more in terms of objective evidence and less on the basis of biased assumptions and misconceptions. This approach consists initially of a precise pinpointing and discussion of the patient's distortions and illogical conclusions. Then, an attempt may be made to correct his erroneous judgments by focusing on the nature of his observations and logical operations and by the consideration of alternative hypotheses.[11]

The major difference between this style of psychotherapy and our method of consultation is that Beck tries to help his patients gain an understanding of the nature and unfortunate implications of their recurrent patterns of thought, while in consultation this step is left out because it would upset the coordinate relationship of consultee and consultant, and also because it might undo the defensive displacement and reveal the personal underpinnings of the consultee's problem with his client.

It is the maintenance of this displacement that provides the leverage for achieving rapid results in theme interference reduction. Because the theme is displaced, it can be handled by the consultee with less anxiety than if its contents were confronted directly in relation to its personal implications. At the same time, the consultee has unconsciously tailored the client's case to the cognitive content of his theme, partly by selecting a client from his case load with appropriate characteristics, partly by selective misperception of items in the case to make them conform to his own cognitive pattern, and partly by manipulating the actors in the client's drama to behave in consonance with his own requirements. All this leads to the "test case" situation, in which the consultee expects once more to validate his fears, even if in a condition of lowered intensity because it is "once removed" from his own problem. This provides the consultant with his very special opportunity for invalidating the thematic expectation. He does this by virtue of the leverage of the consultation relationship. The consultee has accepted the consultant as a supplementary ego figure. The consultant, therefore, is able to provide focused ego support in relation to a highly significant segment of the consultee's ego functioning, namely to improve his capacity for reality testing regarding the expected outcome category.

The effect of this is to reduce the cognitive distortion and to move the theme to some extent into the autonomous conflict-free part of the consultee's ego. This shift is stabilized by continued contact with the client. The consultee confirms experientially that what he previously thought inevitable is not in fact so but only one of a series of alternative outcome possibilities that can be modified by choices open to the client and by the effective intervention of the consultee. This experience produces an important change in the consultee's feelings about the theme and about his own underlying conflict. The details of the latter are not altered, as they might be by uncovering types of psychotherapy, in which they are brought out into consciousness and new ways of resolving the conflict worked out. Instead, the consultee, as a result of the emotionally corrective experience of the consultation, develops a feeling of increased ego mastery and autonomy, so that he learns that he can maintain his integrity and his capacity for effective functioning in dealing with that sensitive aspect of his life, even if the original conflict has still not been resolved and if it continues its pressure to interfere with his cognition.

This process is helped by a concomitant relaxation in the consultee's superego pressures relating to the underlying conflict. This is produced by his identification with the consultant as a superego figure, and by his awareness of the consultant's lack of tension in dealing with the theme and with the actors in the client's drama who personify it.

The combined effect of all this is a segmental improvement in the autonomous ego functioning of the consultee, so that he no longer needs to use clients vicariously to relieve the pressure of the underlying conflict. As indicated earlier, this therapeutic effect often does not occur in one step during a single consultation but may require two or three corrective emotional experiences in successive consultations. Psychotherapists, who know how long such a process often takes in a traditional treatment setting, may be surprised to learn that it can be accomplished so quickly in consultation. The explanation lies in the special setting in which consultation takes place.

First, the consultee, unlike the usual patients who come for psychotherapy, has a fundamentally healthy ego structure. The conflict underlying the theme, even though long unresolved, had been mastered and kept under control until recently by his ego. Second, he comes for consultation under circumstances that render him ripe for the leverage of a short intervention—namely, he is self-selected by virtue of his using the defense of displacement onto his work, and he himself unconsciously set up the "test case." Last, in addition to his receiving the specific ego support available through the consultation relationship, his increased ego autonomy in one segment of his functioning is buttressed by the generalized supports of his professional culture. Improved functioning on this case is likely to be rewarded by a rise in the esteem in which he is held by his organization and by a reciprocal rise in his own self-esteem. He will also experience an increased feeling of competence because of a subjective awareness that he has succeeded in handling a difficult professional case, one that previously was beyond him.

NOTES

1. F. Deutsch, "Associative Anamnesis," *Acta Psychotherapeutica Psychosomatia, 6,* 289–306, 1958.
2. A. T. Beck, "Thinking and Depression I. Idiosyncratic Content and Cognitive Distortions," *Arch. Gen. Psychiat., 9,* 324–333, 1963; A. T. Beck, "Thinking and Depression II. Theory and Therapy," *Arch. Gen. Psychiat., 10,* 561–571, 1964.
3. J. Piaget, *The Moral Judgment of the Child,* trans. M. Gabain (Glencoe, Ill.: The Free Press, 1948).
4. D. Rapaport, *Organization and Pathology of Thought* (New York: Columbia University Press, 1951).
5. L. Postman, "Toward a General Theory of Cognition," in J. H. Rohrer and M. Sherif (eds.), *Social Psychology at the Crossroads* (New York: Harper and Bros., 1951).
6. J. S. Bruner, J. J. Goodnow, and G. A. Austin, *A Study of Thinking* (New York: John Wiley and Sons, 1956).
7. T. R. Sarbin, R. Taft, and D. E. Bailey, *Clinical Interference and Cognitive Theory* (New York: Holt, Rinehart, and Winston, 1960).
8. O. J. Harvey, D. E. Hunt, and H. M. Schroder, *Conceptual Systems and Personality Organization* (New York: John Wiley and Sons, 1961).
9. Beck, "Thinking and Depression II," pp. 562–563.
10. *Ibid.,* p. 563.
11. *Ibid.,* p. 571.

[9]

An Example of Consultee-Centered Case Consultation

INTRODUCTION

The following is a verbatim transcript of a tape recording of a consultation interview. It has been altered slightly to disguise the identity of the client. I have also deleted a few expressive vocalizations that bridged pauses in the interview but did not add to the comprehensibility of the written document. As I carried out this minimal editing of the tape, I was impressed by the richness of the sound record in contrast with the text of the transcription. Much evidence about the interaction between consultee and consultant that comes through clearly on the sound track is hardly discernible in the text. A film would provide further evidence; and, of course, presence during the interview and participation in it would add other dimensions. The reader of the case record must therefore manage with much less information than was available to the consultant. I hope it will be sufficient to give an impression of a typical consultee-centered case consultation that will be good enough to provide a dynamic understanding of the problems of the consultee and of the techniques of the consultant.

The consultee in this case was a public health nurse of about twenty-five years of age, who asked for consultation regarding one of her current patients. He was suffering from terminal carcinoma of the bladder, and she was visiting him daily to change his surgical dressings and to give him general nursing supervision. As usual, this nurse extends her professional focus beyond her primary patient to the whole family; and

191

about four months earlier she had asked for consultation about a problem involving this patient's twenty-year-old son, who was struggling with a conflict over achieving independence from his parents.

The nurse had known the consultant for eight months and during that period had consulted him on several occasions about different cases. She had built up a warm collaborative relationship with him.

The consultant was an experienced psychiatrist, who had had special training in consultee-centered case consultation. In this case he demonstrates a more than average level of technical competence, but the case itself is fairly typical, and I have chosen it as a characteristic example of this kind of consultation.

In order to afford the reader an opportunity to appraise the data and to make up his own mind about the dynamics of the case without being biased by my ideas, we present the entire interview transcript on the left-hand side of the page; and we offer my discussion on the right-hand page, primarily in the form of a series of annotations, numbered in reference to the relevant line of the transcript. I suggest that the reader first read the entire transcript on the left-hand pages and then repeat the reading, with the addition of my annotated comments on the opposite pages. The nurse is referred to in the transcript as N, the consultant as C.

TRANSCRIPT   N: I want to talk with you about Mr. and Mrs. Wood and I spoke with you four months ago about them. He had terminal cancer of the bladder. And this is a family of four children, three still living in the home: an older daughter who is in her middle twenties; another
5   daughter, who is younger, and has been married for a couple of years; a twenty-year-old son who is working as an electrician; and a younger son who is around seventeen and is still in high school. His wife had always been the homebody type of woman until a few years ago when his illness became severe and he wasn't able to work
10   for about four years and she started working part time in a store. And on our last visit I was talking with you about Mr. Wood's reaction to his illness, whether he lorded it over his family, and their reaction because one of the boys had mentioned to one of the hospital nurses about how he was having quite a lot of emotional stress
15   about wanting to leave the family, wanting to set out on his own, start his own business and get serious with a girl, and yet he felt obligated to stay at home because of his father's illness and financial needs, etc.

Because she had discussed this case previously with the consultant, DISCUSSION
and because there was already a well-established consultation relationship, the nurse immediately launched into her story without the need for
introductory remarks. The sound of her voice on the tape indicated
heightened emotional tension, and she was speaking quite tensely and
rapidly.

19, 21, 49. These three questions by the consultant are not really requests for information. They are attempts to break up the nurse's flow of
talk and to slow her down to a more reflective pace. It is important in
the early stages of a consultation session to establish its pattern as a dialogue; and sometimes, rather meaningless questions help to achieve this.
At the present stage, the consultant does not have enough information
about the case to say anything significant, and he must be careful not to
ask any question that might imprint his own pattern on the projectively
determined story of the consultee.

67. "Two persons dying instead of one" is a strange statement. It
might indicate a possible theme, especially as the first part of that sentence is rather vague and confusing. Was the nurse giving her own
projectively distorted interpretation of what the hospital people said, or
was she reporting accurately their statement that "in effect" two people
will be dying? Such a lack of clarity is often a good clue, especially in a
consultee who normally talks as clearly as this nurse does.

It is noteworthy that the consultant did not intervene at this point to
clarify the matter. He certainly noted it, as we will see later in the interview. His technique was good, because if "two persons dying" is an important hint about an unconscious theme, it would not be advisable to
focus the consultee's attention explicitly upon it at this early stage, for
fear of unlinking.

82. Again the consultant's question does not have much meaning. The
tape recording at this point demonstrates a rise in the consultee's emotional tension. Her voice is getting louder and her presentation speeds
up. The consultant intervenes to slow her down and to remind her, as it
were, that the two of them are engaged in a joint appraisal of the situation.

By this time, it was probably clear to the consultant that he was dealing with a case of lack of objectivity. The nurse's dramatic style of presentation, her pressure of talk, and her emotional arousal all pointed to

c: Can you use their first names so that we know who . . .

20 N: O.K. Peter is the name of the father.

c: And the boy?

N: This is George. At that time we weren't sure whether this was premature on George's part, whether this was a feeling that the whole
family was going through or whether this was just George and he
25 was sensing it earlier than the rest of the family. Now later, just a
few weeks after I spoke with you, Peter was admitted to the hospital
because of increased bleeding from his wound—he has a suprapubic
wound from radiation therapy on the cancer and he was hospitalized
for about six weeks. During that time he had two cordotomies for
30 the intense pain he was going through prior to his admission. And
he went through quite a lot of changes. The cordotomies and all led
to incontinence. He has his ureters anastomosed to the bowel. Prior
to his admission to the hospital he had a lot of problems about having to evacuate his bowels quite frequently. But this was even in-
35 creased because then he felt no urgency and he was incontinent
completely. Also he lost his ability to walk. And previously at home
he had been able to stay home all day long, while his wife and
children were out, and take care of himself. They rehabilitated him
quite a bit in the hospital—they taught him how to walk with a
40 walker and now he's walking with a cane. Yet he still is quite incontinent. He uses diapers as a means of controlling it. So he came
home about a week and a half ago and I visited him and I could see
a complete change as to his outlook on things. Before, he was depressed, but not this downtrodden, beaten look to him, as he has
45 now. Before, he seemed to feel that he wanted to stay home during
the day alone, because he wanted his family to go out, to be away
from him. Now, his wife has taken two weeks' vacation now that he
has come home, so in talking with the hospital . . .

c: Is this the vacation from her job?

50 N: Right, to stay home with him for these two weeks, the first two
weeks that he's home. And in talking with the hospital, I've gotten
the feeling that they have discussed this among their social workers
and all, and they feel that she should keep this job no matter what.
They fear that this two-week vacation may lead to possibly her
55 never going back again. And they told me that if I see any signs
of this, I should tell them because they will readmit Mr. Wood un-

some type of subjective involvement interfering with her professional
poise. The consultant's previous experience with this consultee would allow him to differentiate these signs from her expectable normal behavior in a case of this type. Although readers have not heard the nurse's voice on the tape, they can get some feel for the difference between her verbal behavior at the beginning of this interview and her normal functioning, by comparing the text at this point with her recorded statements toward the end of the session, which are considerably less vivid and less affectively loaded.

109. The manifest content of the nurse's story focuses on a conflict between her and Mrs. Wood, whom she is describing dramatically and in negatively stereotyped terms. The general pattern might be seen as Oedipal, with the young woman in rivalry with the mother as to who should care for the father. Might this Oedipal rivalry not be a theme that is interfering with the nurse's capacity to handle the case? The consultant must have considered this because it is so obvious. The continuation of the record shows that he probably did not judge it to be important, and I agree with him. The nurse's story of her conflict with Mrs. Wood is too open and obtrusive to be the expression of an unconscious theme. She is, in fact, fully aware of the problem and seems to be handling it quite well—"I told her then that I realized that she had been taking care of him for a long time and that possibly she didn't need any suggestions from me in his care but that if she ever ran across any problems to please tell me." This certainly sounds like effective professional behavior.

Why, then, is the nurse so dramatic in telling her story about Mrs. Wood's overbearing and suppressive behavior toward her husband, and why does she speak about her so negatively? At this juncture there is no evidence on which to base an answer, but the question must have been in the consultant's mind.

115. The consultant begins asking some questions to explore this issue. Inadvertently he asks a question, "How had she used to sound?" which provokes a defensive response from the consultee—"Well, I never really observed her." The consultant shows how sensitive he is to the nurse's feelings by immediately interrupting her to get her off the hook. He clarifies that he wants to know, not what the nurse observed, but what the husband had told her about his wife. This is apparently a small point, but it is from the accumulation of such interventions by a consultant that a consultee learns that he is interested in finding out about the client and not about her professional performance, and that he is not sitting in judgment upon her.

der real or false reasons—just to get him out of there. So that then possibly they will reconsider a recuperative center or something like this for the time being.

60 C: Have they told you why they feel it's so important that Mrs. Wood work?

N: Yes. Not only for financial reasons, in that she's in her late fifties and after he dies she will need some sort of support of her own, and to retrain her and she's a little bit elderly to start with. And also
65 for the fact that they think that this gives her a little bit of an out on him. If she is there all the time with him, they said, in effect, there will be two persons dying instead of one. Because she needs to get out, to have this job to leave home and in order to tolerate the whole situation. Previously I hadn't seen her very much because
70 she worked. But my idea of what she was like and I think, from what Mr. Wood said, she has completely changed. He pictured her to me, prior to the hospitalization, as the woman who was the staff of strength in this family. She held the whole thing together. She did everything. She was wonderful. She could anticipate his needs
75 before he even said anything. She worked, but she did all the ironing, washing for all the children—his older girl who is in her twenties too and—for both the boys and all of them. She refused to let any of it be sent out to the laundry. I pictured her as a woman who had strong family feelings, strong responsibility to the family.
80 So now that she has come home from work, the first day I went there, she spoke and yelled—a scream—the whole time I was there.

C: Screaming at who?

N: Just anything she said was a yell.

C: Oh, I see.

85 N: Mainly, to a large extent at him. He said to me, "I'm a changed man, these last two weeks or so. I'm not the same man at all. I've lost a lot." And so I said, "Well, what do you mean?" I was trying to get him to talk about it but he seemed so depressed. And she said, "Don't bother her with that, don't gripe!" You know—she just
90 wanted to shut him up every time he opened his mouth to say anything, particularly as a complaint. If he seemed to be heading at a complaint or a problem, she wanted to cut him off. An instance of this was when the son brought home a bedside commode for him to use during the night and he was talking to me about the problem

124. The consultant has asked about Mrs. Wood. The nurse begins to
answer and then switches to talk about herself in relation to the patient.
The consultant interrupts and tries to get the nurse to talk about Mr.
and Mrs. Wood.

127. Again the consultee, instead of focusing on the patient and his
wife, begins to obtrude herself. This time the consultant is more directive. His question specifically mentions the patient and his wife. This interchange demonstrates that the consultant is controlling the content of
the interview. He is insisting that the nurse talk about the client and his
family and not about herself. Such firmness on the part of a consultant,
as long as he is tactful, is usually not resented by a consultee. On the
contrary, the consultant is maintaining a framework that provides the
consultee with a fuller defensive structure than if she were talking also
about herself; and she is likely to feel more comfortable.

131. The nurse corroborates this in her next statement. For the first
time she begins to talk with some sympathetic understanding about Mrs.
Wood. I here get the feeling that the initial negatively stereotyped description of Mrs. Wood is perhaps a cover for the nurse's underlying
identification with her. When the consultant refuses to allow the nurse to
bring herself into the drama, and when he does not accept her unconscious gambit of focusing on the conflict between her and Mrs. Wood,
she begins to take herself off the stage and simultaneously she invests
Mrs. Wood with her part.

153. As the nurse continues along this line, she agrees with Mrs.
Wood's opinion that her husband has the capacity for more independence than he is currently showing. The consultant then openly refers to
the nurse's not wanting to take Mrs. Wood's place with the patient. To
me this makes it clear that the consultant has decided that the manifest
topic of rivalry between the nurse and Mrs. Wood in regard to caring
for the patient is not a substantive issue in the consultation. Otherwise,
he would certainly not have put it so explicitly into words. If I had been
the consultant, I doubt whether on the evidence so far I would have
taken the chance that I might be wrong. I would not have spoken out so
clearly, although the nurse's relaxed response to the consultant's intervention validates his judgment. If the issue of Oedipal rivalry were salient, the nurse would almost certainly have responded defensively to the
consultant's explicit formulation. Instead, she continued to talk with increasing sympathy about Mrs. Wood.

166. I imagine that at this phase of the interview the consultant must
be doing some hard thinking about the meaning of what the consultee
has been saying. He now has confirmed his hunch that rivalry between

96 of having to get up during the night so many times. Then she really yelled at him, "Don't take that to her. You don't have to; I'm your wife. I'll handle that. We'll do this." And so he said that he had always talked to me about anything that ever bothered him. And she says, "But you don't have to bother her with this," and

100 for a minute I wondered if maybe she was feeling that I was not trying to take her place, but that she wanted to make sure that she had a place, now that I was coming in and yet she was home. I told her then that I realized that she had been taking care of him for a long time and that possibly she didn't need any suggestions

105 from me in his care but that if she ever ran across any problems to please tell me. And she said, you know, that she would. Well, since then every time he has commented on anything like about his weight losing, she tells him, "Oh, shut up, you'll be getting better. It just takes time."

110 C: This has been something you never saw before. "Oh, shut up." None of that?

N: Never!

C: How had she used to sound?

N: Well, I never really observed her. But from what . . .

115 C: From what he tells you . . .

N: From what he tells me, she was more understanding. She would at least let him express himself, and now she seems to be taking the attitude, "I know it's that way, but if you just don't talk about it— don't say it—maybe it won't be true." You know, "If you don't talk

120 about it, it would be better." An instance when he was lying on the couch right across the room and I said, "Can I help you up?" just to give him a hand, and she says, "Oh, no, he can do it by himself. He's just got to try." And . . .

C: What happened after that?

125 N: I, you know, backed off, because, obviously, I don't want to say, "Yes, I'm going to help him." After all . . .

C: But does he, in fact, get up by himself or does she . . .

N: He gets up by himself. She sort of beats him into, you know, verbally being independent, being on his own; and in a way, I've

130 thought about it—whether this is her way of trying to make him be on his own so she can still go out and work.

the nurse and the patient's wife is not a central issue, and that the consultee may really be using Mrs. Wood as an identification object. While
he continues to think, he asks some questions to elicit from the consultee a more detailed story about the rest of the family, in order to explore for the emergence of some meaningful pattern. When the nurse
mentions George, about whom she had requested consultation four
months earlier, he allows himself a digression to get some follow-up information. Such a casual follow-up inquiry about the outcome of a previous case is quite a usual procedure in this kind of consultation. It also
elicits some information from the consultee that the consultant does not
have to strain himself to understand, and this frees him on a deeper
plane to concentrate on the elucidation of the central issue of the case
—namely, what is going on in the consultee that is affecting her professional objectivity?

177. The consultant moves his exploration forward. He accepts the
centrality of Mrs. Wood, by his statement that she "seems to be the
focus," and then he continues by asking about the children. The nurse
responds by continuing to paint a picture of the whole family's behaving
as though they do not have much feeling for the father.

If I had been the consultant, I would by now be getting suspicious
that the nurse had been talking for almost half the interview about the
reactions of the wife and children of a man dying of cancer without
focusing on the issue of his imminent death.

195. The above point must also have struck the consultant, because in
responding to the nurse's description of the children as "not caring," he
raises the alternative possibility that "they're scared." He does so not in
the form of a direct question to the nurse but by using the mother as a
displacement object and asking the nurse to imagine what the mother is
thinking concerning the children's attitude to their father. This introduces the topic in a safe way for the nurse to talk about. If she felt too
uncomfortable to confront the issue, she could easily have evaded it by
saying that she did not know what Mrs. Wood was thinking. The consultee responds immediately and to the point. She says that Mrs. Wood
showed no sign of having considered the significance to the children of
their father's impending death.

205. The consultant's direct allusion to Mr. Wood's approaching death
does appear, however, to have made some impression on the consultee.
She says that as the mother talks about the behavior of George "she
interprets this as not caring." By using the word "interprets," the
nurse is tacitly admitting that there may be another interpretation and
that Mrs. Wood may be evading or denying the effect of the impending
death on the family.

C: Mm hmm.

N: So I—I talked to him about how he feels about it.

C: Yeah.

135 N: About her working—and he says—you understand we can't talk too freely because she's there all the time—so he says, "Well, I want her to work, and I know it's important to her, but I'm afraid." Now, before he never—ah—showed me this wanting to hold on, you know, wanting to keep people there. And I think a lot of it is his 140 fear of what's going to happen to him, but he said, "I just don't know what I'm going to do when she leaves." Now to me his physical abilities haven't changed that greatly from before, to where he should have this fear purely because of feeling he's helpless. He's able to get up and down from the chair and the couch by himself. He is 145 able to walk around. He might not be quite as strong, but he is strong enough. He became quite weak in the hospital. My problem is not only interpreting how she is reacting to this—to his coming home, whether this is a change in her—but also how I should react to it. Because in one instance, I feel I should give him a little sym- 150 pathy, you know, give him a little coaxing along. Yet I don't want to seem like I'm going against her wishes as far as how to handle him.

C: Or taking her place, for that matter?

N: Yes, or trying to tell her that she's wrong, in effect. So, I'm sort 155 of—caught in between. And another factor is, before he had said how she prided herself as to how she cared for her children and did all these things for them, and just the other day she started crying, tears, telling me how she was just so overworked—the chil- dren just never did a thing for themselves. And I told her that, you 160 know, that there are times, especially at this age, they become very selfish, that they think that they have to assert themselves. She was talking about how the sons leave the house, any time they have any spare time they leave, they don't stay home.

C: Was she talking about George specifically then?

165 N: George more than the younger one.

C: What's happening?

N: Well, he is still working at the same job, still going with the girl, and evidently it's much the same as it was before. And while I was

221. The nurse's defensive pattern now begins to be obvious. As she DISCUSSION
probably unconsciously continues to associate to the issue of her patient's death, she again repeats her account of Mrs. Wood's denying and
suppressing behavior and of her own conflict about whether to show
sympathy for the patient which will ostensibly push the wife aside. She
feels she can't do this because underneath she recognizes that the family's
rejecting behavior is not really due to their not caring but to the opposite—"they love him, you know." And yet, the nurse, too, as it now begins to be clear, cannot bring herself openly to confront the issue of her
patient's impending death. She hides behind the distancing behavior of
Mrs. Wood and the children that fills her consciousness and the content
of her story. She is half condemning them and, by this stage of the consultation, half sympathizing with them. When she says about them,
"They care, but they are in a lot of turmoil right now," she appears also
to be talking about herself.

Perhaps the nurse's difficulty with the case is that she cannot bear to
face her own feelings about the impending death of this patient and instead becomes preoccupied with the similar behavior of his family. She
does not approve of the family's behavior but is ineffectual in handling
it, because to do so successfully would demand that she confront explicitly the issue both they and she are evading. If this is correct, what can
the reason be? A public health nurse, even one as young as the consultee, has encountered death in many patients. What is it that makes her
evade the issue? At the beginning of the session she talked quite clearly
and objectively about Mr. Wood's surgical experience, and occasionally
she has alluded to his "terminal" condition with no special signs of emotional upset. Perhaps it is not Mr. Wood's death that is the sensitive
issue for her but the implications of his death for those nearest to him.
In effect, the whole story about her rivalry with Mrs. Wood might imply
that she too considers herself a member of his emotional entourage.

At this point in the interview these are some of the thoughts that
would be running through my mind if I were in the consultant's shoes.
The ideas are vague; they are just beginning to take on a pattern. I
would continue my exploration in search of further projective material
from my consultee in order to develop the pattern and to specify its details. Let us follow the transcript to see how the consultant handled this
process.

226. The consultant, having failed to elicit the desired material from
the consultee by asking about Mrs. Wood's ideas about the effect of the
impending death on the children, now addresses the nurse directly and
asks for her own observations about Mr. Wood. He was apparently ex-

170 there one day, she wanted him to take one of his little nephews to nursery school and he had said he had to pick up his girl. And she said, "Boy, you have time to pick up your girl, but you can't pick up your nephew." And so I feel that with the strain between her and him becoming more, also with Mr. Wood and between him and all the members of the family, you know, like a five-pointed

175 star instead of two, you know, and . . .

c: The mother seems to be the focus. She seems to be kind of strained with sons, husband—how about the daughter?

n: The married daughter evidently is a help. She tries to help, not only emotionally, but tries to give them some financial support; but

180 the older daughter lives in the home and evidently does nothing, and this was one of Mrs. Wood's complaints. She says, "I have a daughter who does nothing." Evidently she has never assumed her responsibility. So I don't know what answer to give them. I don't know how to react in the presence of both of them. And when she

185 leaves, and when I go in to see Mr. Wood alone, I don't want to —don't want to undo any good that she has done as far as being out of the home. I don't want him ever to feel that I feel she should be home taking care of him. Yet, I feel that if I don't give him a little bit of—not really sympathy, but understanding—show some

190 understanding of his feelings, that he has no one then, because she shuts him off every time he says anything. The children are never there to listen to anybody.

c: Mm. This seems that the mother is complaining that the children never give her a hand, that they really don't care too much, is it

195 that kind of flavor? They don't care or they're scared, or they're . . .

n: Well, I don't think she's looked that far, to feel that they are scared of the situation. But, after all, they're younger, and dying father . . .

c: And their worries at that time?

n: No, I don't think she has looked that far. I think she looks to them

200 that they just don't care, you know. The boy, George, has given quite a lot of financial support, especially since he's come home. He brought in a lot of supplies and all these things and has gone out hunting. You know, you have to go to all these different supply stores to buy special things for him. Yet, he doesn't want to stay

205 home with the father, and she interprets this as not caring.

ploring to see whether the nurse felt that her patient was worrying about
dying.

232. The nurse responds well to this approach, graphically describing
the patient's psychological withdrawal from life. The sound of her voice
on the tape takes on a depressed quality; and once again, as in the earlier part of the interview when she was quoting Mrs. Wood, she mimics
with dramatic vividness the depression of Mr. Wood as he says, "Just
been laying around."

241. Once again, as the nurse's feelings about Mr. Wood's fatal condition come close to the surface, she defends herself by a brief recapitulation of her defensive "chorus" about Mrs. Wood's cutting her husband
off. This time, the defense is not working properly; and instead of continuing with criticism of Mrs. Wood, the nurse switches to herself. She
identifies with Mr. Wood as someone being "cut off" and in this guise
talks about something preying on her mind. The consultant immediately
intervenes and asks a direct question about the wife, in order to stop the
nurse from talking further about herself and to get her back onto the
topic of the patient and his family. The consultant also breaks up the
flow of the interview by a number of questions that demand short responses from the nurse, apparently to give her an opportunity to reduce
her level of emotional tension. This is an important consulting technique
and runs counter to customary procedure in analytic psychotherapy in
which, unless one is treating a patient with a very fragile ego, the therapist tries to maintain as high a level of emotional tension as possible.
The purpose of this in psychotherapy is to force unconscious material to
the surface and to stimulate the patient's awareness of the personal significance of what he is saying. In consultation, we are trying to understand the nature of the consultee's unconsciously derived distortions. We
do not, however, want the consultee to confront these consciously but to
continue handling them by defensive displacement. Because of this, a
consultant must closely watch the level of his consultee's tension; and
when it approaches the safety threshold, the consultant must take steps
to reduce it. In this case, the consultant apparently judged that the nurse
was expressing a too intense feeling of depression as she talked about
Mr. Wood's mood on his return from the hospital. He therefore asked
her a number of questions designed to get her to recapitulate elements
of the story she had told earlier in the interview.

265. As the nurse retells her story, she once again attacks Mrs. Wood.
This time she uses a characteristic stereotyped phrase, as she says that
Mrs. Wood beats her husband "like a whipped dog."

266. The consultant does not allow the consultee to continue along

C: In a way, Mr. Wood also sees this thing going on now and talks about it. Is it still kind of—ah—"They're still great, doing everything for me, I don't need any help"?

N: I think he'd like to talk about how he feels and how his family feels but, like I say, every time he opens his mouth to say anything about how "I feel bad" or "I'm worried," and she says, "No, you aren't, don't worry her with that." So I really am looking forward to the day when she won't be there so I really can talk with him, find out exactly how he feels. But in letting him talk like that I don't want to seem like I'm being the big sympathy and that "You come to me for your sympathy, because you can't get it from your family." Because this isn't the type of family—they have been close. Generally, they have concern for him, they love him, you know. It's not like they were completely disregarding him, and I was, you know, the only one who cared. They care, but they are in a lot of turmoil right now.

C: One thing you've pointed out was when he came home this time after the cordotomies that he's a different person, even to you, and the difference was that earlier he had been a little depressed, but now he felt, I've forgotten how he put it—ah—he looked kind of beat, was it?

N: Very! He looks down and he just seems like he has no interest. Before, he would speak to me about things that were current events, things that were going on. Now it's all turned inward. He has nothing to talk about when they say, "How are you today? What have you been doing?" "Just been laying around," you know. He doesn't go anywhere outside of himself.

C: So he's just kind of talking about himself. Doesn't go out any farther than his skin, you know . . .

N: And she, in some respects, encourages this by—of course when a man has feelings, and can't say anything, I guess he gets told, "Don't say that, don't bother her with that." I know myself if I were cut off every time I tried to say something that it just preys upon your mind more.

C: Sure. Have you seen the wife do anything other than cut him off like this?

N: No. I have not watched her really listen to him—about anything.

this line but directs the nurse's attention to other, more factual aspects of DISCUSSION
the case.

276. The consultant then launches, himself, into a lengthy recapitulation, apparently in order to establish a more objective view of the case; and then he works his way around to begin exploring the issue he had obviously noted, but not dealt with, at the beginning of the interview, concerning the rationale for trying to make sure Mrs. Wood returned to work after her two-week vacation.

278. The consultant's formulation, pretending that he did not remember what the consultee had told him earlier, so as to get her to repeat her story, is a useful technique. It is clear that he picked up the ambiguity in the nurse's original statement about someone's in the hospital saying that, "in effect, there will be two persons dying instead of one," and is now attempting to find out what this meant.

290. The nurse's response seems to indicate that her earlier statement was not an accurate report of what somebody had said but was her own subjective interpretation, namely that "in effect" what they said amounted to their feeling that two people would die instead of one if Mrs. Wood did not go back to work. In her recapitulation, she once again provides some rich projective material, when she says, "I don't know if they feel that . . . he will grab onto her and keep her home . . ." The fact that she does not know means that she has used her imagination to determine what the hospital people think. This type of statement is most useful, since it provides pure projective material uncontaminated by fact.

Once again, the sound of the nurse's voice on the tape shows a rise in tension. This is also demonstrated in the text by her dramatically quoting the words of her dialogue with Mrs. Wood. On the tape she mimics the way she spoke to Mrs. Wood, with a rising inflection in her questions to put pressure on Mrs. Wood to promise that she will return to work according to plan.

299. At this point in the interview the consultant was faced with a dilemma. Should he explore the nurse's views on Mrs. Wood's anxieties about leaving her husband? Or should he explore the mysterious "two persons dying instead of one"? If I had been the consultant, I believe I would have chosen the latter phrase, because it has a more irrational sound and because it emerged projectively within a confused context. It might also lead to an answer to the question I posed previously about the reason for the nurse's possible inhibition about confronting the effect of the patient's death on those nearest to him.

The consultant chose to explore the other avenue. It turned out to be c: And the only feeling you got was that every time someone makes a move to do something for him, she again intercedes.

245 N: Mmmm.

c: The commode business, or when you start to show interest. She kind of indicates that you oughtn't do any of these things.

N: You shouldn't give him any sympathy.

c: Yes.

250 N: She's afraid I'm going to try to encourage him to be dependent.

c: Umm. At the same time she's saying, "Don't do this, though, because he can do it himself." Did I pick that up?

N: Yes. She is—almost like, "You're going to, whether you think you can and—you're going to!" Period. Like, "I'm going to force you
255 to." Now I know he's capable of more than he wants to do.

c: Yes.

N: Like in getting out things by himself. It almost seems—it's more like she's got the feeling that "If you just don't talk about it, and if you just try" . . .

260 c: What's his response when she says, "You can do it if you just try hard enough"?

N: He says nothing and then he goes about it like a whipped dog: "O.K., I will." When he does what he's supposed to—walking, whatever the action is—he does it, but it's—ah—like a whipped dog, you
265 know, like she's beaten him into it now.

c: Can we just go back now and—tell me something about Mrs. Wood in terms of this job? Prior to his illness, she wasn't working, she was at home raising the youngsters, taking care of the house, taking care of him in many ways; and then when he became ill, he had to quit
270 work, and it was soon thereafter that she began to work. And then there was a period in which she was away at work and the youngsters who are now in their late teens and early twenties were beginning to go off on their own. He was kind of seeing himself as being alone in the house but managing all right. Now with the hos-
275 pitalization, she comes back into the house and she's done this on a two weeks' vacation.

N: Um humm.

productive and led him to a formulation about one reason for the discussion nurse's lack of objectivity, which he made the basis for his consultation intervention.

When two pathways open in the middle of a consultation assessment, it does not really matter which the consultant explores first, as long as he then explores the other. Both often turn out to be productive. My reason for choosing the most irrational-sounding or promising lead first is that there may not be time in that interview to deal adequately with both, and I therefore prefer to deal first with the one that appears most significant.

300. With this question, the consultant begins the crucial part of his assessment. He chose to ask the question in relation to Mrs. Wood's thinking, because it was by now amply clear that the nurse was using her as her major displacement object. The nurse's report on Mrs. Wood's statements about her reasons for not wanting to leave her husband is not very revealing.

305. The consultant then presses the nurse for a further statement. He words his question so as to elicit the nurse's fantasies, in the event that she has no information on which to base her answer.

308. The technique works as the consultant probably planned. Mrs. Wood had not told the nurse what she feared, so the nurse filled in from her own fantasy and thus once more produced pure projective material that was most revealing—"he might fall and not be able to get up and . . . he may die . . ." Here, at last, the nurse is beginning to talk openly about the patient's death and to link it to the behavior of his wife.

317. With minimal support from the consultant in the form of a series of sympathetic vocalizations, the nurse then proceeds to reveal her fantasy: "What if he dies while I am not with him?" "If he does, I don't know . . ."

325. The nurse does not complete her fantasy about the fears that are dominating Mrs. Wood. She brings herself into the picture, once more in the rivalry role. And then she says something very strange indeed. She suggests leaving the case—"Possibly we should change nurses—send a new nurse in . . ." From a professional point of view this is an absurd suggestion. Even a public health nurse of only a few years' experience, and certainly a girl with this nurse's level of intelligence and psychological sophistication, should know that continuity of relationship has a powerful supportive effect on a family in the type of crisis faced by the Woods.

If the consultant was surprised by his consultee's suggestion, he did c: And the social worker or—I'm not sure, somebody—feels that she might not go back to work, but she might just stay home and nurse her husband.

N: Yes. It seems that the hospital had a conference with the social worker and the nurses and the doctors, and they seemed to have a consensus that this job was of the utmost importance to her—short term and long range in that after he has gone, for her support— partially her support and umm, they seem to feel that there is a chance that—ah—either they feel, I don't know if they feel that upon her part or his, whether he will grab onto her and keep her home and keep her from going to work or whether she will change her mind and want to stay home and take care of him. Which I don't know . . .

c: Does she comment about her job?

N: I have talked to her about this—"You are on a two-week vacation, right? You will be going back to work Monday?" And she says, "Oh, yes," you know—I think she still wants to go to work but I'm worried that even after she does go to work if anything happens during the day, she could possibly quit her job to come back. Because she—ah—she's not the type of woman that would do it at any expense to him; I believe she'd do that.

c: Did she suggest any fear as to what would happen if she were not at home?

N: She has gone out shopping and said that she knew I was coming at any minute so she felt safe to leave, but she says he's gotta stay here by himself a little because I'm going to go out to work. But she doesn't feel completely safe about leaving him.

c: Does she give you some clue as to what she is so fearful about?

N: No. Not like—whether she feels that he might fall and not be able to get up and whether if she feels he may die or she thinks it's that far along. But—she just hasn't said what she fears. Well, I do know I think the whole family now is more certain in their feelings as—before, I thought he knew his diagnosis and he talked about death with me. I knew he more or less knew his outcome—what it would be eventually, but I didn't know really how the family . . .

c: Yeah.

N: But now I think they all realize it—that this is eventually going to lead to death and—or whether the idea that now she has to realize not show it. He just said, "Sure," and made no attempt at that time to DISCUSSION find out what the nurse meant. He may have interpreted it as another attempt on her part to escape from the conflict with Mrs. Wood.

328. The consultee apparently corroborated this by once more raising the issue of Mrs. Wood's feeling the nurse "was trying to take her place." Again, I get the impression that the nurse brings up this rivalry to distract herself when she gets close to the emotionally tense topic of the patient's death and its link with his wife.

This interchange leaves me less than fully satisfied. I feel that the nurse's suggestion that she might drop the case in the middle—and especially a case that clearly means so much to her—is so peculiar that it surely needs a good deal of further exploration. But as I read the record and follow the tape, it appears that the consultant had by now made his consultation formulation on the basis of all that had gone before, and was about to start his intervention. The nurse's statement about dropping the case came after he had made up his mind, and he seems to have to some extent brushed it aside. Also, he appears to have neglected, or forgotten, the other avenue he still had to explore about "two persons dying."

So far, I have been in substantial agreement with the manner in which this consultant has been conducting the consultation. He has shown great sensitivity to the consultee's feelings of involvement and has supported her continually in her use of defensive displacements. He has also carried out a low-keyed assessment, which has uncovered a satisfactory amount of information about the subjective distortions in the nurse's perceptions of the case without upsetting her or endangering her defenses. And yet, at this point I feel that he is starting his intervention before he has completed his exploration of at least two striking issues—the "two persons dying" and the change of nurse. If I had been in his shoes, I would have delayed my intervention until I had obtained more information.

338. The consultant starts his intervention gently. He makes a formulation that pulls together a number of pieces of information that the consultee has given him—"So there is some distance developing between . . . Mr. Wood and almost everybody that's around."

341. The nurse responds immediately and confirms that he is on target by amplifying the intent of his formulation—"This withdrawing from him is kind of a cushion for the blow."

342. The consultant drives the point home and for the first time in the interview explicitly links the behavior of the family with the impending death—"Like anticipating his going?"

352. The nurse now is prepared to confront this issue consciously, in

that he is going to die has brought more fear into her. "What if he dies while I am at work? If he does, I don't know . . ."

C: Mmm.

N: My problem was in trying to interpret her actions—whether or not
320 it was possibly me, in that he had become very dependent—possibly he had become very dependent upon me before he would go into the hospital. She might have resented this a little—this all entered my mind. Possibly we should change nurses—send a new nurse in there where this—post-hospitalization could build a new relationship
325 rather than feeling that he had to be back dependent upon me.

C: Sure.

N: And I wondered about whether she could possibly have misinterpreted my actions—feeling I was trying to take her place.

C: Well, whatever is operating here, she kind of is saying to people,
330 "Stay away." Like, for instance, you come in as the caretaker and she says to you, "Don't take so much care of him." But she also complains about her children not caring enough or somehow not letting them get close. Hmm? And then you noted also that she seems to be keeping her distance in a way. Like, you know, "Do it
335 yourself," or, "He can do it." At any rate in some way it's a bit more edgy when she is with him. So there is some distance developing between them—ah—Mr. Wood and almost everybody that's around.

N: Could she be doing this as—ah—I've seen this in families sort of
340 preparing for the fact that he will die some day. This withdrawing from him is kind of a cushion for the blow. Ah . . .

C: Like anticipating his going?

N: Yes, and that maybe if we just draw back a little, it will be easier. You know, not consciously thinking this but a little bit of that re-
345 action, like when a patient gets closer to death in a hospital the family makes less and less visits—shorter and shorter periods of time until the very final few hours—you know, this sort of insulation, a way of insulating themselves from the unpleasant. It's the daughter who is not living at home that seems to be fulfilling both
350 her and his expectations, while the ones who live in the home just don't do a thing according to their words. She seems to be doing what they want her to.

contrast with her evasions earlier in the interview; and she once more DISCUSSION
validates the consultant's formulation. She gives a penetrating and sensitive description of the visiting behavior of relatives of dying patients in
hospital. This shows her to have taken a good deal of interest in such
situations. She also makes an excellent interpretation of the reaction of
the Woods' married daughter, who does not live at home and therefore
does not have the same need as the rest of the family to pull away from
the dying father.

357. "I don't know what they think that nurses have" seems to indicate some self-consciousness on the part of the consultee about Mr.
Wood's idealized expectations of her.

373. The consultant develops his intervention further, utilizing the
exact words of the consultee's previously expressed fantasy—that Mrs.
Wood is afraid to be away from her husband "if he were to die . . . or
if he were to fall . . ."

389. I am not sure how wise this is in consultation. It is a good technique in psychotherapy, as Felix Deutsch has pointed out, because the
patient's words carry unconsciously determined emotional connotations
that may be especially meaningful if used by the therapist—a sort of key
to the patient's unconscious that bypasses the patient's ego defenses.
This is just the opposite of what we are trying to achieve by our consultation technique. In any event, the nurse's reaction to this formulation by
the consultant is not as positive as her previous responses. She tells a
rather confusing story about Mrs. Wood's claiming to be self-sufficient
in the face of the nurse's attempts to help the patient, and ends with her
usual defensive statement about being an intruder.

391. The consultant, in a *non sequitur,* returns to his message—"the
whole family seem to know that he is going to die now . . ." He then
twists the intruder topic into the pattern he is developing, and he formulates the conflict of Mrs. Wood as being between pulling away from her
dying husband in order to cushion the blow of his death and the fear
that if she pulls away from him "something terrible is going to happen."
The nurse's response to this does not come out clearly in the text, which
transcribes her vocalization merely as "Yeah." In the tape, however, the
sound she makes is clearly one that signifies a considerable lowering of
tension, as though the consultant has just taken a great load off her
mind.

412. The consultant repeats his formulation in other words and manages to link the family's reaction with Mrs. Wood's statement, "We can
do it . . ." In this manner he succeeds in weaving the nurse's repetitive
allusions to Mrs. Wood's claim of self-sufficiency in regard to caring for

c: Does he say that?

N: No, he thinks that the daughter who is married and doesn't live
355   there understands him. But he has interpreted it that she has a—that
little bit of—like he said, she could have been a nurse. I don't know
what they think that nurses have—"She could have been a nurse,
she understands these things. My other one is weaker—she can't
take being around me while I am sick." The daughter who is mar-
360   ried seems to be fulfilling their idea of what she should do. While
the other ones are not. Um. The youngest boy, William—I only get
the idea that he is not there because of school, but they sort of
excuse him in some way, I think, because he is younger. So it's the
three children, but mainly the two older ones.

365   c: I get the feeling that Jean, George, and William aren't around very
much so you don't get a chance to talk to them.

N: Right.

c: But the mother has said that—ah—she really doesn't feel comfortable being away from her husband, and the only way she promised
370   herself to get away is, for instance, if you're coming and she puts
it on the basis that maybe something will happen so "I ought not be
away." She would feel very bad if something happened while she's
away, like if he were to die or something—or if he were to fall . . .

N: One of the answers which really brought to my mind the feeling
375   that she has is "We, the family, can handle this." We were talking
about transportation to the hospital and he was talking about how
he had trouble going downstairs—they do live on the third floor.
This man who's a little bit wobbly on his feet anyway, trying to do
three flights of stairs. So he was saying how his strong side seems to
380   be on the right side, that's where the banister is; if he had it just
the opposite, he would feel better going down. So I even told him
that as long as he had somebody right there with him, possibly going
down backwards, look down straight and step down backwards.
You know, if he had somebody strong there holding him, don't try
385   it by himself. So she says, "Well, we'll work out something, we'll
work out something, we'll do that. We will handle this, thank you."
So I really wonder about sometimes whether it's me or whoever
goes in there. Especially as long as she is there, any reaction as
far as not being the intruder . . .

390   c: Yeah. What you're suggesting—the whole family seem to know that
he is going to die now, and he himself has talked to you about death.

her husband into her central conflict. This notion of the consultant
sheds a more sympathetic light on Mrs. Wood's motivation—that is, she
was not being bitchy but was trying to master her emotional turmoil.

415. The nurse immediately picks this up and repeats the idea in other
words. Her voice on the tape sounds most sympathetic as she expresses
her understanding of Mrs. Wood.

416. "It all, you know, eventually fits together." This is a kind of expression of gratitude to the consultant for clarifying what had previously
been so confusing.

419. The consultant repeats his statement that Mrs. Wood's distancing behavior must not be interpreted as meaning that "she doesn't care."
But this formulation introduces an additional message. It implies that
people are watching Mrs. Wood and judging her. The consultant is defending Mrs. Wood against those who might make the mistake of thinking that she does not care for her husband. His use of the expression
"doesn't spend twenty-four hours a day with this guy" may also be an
attempt to say something about Mrs. Wood that might also apply to the
nurse.

428. The consultant copies the nurse's pattern of role playing the part
of Mrs. Wood and expresses the other side of the conflict, bringing out
more clearly the guilt Mrs. Wood would feel if her husband died while
she was not with him.

434. The nurse follows the consultant's previous hint and makes explicit the issue of Mrs. Wood's worrying about being blamed. Note that
she is now role playing Mrs. Wood's part, and putting words in her
mouth that clearly come straight out of her own fantasy, since she has
absolutely no evidence about how Mrs. Wood really feels on this issue.

442. The consultant again is saying things about Mrs. Wood that
apply also to the nurse. He probably has in mind the consultee's earlier
aside about Mr. Wood's high opinion of nurses—namely of her.

446. The nurse follows suit and talks about Mrs. Wood's appearing
ideal but having underlying weaknesses unrecognized by her husband.
Her words might equally apply to herself.

448. Another vote of thanks! Her statement, "You have to remove
yourself from the situation so you can understand it," is a good explica-
tion of how consultation works.

461. It seems that the consultation is coming to a satisfactory close.
The nurse is relaxed. She talks objectively and sympathetically about
Mrs. Wood, whom previously she was stereotyping. The consultant has
helped her understand what was initially a confusing and emotionally
upsetting situation. He is now apparently proceeding to terminate the interview.

And there is a kind of atmosphere of people perhaps anticipating this and pulling away from one another just a bit and if not actually physically pulling away, managing to do that by building little ten- sions between them. And it might well be that anybody who comes into this—ah—setting and moves closer to, would be kind of going up stream. But they also have some kind of feeling about it if they pull away from him, something terrible is going to happen. They can't quite at this point see it as a fairly frequent phenomenon where as people approach death, there is a kind of pulling away. And I think the mother illustrates this most vividly by—how was it?—she kind of blames the kids for not being around and supporting, but somehow she does not link it with Dad's severe illness.

N: Yeah.

C: She puts it more on the basis that they are young, they have a lot of things of their own, have a life of their own to lead. And she doesn't link it with his possible dying and how would they feel after- ward. Which seems to be something she is concerned about, how would she feel if she didn't do enough for him? There is kind of a clue, isn't there, where she says something like—"We can do it; the family can do it"? She's kind of talking about her son—doing things for him.

N: Possibly in her own way because she'd be saying that even though we maybe appear to not care at times, we still do, you know, and wants to make that clear to me—doesn't want me to interpret them as not caring. It all, you know, eventually fits together.

C: Well, just because she doesn't spend twenty-four hours a day with this guy, and take care of everything, does that necessarily mean that she doesn't care?

N: She might be wondering this. I mean, you know, battling this in her mind. Whether Mrs. Wood interprets her working as not car- ing about him especially now that he seems to need me so much, whereas before she felt really safe to leave him.

C: Suppose she did go back to work—it's this Monday, right? Is she scheduled to go back, or next Monday? This coming Monday—and something does happen to him, then it's—does she kind of see it that "It might be my fault, that I wasn't there; if I were there I could have done something about it"?

N: She could possibly. Or even she could feel that possibly "Would someone else blame me?" You know, she might have it resolved in

At this point we are in a position to appraise the consultant's proba- ble formulation of the case. He must have ascribed the consultee's difficulties to her wishing to avoid the pain of continuing to be in close contact with a favorite patient who was about to die. At the same time, she was afraid that the patient, who idealized her, and his family, would criticize her for allowing the man to die, for not treating him so well that death would be kept at bay. She herself and possibly others might have similar critical feelings.

This possible conflicted reaction of the nurse represents a common human response to the death of a person with whom one is emotionally linked. In our consultation typology it represents a form of personal involvement, in that the nurse's professional distance and objectivity were being upset by her becoming personally involved with this dying patient. She was, however, not conscious of her feelings but was defending against them, both because they were painful and because they would not be professionally appropriate. Her defense was that of displacement. She chose Mrs. Wood as her identification object and was as confused and condemnatory about her as she would have been about herself, if she could have confronted her feelings directly.

An alternative formulation would categorize the case as one of theme interference. The theme would be "All people who care for a dying man will be blamed when he dies, because they did not succeed in saving him."

The consultant accepted the Initial Category and emphasized that Mrs. Wood did indeed care for her husband, although she pulled away from him to some extent in order to cushion the blow. He then invalidated the Inevitable Outcome by showing the nurse that people would not necessarily condemn the wife when her husband died, because even twenty-four hours a day of care could not prevent him from dying, and people would realize that.

Whether the consultant classified the case as personal involvement or theme interference, his intervention was well planned and effectively implemented. It led to an obvious lowering of tension and improvement of professional objectivity in the consultee.

Unfortunately, there appear to be some loose ends! As the consultant tries to end the session on a relaxed note, the nurse inexplicably raises once more the issue of a change of nurses. This sounds a rather sour note. If our previous formulations had been adequate, the nurse should now be perceiving the case and conducting herself in line with her customary level of professional skill. The suggestion to "send different nurses and give him a little bit of a change of face" certainly does not conform to this pattern.

her mind that "I had to go to work. That this was not only for my interest but for his well-being—not only emotionally and economically. But, would other people blame me for leaving my husband and going to work?"

435 C: Yes, like the social worker and like the nurse and other people.

N: She's lived here quite a while, they have friends and all; I think she even has other than the people who are directly connected with his illness, possibly she has the layman's idea of it. What friends and family expect . . .

440 C: Any expectations—just thinking back to what Mr. Wood was saying about his wife. Wasn't he kind of turning on pretty strongly about what a terrific supporter she is?

N: She seemed to be ideal in every way. Maybe she realizes that he thought this of her and she is trying to be more realistic about it in
445 showing that she has some feelings. Maybe she hid something previously or tried to, when he was first ill.

C: Um humm.

N: This helps me quite a bit. It seems possibly why she's staying away from this. Because like when I went in there every word she says is
450 in a shouting tone and, you know, it's hard to—to look through. You have to remove yourself from the situation so you can understand it.

C: Especially your visiting after he had been in the hospital for a couple of months and then suddenly finding things so apparently different.
455 We had the picture of a family that is well knit and supporting one another with a mother who is just as strong as all that. And suddenly finding her kind of crabby and griping and being curt. Will you be visiting next time when he is not with his wife?

N: Yes. I thought I would keep following it until we got him fairly well
460 established. And then possibly send different nurses and give him a little bit of a change of face. But for the time being we are trying to keep it the same nurse, and I go every day, Monday through Friday. So there will be the opportunity to see a change.

C: So that right now, he does require a fair amount of nursing care?

465 N: Yeah.

C: And this is stuff that the family cannot do?

463. Perhaps I am expecting too much! The nurse's next statement DISCUSSION implies that she is not thinking of leaving the case as quickly as she had previously intended. Perhaps the consultant's intervention had not solved her conflict or invalidated the interfering theme entirely but had very much weakened it.

464. The consultant seems to have been alerted to the possibility of unexpected loose ends, because he begins a new exploration to get the nurse to tell a fuller story of her nursing procedures in the case.

482. As the nurse reports on what she does for the patient, we appreciate her regular and intimate professional involvement in his care. We also confirm the improvement in her professional objectivity as she clearly differentiates the appropriate roles for herself and Mrs. Wood. There is now no sign of rivalry. On the contrary, she sees their roles as complementary.

513,517. The consultant has not uncovered new material from this exploration but rather has confirmed that all seems to be well. He therefore repeats one of his main messages about Mrs. Wood's irrational doubt that whatever she does for her husband will not be considered sufficient.

519. He also validates that Mrs. Wood (and by implication also the nurse) is in fact doing a great deal for her husband.

524. The nurse responds well to this reassurance and brings into the open the discrepancy between Mr. Wood's idealization of his wife and the reality of her human frailty—a clear allusion to the nurse's new mood of relaxed acceptance of her own humanity.

528. The consultant now delivers the new message he has been working up to. He obviously has interpreted the consultee's suggestion about leaving the case as being due to her feeling that in this case she cannot live up to her expectations of herself. He deals with this by talking of Mrs. Wood's having difficulty living up to her "big image" and because of this having the impulse to pull out.

532. The nurse reacts with some surprise to the idea that Mr. Wood might be disappointed in his wife. Hopefully, this is the kind of surprise that analysands often express when the analyst makes a successful interpretation—it is due to the feeling of strangeness at confronting previously unconscious material. We cannot validate this, or differentiate the nurse's reaction from that of someone hearing something irrelevant, because the interview has now come to its end.

533. This remark of the consultant is ambiguous. I believe it refers to Mrs. Wood and is a further expression of the consultant's sympathy with her. The nurse only a couple of minutes earlier had been commenting on "the pressure of all these things" on Mrs. Wood.

N: Well, not so much that they cannot do. Really the only actually nursing care is the dressing which is washing it out and packing it and putting a dry dressing on it. And Mrs. Wood does this over the weekend; she is capable, so right now this is not absolutely necessary. But we were going in because we didn't know how long she would be off of work. And as a break for her, to give at least this one task she doesn't have to do for him right now. Of course, when she goes to work it will be necessary for me to continue watching him such as like if he starts running a temp, possible kidney infection, and also the possibility of hemorrhage. He was bleeding quite a bit—it wouldn't be just a little. It's all these things we have to keep an eye on so we do. Previously there was always daily change. . . . One day he would be good and one day he would be bad, you know; we had to go in every day and he seems to be more established possibly. And if she wanted to change it when she comes home at night we could cut the visits down.

C: There are a lot of things then that not only you people but the wife can do for him. It's not as if she has to pull away entirely.

N: Um humm.

C: Even though sometimes it might be hard to make things as they used to be, there are still a lot of things that she can do for him.

N: Like his bath and things like that. She's been doing this for a long time, ever since he had trouble getting in and out of the tub; she used to put a chair in it for him to sit and those sort of things. I don't feel that right now she is interested in any actual physical— as changing himself, he has to change himself because he needs it so frequently, probably every hour he will have to change his padding—his diaper. So this he is handling mostly himself. He just needs a little help—if he needs anything in one room for him to go get it and come back, if he needs it right that minute . . .

C: Do you suppose the wife feels that she has to do all these things even though he can do a lot of these things?

N: No. I think that's part of her—thing that she's wishing him to do whatever he can on his own and . . . He doesn't appear to be ready for . . . She in some ways is a better judge than I am whether he can do it, to make him do it right now, start out in the beginning doing it instead of having him get used to someone else doing it for him.

The wording of the consultant's comment is, however, rather unfortunate. He could have meant, and the consultee could have thought he meant, that the *nurse* was under a lot of pressure and that he was sympathizing with *her*. I have listened carefully to the tape but am not certain which it was. Of course, if the consultant was sympathizing with his consultee, this would be a major error in technique and would undermine, at the very end of the session, the coordinate consultation relationship that he had been at such pains to foster throughout the interview.

536. The consultant closes the interview with a relaxed invitation for a further contact. His lack of pressure is an important nonverbal communication. At the same time he demonstrates his continued interest in the case; and if he believes, as I think he may, that there are elements in it which he has not yet uncovered, he will have another opportunity to work on them. Unfortunately for the satisfaction of our curiosity about these, this consultation took place some years ago, and the only record available to us for analysis is the tape of one session. Neither the consultant nor the consultee can be contacted to answer any of our questions. We must therefore accept the transcript as our only material, without the possibility of further validation of our ideas.

Before ending my discussion of this consultation, I wish once more to emphasize that the mystery of the phrase "two persons dying instead of one" still remains unsolved. Also, I am not satisfied that the consultant's explanation of the nurse's wish to leave the case was correct. As I ponder these two issues, it occurs to me that in addition to the theme interference identified and dealt with by the consultant, there may have been a second theme interfering with the consultee's work performance that was of more importance than the first. It escaped detection by the consultant because he chose the wrong avenue to explore at that crucial parting of the ways during his assessment. Since I would need the kind of material to validate my hunch that could come only from an exploration that was not made, my ideas have the weight only of pure conjecture, but they seem plausible to me, and they have the merit of pulling all the loose ends into a cohesive pattern.

I believe that the main clue was the nurse's fantasy that if Mrs. Wood stayed at home with her husband and did not return to work after her vacation, "two persons would die." This raises the possibility that the nurse fantasies that someone who is emotionally and spatially close to a man during the last moments of his life is in danger of being carried into the grave with him. In one of her more projective statements, the nurse says about Mr. Wood, "I don't know . . . whether he will grab onto her . . ."

C: Um.

506 N: She is there twenty-four hours a day, and she knows even better than I what physically he is capable of.

C: The thing you point out is that she does push him all the time to do as much as he can. I suppose one possible thing is that all the 510 while she keeps pushing him to do as much as he can for himself, that there is some part of her feeling that she ought to be doing more for him. She could get very hung up on these things, of how much to let him do for himself and how much she ought to do.

N: So this would be something to watch when she goes back to work, 515 what she wants—how she . . .

C: If she goes back to work, then this other notion will come up: "I'm not doing enough for him."

N: As she doles out the work—she, ah . . .

C: And she does do a lot, apparently.

520 N: Quite a bit, and this was never any problem. She did it because she wanted to. Now it's starting to show that this was not a realistic viewpoint on his part because she evidently is feeling the pressure of all these things. She wasn't so strong physically and mentally as he thought she possibly was.

525 C: Um humm . . . He seemed to have built a very big image that she had to struggle to keep up with that image. She could end up feeling that, like "No matter how hard I try, I can't quite meet his image." And one way to deal with that is by pulling out.

N: Um humm. I try to keep that in mind in going in there. If he ever 530 mentions anything about being disappointed in her—that's something I never really thought of, that he might be feeling disappointment in her.

C: It's a lot of pressure, isn't it?

N: Kind of bad . . .

535 C: After you have a chance to see him again when she goes back to work, let's plan to talk about it a bit more.

N: O.K.

In the light of my hypothesis, many aspects of the nurse's story and
behavior take on new meaning. Mrs. Wood's efforts to distance herself
from her husband become, not ways of cushioning the blow, but attempts at self-preservation. The nurse's ambivalence about taking the
wife's place becomes a manifestation not of rivalry, but of exposing herself to the danger from which she is helping Mrs. Wood to escape. In
fact, the nurse's attempts to push Mrs. Wood out of the house can now
be interpreted as being motivated by rescue efforts for an identification
figure.

The hypothesized theme also solves the mystery of the proposed
change of nurses. The consultee must leave the case in order to escape
herself from being sucked into Mr. Wood's grave. This danger increases
as the first theme interference is reduced and the obstacles to the nurse's
becoming emotionally close to Mr. and Mrs. Wood are overcome. In
fact, the nurse's previous confusion and preoccupation with the dramatic
rivalry with Mrs. Wood can now be seen in their true defensive perspective—as a way of producing psychological distance from the dangerous
closeness with the dying man.

The nurse's perceptive description of the pattern of visiting behavior
in hospitals of the relatives of dying patients indicates a long-standing interest in this issue and adds a little extra weight to my conjecture.

My formal statement of this theme would be, "Any person who remains emotionally and spatially close to a man during the process of his
dying will inevitably be captured by him and taken with him into
death." The only remedies are to distance oneself emotionally or to
leave the scene.

If I had been the consultant in this case—and if I had been perceptive and quick-thinking enough at the time to have thought then what I
now have worked out by my leisurely analysis of the transcript—I
would have validated my hypothesis by asking the nurse to talk more
about Mrs. Wood's reasons for distancing herself from her husband. I
would have phrased my questions in order to elicit the nurse's fantasies
about Mrs. Wood's possible thoughts in much the same way as the consultant did on a number of occasions during the session. Since the theme
expresses an obviously bizarre fantasy, I would have supported the
nurse in verbalizing it by pointing to the obvious emotional burden
under which Mrs. Wood was laboring, and saying that under such conditions of turmoil people often harbor quite irrational fantasies about imaginary dangers that lurk in their path.

If the consultee had produced material to confirm my hypothesis, I
would then have invalidated the theme expectation by helping the nurse

DISCUSSION see that although it is far from unknown for near relatives to die shortly after a bereavement, and although this theme is enshrined in some cultures which prescribe that the widow should be burned on her dead husband's funeral pyre so that she can accompany him to the next world, Mrs. Wood's fantasy of dying with her husband is an irrational fantasy. Since at the moment I am not in possession of the nurse's projective material on this issue, I cannot be sure how I would formulate this message so as to make it meaningful to the consultee. Clearly, it would have to be communicated not as an abstract concept but in concrete terms. I would expect to derive these from the content of the nurse's discussion of Mrs. Wood's ideas, and of Mrs. Wood's reasons for being so scared of her impending doom.

It is not unusual in consultee-centered case consultation to identify two or more interfering themes that have almost equal salience. Often the themes are linked, as in this case. The consultant must make a choice about the order in which to explore and deal with them. If, as probably happened here, the consultant misses one, there is no great harm done. As long as he maintained a satisfactory relationship with his consultee, the consultant can rest assured that he will be called upon in the not too distant future to deal with it, either because of continued problems with this client or because of difficulties with someone else drawn from the consultee's work load.

[10]

Program-Centered
Administrative Consultation

INTRODUCTION

In program-centered administrative consultation, the consultant is invited by an administrator or by a group of administrators to help with a current problem of program development, with some predicament in the organization of their institution, or with the planning and implementation of organizational policies, including personnel policies. He is expected to come into the organization, study its problems, assess the significance of the relevant factors, and then present a report containing his appraisal of the situation and his recommendations for dealing with it.

This type of consultation is usually requested on an *ad hoc* basis, and it is expected that the consultant will present his report in writing after a fairly short period of study—ranging from a few hours to a few weeks in duration.

In many respects this type of consultation resembles client-centered case consultation, except that instead of a client the consultant focuses on the problems of an organization; and instead of recommendations in regard to case management he presents a plan for administrative action. In both types of consultation, the consultant is personally responsible for correctly assessing the problem and for giving a specific action prescription or range of alternatives to be carried out by the consultees. In both it is therefore essential that the information upon which the consultant bases his recommendations be accurate and that he have the expert knowledge to deliver a wise plan. He does not in this regard have the leeway of the consultee-centered case consultant or administrative consultant whose contract calls for him only to improve the understanding and operational effectiveness of his consultees.

The skill and techniques of the mental health consultant in collecting information and communicating his plan in an acceptable way to those who have responsibility for the action outcome are the main focus of this chapter. The success of the consultation also depends on the expertness of the consultant in regard to the content matter of the problem on which he is being invited to help. A consultant who has excellent fact-finding and communications skills will fail if the content of his messages is poor because of lack of expert knowledge of the issue.

In client-centered mental health case consultation this situation is relatively simple. The mental health specialist is likely to have a more than adequate background of training and experience in psychiatry, psychology, psychiatric nursing, or psychiatric social work to enable him to make a correct clinical assessment of the client's condition and to develop a valid recommendation for remedial action based upon the current state of the clinical art. In administrative mental health consultation, on the other hand, the nature of the program or policy problem is likely to be such as to demand knowledge and experience in the fields of organizational theory and practice, planning, fiscal and personnel management, and the ramifications of general administration, in addition to the clinical area. This requires that the mental health consultant equip himself with this additional knowledge if he wishes to offer his services as an administrative consultant, even if he tries to restrict his operations to the "human relations" aspects of administration.

WHY SHOULD THE ADMINISTRATIVE CONSULTANT BE A MENTAL HEALTH SPECIALIST?

When a human services organization seeks administrative help, the question sometimes arises as to the relative advantages and disadvantages of calling in a management consultant, such as a specialist in business, industrial, or governmental administration, as against a mental health specialist with administrative competence. It is probable that many problems could be dealt with equally well by each of these specialists. There are generic aspects of the operations of all organizations, irrespective of their specific goals, so that many problems of planning, budgeting, personnel policies, and managerial controls in a program dealing with the prevention, treatment, and rehabilitation of mental disorders can be competently handled by an organizational specialist who has a modest knowledge of psychiatric issues. On the other hand, a mental health specialist is likely to have a more intimate and extensive knowledge of how such problems have been successfully and unsuccessfully dealt with in other settings and may be in a better position than a generic consultant to suggest an approach that is particularly tailored to the content area of the program.

For instance, a traditional management consultant might give as good advice as a mental health consultant to a state mental health department on how to organize a statewide program of decentralized community mental health center facilities through contracts with general hospitals. The community mental health specialist, however, may be more likely to question some of the consultees' basic premises in relation to the likelihood that such a system would lead to an innovative approach in reducing community rates of mental disorder in contrast to an alternative system that supplements the medical model with sociological and educational models. The latter models might point to developing services based in nonclinical community facilities, such as multiservice centers and community action programs for urban renewal.

A similar problem is not infrequently encountered in reverse. An organization or institution that has little or no explicit mental health "product," such as a general hospital, an army unit, a federal or state public health unit, or an industrial firm, may seek consultation on account of lowered efficiency, difficulties in planning and program development, and problems in personnel management. Such problems may involve a significant human relations factor—poor leadership, lowered morale, or communication blocks. All organizational consultants must deal with such issues in their everyday work; but when these issues are particularly obtrusive, there may be special merit in invoking the aid of an administrative consultant who is a mental health specialist. Some administrators think so, and increasingly over the last few years community mental health specialists have been called in to give advice on human relations aspects of administration. As someone who has had experience in such cases, with apparent success as judged by the implementation of my recommendations and a concurrent improvement in the problems for which I was brought in, I have sometimes asked myself whether there was any difference between what I did and what would have been done by an organizational consultant, such as someone from a management consultant firm or from Harvard Business School.

I have not yet been able to answer this question to my own satisfaction, except to say that perhaps my image as a physician competent in mental health makes it easier for me to penetrate the social system quickly and to develop relationships of trust and free communication with informants at different levels who rely on my confidentiality and on my not acting as an agent of the authority system in infringing on their individual interests. My clinical background in differential diagnosis allows me to focus quickly on salient issues without losing the implications of the whole complex of social system, subsystem, interpersonal, and personality factors in which they are embedded. My psychiatric knowledge allows me to place personality and interpersonal issues into perspective against the backdrop of organizational matters. And my community mental health practice skills enable me to collect and analyze data at the population level to complement what I pick up from individual and group interviews.

What emerges is a style of working and of communicating that may differ qualitatively from that of many consultants drawn from business management or organizational sociology, although I suspect that those whose personal talents are comparable to mine would probably focus on similar issues and make roughly similar recommendations.

RELATIONS WITH STAFF OF
CONSULTEE INSTITUTION

An important difference between administrative consultation and case consultation is that in the latter it is usually possible for the consultant to collect most of his data himself by conducting an appropriate clinical investigation of the client. Occasionally help may be needed from another specialist, such as a psychologist or psychiatric social worker, but these will probably be operating within the jurisdiction of the consultant. In most examples of administrative consultation, on the other hand, the consultant must rely for much of his data on the collaboration of the staff of the consultee institution. He gets some of his information directly from individual and group interviews in which he taps their opinions, but he also usually needs additional information about the internal and external affairs of the organization which comes from data that others must collect and assemble for him.

This means that administrative consultation often involves the expenditure of much time on the part of the institution's staff, and also that information which is usually not available to outsiders must be released for the consultant's use. These aspects must be specifically sanctioned by an appropriate authority in the hierarchy of the organization, and this sanction must be clearly communicated to all concerned.

It is important that an administrative consultant, who is being called in to deal with a particular problem, should initially appraise the area of the organization that is likely to be covered by his investigation and ensure that he is being called in by someone sufficiently high up in the organization so that he will be given sanction to move freely and to utilize staff time throughout that area. For instance, a consultant was called in by the assistant director of a state department of public health, who was in charge of the mental health unit, to advise on the reorganization of this unit in the light of developments in federal funding and state planning. A short preliminary discussion by telephone alerted the consultant to the fact that the problems of reorganization of the mental health unit were much affected by current plans for developing the alcoholism and the crippled children's programs of the state health department, which fell outside the jurisdiction of the assistant director in charge of mental health. The mental health specialist accordingly stipulated that he would be prepared to come only if he was called in by the director of the whole department as his consultant, so that he could be assured that all relevant operations of the organization would be open to his investigation, and so that the person to whom his recommendations would be addressed would have the necessary authority to implement them if they were found acceptable.

The usual necessity for the administrative consultant to operate collaboratively with wide sections of the staff of the organization involves two issues that sometimes lead to methodological difficulty.

First, the program-centered consultant must realize that he personally is the one who is responsible for collecting and analyzing the necessary information about the organization and developing the remedial recommendations. He should not be misled by the format of group discussions and the need for motivating staff to collaborate, through the utilization of group dynamics skills and knowledge of group process, into the belief that his role is to catalyze their collecting only the information they think relevant and working out their own solutions to their problems. The consultant will probably get as much out of such an approach as possible and will be interested in the staff's spontaneous suggestions and recommendations. But he must usually go beyond this, both in fact finding and in problem solving, because he will be held responsible for the content of assessment and of remedial recommendations and these must be based upon his own expert judgment and not restricted in any way by the limitations in knowledge, skill, and objectivity of the staff. Moreover, because program-centered administrative consultation is usually a relatively short process of a few days to a few weeks in duration, the consultant is operating under considerable time pressure, and he cannot afford to move at the slow speed that is likely to be comfortable for a staff which is confused and is struggling with communication blocks, or is relatively ineffective because of reduced morale associated with the problems that stimulated the request for consultation.

This type of approach is in marked contrast to the operations of an administrative consultant in consultee-centered consultation, in which the consultant's primary goal is, not his own rapid assessment of the administrative problems as a basis for a written report that lists his remedial recommendations, but working with the staff at a speed which is most comfortable for them, so that they may improve their own capacity to understand and master the problems they perceive within their administrative jurisdictions.

The second, and related, issue is that of the consultant's use of authority with the staff of the organization. It is important to realize that his consultee is not the staff group but the administrator who called him in. His relationship with this consultee must be a coordinate noncoercive one, as it is in all types of consultation discussed in this book. This administrator must be free, and must feel free, to accept or reject part or all of the consultant's recommendations.

On the other hand, the consultant's relationship to the administrator's subordinates is not coordinate. In order to accomplish his mission he must have authority to move freely within the organization, to obtain information, and to require the participation of its staff in his efforts, whether or not they agree with his plans and methods. Of course, in most instances he will be well advised not to throw his weight around and behave in an authoritarian manner, because this will arouse resistance and prevent him from obtaining the willing cooperation of the staff. Moreover, he cannot utilize more power that the administrator has given him; and the authority of his consultee may be limited and subject to sanction by people higher in the power network inside or outside the organization. But the consultant's friendly appeals for collaboration from the staff must be understood by him and by them to be underpinned by the authority vested in him by the chief; and occasionally this power must be clearly and quickly invoked in order to overcome an obstruction and get the job done.

For example, a consultant was called in by the head of a governmental department to advise on the reorganization of a certain division. On his arrival, after a long airplane flight, he had a short conference with his consultee, who told him that all the technical arrangements for his seven-day stay would be handled by the division chief, who was not available that afternoon but who would meet with him the following day. The next morning the consultant was surprised when, instead of the division chief, the latter's secretary came around to his hotel to welcome him. She brought a schedule of his appointments over the next five days that the division chief had prepared for him with exemplary efficiency. This program scheduled him in two-hourly blocks to meet with most of the unit heads of the entire department; but the list included very few of the line workers or even the supervisory staff of the division. The secretary hoped that the schedule met with his approval and had a car outside to convey him to the head office of the department to begin his program. The consultant asked whether he could first meet with the division chief and discuss the schedule, because at first sight it did not seem to be the best way of utilizing his time. The secretary replied that her chief was busy on some urgent business that morning and would not be available till later that day for such a discussion.

This situation presented the consultant with a dilemma. Apparently, the division chief was defensive about his visit and was possibly avoiding him. There was nothing obviously wrong with the schedule except that it filled his time completely and left him little room to maneuver, as well as leading him mainly into the general field of forces in the department rather than into the internal affairs of the division that he had been called in to investigate. And yet it would obviously be rather rude to question the arrangements that had been so efficiently made on his behalf and that were being so obligingly pressed upon him by the charming girl who had been sent to guide him. To accept the arrangements graciously would calm the fears of the division chief, and perhaps there would be time later that day to discuss the program and negotiate its modification. On the other hand, it might be that the absent division chief would persist in being otherwise engaged—his own name did not appear on the interviewing schedule until the fourth day! By then it might be too late to collect enough information about the division to make a valid assessment of its problems. Perhaps the price of being non-threatening was to accept a role of impotence.

The consultant asked the secretary where her chief was at that moment. With some reluctance, she divulged that he was chairing a meeting of the unit chiefs of his division at one of their divisional office buildings on the outskirts of the city, several miles away from the headquarters of the department where the consultant's scheduled interviewees were awaiting him. The consultant then told her that he was sorry that he could not accept the schedule of interviews and asked her to drive him to the divisional office and then to inform his interviewees at headquarters that he would see them at a later date. He dealt in a friendly but firm manner with her protests, and she took him to the divisional office.

Once there, he found out where the meeting was being held and, without more ado, marched into the room. To the consternation of the division chief, he interrupted the meeting; introduced himself to the assembled group; told them about his mission and about his mandate from the head of the department; and said that their meeting provided him with an unexpected and marvelous opportunity to meet immediately with the principal people whose views on the problems confronting the division he was eager to obtain. He then said that if the division chief had no objection, he would like to pre-empt the meeting time to discuss these matters, since he had traveled several thousand miles to get there and had very little time available to reach the core of the situation. The division chief was obviously furious but could do nothing but meekly go along with this *fait accompli;* and there followed two hours of explosive and illuminating discussion, which laid bare the fundamental problems of the division that underlay the request of the department head for consultation help.

This dramatic action on the part of the consultant initiated a process of rapid fact finding. He was able to overcome the initial authoritarian impression he had made on most of the staff when they became familiar with his style of conducting individual and group interviews. The division chief, however, not unnaturally, never completely warmed up to him, although by the end of the visit even he began to respect the competence and sincerity of the consultant and to realize that his worst fears about him were ill founded.

Such highhanded and defense-attacking coercive behavior should be an infrequent occurrence in this type of consultation, but a consultant should feel free to make use of it whenever the situation so demands. More frequent is the need to influence the staff of an institution to realize that although the consultant carries the authority of the director, and although the latter may perhaps be correctly or incorrectly perceived as authoritarian and coercive, the consultant normally holds his power in reserve and conducts his business on the basis of a free interchange with staff, to whose needs he is sensitive and upon whose personal and professional rights he takes pains not to infringe, within the relatively wide range of latitude that his role usually affords him. Only if there is an obvious attempt to obstruct him or to manipulate him too far off course must he invoke his power.

CONSULTATION PROCEDURE

Preliminary Contacts and Negotiating the Initial Agreement

The first contact is usually by telephone, and if by letter this is usually a short and vague communication, which is best followed up by a direct telephone conversation.

The representative of the potential consultee institution who first writes or speaks to the consultant is rarely its director but usually one of his staff who has been deputed to explore whether, and how, consultation may be arranged.

It is always worth trying to find out how the consultant's name came up for consideration in this matter, because it throws light on the expectations of the administrators in trying to involve him in their predicament. Often they say they heard of him through some personal contact —one of his former students or a mutual acquaintance—that they have read some of his contributions to the mental health literature, or that they have heard of his successful consultation to a similar institution or with a comparable problem.

Occasionally, the initial request may not be explicitly for a consultation but to give a lecture or conduct a seminar; and only as this request, which is usually expressed in vague terms, is clarified, does it transpire that what the administrators really want is to get to know him and to find out whether he is competent and willing to help with their administrative problems. In such a case, the consultant may agree to come out to give some lectures; but he would be well advised to offer in addition that he would be willing first to explore the program and reality situation of the organization in order to discover how his visit can be most useful to them, and what content should be included in his educational efforts in order to make sense to their staff. Such a discussion often rapidly leads to a reformulation in which the basic need of the administrators for consultation begins to take precedence over the request for the in-service education of their staff.

The preliminary exploratory telephone discussions are usually helped by the consultant's very free admission of his ignorance about the problems posed by the administrators. His posture should be the realistic one that although he is a specialist in mental health and in consultation, he cannot initially judge to what extent his knowledge and experience may be relevant and helpful in the current situation. He must therefore find out more about it; and even if he agrees to come on a visit, he cannot guarantee to do more than explore the problems and be as helpful with as many of them as time will permit.

If the organization is one of a type that he has not yet worked in, he should frankly say so. He should indicate his hope that his experience with roughly similar organizations may be of help in this situation, but that he will need quickly to learn some of the elementary information about the culture and traditions of this new institution and its program elements. He should emphasize, and in this he should be sincere, that he has no pat formula or prearranged administrative pattern or system into which he can fit the problems of an unfamiliar organization.

This reality-based modesty begins to mold the expectations of the administrators about the kind of assistance they can get from him. It also sets the stage for a series of exploratory telephone conversations, during which the rough outlines of the consultation problems are mapped out against the backdrop of the organizational setting.

As already indicated, one initial goal of the consultant is to identify the level in the authority hierarchy of the organization from which he should draw his consultee. Whenever he is in doubt, he should go for the man at the top, at least in the locality from which the call is coming. This is usually the man who was involved in the decision to contact him. For instance, when I was phoned by the Head of Professional Services of the Indian Health Area in Arizona, I suggested that I would be willing to consider coming as the consultant to the director of that area, who I discovered had considerable local autonomy over his program; and I did not feel that my consultee should be the Head of the Division of Indian Health in Washington, who was his immediate superior.

The person making the initial contact with the consultant is usually not upset by the suggestion that the primary consultee be his administrative superior. On the contrary, it has been my experience that this is usually welcomed, since it shows that the consultant recognizes the need for adequate sanction for his entry into the organization and for direct contact with someone empowered to carry out his recommendations.

If the initiative for the first contact did not come from the director of a service but from one of his subordinates, and if there is reluctance in involving the director, the consultant should think twice before accepting the invitation. He will almost certainly encounter insurmountable opposition from other unit heads in the organization who are at the same level as the person or group who called him in and whose interests conflict with theirs. In such a situation the most the consultant should promise is to come for an exploratory visit to ascertain the nature of the problem and to recommend with whom it would be advisable to consult.

It will then be necessary to identify on the spot the person with power to sanction his fact finding and to implement his recommendations and then to find out whether this man wishes to accept him as his consultant.

Two other issues must be settled during the preliminary telephone negotiations. First, the length of the consultation visit must be determined, and whether the consultant will come alone or with a team of assistants. This depends on the amount of ground to be covered in the assessment of the consultation problem; the availability of consultant resources; and the financial constraints, which should be very frankly discussed and decided. The second point is to set up arrangements so that the consultant may learn as much as possible ahead of time about the consultee organization and its current administrative predicament, and so that relevant members of its staff should begin systematically to think about the nature and boundaries of the problems on which they and their director would like the consultant's help.

I have found it useful to have a telephone talk with the director in order to initiate the consultant-consultee relationship. During this discussion, I usually suggest that he appoint a task force, drawn from different units and administrative levels of his organization, which will work with me in clarifying the nature of the problems as seen by his staff. I say that I will eventually discuss my recommendations with this task force, so that they may be evaluated and modified in the light of the current realities of the day-to-day operations of the program. I then ask the director to send me as much written material as possible, which I can read in order to brief myself on the structure, history, traditions, and problems of his organization. I ask particularly for organization charts, with the names of current officeholders, and copies of recent internal memoranda that deal with relevant issues. I also ask the director and his staff to send me a rank-ordered list of the administrative problems on which they want my consultant help; and I make it clear that the relatively short duration of my consulting visit, which is all that we can afford in the light of mutual time and financial constraints, is not likely to be enough for us to work on more than a few of the problems at the top of the list.

Following these telephone discussions, there should be an exchange of letters between consultant and consultees, so that the details of agreements can be recorded and specifically ratified by both sides. This ensures that when the visit takes place there is a maximum opportunity for consensus on what each side should expect to give to and receive from the other, and so that the time can be most productively used to solve the mutually agreed upon tasks.

Preparation for the Consultation Visit

Once the consultant has agreed to visit the consultee organization, he should use the intervening time to learn as much as possible about the setting and the problems of the consultees, as well as to anticipate the predictable issues in the consultation and how to deal with them.

He will be helped by reading the documents sent by the consultees. It is important to study these, not only as a factual account of the consultee organization and its personalities, but also as a preliminary opportunity to understand the value system, operating style, and preoccupations of its staff.

If the consultee organization deals with a content area with which the consultant is unfamiliar, he should also use the lead time in doing some library research. For instance, before my consultation visit to Arizona, I read a number of books about Indians; and while preparing for a consultation visit to Alaska, I read some books about Eskimos and an ethnographic account of one of the native villages I was being asked to visit as part of my field observations. In both cases, I found the knowledge I had gleaned, superficial though it was, of great value in orienting me to what I should look for in exploring the work of the health services with which I was consulting.

The more ignorant a consultant is in regard to the content area of the consultee institution's mission or about the social, cultural, political, or geographic setting in which it operates, the bigger the potential return from reading a few books ahead of time. Not only can he "tune in" more quickly to the realities of the consultee setting, but he can impress the consultees with his serious approach to understanding their situation and his awareness that he has a lot to learn from them. He can capitalize on his initial naïveté in arousing their trust, but by "doing his homework" he shows that this naïveté is not synonymous with simple-mindedness and so he also stimulates the building of respect.

In addition to books and local documents, the consultant should also try to use collateral informants. If he searches, he will often find others in his city who have a specialized knowledge about the consultee institution or profession, or about the sociocultural and ecological setting in which it operates. Such informants may also be able to suggest others to whom he can turn for guidance and advice. Naturally, he will preserve the confidentiality of his assignment; but this is not difficult, because all he need divulge is that he is going out to study the local situation or give some lectures. Especially if the consultee institution is in some distant place or unusual setting, I have found it very easy to get a lot of information from others who have been there before me, and who seem delighted to have the opportunity to talk about their travels and to share their ideas on local customs or about relevant books. They may also provide the names of some of their own contacts out there, and sometimes these can be useful; but I have often found that when I arrive on the spot it may not be politically expedient to look up these friends of my home contacts, because they are outside the circle of my consultee group or sometimes are members of opposition groups in the community.

In addition to these general informants, an experienced consultant usually develops a network of specialized informants, some of whom can give him confidential background information about the field of forces in the consultee agency and possibly about recent events that may have led up to the request for consultation. The telephone is a useful device for getting such information, and my long-distance telephone bill always rises steeply during the weeks before I travel to a program-centered administrative consultation. Confidentiality is still an issue in such communication, although the nature of the relationship between the consultant and his specialized key informants may permit him to go into more detail about his assignments because he can trust the other person not to divulge the information. Even with close friends, however, I make it a practice to be explicit to them and to myself about the boundaries of confidentiality in discussing the details of the preliminary data on a consultation case. Such self-discipline is valuable in preventing the little slips of the tongue that can have major negative consequences to a consultant's reputation and effectiveness.

During the preparatory period the consultant should also try to initiate meaningful communication with some staff members of the consultee institution, either by an exchange of letters or telephone calls with individuals to clarify specific issues, or by starting a dialogue with the advisory committee that may be set up by the director. In my experience, these attempts usually do not get very far. The consultee institution staff is busy at its day-to-day activities, and the consultant becomes a reality to them only after he has appeared on the site. Apart from the liaison person with whom the initial negotiations were carried out, it is unlikely that many other people in the consultee institution can be significantly involved in building up relationships at a distance. But some effort along these lines is worth expending, if only to improve the consonance of expectations on both sides, so that when the consultant arrives he can as soon as possible begin to work collaboratively with the consultee group. I like to think of this as "getting on the same wave length," which implies recognizing what issues seem significant to the others and learning something about values and semantic barriers that will have to be surmounted.

In administrative consultation, time is usually of the essence; and anything that can be done, however slight, to accelerate this process before the consultant arrives is of potential value.

Initial Process after Consultant Enters Consultee Organization

Negotiating the Contract

The first goal of the consultant on arrival in the consultee organization is to confirm the identity of his consultee and to negotiate the final consultation agreement or contract with him, based upon the provisional contract that was decided upon ahead of time. The length of the visit, the remuneration, and the nature of the consultation report will probably already have been fixed, but within this framework much still has to be decided.

The consultant must confirm the direct line of communication between himself and the authority figure with whom he is consulting and ensure that this communication will not take place through intermediaries, important as it will be for the head of the institution or department to delegate one or more members of his staff to help the consultant implement his plans.

I have found it valuable to meet alone with the director as soon as possible after my arrival in his organization, and to have a confidential chat about his view of the administrative problem and of my possible contribution to its solution. Involved also are the initial steps in building the consultation relationship. The issues in relationship building in administrative consultation are similar to those in other types of consultation and have already been discussed in previous chapters.

In this initial conversation, the consultant must ascertain what problems are of most importance to the administrator and must quickly judge which of these he is likely to be able to handle within the time limits of his visit. He should share with the administrator the predictable limitations of his contribution and should involve him in a joint decision about priorities. The consultant should be alert to avoid undertaking a commitment for help with problem solving outside the jurisdiction of the administrator, both because of the greater difficulty in getting information quickly from people whom the administrator does not control and because the administrator's power to implement the consultant's recommendations will be limited outside his own domain. On the other hand, it is important for the consultant to allot some of his time and energy for independently assessing, if only superficially, the external field problems faced by the organization in fulfilling its mission. In his initial conversation with the administrator, as they are planning how the consultant will spend his time during the visit, he should emphasize the necessity for this.

For example, during a recent ten-day consultation visit to the Alaska Native Health Area in order to advise its director on interpersonal aspects of administration, I felt that, despite my prior reading, I knew so little about the realities of Eskimo and Indian life and health problems that I could not make sense of the internal predicaments of the staff in relation to morale, communications, and personnel policies unless I obtained some firsthand experience of conditions in native villages and small towns. I had communicated this view during preliminary telephone discussions before my visit. But in a conversation with the area director shortly after I arrived, we discussed the optimal ratio of deployment of my time in native villages, field units, and the area office in Anchorage; and we decided that after half a day's meeting with the core staff in Anchorage I should spend three days at a field health station about eight hundred miles away and go by boat up a nearby river to visit four Eskimo villages and fishing camps. This turned out to be a wise allocation of my resources, because by the time I got back to Anchorage I had obtained considerable information about the realistic aspects of the mission of the program that served as a framework within which to explore the problems of the Anchorage staff in carrying it out.

Another goal of this initial discussion with the administrator is to achieve consensus on the ground rules of the consultation process, particularly in regard to the consultant's way of working with the staff of the organization. The consultant should ask the administrator to sanction his obtaining information from them relevant to the exploration of the problems on which the administrator is soliciting his advice. This request should include discussing how this sanction is to be communicated to the administrator's subordinates in order to ensure their collaboration. But the consultant must also emphasize that he can operate effectively only if he can encourage staff to talk freely without fear that "incriminating" details will be divulged to their superiors. The administrator must not only explicitly sanction the consultant to withhold from him material that may reflect on personalities in his organization—at least information communicated in confidence by them to the consultant —but he must also let his staff know that he has guaranteed this privilege.

Another point that should be clarified in the initial interview is that the consultant will probably arrive at his formulations by progressive approximations. He will collect some data, develop a currently meaningful formulation of a problem and some possible solutions, and then share these ideas with relevant individuals and groups of staff in order to get their reactions and suggestions for modification both of his statement of the problem and his range of solutions. This will then lead him to collect further information to refine his formulations, which will again lead to feedback and modification.

The administrator should be asked to what degree he personally wishes to be involved in this process. He may wish to wait until the end of the visit. If possible, the consultant should encourage him to make himself available on his own, or with some of his senior staff, from time to time during the course of the consultation process, so that his own reactions to the unfolding pattern can mold the consultant's ideas. In many of my consultations I have arranged to meet the administrator for lunch or dinner intermittently during my visit; and I have found these opportunities for informal interchanges invaluable, both in keeping him informed and maintaining my sanction, as well as in checking out my hunches and involving him in shaping my plans.

It is also advisable at this initial meeting to set up some formal channels for presentation of the consultation report. The consultant will usually be asked for a written report, and this will be included and paid for in the contract. Preferably, it should be submitted within a couple of weeks after the visit, so that it can capitalize on the interest aroused by the consultant's personal interventions. The consultant should let the administrator know that all the points raised in the written report will have been discussed with him before the consultant leaves. The administrator should decide not only on a private reporting session but usually also on a formal session to include the key staff at which the consultant, in the presence of the administrator, will present and defend his recommendations.

Getting a Bird's-Eye View of the Problem and Its Ramifications

In order to plan the consultation program, the consultant must be prepared to make a rapid initial assessment of the structure and culture of the consultee organization and of the nature of the predicament in which his help has been invoked. He will already have some vague ideas on this before he arrives, and his confidential talk with the administrator will have firmed up the picture. He should, however, be particularly alert, in his initial formal and informal contacts with everyone connected with the organization, to modify and then reformulate the main outlines of this picture. At this stage he should not be particularly interested in details but in a general pattern, which will guide him in regard to the people and units that he should explore. The consultant should not be afraid to "play his hunches" in formulating this initial *gestalt,* even on flimsy evidence; but he should be equally quick and confident in modifying the pattern in response to discrepant information, to which he should be particularly open.

Because of the time pressure, and because of the inevitable confusion in the mind of anyone entering a social system that generates numerous and complex stimuli on many different levels, especially as the newcomer penetrates deeper into its life, the fate of the whole consultation may hinge upon a valid initial orienting formulation that will guide the consultant in choosing avenues to explore. More than any other aspect of consultation, I have found this to be most demanding on the native talent of the consultant. Increasing experience will give a consultant the confidence to react intuitively; seminars and supervision during consultation training will help him increase his sophistication in regard to systematic ways of exploring the field; clinical and community mental health training and skill will enable him to be more comfortable in judging the relevant emphasis to place on personality, small-group, and organizational factors; but in the last analysis I believe that consultation is an art, and that the basic asset which enables a man to be an excellent consultant is an elusive fundamental attribute of his total personality. It is this that molds his perceptions and enables him to react intuitively to his initial impressions.

I am aware that my approach to this issue is that of a clinician, who is trained to make a differential diagnosis by a process of successive approximations; and it may be that a consultant who comes into this field from social science may use a different approach, based upon the systematic collection of data and upon suspending judgment until these data are analyzed. It would be interesting to explore this issue but, as elsewhere in this book, I am aware that I am presenting principles which are derived from my own experience and that of like-minded colleagues and which therefore are consonant with our own style. Many students have validated that this is not entirely idiosyncratic, but I particularly do not claim that these principles are universal; and I am confident that there are other styles of consulting which are likely to achieve as good or, in certain situations, better results.

Fact Finding

Once the consultant has a clear idea of the principal problems to which he must address himself, he must collect the information needed in order to understand them and to clarify the possible solutions. He does this mainly by talking to individuals and groups both formally and informally, as well as by observing the behavior of the staff of the organization as they go about their daily work and as they interact with each other socially outside the job setting.

Some consultants supplement relatively unstructured individual and group interviews by developing interview schedules and questionnaires for use by auxiliary field interviewers, especially in assessing the attitudes and opinions of the staff of a large organization. I make little or no use of such survey techniques, and rely on a more "clinical" approach based upon data collected by personal interview or direct observation from individuals and groups that I judge to be representative of the whole organization or to be of key importance in relation to the problem under study.

I begin my interviewing by working through a list of key people and groups that I have drawn up in collaboration with the director or his assistant. My first interviews are usually rather long and full; but as I learn more about the situation the interviews become shorter, and I search only for supplementary information or for items that validate my hunches about particular patterns or issues. I often ask interviewees to recommend other informants both inside and outside their section of the organization, and once a pattern clarifies I cross check by a kind of triangulation process—that is, I try to get perceptions of it from people with different points of view.

The process of fact finding usually goes through three phases. Initially, I have a relatively clear idea of what I am looking for—for example, information about the causes of low morale in a certain unit, or about poor communication and collaboration between two divisions, or about ineffective performance in a particular department. This clarity emerges from the stated perceptions of my consultee or from my reformulation of his problem.

The second phase begins as I collect information from various people about their perceptions of the issue and their explanations of the factors involved. Characteristically, these stories conflict, and each interview brings to light fresh dimensions and reverberations of the problem. My initial clarity gives way to confusion. It is important that I accept this confusion and do not try too early to resolve it by accepting one or another ready explanation put forward by my informants or derived from my own experience of similar situations I have encountered in other places. The confusion is cognitively and affectively burdensome, but I have learned to avoid premature closure and to allow it to continue until it resolves spontaneously as further information comes to light and is intuitively organized into a meaningful *gestalt*. The pressure to premature clarification is aggravated by the need to produce a quick answer to the consultation questions. Much experience has taught me a practical time perspective in this regard, which I use to maintain my equanimity during the phase of confusion.

I have found that, leaving aside the period of preliminary exploration and fact finding about the external field of forces within which the consultee organization operates—for example, in the Alaska case, the three days I spent visiting Eskimo villages and observing the work of a peripheral health unit—I can safely allow one third to one half of the remainder of my consultation time to be spent in a state of greater or lesser confusion. During this phase I purposefully do not attempt to pin down a conceptual pattern or to tie ends together and to reconcile apparent incompatibilities in the data. Nor do I focus too narrowly on the lines of inquiry that I originally set up; but I allow myself, as it were, to roam the field in response to whatever cues appear of intrinsic interest. This is a process not unlike the unfocused attentiveness of an analyst to the free associations of his analysand. And as in that situation, I rely upon my unconscious or my "intuition" to produce the integrating pattern.

The third phase is that of the *gestalt closure*. Suddenly or gradually, the pattern takes shape and I begin to see what appears to be happening and how different strands of factors on a variety of parameters associated with different systems and subsystems are meshing to produce the presenting situation.

In phase three, which can be called the phase of cognitive organization, the whole picture in all its ramifications is rarely seen immediately. Most often, part of the picture becomes visible and then in successive insights additional facets clarify and articulate with the rest, often as a result of looking for and finding supplementary information.

The list of informants varies with the three phases. In the first phase, a logical list is drawn up that mirrors the formal organization chart and is made up of people and groups who would be expected to relate to the problem at issue. It is rare for a consultant to interview everyone on this original list, so he should make it clear that it represents only a tentative plan or else some sensitive members of staff will be insulted because he has bypassed them, implying that he considers their views to be unimportant.

The reason why the consultant does not complete these scheduled appointments is that he moves into the second phase, and then he no longer is certain that he understands the focus of the problem. It is important that he not waste time by, as it were, perseverating with his initial list, because this will probably lead to the collection of redundant data. In fact, it is an awareness of this redundancy which usually alerts the consultant to the fact that his original choice of interviewees is ceasing to be productive. At this stage, the consultant should begin to work on an *ad hoc* basis, and he should choose his next couple of informants on the basis of leads suggested by his current interviewee.

When he reaches the third phase, the consultant will once again develop a clear idea of the relevant people to interview, because he will know who can be expected to validate his thesis or what new avenues he must explore in order to enrich or round out the picture. Some of these will be people he has previously seen and from whom he requires specific additional information or opinions.

During the second phase, of confusion, some consultants maintain their composure by going through a systematic set of explorations of issues, such as the quality of morale of the unit, the nature of its leadership, how power is allotted and used, and the nature of the communication process within the unit and between it and its surroundings. I feel that any system of this type, while supportive to the consultant, is often rather a waste of effort. I rely instead on my hunches and on cues of the moment to determine pragmatically what to do next.

In all phases of data collection, chance informal contacts often reveal valuable information and insights. At social gatherings after working hours the consultant's presence usually catalyzes discussions that overtly or covertly deal with the salient issues of the organization. The consultant need feel no guilt about receiving information informally from the families and friends of the staff, or from workers in other branches of the organization, as long as he introduces himself clearly as someone who has been invited to study local organizational problems. On such consultation visits a consultant is "on duty" twenty-four hours a day. This is quite fatiguing, but just as patients often make their most significant remarks as they are leaving the office, so the informal aside of a peripheral person at a social gathering may be the key to the consultation puzzle; and the consultant's professional alertness on all such occasions may reap important harvests.

For example, a consultant visiting the home of a senior staff member was introduced to another member of staff who had just returned from vacation and so had not been on the list of interviewees. This individual, who had not heard about the consultant, was told briefly about the purpose of the visit and immediately launched into a list of the many administrative problems he was encountering in his communications with the specialists at headquarters. Among his complaints was his anger at being forbidden to use the telephone to consult with his senior colleagues about difficult cases. Instead, allegedly in order to reduce the expense of the telephone bill, he had been instructed to make such communications in writing. But the overworked specialists at headquarters usually did not reply for several weeks, and this often meant that his patients were ineffectively treated in the meantime, and some of them were kept in the hospital unnecessarily, which represented a much greater waste of money than the cost of a telephone call. When the consultant returned to headquarters she inquired from the director of the department why there needed to be such tight control over telephone expenses in an organization with a far-flung system of field stations. The director was amazed at the question and maintained stoutly that he actually encouraged telephone communication as a way of reducing the travel costs of his central specialist group. Without revealing the identity of her informant, the consultant pressed the director to try to explain the discrepancy between his views and the complaints of the man in the field. Eventually, it emerged that the director had some months previously been interested in analyzing the pattern of telephone communication in his department and had sent out a request for information from field units about their use of telephone communication in contrast to written communication with specialists at headquarters. He was amazed that this innocent request had become garbled as an authoritarian message prohibiting telephone communication.

This incident led the consultant to the realization that the director, who was a quiet, nonauthoritarian person, was being misperceived by many of his staff, especially by those in field stations who had little chance of getting to know him personally, as a kind of "gray eminence" who was exercising an iron control over their every activity. This finding, in turn, illuminated other aspects of the administrative climate of the organization; and the consultant began to understand how the image of the director among his staff was being molded, not by his actual personality, but by some of his subordinates who acted as his intermediaries with the organization at large and who were influencing the development of a rigid authoritarian atmosphere.

This example raises another issue. A mental health consultant who is called in to help deal with human relations problems in administration is expected to emphasize the influence of the personality of administrators, particularly personality disorders, upon the problems of the organization. Information relevant to this factor is often pressed upon the consultant, and sometimes it is sufficiently dramatic and diagnostically intriguing to persuade the consultant to see it as the focal point of the predicament. Such a formulation is usually an oversimplification and often leads to missing the main point of the etiology of the administrative impasse.

The key person may in fact have a personality disorder, and this may be one factor in the situation; but usually there are also many other factors operating, and it is the constellation as a whole that is determining the sequence of events, including why the administrator's idiosyncratic quirks are being currently stimulated and why he is being allowed or encouraged to distort his role functioning. The special merit of having an administrative consultant who is a mental health specialist is that his expert knowledge should enable him to see a personality idiosyncrasy in proper perspective, not as a stereotyped fixed "thing" but as a function of a person in a field of forces. The consultant must not be so impressed by the dramatic or peculiar aspects of one person's behavior that he does not search for the interpersonal, intergroup, and system factors that are also operative in the situation.

For example, in a social welfare agency the morale in a particular department was very low, as evidenced among other facts by a high turnover rate among the junior staff. When the consultant interviewed the agency director and a number of the caseworkers, the consensus appeared to be that the prime cause of the low morale was the rigidly obsessional personality of the chief supervisor of that unit. This was apparently confirmed by her behavior and statements when she was interviewed. On the other hand, whether or not she had personality difficulties, it seemed clear from her account of the predicament of her unit that she was confronted by an extremely complex and difficult set of reality factors, related to the attitudes and problems of her client population, which was in a state of violent upheaval.

The consultant was not satisfied that the personality disorder of the supervisor was the main cause of the low morale of her staff, and he asked the director to obtain the figures for staff turnover in that unit over the previous ten years. These revealed that the attrition rate of line workers had started rising five years previously; and even though it was higher now than in units dealing with other parts of the city, it had fallen significantly during the two years since the supervisor had taken over the unit. Moreover, it appeared that the supervisor's personality difficulties were well known in the agency, and she had been transferred to this difficult unit as a kind of punishment after having a difference of opinion with the director about her handling of a personnel problem in another part of the agency.

The headquarters staff were frustrated because they could not fire her on account of civil service protection, and they were expecting that she would make trouble wherever she was placed. In addition, the consultant felt that the advisory board of the agency was ambivalent about its service to the client population served by that unit. This mirrored a major conflict in the community. It had resulted in the deployment of a smaller slice of the agency's resources than might be considered optimal for dealing with that population—including the appointment of a supervisor with a poor reputation. Also, the supervisor was given less administrative support by headquarters staff than other supervisors in grappling with current difficulties.

By widening the focus of his data collection beyond the nature and effects of the supervisor's personality disorder, the consultant was thus able to understand the richer complexity of the agency system and community supersystem problems, and within this framework to assess the significance of the various factors in developing suggestions for amelioration.

During the third phase, of cognitive organization, and while the consultant is beginning to develop recommendations for solving the administrative problems, it is often valuable to assemble *ad hoc* groups drawn from the various units of the organization that have a bearing on the issue. One or two meetings with such a group will allow the consultant to pose the salient problem and get all the staff talking about their perceptions of it and their suggestions for a solution. Such horizontal communication cuts across the usual boundary lines of vertically organized units and allows the consultant to validate his hunches as well as to understand more clearly why certain "logical" remedies may not work because of current realities in the agency.

The consultant must use such *ad hoc* groupings sparingly. These meetings interrupt the usual routine of the organization, especially as they have to be convened at short notice and primarily at the convenience of the consultant rather than fitted into that of the staff. Moreover, it is not unusual for such meetings to endanger the participants' defenses that have been maintained by selective inattention to certain aspects of the problem and by lack of communication between particular units. The meetings may therefore be burdensome both for task-oriented and for affective reasons. It is well that the consultant should delay the use of such meetings till the final stages of his visit, by which time he has hopefully built up a good relationship with the staff of the consultee institution and has begun to demonstrate that they can expect some concrete benefits in return for the upsets and burdens he is causing them.

A small but important practical issue in regard to fact finding is that of record keeping. A vast amount of data in the form of verbal and nonverbal communications, as well as documents and statistical tables, is usually rapidly accumulated. The consultant will be expected to keep the relevant issues constantly in focus and to have various details and facts readily available for use in his verbal and written reports.

An excellent memory is a useful asset for an administrative consultant. Since I, unfortunately, have a poor memory, I have had to develop ways of compensating. Taking notes is the obvious answer, but this interferes with the spontaneity of the consultation process and adds a special burden to the consultant who wishes to focus his attention on the many complicated issues of an interview or a group discussion. I have sometimes been lucky enough to have an assistant who acts as a recorder, and this has been invaluable—although apart from using the records as a source of information about names and titles of interviewees, I must admit that I only really utilize them to check my memory for a few details. Their value is mainly psychological—I do not have to be concerned that I won't remember some detail, because it is being recorded. This frees me to remember what I need. Interestingly enough, I do seem to remember the important things. The reason probably is that I immerse myself experientially so completely in the consultation situation and in the current life of the consultee organization that for a while it is my life; the details do not have to be remembered as an explicit act, like, for example, trying to recall something one has read in a book or heard in a lecture.

When I have no recorder I take notes myself at the time. These are usually quite rough and consist mainly of cue phrases about topics or personalities. The only specific information I record meticulously is the name and title of individual interviewees and group participants. At the stage of writing my report, this information is essential, and it is quite frustrating not to have it readily available.

Another practice that I have found useful is to spend a little time at the end of each day, or occasionally during a rest period while waiting for an interviewee, to summarize in writing the main points of the day's events and issues. The time is mainly taken up in thinking rather than writing. And the latter usually involves only jotting down a series of rough notes to remind me subsequently of the points. They are in no sense a narrative that would be understandable to anybody else.

Developing the Recommendations—Repeated Feedback and Modifications

As previously indicated, the consultant's recommendations are developed and refined as a series of progressive approximations. He should discipline himself to avoid starting this process until phase three of his fact finding when he begins to get a clear idea of the dimensions and etiological constellation of particular problems. Suggestions for action during the phase of confusion are usually attempts at premature closure to escape the frustration of that period; and ideas for solution that emerge during the first phase of initial clarity should be studiously inhibited, because almost inevitably they will be based upon oversimplifications and preconceptions that miss the main obstacles of the situation. If the predicament were so simple that an outsider could arrive at a sensible plan from a cursory review of superficial information, it would usually have been handled by the administrators without his help. In fact, the quick *tour de force* of a visiting expert, even if occasionally sensible, will have a noxious effect on the development of the consultation relationship, because the consultees will feel that the consultant does not have a proper respect for their intelligence and commitment to their task if he believes that he can immediately produce an answer to the problems that perplex them. This is complicated by the fact that consultees often test out the consultant by demanding such an immediate answer from him. Their ambivalence will become apparent if he falls into the trap of accepting the gambit!

Initial formulation of recommendations can also be delayed too long, with negative consequences. The consultant must continually pace himself in relation to the trajectory of his site visit. He must leave adequate time to refine his recommendations by discussing them with the staff of the consultee organization. Under all circumstances he should try to avoid developing a plan and including it in his report without giving the staff a chance to discuss it. This is not merely a relationship-building issue but is based upon our experience that unless people are personally involved in collaborating with the consultant in developing a plan, they are less likely to accept it and work toward its implementation. The main issue is that in the short time at his disposal the consultant cannot possibly obtain more than a superficial view of the life of the organization; and although this may be sufficient to enable him to foresee the main impact of a recommendation, it will not be enough to tell him about its side effects and about the consequences for the plan of reactive reverberations within the system. Only those who have a living experience of the organization are likely to be able to predict in detail the practical implications of the changes the consultant is recommending.

The seductive aspect of the undiscussed recommendation is that it usually seems clean cut and logical, precisely because the ideas do not get confused and obscured by discordant facts and probabilities.

Having regard to all these considerations, consultants should aim to begin formulating their recommendations piecemeal and in tentative terms shortly after the beginning of the third phase of their fact finding —that is, as soon as they begin to understand clearly what some of the problems are and which etiological factors are involved. I make it a practice to open most of my interviews and group meetings from that stage on with a brief formulation of how the situation seems to me and what I think might be done about it; and then I ask the staff to react to my ideas, correct or modify them in the light of their more intimate knowledge of the local situation, and provide more information to broaden and deepen my understanding.

In such an interchange, it is important for the consultant not to hide the tentative and exploratory nature of his ideas, and for him to be completely sincere and frank in soliciting divergent opinions. Many people are concerned lest a consultant, and especially a mental health consultant who is often stereotyped in Machiavellian terms, manipulate them by forcing his ideas onto them. They will be particularly alert to evidence that although he solicits their reactions, he is not really interested in any ideas that negate his own. Because of this, the consultant should be perfectly open about what he is doing, and about the degree of his own commitment at that time to any of the ideas he puts forward. And he should let people know whether or not he accepts their suggested modifications.

The consultant should not modify his plans merely because they disturb or arouse opposition among the organization staff. His recommendations almost inevitably will imply changes from accustomed patterns of thought and practice, and such changes often make some people uncomfortable. It is important that the consultant neither accept nor reject discordant ideas merely because of this factor. Instead, he should pay careful attention both to the emotional and cognitive response to his tentative recommendations and in the light of this added information decide whether and in what ways to modify his recommendations.

A consultant's recommendation develops by accretion, like a snowball, getting progressively richer, more detailed, and more complicated, as the consultant discusses it successively with different members of the consultee organization's staff. It is useful to conduct these discussions systematically at as many levels of the administrative structure as possible, and to feed back and forth between them.

The consultant might identify a problem at the level of a unit chief and explore it by talking to the chiefs of other units of that and other divisions and departments. He shares his tentative formulations and suggestions with them and then with the division and department heads and with the staff of the director's office. At each higher level of the structure he discovers new constraints and demands and modifies his plan to conform with them. Then he takes it back to the unit chiefs to see how it looks to them in its revised form, and whether it is generalizable across units with different clienteles and working conditions. Eventually the consultant presents the latest revision of the plan to *ad hoc* groups which are composed of representatives of different levels of the structure and in which its horizontal and vertical reverberations can be assessed.

For instance, in my consultation with the Alaska Native Health Area, I was asked by the director to advise on the recruitment and training of village health aides. I discussed this issue with the head of the Area Office of Training Services, who told me of his plans to establish a training program at the Native Medical Center in Anchorage, where Eskimos and Indians would be trained in elementary medical and surgical procedures and in practical nursing and then deployed in native villages, where they would be the local representatives of the doctors and nurses of the health service units.

When I visited a health service unit in the field and some Eskimo villages I discussed the problem as seen from those levels; and what had started as a simple matter of curriculum development and of training techniques began to take on a different shape. It became clear that because of the vast distances involved and the difficulties of travel and transportation, the village representative of the health service should not only be a technical assistant to the doctors and nurses but should have considerable capacity for independent judgment, even though he could operate under the control of the medical and nursing staff of his district by means of daily radio-telephone contact. Optimally, his duties should extend beyond first aid and simple nursing and doctoring in cases of acute illness and accidents to the important area of health education and disease prevention. This was all the more necessary because of major cultural barriers between the villagers and the staff of the health services; the latter were not succeeding too well in communicating the most elementary notions of hygiene relating to clean food and water, personal hygiene and communal sanitation, and isolation of infection. It further became clear that since the health aides were either volunteers or poorly paid, they were mainly recruited from low-status people in the villages. This meant that they had little influence among the villagers and achieved little effect in modifying the conditions of village life that were associated with high morbidity and mortality rates.

By the time I returned to Anchorage, I had developed the idea that the village health workers should not be relatively low-level, poorly paid medical and nursing auxiliaries but high-level and high-status village officials who would be members of, and responsible to, the village councils, the governing bodies of the villages.

Both in the field and in Anchorage I then discovered that my simple plan would be complicated (a) by lack of funds to pay such village workers, (b) by difficulties in gaining the collaboration of the village councils, (c) by difficulties in deciding how the workers should be supervised, and (d) by the fact that a number of other federal and state departments, such as the Bureau of Indian Affairs and the State Health and Welfare Departments, were also currently planning the development of a network of village representatives. Moreover, there was already a budgetary allotment for training village health aides, and this money had to be spent within the budget year or it would have to be returned.

The problem now seemed to extend beyond the domain of the Office of Training Services and into the domains of other units of the Anchorage staff, such as Health Education, Environmental Sanitation, Public Health Nursing, Professional Services, and the Office of the Director, including his Native Affairs Officer; as well as involving issues of the relationships between the Alaska Native Health Area and the Alaska branch of the Bureau of Indian Affairs, the Alaska State Health and Welfare Departments, and a variety of other federal and state agencies, including a special Federal Field Commission, established to coordinate economic and social planning for the state, and a task force of the Office of Economic Opportunity and other federal agencies within the framework of the President's Economic Advisory Council. The dimensions and implications of the issue certainly seemed to be rapidly escalating.

Since by this time I had only about four more consultation days left, and a variety of other problems also on my agenda, I rapidly initiated a series of exploratory and feedback sessions with relevant members of the Anchorage staff. I requested a meeting of all the unit and division chiefs most immediately involved and started a discussion of my evolving plan. I then discussed with the Native Affairs Officer how statewide native organizations and village councils might best be involved, and how the

plan might be modified to secure their collaboration. With his cooperation, I met with leaders of statewide native associations. I talked with
the Director about possibilities of collaboration between his agency and
the other major federal service agency involved, the Bureau of Indian
Affairs; and he arranged for me to discuss the plan with its director in
Alaska. He also arranged for me to talk to an appropriate representative
of the Federal Field Commission for Alaska.

In the light of these discussions I then met again with the Director of
the Office of Training Services and suggested that whatever the outcome
of my ambitious plans for village workers, he should, as an interim measure, move his upcoming training program for health aides from Anchorage to one of the health service units in the field, and if possible organize some of the training sessions in native villages; and that he
should enlarge the focus of his training from first aid and practical nursing to health promotion and maintenance through community development and health education. I also suggested the advisability of involving
health educators and native leaders, as well as Bureau of Indian Affairs
community development personnel, in the planning and implementation
of the training program, as a step toward the eventual goal.

The following excerpt from my final report indicates some of the recommendations that emerged from these discussions:

Problem 1.1. *Low Salience of Health Issues for*
                Villagers and Leaders

The outstanding problem in the village is the low importance ascribed to
health matters by the villagers and their leaders. This is mirrored in their
ignorance of fundamental health issues, their inconsistent and ineffective
practice of communal and personal hygiene, and the relatively low prestige and influence of the local representative of the Area Native Health
Service, the Health Aide. This person is usually unpaid and is often a
woman or a young man, who works at a technician level in relaying information about sick villagers by radio communication to the doctors at
the Service Unit and then in dispensing the prescribed medication.

RECOMMENDATION 1.1.

I suggest a revolutionary change in the approach of A.N.H.A.* to the villages—mainly with the goal of making the promotion of health and the
prevention and early treatment of illness a matter of immediate importance to the villagers and their leaders, so that they will actively collaborate with the A.N.H.A. and other professionals in implementing programs
in which the improvement of health will be seen as an integral part of

* Alaska Native Health Area.

total village development, economic, social, educational, cultural, legal, and political.

(a) *Generalist Village Workers.* As the spearpoint of this new approach I recommend the organization of a network of Village Workers, similar to the community development workers of India, Pakistan, and the Philippines. A Village Worker should be a mature Native man, or occasionally a woman, of prestige and influence in the village. He should be paid a good salary to release a major part of his working day from fishing, hunting, and trapping; but he should continue these occupations to some extent in order to remain identified with the day-to-day life of his neighbors.

His main duties should be broad community development and adult education, within which the promotion of health and the prevention and control of disease would be integrated. As a village leader, he would have special skills derived from his knowledge of local culture, politics, and personalities. In addition he would be given extra knowledge and skills by A.N.H.A. and other interested Federal and State organizations, such as B.I.A.,* O.E.O.,† the State Department of Health and Welfare, the Court System, etc., who would wish him to act as their collaborator and agent at the village level. According to the size of the population, he would recruit and supervise full-time or part-time assistants, one of whom might be similar in role to the present Health Aide, and assist him at a technician level to collect and relay information about sick people and to dispense drugs in line with the orders of doctors and public health nurses.

The Village Worker should be treated as a *non-professional collaborator,* and not as a sub-professional agent, by the A.N.H.A. and other Federal and State agencies. He should be given a certain amount of technical orientation by each of them, but his development should mainly arise on the job as he collaborates with representatives of the agencies in his day-to-day operations. Rather than lengthy systematic training in Anchorage or Juneau, he should be involved alongside small groups of Village Workers from neighboring villages in repeated seminars of a few days' duration at Service Units or other regional centers, or in representative villages. These seminars should focus on greater understanding of specific issues and not upon acquiring professional frames of reference and techniques. The community development work of Fred and Carmen Wale in the Division of Adult Education of the Department of Agriculture in Puerto Rico can be used as a model.

The Village Worker should operate under the control of, or within the framework of, the Village Council, or some other accepted representative governing body of the village. In certain villages one of his main tasks would be to revitalize such a Council, so that through its operations the villagers would improve their self-respect and their ability to exercise greater control over their own destinies.

There should be only one Village Worker responsible for "human services" in each village, through whom the Federal and State agencies should

* Bureau of Indian Affairs.
† Office of Economic Opportunity.

operate locally. This should be ensured by coordinated agreements at the various levels of government. The alternative will be confusion and chaos for the villagers, as each agency competes for the interest and allegiance of villagers and pours in discrepant information and funded demands.

Ways of paying the Village Workers should be investigated which would enhance their generalist role and their bridge function between village, State, and Federal governments. One alternative would be for A.N.H.A. and B.I.A., as well as other agencies, each to provide salaries for a few Village Workers, and then to pool them, so that each agency in the consortium would freely use the other's workers. This unfortunately leaves the Village Council in a position devoid of realistic power. Another alternative would be for each agency to contribute funds to a consortium which would sign a contract with the Village Council. The Council would employ and pay the Village Worker, subject to effective controls from the funding agencies to ensure proper criteria for selection, working arrangements, and tenure, so that the vicissitudes of local politics would not upset the scheme.

Because of its novelty, I recommend that this program be tried out to begin with only in particularly appropriate areas on a pilot demonstration basis; and that only those agencies be involved which are prepared for unambivalent cooperation. I believe that A.N.H.A. and B.I.A. could make a start, possibly with the addition of O.E.O.

My report went on to discuss the back-up support of the village workers to be provided by the Service Units and the Area Office of the Health Service, and the negotiations with other units of federal and state government which I hoped would lead to organizing a consortium of agencies that would pool resources and establish a joint statewide program of village workers in collaboration with an advisory council drawn from leaders of the native associations.

As I moved among the individuals and groups at the different levels of the health agency and in the client population and contiguous agencies, I was not only gathering information about their individual, group, and organization needs and resources and their criticisms of my formulations of the problem and my successively more sophisticated suggestions for solving it, but I was being stimulated to bring to bear on this issue my background knowledge of psychosocial and sociocultural processes. What eventually emerged in my mind, and was discussed and then committed to paper, was not only a series of concrete suggestions but also a statement of some philosophical principles that I felt were relevant guides to planning. The following excerpt from my report illustrates this:

A fundamental problem will be how to pool the agency contributions in order to pay the salaries of Village Workers and how to involve Village

Councils in their selection and supervision so as to provide Councils with the real power that is indispensable for full involvement, and yet protect the program from the changing winds of local politics and ensure that the governmental agencies fulfill their several goals. The Native people must be given sufficient power so that they can control the type and rate of delivery of our professional offerings, and tailor them to the currently perceived needs of the village population. We must provide them with the community organization skills so that they can effectively resist those of our well-meaning efforts which they realize are not in the best interests of their people. In the 1890's the Moravian missionaries made very effective use of village "helpers" who were recruited and trained along similar lines to those which I am advocating. They used these workers, however, to destroy the essential basis of the village cultural system. They did much good, but they have left us and the villagers with a legacy of demoralization because of their indiscriminate attack on the cornerstone of Native life. We must avoid their mistakes even though we make use of social techniques similar to the ones which they proved to be so effective.

The only people who have a deep enough understanding of the essential needs and conditions of Native life to know how far and how fast to go in supporting and supplementing indigenous strengths by means of the professional rssources and knowledge of our modern civilization are the Natives themselves and their leaders. We must therefore develop such a system that protects them against our enthusiasm and drive and against our professional and bureaucratic blind spots—even though this will inevitably frustrate some of our most cherished schemes and timetables. Paradoxically, true and lasting progress with a minimum of unexpected bad side effects will be quicker and surer that way.

We must be prepared for the villages to move at widely differing speeds in their capacity to make proper use of our assistance. I believe that of the more than 300 villages in Alaska we will find at the present time no more than about 50, in which the Village Councils are already well enough organized and led to be able to collaborate effectively in the Village Worker program. I feel that we should restrict our initial efforts to this sub-group. At the same time, the regional community development workers should begin to work with the most promising of the remainder in order to help the villagers identify their natural leaders and to organize their community life under their direction. Only when a Village Council achieves an appropriate level of development and power should the village be admitted to the program.

Continuing Contact with the Director

As already indicated, the consultant should arrange to have as much contact as possible with his principal consultee during the development of his assessment of the consultation problems and of his recommendations for solution. This is partly in order to ensure that in the rapidly expanding field of his interest in a particular problem, as demonstrated in the above example, he remains in touch with the practical realities of his consultee's preoccupations. This is important so that he can receive the guidance of someone whose role encompasses an overview of the relationships and complementarities of the subsections of the consultee organization and also of its connections and overlaps with other systems. The director's reactions also allow the consultant to assess the short-term and long-term acceptability of his recommendations.

In Alaska, for example, my daily contacts with the director of the health agency not only helped me to decide quickly whom I should interview and smoothed my path in making contact with key informants and critics inside and outside the organization—and some of the latter were important and busy people, whom I could not have succeeded in meeting at short notice without influential backing—but also reassured me that my broad and innovative approach was in line with the task demands. Whether or not my ambitious suggestions will ever be accepted or implemented, I was convinced from my discussions with the director that they fitted within the framework of his own conception of his mission and of that envisaged by his superiors in Washington. In fact, he urged me to feel free to reappraise the policies of his agency in the light of whatever fundamental principles my own past experience and basic philosophy made relevant. I was able to validate that he meant what he said by his reactions of interest and his practical suggestions for the elaboration of my recommendations during our daily informal discussions.

In other cases, a consultant may not be so fortunate in gaining such frequent access to the head of the consultee organization, who is usually a busy man with many pressing demands on his time in addition to those of the consultation. In such instances, the consultant should make a determined effort at least to "touch base" with him now and again during the consultation visits. This will ensure that at the formal reporting sessions before his departure there will be consonance between the focus of consultant and consultees. At that advanced hour it is too late for the consultant to make a major readjustment in his views of problems and solutions in order to make his appraisal and recommendations seem salient and feasible to the consultee group.

The Consultant's Recommendations

It must already be clear that the recommendations that the consultant eventually formulates have been developed collaboratively between him and various individuals and groups within and outside the consultee organization. Some of the ideas may even be taken directly from one or more of them. They are likely to have a different impact when they are reformulated and enunciated by an outside specialist from when they were originally proposed by somebody, possibly of low status, in the organization.

The consultant should acknowledge privately his indebtedness to individuals whose ideas he incorporates in his recommendations, but he should preserve the confidentiality of these, as of other, communications. He might embarrass both the staff member and himself by publicly announcing that of all ideas he had heard he was in favor of those of Mr. X. Moreover, he will almost certainly have changed the content or emphasis; and in any case, he must accept the entire responsibility for anything he recommends.

The best way of dealing with the question of acknowledgment is for the consultant to make a blanket admission of his debt to various members and groups of collaborators among the staff of the organization and to his other interviewees as an introduction to his remarks at the reporting sessions and in his final report.

No consultant worth his salt will merely sift the suggestions of the consultee group and piece together those that seem most sensible into a set of recommendations. This may be useful, but it is not sufficient. The consultant is expected to add ideas of his own, both to deepen and broaden the understanding of the problem by bringing into focus forces and issues from hitherto unrecognized relationships within and outside the organization, and also by suggesting novel avenues of exploration or of remedial action.

In formulating recommendations for action, the consultant should usually have a double focus. First, he should recommend what should be done immediately, or in the near future, with resources currently available. Such action should be sensible in regard to achieving a specified goal; it should also be acceptable within the framework of existing assets, liabilities, and values of the staff of the organization.

Usually this type of recommendation will involve additions to the existing duties of staff, or modifications of role that make their work more complicated. The consultant should ensure that he is not asking more than they are able or prepared to accomplish, and that he has also suggested how they can be helped to learn and be supported in their additional or new responsibilities.

Not infrequently this type of recommendation will not be popular in certain quarters. Change is often painful. Addition or redistribution of responsibilities to a segment of the organization may involve reducing the domain and the status of other segments or individuals. Some people may be demoted or even lose their jobs as an immediate or eventual result of the recommendation.

A mental health consultant will be particularly sensitive to the possibility of infringing on the rights or well-being of individuals as a consequence or side effect of his recommendations for organizational change. He will try to prevent this as much as possible; or if it is inevitable, he will try to suggest ways of preventing or remedying the damage by such means as discussing with the administrators ways of finding a new job inside or outside the organization that is more in line with a person's capacities. Wherever possible, he should give the individual or group whose status may be diminished as a consequence of his recommendation an opportunity to confront him and express their feelings and ideas. If they do not persuade him to modify his recommendation, he should frankly say so and explain his stand. He should, however, not change his position merely because it is not acceptable or welcome to particular parties. These will have their chance after he has gone to protect their rights and values during the administrative process that will be involved in institutional decisions to accept or modify his plans.

It is not part of the role of an administrative mental health consultant to allot blame for an administrative impasse or failure; but although he could communicate his observations and suggestions carefully and in system terms so as to reduce to a minimum the possible harm to individuals, he should objectively and honestly analyze difficulties and recommend remedies that replace areas of organizational weakness by opportunities for strength.

For example, a consultant who was called in to advise on the reorganization of a state mental health department developed a series of recommendations focused on decentralizing many of the activities of the headquarters unit. Among his suggestions was that of replacing the line positions of Chief Psychologist and Chief Social Worker, each of whom administered a relatively large division of personnel deployed in a variety of units, by the staff positions of Senior Psychologist and Senior Social Worker. The majority of workers of these professions would be incorporated under the line authority of the heads of individual units such as hospitals, clinics, and rehabilitation centers. The staff specialists at headquarters would, according to the new plan, provide their colleagues with technical guidance and consultation and would be responsible for in-service training and assistance in professional development. They would also help directors of peripheral units recruit and select workers in their discipline.

The Chief Psychologist was quite upset when the consultant told him about his ideas. He argued that to put psychologists under the direction of heads of units, who were mostly psychiatrists, would stifle their professional creativity. He pointed with pride to the record of his division in terms of growth in size and of research publications. He felt that the maintenance of a compact reference group improved morale and increased recruitment possibilities. When none of these arguments seemed to convince the consultant, he raised a personal matter. He reported that the state government was about to reorganize its civil service rating system as part of the general developmental program that had stimulated the request for consultation about the department of mental health. Civil service grades in that state were based upon the number of subordinates over whom a worker had line responsibility. If his job were changed from Chief Psychologist to Senior Psychologist and from line to staff on the organization chart, the probability would be that it would be recategorized to a lower civil service grade, involving loss of status and salary. The consultant said that this would be most regrettable and that he would raise this matter with the director, who might be able to protect the rights of the key member of his psychological staff, but that this personal issue did not persuade him that his basic advice to decentralize was not in the best interests of the department as a whole and eventually also of its psychological staff.

The consultant made his recommendation, which was accepted by the director and by the state authorities. Unfortunately, the psychologist did not wait to see whether his civil service grade would be reduced but resigned shortly after and took another job with higher pay and increased responsibilities. In fact, the new state post of Chief Psychologist probably did not demand as high a level of research and administrative competence as he had, and his decision to leave was valid. Neither his career nor the interests of the department were apparently harmed by the changes catalyzed by the consultant.

The second focus of a consultant's recommendations goes beyond the immediately feasible changes to an eventual or ideal situation which he deems possible and desirable in that setting. The consultant should make it clear that he is taking a distant view and is envisaging long-term goals that can be attained only with different or increased resources of staff, finances, and administrative structure. His own freedom from the preoccupations and conceptual constraints of the day-to-day job demands felt by the staff of the consultee institution, as well as his breadth of vision related to his special expertise, frees him to look to the future. This aspect of his functioning is usually much valued by the consultees, as long as his long-term recommendations have some practical feasibility and do not seem too much like "pipe dreams," and as long as they are supplementary to a series of down-to-earth recommendations for achieving short-term goals. I have found that most consultees appreciate a consultant with his head in the clouds as long as his feet are firmly on the ground.

The Consultation Report

As previously indicated, the report should be a communication in writing of material that has already been discussed in various forms with the key people involved. In addition, it is a document that can be disseminated widely to relevant parts of the organization and can be shared with higher authorities who may be involved in the implementation of plans for administrative changes that may emerge from the consultation. Because of this, the final report should be written in a rather formal style and should contain enough information about relevant issues so that it can be understood by those who have had no personal contact with the consultant. It is a document that may become part of the archives of the organization and that may, especially in respect to its long-term recommendations, be consulted for years to come.

Each consultant will undoubtedly develop his own style of reporting. My own reports, over the years, have begun to take on a consistent structure. I begin with an introductory section that briefly describes the setting, the reasons for my being invited in, and an outline of my activities during the consultation visit. In an appendix, I list the individuals and groups with whom I had contact. I usually end this introduction with some personal remarks of appreciation of the people and the organization and of thanks to those whose hospitality I enjoyed. For instance, in my report on a consultation visit to the Indian Health Service in Phoenix, I mentioned the "general atmosphere of warm welcome extended" to me and my family by its director and his staff and also said, "We were especially impressed by their solicitude for our religious dietary requirements, a sensitivity to our cultural idiosyncrasies which I feel is an indication of their basic respect for others with different ways of life. This must be a significant element in fostering good relationships with the Indian population."

In the introduction to my report on my Alaska consultation, I said:

During my stay I was happy to be invited to participate in some of the recreational activities of the staff of the Service Unit. I attended a farewell party for the Deputy Nursing Director, at which I watched a fascinating demonstration of Eskimo dancing. One morning I went out fishing for salmon on the Kuskokwim with Dr. Eneboe and his family. We fished Eskimo style on the incoming tide with a drifting gill net, and had what I was told was a moderately successful catch for the time of the year—10 silver salmon. I took the prize of the catch, a 17 lb. fish, back to Boston as a memento of my visit.

We returned to Anchorage on August 28th carrying a severely ill infant complete with intravenous drip on the plane with us. This I was told was frequent practice in order to conserve travel costs of accompanying staff.

Such personal items are not only a sincere expression of the appreciation of the consultant for the human interchanges during his visit but serve to introduce him and the staff of the consultee institution to those readers of the report who have not met them, as understandable people with whom they can empathize.

Following the introductory section, I occasionally include a short theoretical or "philosophical" section, to present my point of view about a central theme of the consultation. For instance, in one consultation, in which I was called in to advise on methods of in-service training in consultation and supervision for the staff of a headquarters unit, I wrote a short section on "Definitions," in which I summarized my approach to consultation and differentiated this process from administrative direction, administrative supervision, technical supervision, and educational programs. My dealing systematically with my use of these terms in this initial section set the stage for me to use them without the need for repeated explanation later in the report. Where such conceptual expositions are not necessary as a systematic foundation for the whole report, communication of my values and philosophy may be of significance in particular sections or in relation to a discussion of specific issues. The quotation earlier in this chapter from my Alaska report about my views on the importance of ensuring and safeguarding the power of dissent among villagers is a good example.

An administrative consultation report is not a book or a literary magazine article but a business document. On the other hand, many of the consultant's recommendations are heavily value-laden; and his personal assumptions and beliefs should be made explicit wherever possible, so that consultees can take them into account in deciding whether or not to accept his ideas. All communications by the consultant should be designed to maximize the consultees' freedom of choice and to reduce their tendency to accept suggestions because of dependence on higher authority, apart from the "authority of ideas" that make sense to them.

The body of the report consists of a systematic statement of problems and of short-term and long-term suggestions for grappling with them. I usually classify and group the problems—for example, according to the level of the organization involved, or in regard to geographically situated units. In my Alaska report, for example, I dealt successively with problems at the village level, the service unit level, the Native Medical Center in Anchorage, and the area office. Since the whole organization is seen as a reverberating system of interdependent parts, any such classification makes for difficulties, and there must be constant cross reference and not a little repetition; but I find that the alternative approach of system-wide exposition usually leads to greater confusion.

It is my practice to follow my exposition of each problem or subproblem with a list of suggestions and recommendations, rather than to deal first with all the problems and then to discuss all my recommendations. I also have found it useful to enumerate the problems and suggestions systematically, with appropriate headings and subheadings, so that the consultees can use my report more easily in their follow-up discussions. For example: *Problem 2.2. Low Morale of Social Workers.* Reasons for low morale listed successively (a) to (e). *Recommendations 2.2. Practical Steps to Raise Morale.* Steps listed successively (a) to (g).

Whenever I see no clear way of dealing with a problem, I do not hesitate to confess my uncertainty and to provide a series of alternative suggestions for further exploring the issue or trying to develop a solution. When I am a little more sure of myself, I give a list of tentative suggestions. When I am confident that I have some workable ideas, I offer firm and detailed recommendations. If I see alternatives, I say so. If not, I express a definite opinion. I do not believe in pretending to be uncertain in order to preserve a coordinate relationship with my consultees. On the other hand, my style and the whole tone of my report are explicitly nonauthoritarian and calculated to open questions rather than to close them off. For example, in a consultation report about a county health department I wrote:

Problem 2.4. *Difficulties of Communication among*
                    Specialists and across Administrative
                    Boundaries

A problem perceived by most of the specialists, with whom I talked, is that of promoting better communication among specialists and across administrative boundaries. In particular, there was dissatisfaction with the amount of communication among the four chief units in Centerville—the Offices of Program Services, Environmental Health, and Administration, and the group of department heads of the County General Hospital. Each of these units encompasses specialists who could be making more of a contribution to the work of the others, and each seems to be operating in too self-contained a manner. Some specialists felt that they were not being called in often enough by those in other units. Some felt that other units did not respond adequately when asked for assistance. An example of the former is the feeling among staff of the Office of Administration that they usually become involved with other units only to communicate the constraints of State policy. They are thus often seen negatively as opposing and limiting the plans of their colleagues, and as exercising undue control over professional decisions because of their fiscal knowledge and power. Since they are not health professionals, they feel that they are often perceived as non-professionals, that their expertise in such fields as systems organization, program planning and personnel management is not respected, and that consequently their guidance in such matters is not sought.

SUGGESTIONS 2.4.

(a) This problem is common to all organizations, and is no more marked in Centerville than elsewhere. I know of no ideal way of dealing with it. Differentiation of function, and bounded units, are essential in the structure of complex organizations; and lower communication across boundaries than within them is an inevitable aspect of the operations of a sub-system.

It might be useful for Dr. Jones [the Health Officer] to devote special attention to counteracting this difficulty in his organization. He might develop formal ways of ensuring that people from different units worked together on specific tasks, so that they would have to learn to talk to each other, and thus discover each other's specialist capacities. This might be done by establishing *ad hoc* task forces whose members are drawn by design from each of the four main units, as was done in preparation for my visit. Such groups should be given a concrete short-term task to accomplish, and should then disband, in order both to prevent the erection of new ingroup boundaries, and to provide an opportunity for involving others in this kind of activity.

(b) One type of task force which has special relevance for my theme is that of a group of colleagues from Centerville who travel together to a District Office. At present such joint trips are encouraged, but are left to individual initiative, and they occur less often than they might. Such joint trips do not necessarily involve a saving in staff time, because if three specialists all want to talk to the same person at a District Office they may block each other in the field. Team consultation in group meetings is expensive in staff time and should be used only when specifically indicated. No person should attend a consultation or supervisory session whose presence is not absolutely necessary—spectators waste the agency's money.

Despite these cautions, I believe that Dr. Jones might well consider convening task-forces of specialists to make joint trips to District Offices— either as part of a long-term plan or in reaction to a current crisis.

(c) It might also be worth exploring a team approach to consultation with an appropriate District Office on a demonstration basis. In this case a core group of consultants could be assembled from the four main units, and given the long-term task of systematically exploring and handling the problems of the District Unit and its catchment area. This would involve both group and individual contacts with its staff, as well as planning and evaluation meetings which could take place in the car travelling to and from the site. Such a project would have both the goal of helping the staff of the District Office and also the function of promoting communication among Centerville specialists.

Follow-up

In this, as in other types of consultation, efforts should be made to get follow-up information in order to try to assess the impact of the intervention. This assessment is somewhat easier here because it is likely that formal administrative action will be taken to implement all or part of the consultant's recommendations, and this will be a matter of record.

The consultant should discuss, during his last conference with the head of the organization, his interest in learning what transpires. His request that he be informed about results is likely to meet with a positive response, since it will be received as evidence that he has become committed to the organization and interested in its future welfare. I feel that the highly cathected relationship between the consultees and myself should continue after my departure, and remain a significant bond during the writing of my report and its subsequent consideration by the consultee group. Their communication to me of their reactions to the report and of their plans to deal with the issues I have raised brings the consultation to a close; and after that, the vividness of the emotional encounter begins to fade into memory.

In some instances, I have been called back as a program-centered administrative consultant for a second and third visit. Sometimes, this is for continued consultation on problems raised during the first visit which time did not allow us to handle adequately. More often, the return visits were made after several years' interval and dealt with fresh problems. The staff by then had usually changed; and apart from some familiar figures, the consultation relationship had to be rebuilt from the beginning. Such experience confirms my feeling that this type of consultation should usually be considered a circumscribed encounter, in which both consultant and consultees rapidly develop an emotionally charged working relationship in order to accomplish a specific task, and then bring this relationship to a close with the accomplishment of the task.

As in other types of consultation, evaluation of the consultant's success is very difficult. That administrative changes take place following his visit, and perhaps in line with his recommendations, may be a sign of success, especially if long-term follow-up indicates that the underlying problems seem to have been resolved. Unfortunately, such long-term follow-up is rarely possible, because once the consultation report has been acted on in whole or in part, there is a reduction in the level of communication with the consultant and it is hard for him to get valid detailed information. Moreover, he can never be sure that the same changes might not have occurred even without his intervention. This is complicated by the frequently occurring changes in the staff of organizations, so that it is hard to differentiate the effects of such changes from those initiated or catalyzed by an administrative consultant.

It is, however, possible to be fairly confident about negative results. If the consultation report is quickly shelved, and if few of the consultant's suggestions are accepted in the post-consultation discussions by the consultee group, this should be obvious, although it may sometimes be difficult for the consultant to obtain such information from people with whom he has built up a friendly relationship and who may wish to protect his self-respect. It is important for consultants to try to get this knowledge, because they can use evidence of lack of success in certain aspects of a consultation to learn what to avoid in the future. By and large, we learn more from our failures than from our successes, if we have the courage to confront them and try to analyze the reasons why things went wrong.

Finally, it must be admitted that many administrative consultants do not have a good record either in adequately following up or in trying to evaluate their consultations. Yet somehow they develop a good reputation, which convinces them that they have been successful. Presumably, satisfied consultees talk about them to their friends, and this leads to new consultation requests. This is a less than perfect basis for professional development, and I hope that eventually we will develop more systematic follow-up procedures and better evaluative techniques, but I see no signs of a likely breakthrough on this front in the near future.

[11]

Consultee-Centered Administrative Consultation

INTRODUCTION

Consultee-centered administrative consultation is probably the most complicated, interesting, and demanding type of mental health consultation. The consultant is called in by the administrative staff of an organization to help them deal with current problems in organizational planning, program development, personnel management, and other aspects of the implementation of organizational policies. It is expected that he will help them to improve their capacity to handle such problems on their own in the future. The consultant centers his attention primarily on the work difficulties of the consultees and attempts to help them improve their problem-solving skills and overcome their shortcomings. He is interested in collecting information about the organization, its goals, programs, policies, and administrative structure and functioning, not in order to work out his own recommendations or a collaborative plan for improving these, but as an aid in assessing the problems that impede the operations of the consultees and as a vehicle for assisting them to improve their ways of overcoming their work difficulties.

A mental health consultant who is asked for this type of administrative consultation may be invited to consult with a single administrator or he may be asked to help part or all of the staff of the organization. There is usually the expectation that his work will continue for a substantial period of time—months or years—unlike program-centered administrative consultation, in which he is usually expected in a relatively short period of time to provide a concrete plan to solve a particular administrative problem.

If the consultant is asked to offer help to part or all of the administrative staff of the organization, rather than just to an individual administrator, he will work with individual consultees and various established groups, as well as possibly dealing with the problem of reaching the general population of administrators. The number of administrators in the organization may be too big for him to be able to talk to all of them directly. This population may, therefore, have to be sampled in specially arranged *ad hoc* consultee groupings. The possible multiplicity of consultee individuals and groups is one of the factors that makes this type of consultation so complicated.

The knowledge and skills demanded from the consultant include not only individual and group methods but also a specialized understanding of social systems and of administration and organization theory and practice, with special reference to their implications for the mental health contribution of the organization to its community and to the satisfaction of the individual and group psychological needs of its staff.

Over the years my colleagues and I have engaged in many examples of consultee-centered administrative consultation, and it is largely upon this experience that this chapter is based. Our experience has included individual consultation to the head of a health organization on problems of establishing a community mental health program; ongoing group consultation for several years with the nursing directors and supervisors of a general hospital about current interpersonal problems in their administrative work; consultation with the senior administrative staff of the Peace Corps on policy development that has significance for the adjustment of volunteers, as well as for mental health programs in host countries; consultation with commanding officers and their administrative staffs in a variety of army settings on problems of maintaining the morale and efficiency of their units and of reducing the incidence of ineffective functioning due to psychiatric disorders; consultation to the directors and supervisors of public health nursing agencies on psychological aspects of personnel management and the development of agency policies in the mental health field; consultation with the total administrative and instructional staff of a Job Corps camp on staff morale and on policies and procedures related to the mental health of students; consultation to the staff of a religious diocese on how to improve the morale of clergymen in the parishes and their effectiveness in dealing with the mental health problems of their parishioners; consultation with the administrators of several school systems about problems of curriculum development and personnel management that have implications for the mental health of teachers and students; and consultation to the administrators and staff of several departments of a state mental hospital on program development in community mental health.

In some of these programs, single consultants have been involved. In others, a number of consultants have operated in teams, either to increase the range of knowledge about the subject matter of the administrative problems by means of a multidisciplinary approach or simply to cover more ground quickly in a large organization in which many contacts at a variety of levels are needed in order to produce the best results.

OPERATIONS OF THE CONSULTANT

The general principles discussed in previous chapters in relation to consultee-centered case consultation apply also to consultee-centered administrative consultation. An administrative consultant is usually asked also for help in dealing with individual cases, so his operations usually include consultee-centered case consultation, as well as occasional client-centered consultation. At times he may be asked to make specific recommendations for planning a circumscribed program in the mental health field; and if he feels the change of role to be appropriate, he may temporarily engage in program-centered administrative consultation or in administrative collaboration.

Choice of Consultees

The most characteristic aspect of consultee-centered administrative consultation is the need for the consultant to be mobile and flexible in his choice of consultees. Occasionally, this choice may be predetermined by the consultee organization, as when the consultant is restricted to helping an individual administrator. He may then have little contact with other members of the organization staff, and his operations would be similar to those of individual consultee-centered consultation, except that instead of focusing on the case of a client and his management, he would be dealing with a current administrative problem. On the other hand, the administrator may ask the consultant to talk with some of his subordinates, in order to gain a deeper understanding of the organization. This would be analogous to interviewing the client of a consultee in consultee-centered case consultation. In administrative consultation such action may be more helpful than in case consultation, because the consultant is not likely to know as much about the content area of the discussion as if this centered on the psychological aspects of an individual or family, the field in which he has had years of professional experience.

If he does agree to see the administrator's subordinates, the consultant should beware of the trap of thinking they too are his consultees. If he has been invited to offer consultation only to the director of the enterprise or the unit, rather than to the total administrative staff, this should have been made explicit to the rest of the organization; and his contacts with other workers should be clearly structured so as to enable him to collect information for the purpose of advising the director.

Another example of predetermined choice of consultees was the invitation to offer consultation to the group of directors and assistant directors of the nursing division of a general hospital. This group had a regularly scheduled three-hour meeting every Wednesday morning, and the mental health consultant was asked to meet with them for half of this time every other week. In the same hospital, the consultant was invited by the nursing directors to offer consultation to twenty to twenty-five nursing supervisors. Since this group had no regularly scheduled meetings of its own, a time was chosen that was most convenient for the day, evening, and night shifts, and all the supervisors were invited to attend a special group consultation meeting at two-weekly intervals. Over a seven-year period the attendance varied from ten to twenty.

The usual pattern encountered by administrative consultants in large organizations, such as the Peace Corps, universities, Job Corps camps, large mental hospitals, school systems, and industrial firms is quite different. Here the consultant may be invited to offer help to the entire organization, and he may be expected to play an active part in deciding which members of its staff he will engage in consultation discussions. Usually, the director of the organization and his senior staff will have specific ideas on this subject and may wish to be seen individually, as part of regularly scheduled meetings, or in specially convened consultee groups. They may suggest that the consultant attend regularly scheduled meetings of various work units, interdepartmental task forces, or layers of the administrative hierarchy; and they may also convene special consultation groups, such as the nursing supervisors in the previous example.

It may be expected, in addition, that the consultant will collect information about the organization on the basis of which he might suggest from time to time other individuals and groups whom he would like to involve in consultation, so as to make the maximum contribution to the organization. In this aspect of his work the consultant is guided by principles of salience and feasibility similar to those on which he bases his operations in developing his program in the outside community, as discussed in Chapter 3. This means that during his period of consulting in the organization, there will be changes in the roster of his consultees. Whenever he moves to a new group of consultees, the consultant must carefully build up relationships of trust and respect and negotiate with them an agreement on mutual goals and rules of procedure. He can never rely on their effective collaboration merely on the basis of sanction obtained from their administrative superiors, although this is, of course, a necessary precondition for initiating consultation contacts.

Negotiations and Initial Contacts with the Organization

Many programs of consultee-centered administrative consultation have developed logically out of earlier mental health programs that have gone through stages of collaboration, education, client-centered case consultation, and consultee-centered case consultation. More and more, however, as the achievements of mental health consultants in organizations such as the army, the Peace Corps, and industrial firms have been publicized, organizations are beginning to ask for this type of consultation from the beginning, either on its own, or more usually as part of a general program that includes mental health education and other types of consultation. For example, the director of a Job Corps camp, a number of whose senior administrative staff had had satisfactory experiences with mental health consultants during earlier service in the Peace Corps, asked a community mental health center for a program of consultee-centered administrative consultation for himself and all his staff. He also wanted case consultation on problems among his students and assistance with the in-service training program of his instructors and counselors. In this, as in a number of recent instances, we have been impressed by the sophistication of the administrators in understanding just what kind of consultant help they want and in placing their highest priority on consultee-centered administrative consultation, rather than first seeing the community mental health agency, as used to be the case only a few years ago, mainly as a vehicle for referral of individual problem cases.

In negotiations with such knowledgeable and highly motivated administrators, each side must first learn as quickly as possible what the other wants and has to offer, and what is its basic approach to organizational problems and to community mental health. They will no doubt amplify and corroborate their personal impressions of each other with additional data from other informants. For instance, the Job Corps's director and his colleagues made a number of inquiries into the reputation of the mental health agency through their contacts in the local psychiatric community; and the agency director collected information about the history of the Job Corps camp and the reputation of its senior staff from a variety of local and Washington informants. This is like obtaining credit ratings in business dealings or getting letters of reference in appointing a new member of staff—it is a process of corroborating the *bona fides* of the negotiating parties.

If these preliminatry explorations are satisfactory, and if the needs, capacities, and philosophies of the two sides seem compatible, there is no point in prolonging the initial negotiations. The consultants should pay a quick visit to the organization and then agree to a contract for a trial period. This contract need not be a particularly formal document, although in the case of a governmental or other public organization, amounts and types of services to be rendered and fees to be paid may have to be stated. The agreement should be written in general terms, so as to allow the details of the operations to evolve collaboratively in the light of joint experience.

One detail of the initial agreement is important, whether or not it is explicitly mentioned in the contract: the consultants should ensure that they have direct access to the top administrator of that part of the organization in which they will be working. In offering consultation to the nursing division of the general hospital, for example, the consultant related primarily to the nursing director and not to the director of staff education who made the arrangements for his consultation sessions with the supervisors; and in the Job Corps camp his basic relationship was with the camp director, and not with the program coordinator or head counselor, who had been sent by the director to conduct the initial stages of the negotiations. This ensures that the consultant has the backing of the top man in moving freely through the whole of the social system for which he is accepting consulting responsibility. Otherwise, he may become isolated in the part of the organization that is under the administrative jurisdiction of his chief consultee and may be unable to gain access to administrators in adjoining departments who are of direct relevance to the problems at hand.

This sanction from the top gives the consultant his fundamental mandate for free movement across intra-organizational boundaries and for contacts with all its staff. It does not automatically give him sanction from the lower levels of the power structure; and one of his first tasks after starting work in the organization is to negotiate sanction through all grades of the administrative hierarchy down to and including the various levels at which he intends to consult. This top sanction, however, although indispensable in allowing the consultant freedom of movement and authorizing the staff to take time off their regular jobs to consult with him, is not an unmixed blessing, because the consultant is likely to be seen as the agent of the director, and this may inhibit or distort communication by lower-level staff.

It is essential, during the initial negotiations with the director, to obtain his explicit assurance that he will not ask the consultant to act as his agent in either giving or receiving communications. This does not mean that the consultant will not discuss salient program or policy issues with the director, basing his comments upon his observations of the predicaments of the staff in managing their daily work problems; but it does mean that the consultant will be empowered to maintain the confidentiality of information given him by individuals and groups and that the director will not expect him to divulge details that may reflect on the behavior of particular individuals and groups.

The initial negotiation of sanction to operate is part of the first two tasks of the consultant in the consultee organization: (a) building his relationships with its staff and (b) learning about its social system, including its organizational structure and functioning and the values and traditions that bind its members together.

Building Relationships with Consultees

The fundamental goals in this as in all types of mental health consultation are for the consultant to stimulate the development of a coordinate relationship of mutual trust and respect. This must be based upon the consultees' perceiving him as a reliable professional who has specialized knowledge and skills that he is prepared to put at their disposal to enhance their working capacity, without infringing on their authority and responsibility and without endangering their occupational status and personal self-respect.

The main technical problems, in addition to those already discussed in Chapter 5, are related to the role of the administrative consultant as a change agent who is empowered to cross boundaries between individuals and groups and across levels of the organizational structure. This may interfere with the orderly patterns of communication and perception that usually act as an organized system of defenses against an undue rise of tension in individuals and groups in their daily work. How staff perceive each other, and how they behave toward each other and toward their clients, are parts of a complicated sociocultural equilibrium involving individual, group, and organizational factors that have so far resisted the efforts of organizational theorists to understand completely. The entry of an administrative mental health consultant, who is authorized to question accepted values and traditions and customary patterns of communication and perceptual distortions, may be particularly threatening to all concerned. This is analogous to the perception by an individual patient of a psychotherapist as potentially dangerous because he is likely to weaken or destroy defenses, which, although costly, nevertheless protect the patient against the anxiety that would be aroused by his facing the unacceptable impulses and fantasies which they cover.

Besides this, there are three other dangers. One is the possibility that the consultant may be seen as a spy for the director. A second is that he may be perceived as the agent of the director in using specialized psychological techniques to exert undue influence on the staff. In this connection, it may be feared that the consultant will use his power to side with certain factions in the organization against those who for their own good reasons oppose current policies of the top administration. And third, the consultant may indeed have his own axe to grind. He may have his own ideas and values about organizational structure and functioning. He is interested in promoting mental health. Perhaps he has some blueprint of an ideal organization at the back of his mind; and he may be trying to manipulate the organization to conform to his pattern. His lack of experience of the administrative realities and feasibilities of this particular organization, and the unproven and possibly fallacious value-laden premises upon which he bases his ideal pattern, may make his plan unworkable.

These are all significant reasons for reservation in welcoming an administrative consultant; and they supplement many less rational suspicions and stereotyped expectations that have been discussed in previous chapters. It is clear, therefore, that it will not be easy for the consultant to establish himself as someone whose help may be accepted without danger; and he should intervene cautiously as a change agent lest he indeed do more harm than good.

The consultant's fundamental method of initiating and building relationships is the same as for other types of consultation. He establishes proximity and promotes a process of mutual exploration so that the consultees can get to know him as he really is and not as they imagine or fear him to be. In a large organization, and especially in one in which the main factor influencing the request for administrative consultation is current organizational turmoil, rumors are easy to start and the fixed stereotyped expectations they produce are hard to undo. It is therefore important for the consultant and his team to move about as quickly as possible after the start of the program to all levels of the social system, so that most of the staff see them personally in individual or group situations. This allows the consultant to meet many of his potential consultees and to get a preliminary overview of the structure and functioning of the organization.

In these early contacts, it is advisable for the consultant to move along established channels of communication, at least in relation to group meetings. He should sit in at meetings that are convened for regular organizational purposes, and make as little use as possible of groups called by the authorities expressly for the purpose of consultation. When such a special meeting is convened, the consultant should be careful to give its members an early opportunity of defining some of their own needs that might be satisfied by this discussion, rather than taking it for granted that they have assembled only to enable him to see them and their work. In this way he can show his respect for them and his realization that, whatever advantage they may eventually derive from his efforts, his entry into their system is an interference with their work day and is a distraction, if not a burden.

In all his initial contacts, the consultant should emphasize his wish to be helpful and his interest in learning more about the organization. He should stress also that he still has no clear idea how the consultees can best utilize his knowledge and skills. On the other hand, he should not hide the fact that he has a store of expertise that he is willing to place at their disposal. This message is best communicated, not by immodest accounts of past consultation successes or by lectures on mental health, but by the kinds of questions he asks as the discussion progresses. In previous chapters I have referred to the special style of consultation questioning that is particularly effective in demonstrating a consultant's potential contribution. It consists in aligning himself with the consultees in facing the issue of the moment and then raising questions that widen or deepen the focus of the discussion. One consultant has referred to this as "complicating the thinking of the consultees." Essentially, it involves throwing light on the topic by bringing additional information to bear or suggesting further avenues for collection or analysis of information. This is a safer method of presenting one's credentials of expertise than trying to give specialist answers to questions at a stage when the consultant's knowledge of the realities of the organization is bound to be inadequate and when he cannot differentiate a legitimate task-oriented question from a testing-out gambit.

A relationship-building problem characterizing most types of consultation, but particularly obtrusive in consultee-centered administrative consultation, is that of maintaining a coordinate relationship with consultees in the lower echelons of the organizational status hierarchy. This is especially so in institutions in which status differentials are marked, such as in the army or in a traditional mental hospital or public health agency. It is hard for the staff to see the consultant as having only the authority of ideas; and it is hard for the latter to divest himself of the mantle of power handed over to him by the director, as well as invested in him by social evaluation of his professional status. Experience shows, however, that a coordinate status can be achieved by an informal, modest, sympathetic, and friendly manner as well as by meticulous avoidance of authoritarian or coercive formulations, and by the consultant's aligning himself with the consultee to face joint problems rather than investigating how the consultee deals with his problem. The consultant must also show in the privacy of the interview setting that he sets aside his mantle of status and power while retaining his potency as an expert colleague. Team consultation provides a supplementary approach to the solution of this problem. The professional status hierarchy of the team can be matched against that of the organization, so that each consultant works at his own level in the consultee hierarchy.

Relationship building in an organization is a never-ending process. Apart from the continual addition of new groups of consultees as the consultant moves from level to level and unit to unit of the organization, the staff of the latter is usually changing. Gradually, the consultant's reputation becomes part of the culture of the place, and it is easier for new consultees to perceive him in his true colors; but the consultant must never rely upon this. Each time he begins with a new individual or group of consultees, he must start again on the process of mutual exploration, role definition, and relationship building.

Studying the Social System

In consultee-centered case consultation, as we have seen in Chapters 7 and 8, it is important to learn a great deal about the social system of the consultee institution and to keep abreast of current issues in order to understand the institutional implications of the problems of the consultee with the individual case he brings for discussion. In consultee-centered administrative consultation this knowledge is even more important, because it forms an integral part of the content of consultation intervention. It might be argued that a skilled consultant should be able to pick up enough information just from his interviews with his consultees to assess the nature of their work problem and to plan how to help them. This might be true if the consultant were to limit himself to theme interference reduction with a regular group of consultees; but the essence of consultee-centered administrative consultation is that it may have a wider focus and may include intervention beyond the limits of the patterns of perception or role performance of specified consultees. It is this need to obtain a view of the total organization, in order to identify issues that are not brought to his attention by his consultees and that he might deal with by initiating an approach to other members of the organization who might be encouraged to ask for his consultation help, that sets its stamp on this type of consultation in contrast to consultee-centered case consultation.

This is vital to the administrative consultant. By widening his range of data collection and by accepting responsibility for identifying and dealing with problems in the organizational structure beyond those brought to his immediate attention by his current consultees, he is faced by the question of how far to go in initiating action to achieve organizational change through his influence on consultees. The more specific he is in his planning of solutions for the difficulties he sees in the organization, the more he is likely, consciously or unconsciously, to manipulate his consultees to carry out his plans. My personal feeling is that an administrative consultant who develops his own plans for changes in the organizational structure should state these recommendations openly, in which case he will be engaging in program-centered consultation. It is then up to the consultees whether and to what degree they accept or reject his recommendations.

I do not like the idea that the consultant may develop his plan and then manipulate or influence his consultees to accept it. This does not fit into my concept of consultation as a coordinate process, in which the consultant exerts no coercive power. Perhaps this point of view is based upon my doubts that a mental health consultant has a valid enough base of theory and experience for directing specific patterns of organizational change, nor is the mental health dimension in which he is an expert necessarily the only or main issue in the organizational predicament. Perhaps this is a carry-over from my professional style as a psychotherapist, in which I identify difficulties in a patient's emotional life and then intervene to increase his power to overcome them, but always leave to him the final choice of which specific path to take in resolving his conflicts.

In consultee-centered administrative consultation I feel most comfortable if, after I have identified organizational problems and have made consultation contact with staff members who are involved in them, I restrict my intervention to increasing the range and depth of their understanding of the issues and to augmenting their emotional capacity to use such knowledge productively. It is then up to them to work out solutions in the light of their own personal and role-related choices. I believe this is no small contribution by the consultant. It does mean, however, that although he might forecast the outcome on the basis of his knowledge of the people involved in the decision making, he must be careful to keep an open mind and not commit himself, even privately, to favoring any specific plan of action.

From these considerations emerges the principle, which is common to all consultation, but most salient in consultee-centered administrative consultation, that in the consultant's mind he must separate the three phases of (a) collection of information, (b) making a consultation plan, and (c) implementing the latter in his specific consultation intervention. This conceptual differentiation, which helps him control what he does in a disciplined way, is obscured by the fact that in practice all these mental operations of the consultant may overlap in time, and any of his actions may include elements of all of them, so that an outside observer may have difficulty in separating them. This is particularly true, for example, in the consultant's choice of the kind of data he collects about his current and potential consultees and their organization, and of his methods of data collection.

In *program-centered* administrative consultation, the consultant collects data that he considers relevant to his analysis of the problem he has been invited to solve; and when he reaches the stage of tentatively formulating solutions, he collects further data that will illuminate the possible effectiveness and feasibility of his alternative plans. He uses normal tact and good manners in encouraging the collaboration of the members of staff of the consultee institution in collecting some of the needed information for him, but in the final analysis he relies on the authority vested in him by the director in ensuring their cooperation. In *consultee-centered* administrative consultation, on the other hand, he operates in data collection with many more constraints. First, he has accepted no coercive authority from the director, and so collaboration of the staff, although authorized, must be freely volunteered by them and is more likely in regard to certain issues than others. Second, the consultant is continually aware that while he is collecting information he is also building relationships that will form the vehicle for eventual consultation intervention. In fact, his intervention usually starts at the moment of his first contact with his potential consultees, who may from the beginning be watching such things as his way of asking questions and the areas of his major interest, as part of the process of identification with him that is one of the major ways in which they are influenced. Third, although the area of his inquiry has not been predetermined by a request to deal with a particular administrative predicament, and so is apparently wide open to include any or every aspect of the organization, the consultant realizes that the resources at his disposal are necessarily limited. He must therefore narrow his focus to those issues that the consultees feel to be currently most pressing, and which they are thus likely to want to discuss.

The special skill which consultants develop with increasing experience, and which is similar to the "intuition" of a clinician in following productive leads in psychotherapy, is that of superficially scanning the entire field of the life of the organization and then making quick judgments of the "hottest" areas for deepening his inquiries—that is, choosing those topics that provide leverage points in regard to salience and feasibility for the consultees. An ongoing systematic examination of such statistics as staff turnover in different departments, patient, client, or product movement, or staff absenteeism or sickness rates should form the background of his data collection and may suggest leads for further exploration. But the consultant's main method of scanning will probably be that of moving about as a participant observer within the life space of the organization and chatting with as many people as possible at different administrative levels, so as to find evidence of unusual behavior or preoccupation that may indicate administrative difficulty.

Increasing knowledge of the culture of certain types of institutions, such as Peace Corps training camps, general hospitals, or public health agencies, and increasing experience with a particular organization may alert the consultant to repetitive sources of program or policy difficulty. He will thus be prepared to identify minor clues to be especially followed up, such as difficulty due to rapid staff turnover, lack of complementarity in particular role networks, communication blocks, or interdisciplinary rivalries.

When the consultant does identify a salient problem, or when it is brought to his attention by a consultee individual or group, he is faced, in this type of consultation, by an interesting technical dilemma. The more active he becomes in searching, himself, for more data from additional informants, the more accurate a picture he will obtain but the less influence he will be likely to exert on his consultees during the process. On the other hand, the more he sees himself as an "enabler" and catalyst in stimulating the consultees to obtain additional information, the more likely is his picture to be lacking in clarity and fullness because of the very limitations and blocks in the consultee that his consultation is designed to remedy.

The consultant must judge in each case at what point on that parameter to pivot his approach. If he is working on a regular basis with an individual consultee or group of consultees, he will probably operate closer to the "enabling" end of the parameter, along the same lines as in consultee-centered case consultation. He will rely mainly on identifying distortions in the consultee's story from evidences of theme interference, and on trying to reduce the latter with the hope that increased objectivity in the consultees will enable them to get, and to transmit to the consultant, a more reality-based picture. He will also attempt to increase their knowledge of possible additional sources of useful data. If the consultees do not manage to use this knowledge and professional objectivity with greatest effectiveness in analyzing the current administrative predicament, he will rely on continuing contacts with them on future problems to lead to progressive improvement, and he will be satisfied to move forward at their pace.

For example, a consultant who was meeting regularly, once a week, with a group of educational counselors at a Job Corps camp, was asked by them for guidance in handling homosexuals. The topic emerged for discussion as several of them reported recent difficulties in controlling homosexual behavior among their students. The consultant found it hard to obtain from them a clear picture of the camp policies governing the treatment of homosexuality. He was also not able to ascertain whether there had been a recent increase in the number of homosexuals or whether the discussion was being stimulated by a change in staff attitudes. In any case, he could not identify what factors in the composition of the student group or in the behavior of the camp administration might have contributed to such changes.

The discussion was dominated by an atmosphere of anxiety and mystery. The counselors were apparently inhibited in their contributions either by ignorance of the subject or by reluctance to reveal the extent of their knowledge, in case their peers should suspect them of an undue interest in this subject based upon difficulties in their own sexual identification. Instead of pressing for the collection of objective information about changes in the prevalence of homosexual behavior and about alterations in the social and administrative atmosphere of the camp that might be relevant, the consultant focused on lowering the counselors' anxiety and helping them talk more freely about the topic. He gave them a factual account of the nature of homosexuality; and he initiated a discussion, linked with the details of some of the cases, about the types of homosexual behavior and about problems of individual and social control. In his contributions to these discussions, which continued over three sessions, the consultant presented himself as a model of a professional who could talk calmly about an emotion-laden topic and could analyze the idiosyncratic details of each case without hasty generalization based on prejudice or stereotyping.

Over the three sessions, the anxiety and confusion of the counselors gradually diminished. The consultant hoped that this would lead to a fundamental review of the administrative problems involved. But instead, the group then turned to another topic of current interest; and the consultant followed suit, hoping that they would return to the problem of homosexuality at a later date.

Two months later, the camp was shaken by an incident involving a homosexual assault on a white student of low intelligence by a couple of black students, who were caught *in flagrante delicto* by the head educational counselor. This stimulated a new series of discussions in the consultation group. This time it was possible to analyze the problem, not only in terms of the nature of homosexuality and its control in individuals, but also in terms of factors in the social system and administrative structure of the institution that were instrumental in altering the prevalence of homosexual behavior. The consultant was also able to help the counselors see the need to press their administrative superiors to define their policies more clearly, so that all staff could know what to do in preventing and managing different types of homosexual behavior, and so that students could be informed of the consequences of breaking the rules.

If the consultant is at the stage of moving freely through the life space of the organization on the lookout for intervention points, he will probably orient his data collection to be nearer the other end of the parameter, and he will gather as much information as possible on his own. But even then he will be alert to the need to choose, as quickly as possible, a group of consultees and to mobilize them to survey and elucidate the situation, rather than completing the job on his own and then assembling a group to listen to his report.

For instance, in the previous Job Corps example, the consultant might have taken a different approach. He might have terminated the discussion of homosexuality by the counselors after one session. He might have talked to a variety of other groups and individuals in the institution in order to define the nature, extent, and causation of the problem. Such an investigation would probably have led to discussions with the medical and nursing staff, the chief educational counselor, the director of education, the group of dormitory counselors, the director and the deputy director of the camp. He might also have collected statistics on recent changes in composition of the student population from the records room. On the basis of the information that emerged, he might have identified the reasons for the currently increased salience of this problem. He might then have decided, for example, to raise the matter with the camp director, and from this interview might have emerged a plan to convene a task force to develop some new policies about homosexuality. The consultant would serve as a resource person on this task force. Alternatively, the consultant might have contacted the chief educational counselor and during this consultation the necessity for an inservice training program on sexual deviance for his counselors might have been clarified. He might have talked with the deputy director about the need to coordinate the operations of educational counselors and dormitory counselors so that they would share information about students and be less inconsistent in their standards of dealing with deviant behavior. The consultant's choice among these avenues for action would depend on his appraisal of the meaning of the information he collected and also on the current state of his relationships with the individuals and groups involved.

In each case, the consultant would initiate the discussion by saying he was currently becoming interested in problems of homosexuality and by asking his consultee for his comments. If the consultee appeared interested, the discussion would progress. If not, some other topic would be discussed. The plan, if any, that emerged would be that of the staff member or group involved, and not that of the consultant, who would guide the unfolding of the process only by his choice of contacts, which would determine the area of the social system and the levels of the administrative hierarchy involved. In addition, the consultant would catalyze and facilitate a rational investigation of the issue and the development of an effective remedial plan by supporting his consultees in confronting the problems and by helping them overcome emotional or cognitive obstacles in their reactions.

What makes consultee-centered administrative consultation so interesting—and also so demanding—is the wide range of possible factors and levels that the consultant must be prepared to handle. He must appraise individual personality characteristics and problems among the key administrators, intragroup and intergroup relations in and among the various units of the enterprise, organizational patterns of role assignment and lines of communication and authority, leadership patterns and styles, vertical and horizontal communication, and traditions of participation in decision making. These encompass the full range of individual psychology, group processes, and organizational structure and functioning. Of particular importance are changes induced by intra-organizational dynamics, such as those related to movements of individuals among positions, and by alterations in the relationship between the organization and its external community from which it derives its resources and to which it delivers its products. In the Job Corps, for example, it eventually became clear that a major factor in increasing the salience of homosexual behavior was an increase in the pressure on the camp by the surrounding white lower-middle-class community, whose leaders were worried lest an influx of Negroes and delinquent white students should upset their constituents.

A mental health consultant cannot be expected to be equally expert in all these areas of psychology, psychiatry, small-group processes, sociology, anthropology, administration, and economics. He must, however, develop some generalist working competence in all these areas. He must also make a study of the traditions, values, and customary practices of the organizations with which he consults. His own expertise consists in a specialized knowledge of certain aspects of the field and in his being able to help his consultees strengthen their mastery of those aspects in a balanced relation to the other factors. In this regard, his operations resemble those of a lawyer, who has to learn enough about the details of a wide variety of fields in successive cases so that in each one he can focus his legal knowledge in a meaningful way.

To illustrate the width of this range of factors, the following list of issues raised in successive consultations with groups of general hospital nursing directors and supervisors may be of interest: The question of maintaining discipline among ward nurses in regard to procedures relating to the poison cupboards. Relations of the nursing division and hospital security in controlling drug addicts among nurses and aides. How to reduce nursing staff equitably and effectively because of low patient census. Emotional difficulty of the nurse who resigns or is fired. How to prevent medication errors—how to study their causes by epidemiological methods, and how to deal with nurses who have made serious mistakes. How to encourage nurses to become more productive in a culture that is in transition between authoritarian and participant forms of leadership and decision making. How to increase adequate feedback of information to central policy makers from line workers. The problem of controlling rumors, and the relation of these to low morale due to poor nursing leadership on a particular unit. How to support the head nurses so that they can maintain nursing policies and withstand the pressures of resident physicians who want their own way. The difficult status of the nursing supervisor—her negative image as a "snoopervisor" on the prowl to identify policy infringements and as someone called in only when there is trouble—how to increase her sources of professional gratification and her feelings of self-respect. How to deal with a medical resident who loses his temper with a ward nurse and shouts at her in front of her patients—relations between the nursing division and the medical department concerned. How to promote communication among supervisors on the three shifts who work in different departments and buildings of the hospital. How to handle depressed, and possibly suicidal, patients on general wards. Tensions between nursing service and nursing education in relation to nursing students working on the wards. Effect on the nurses of low morale on a medical unit caused by the impending retirement of a chief of service. Problems of recruitment of new nurses, and relations with the hospital personnel department. How to increase the participation of the nursing division in deciding hospital policy on such matters as increasing bed capacity and census when the number of nurses is thought inadequate.

Planning Consultant Intervention

Although in practice an experienced consultant usually moves smoothly and quickly from his assessment of the administrative problem to his helpful intervention, it is useful if he teaches himself to hesitate, while he reviews the situation and explicitly chooses his goals and his methods of reaching them. This pause for planning should not show as any perceptible interruption in the flow of an interview. As in all other forms of consultation, the consultant must learn to continue talking at the manifest level while cogitating about the latent content and about the process of his operations.

This pause for planning is simplest in those cases in which the consultant is moving freely in the organization and in which he must decide which members of its staff to try to draw next into consultation in regard to an issue he has uncovered. This is not merely a matter of deciding which people are involved in a particular problem and of calling them together for a group consultation. The issue may lie precisely in the tensions and disordered communications among them; and it is often too tempting to try to resolve these quickly by face-to-face confrontation of the members of the staff network, with the consultant acting as a communication bridge or mediator among them. The consultant must recognize that such intervention implies that he is taking an active part in the administration of the organization, and almost certainly is plugging a gap left open by some member of the administrative staff who has not adequately fulfilled his supervisory obligations. This man may be grateful for the consultant's help, but he may also feel less self-confident in his role, and lose face with his colleagues, when he sees during the meeting or, if not present, learns subsequently how easily the consultant moved in and pulled his coals out of the fire.

The consultant may judge that the administrator in question would learn enough from the demonstration and would be so little threatened, because of his stable personality or good relations with his colleagues and with the consultant, that the probable benefit would offset the possible loss. On the other hand, the consultant might choose other tactics. For example, he might arrange for individual consultation with the administrator and help him work through his own role difficulties with his conflicting or noncommunicating subordinates. Or the consultant might contact the man's superior and help him find ways of supporting him in his predicament. Another alternative might be to work directly and separately with members of the network who are not communicating adequately with each other. In all these cases, of course, the consultant has to exercise caution in his own communications with the parties concerned, lest he breach confidence or adopt an "inspector-general" role in relaying information and making a judgment about a specified individual to his superior.

Consultant Intervention

As already indicated, the consultant may intervene at an individual, group, or organization level. His interventions are of a time-limited, circumscribed nature; and whether or not they are prompted by his own awareness of an issue or initiated in response to a feeling of need for consultation by a member of the organization's administrative staff, they must be limited by the boundaries of what the consultees feel are salient current predicaments. This means that although the consultant may be visiting the organization on a regular weekly basis for several years, and having continuing contacts with particular individuals and groups with whom he develops stable relationships of a gradually evolving character, his consultation interventions continue to be of an *ad hoc* type focused on temporary intercurrent episodes. This is so even though the consultant may recognize in his own mind that certain repetitive issues are linked to major continung difficulties in the organizational structure. From time to time he may choose an opportunity for focusing discussion on these major problems; but on the whole, his strategy is to help the consultees handle them piecemeal in relation to the crisis and social system disequilibria they produce. For instance, lack of adequate direction and supervision of junior staff was a continuing problem in the Job Corps previously mentioned. But the consultant did not deal with this except when situations like the homosexuality issue brought it into salience. In this way the consultant capitalizes on the increased leverage of crisis upset that arouses the motivation of participants to ask for consultation help and temporarily increases their susceptibility to outside influence. The details, timing, and speed of change in structure and culture are thus molded by the staff in relation to their intimate living knowledge of the organization and of their own capacity to cope with change. This provides an optimal opportunity to deal with reverberations and undesirable side effects occasioned by the possible weakening of institutional defenses against individual and group anxiety, and permits the staff the time to work out alternative systems of cooperative defenses.

Consultee-centered administrative consultation covers so wide and changeable a field that it is difficult in our present stage of knowledge to do more than indicate a few general principles of interventive technique, with the hope that these will guide other consultants in working out their own individual ways of achieving similar goals. I trust my remarks may stimulate others to conceptualize what they find effective and thus to add further items to the cumulative list of principles.

The following are some of the main types of operation which my colleagues and I have found valuable in our experience of this type of consultation.

Increase Mastery by Extending Consultees' Cognitive Field

The consultant capitalizes on his specialized knowledge of human nature in helping the consultees increase their understanding of confusing and apparently unexplainable behavior among their clients and colleagues. In regard to clients, the discussion can legitimately focus on the details of the presenting case. In regard to other members of staff of the organization, the consultant must judge whether the distance between the consultee and the person under discussion is such, in regard to customary usage in that organization, for the consultation to focus explicitly on this actual behavior. For instance, it might be acceptable to talk with a school superintendent about a particular teacher who would be personally unknown to him; but it might not be acceptable to discuss that teacher with her principal. If such a focus would not be legitimate, or if it would endanger confidentiality or the relationship of the consultant with the individual in question, who might learn through the grapevine that the consultant had analyzed his case, the same goal could be achieved by displacement from the particulars of this individual to the general category of human predicament involved, illustrated possibly by other individual instances drawn from the consultant's memory or imagination. This is like using a parable in consultee-centered case consultation.

The goal of such a discussion is to reduce the consultee's feeling that people behave in mysterious and unpredictable ways. This must be replaced by the confidence that if one gets enough relevant information about the situation, one can understand why a person feels and acts as he does, and then one can forecast how he will probably react if one modifies his situation in particular ways.

Allied to this help in understanding someone else's behavior is that of increasing the consultee's understanding of systematic ways of dealing with confusing problems in general. Although methods of problem solving are not exclusively the professional province of the mental health specialist, he can contribute to this field by his knowledge of ego psychology. In particular, he can help consultees increase their ability to confront rather than evade difficult issues and to realize the importance of persevering with a currently insoluble problem despite initial confusion and frustration. This is, of course, not a pure cognitive issue but is intertwined with the ability of the consultees to master their feelings, an issue that I will discuss in the following section. The particular contribution of the mental health specialist is to help consultees increase their mastery of this borderland where thought and feeling overlap.

In this as in most of the other operations of the consultant, he uses the fact that he becomes a role model or identification object for his consultees. More significant to them than his intellectual analysis of the orderly repetitive process in solving problems of confronting the issue, actively collecting and reviewing information, analysis, planning, action, and evaluation, is his demonstration of the way he himself actually proceeds, as he sits beside his consultee confronting with him the predicament that has occasioned the consultation. Particularly important is the unhurried and calm way in which he perseveres with his explorations of the situation, despite his expression of perplexity and concern and despite his obvious sympathy for those who are inconvenienced or suffering in the predicament.

When the administrative problem relates to a specific issue of mental disorder in a client, or of developing or improving a program of community mental health services, the consultant obviously has the traditional role of adding his expert knowledge to the pool of information upon the basis of which decisions are being made. He can demonstrate the benefit to such a program from adding a specialized outside contribution to the participants' knowledge of the relevant issues involved, and particularly to their fund of information about the contributions of recent research and the results of innovations in other places. Few organizations can afford to train their regular staff to such a high standard of expert knowledge that they can keep abreast of the latest thinking in all relevant fields. No practical method other than inviting an expert to consult on specific areas can achieve the greatest use of a specialist's up-to-date knowledge of his field. Most consultants know more about a topic than they can communicate in a systematic report. When they focus on a particular problem situation, they call to mind many ideas that they would otherwise not think of, and the richness of their associations throws valuable light on the consultee's difficulty.

Increase Mastery of Feelings

The self-conscious utilization of himself as a role model is nowhere more important for the consultant than in helping his consultees increase their tolerance of negative feelings, and in legitimizing the open expression and discussion of emotional discomfort as a natural and expectable reaction of people to the inevitable frustrations and failures of everyday work in an organization. The consultant freely demonstrates his empathy with his consultees and his sharing of their discomfort with an administrative predicament. He openly expresses his own frustration in the situation and his concern and compassion for the clients involved. He also takes the opportunity, whenever feasible, to tell anecdotes about similar professional problems he has himself faced in the past, and to talk about his sense of failure, anxiety, shame, guilt, and even despair when he was unable to find his way out of the mess and when at times he was unable to prevent such dire consequences for his patients as suicide.

This technique avoids the usual hazard of explicit discussion of feelings of anxiety, shame, guilt, and depression aroused in consultees by their work impasse—namely, that of setting up a hierarchical situation in the consultation relationship in which the emotionally stable consultant expresses recognition of, and sympathy for, the emotionally disturbed consultee. Such a hierarchical situation would unduly stimulate the consultee's dependency and might lead to his going on to talk to the sympathetic listener about personal matters that may be linked at some level with his sense of frustration and failure. By putting himself "in the same boat" as the consultee, the consultant maintains the coordinate relationship and confirms the message that all normal people must be expected to feel upset at times of crisis in their work, and that such upset can be experienced and discussed without loss of face and without license to regress into dependency and the role of patient vis-à-vis a therapist.

Another way of showing feelings of upset to be a legitimate part of acceptable adult maturity is to focus on this topic in group situations, in which peers and superiors can provide consensual validation by revealing that they feel the same way. The ultimate legitimization occurs when the policies of the organization take explicit cognizance of the inevitability of negative feelings and prescribe procedures for supporting the temporarily upset individuals during their period of discomfort. This was achieved in our administrative consultation and collaboration in the Peace Corps, when the organization issued a booklet to each volunteer forecasting his expectable tribulations overseas. This message had a foreword signed by the Director, Sargent Shriver, that stated, "This material discusses some of the reactions and feelings you are likely to have during your Peace Corps service. You should be prepared to recognize and accept these feelings as a normal part of being a Peace Corps Volunteer." [1] Shriver's message then went on to enunciate official policy for handling this situation: "Face up to these reactions frankly, and discuss them with your friends. In this way, you will be better able to deal with them. At the same time, you will be enriching your understanding of yourself as a person and of your experiences as a Volunteer." The expression and mastery of feeling is thus not only sanctioned but made an integral part of the educational experience that is one of the main functions of the organization.

The Peace Corps example points to a further goal of the consultant, in addition to the recognition of feeling and the encouragement of ventilation—namely, helping the organization set up mechanisms for supporting its staff in reducing their emotional discomfort. The consultant can stimulate the spread of attitudes and practices that foster the exchange of emotional support among peers, both individually and in groups; and he can help plan the convening of meetings among those involved at times of expectable rises in job stress.

In all these situations, the consultant should emphasize that helping staff with their work-related feelings should not mean trespassing on their individual privacy. Once again, he will use himself as a role model in demonstrating that he is comfortable discussing universal human reactions in himself and others in the occupational setting, while not talking about his own private life and while maintaining respect for the boundary line between the public and private domains of other people's lives. Needless to say, the importance of this issue is related to the culture of the people involved. Attitudes toward personal privacy vary among different ethnic groups and social classes, and the consultant will take into account his assessment of these attitudes among the staff of the consultee organization in deciding how much to emphasize this matter.

Improve Communication

Distorted messages and blocked or inadequate channels and flow of communication are among the commonest causes of administrative difficulty or inefficiency. The mental health consultant has a particularly significant role in detecting and remedying these. His freedom of movement, his image as a clinician who can be trusted to maintain confidentiality, his role as a nonaligned, sympathetic professional, and his adherence to a nonhierarchical coordinate relationship with his consultees all give him a privileged position as the recipient of information from all parties at all levels and positions in a network. He is therefore uniquely placed to identify discrepancies in information about a presenting issue and disorders of communication among individuals and groups.

A fundamental goal for the mental health consultant in an organization is to increase the trust and respect that individuals and groups feel for each other and hence to facilitate free and open communication. Difficulties here are often caused by distortions of perception and expectation based on personalities, interdisciplinary tensions, cliques, and status separatist tendencies. The remedying of these will be discussed in the next section.

At this point I would emphasize that, in addition to trying to relieve such distortions by interview methods, the consultant may also bring the parties together and act as a mediator and communication bridge between them by interpreting the messages of each to the other through his own reformulations. Very often, lack of trust between two people will prevent their coming together because each suspects that the other will take unfair advantage of him. This prevents the invalidation by real experience of their negative expectations. The latter are then intensified and further increase separation. The consultant can influence one or the other to take the first step in breaking this vicious circle, or he can himself initiate the contact, possibly at a meeting to discuss a safe topic that he has chosen as a vehicle for them to get to know each other. Both should be interested in the topic, but it should not be crucial to either.

In many organizations, communication upward is defective and produces ineffective policy development. The consultant deals with this by working with consultees at both levels. He supports the upper echelon to feel secure enough to solicit the feedback that will help them evaluate their plans without seeing this as criticism from below. And he helps the subordinates to realize that they are obligated to contribute to policy development by communicating evidence of inadequate results, so as to help their superiors bring the program into line with reality, instead of restricting themselves to grumbling secretly about poor leadership and feeling that any open criticism will prove their own rebellious hostility. If all levels can be helped to see such feedback as a collaborative contribution to evaluation and planning, and as a form of complementarity in line workers and policy directors, the obstacles on both sides will be overcome.

Reduce Perceptual Distortions

A major contribution in all types of consultee-centered consultation is to improve reality testing by reducing distortions of perception and expectation. Theme interference reduction is frequently applicable in administrative consultation, particularly in individual consultation with key administrators, in whom subjective factors not infrequently interfere with professional objectivity in planning programs, managing personnel problems, or maintaining collaborative relationships with other community institutions.

In addition to such personally idiosyncratic distortions, mental health consultants often identify misperceptions and stereotyped expectations among administrators based upon cultural prejudices, and such as those that relate to rejected ethnic, religious, or racial groups or to members of other professions or occupations which are believed to be inferior. One way of handling this, in addition to acting as a mediator to bring the parties together so that they can meet each other as people rather than as stereotypes, is for the consultant to ask his consultee for a factual account of the professional behavior of the person who is being stereotyped and then to discuss this in such a way that the realities of the situation begin to shine through. In this conversation, the consultant temporarily lends his perceptual apparatus, as it were, to his consultee. He gives him specific ego support by using the leverage of the consultation relationship to enable the consultee to identify with him and to stand back for the moment from his preconceptions and, along with the consultant, take a fresh look at the other person. The consultant will usually have to begin by pointing out some specific details of his own perceptions or inferences about the case, and then he can start to involve the consultee in the joint task of adding items to the list.

Another method, which can be used on its own or to supplement the above, is for the consultant to recount an anecdote from his memory or his imagination about his own experience with a person of the category under discussion. He indicates his respect for this person by his tone of voice and by the admiration with which he talks about him, and perhaps drives the message home by telling of the surprise he felt when he discovered how effectively the hero of his parable operated, and how much he himself had learned from that encounter.

Improve Leadership

Directors of organizations are often lonely people, at least during the working day. There is rarely anyone in their organization with whom they can feel free to share their concerns and doubts about their judgments and decisions. The mental health consultant, as a respected and trustworthy as well as nonaligned person who has no personal axe to grind within the organization, can often act as an objective and sympathetic sounding board and as a source of ego support to a director. This can have a significant effect on the capacity of the director to act wtih firmness and flexibility in his leadership role. The consultant can offer similar support to administrators at lower levels of the power structure, who are likely to be less lonely, because they can discuss their uncertainties with peers and superiors, but who may sometimes, especially in moments of crisis, be inhibited from sharing their hesitations with colleagues inside the organization. At all levels of the hierarchy, the consultant can help an administrator discuss difficult decisions and clarify what should best be done to advance the mission of the organization, despite the fact that this may also create a personal burden for the leader by obliging him to take an unpopular stand—for example, in forcing him to turn down a friend or retire a long-term employee who has grown ineffective.

Leadership style is primarily based on personality; and the consultant's main job is to support each administrator and free him psychologically so that he can act consistently. On the other hand, the administrative climate in many organizations at the present time is conducive to increased participation of lower echelons in decision making, so that the organization can react more quickly and flexibly to the sudden changes that are so characteristic of the times.

Certain administrators may have special difficulties in fostering true participation of their subordinates in the decision-making process. They may believe in this policy as a theoretical dictum, but in practice they may make the essential decisions themselves and pay only lip service to the ideal of involving subordinates. Or they may try to have the best of both worlds by manipulating the latter to arrive "spontaneously" at the conclusions to which the superiors have already committed themselves. A mental health consultant who identifies this difficulty may be able to help such an administrator to recognize the discrepancy between his preaching and his practice, and to support him in modifying his actions. This will probably involve uncovering the administrator's basic doubts about the ability of his subordinates to create a good plan quickly enough to handle the problem. Such a fear may be based upon stereotypes caused by a lack of appreciation of the subordinates' recent improvements in skill. The consultant may also support the administrator while the latter experiments by sharing decision making with his subordinates in matters of gradually increasing importance and urgency. The consultant may then help the administrator evaluate the results in order to test the feasibility of such a system.

Increase Congruence of Satisfaction of Personal and Organizational Needs

The thread that runs consistently through the operations of a mental health consultant, and often differentiates his work from that of other specialists who offer administrative consultation, is that of attempting, in every organizational predicament or planning problem, to keep a joint focus on the personal dimension of the individual or group and the needs of the organization and its goals. His consulting work in reconciling the two sides of this equation is similar to his psychotherapeutic work with his patients, whom he helps develop effective and socially acceptable compromises between the pressures of their instinctual drives and the demands of reality, which have both an environmental and an internalized ego aspect. In all his consultation interventions, the mental health worker fulfills a particularly valuable function for his consultees in their planning and administrative decision making when he keeps bringing them back to the need to keep both sides of the equation in mind, however obtrusive one or the other side may be at the moment.

Often, this work will involve aiding the administrators make a plan with the understanding that the human factor among their staff will affect the efficiency with which such a plan can be carried out. There is a natural tendency among top administrators, who necessarily deal in abstractions and statistics, to dehumanize the human issues involved in their operations. The consultant can continually counteract this by reminding them vividly of what their discussions may mean to the people involved.

When the pendulum swings too far to the other side, there is an equally troublesome problem of administrators who become so preoccupied with the emotional impact of a particular person's upset and pain that they lose perspective on his long-term needs and those of his family. They may also lose sight of the significance of the case for the fulfillment of the goals of the organization. If the organization is hampered, this in turn will have a material and psychological effect not only on this person but on all the other members of the staff. It is then the role of the consultant once again to redress the balance and to help the administrators replace identification with a victim by empathy with a person operating in the complicated system of the organization that is itself a subsystem of the community in which both exist and must work out their fate.

Improve Individual and Group Interpersonal Skills

The mental health consultant has his own special skills, and some of these may be helpful additions to the competences of administrators, in fulfilling the mission of the organization and in catering to the individual and group psychological needs of their staff. Here, the mental health worker will be an educator rather than a consultant.

Ending and Follow-Up

The consultee-centered administrative consultant, whether he meets with an individual consultee, an ongoing group of consultees, or with a variety of consultees on an issue he has uncovered in the general life of the organization, will complete his intervention on a particular problem within a short series of visits—usually one to three. He will thereafter take up some other problem. The regularity of his continuing visits to the organization should not obscure this pattern, or his work will be in danger of sliding insensibly into general emotional support, education, or administrative collaboration. By this last term is meant sharing with the staff of the organization the responsibility of directly effecting program development or of producing plans. Each short series of consultations focused on a particular current problem should be terminated by the consultant when he feels he has made his contribution. He then leaves it to the consultees to make whatever use of his contribution they wish. As he closes each episode, the consultant should express interest in learning the outcome of the problem and should arrange for the consultees to tell him of further developments when it is convenient for them to do so. The timing of this follow-up may well be left vague. This will allow both sides to use the follow-up discussion, if they wish, as a way of initiating future consultation contact.

In Chapter 12 we will discuss evaluation of consultation. Here it may be mentioned that scientific evaluation of consultee-centered administrative consultation seems impossible in our present stage of inadequate evaluative skill. The most that a consultant can demand of himself at the moment is to make a subjective assessment, from the follow-up reports of his consultees and from his observations of their behavior and of related aspects of the ongoing life of the organization, as to whether the administrative problem has been satisfactorily dealt with, and the degree to which his consultation intervention may have contributed to this.

If the problem appears to have been adequately handled, the consultant can never be sure to what degree his own intervention was an important contributory factor, as distinguished from a multitude of other helpful factors in the complicated interrelationships of the individual, the group, the organization, and the outside community systems involved. The consultant is more likely to be confident about a negative assessment—namely, that the problem has not been solved and that his consultation has not resulted in much benefit. This is important, because it allows him to criticize his choice of consultees, goals, or methods and, on the basis of his analysis of the case, to decide on modifications of approach in future administrative problems of this type. He may indeed have a second chance since it is likely that if the issue was not adequately resolved, it will repeat itself in a relatively unchanged form in the not too distant future; and the consultant will then have the opportunity of trying a new approach.

NOTE

1. G. Caplan and V. Cadden, *Adjusting Overseas—A Message to Each Peace Corps Trainee,* reprinted as Appendix A in G. Caplan, *Principles of Preventive Psychiatry* (New York: Basic Books, 1964), p. 279.

[12]

Evaluation

EVALUATION BY THE PRACTITIONER

Repeatedly throughout this book I have emphasized the necessity to evaluate the goal achievement of consultation, in order that the consultant might become aware of the differential effectiveness of various techniques that he uses in particular situations, so that he may improve his skills and learn to operate in a more consistently helpful manner. There are two aspects to such an evaluation. First, the consultant must record, either on paper or in his memory, an account of the consultation predicament and of how he appraised and dealt with it. However spontaneous the behavior of the consultant was during the consultation, this implies developing a professional self-awareness and subsequently recapitulating what took place in the consultation and analyzing this as objectively as possible.

Second, the consultant must develop some method by which he can assess whether and to what extent his particular technical response to the consultee's behavior achieved the desired result in improving the consultee's job performance and accomplishment. This is the more difficult task. In fact, it is so difficult that at the present time we can hope only for an approximate result. Nevertheless, it is so important that even an imperfect result is better than not making the effort at all.

Fundamentally, the goal of consultation is that the mental health of a client or a client population will be improved as a direct result of improved behavior of a consultee or group of consultees produced by the intervention of the consultant. Ideally, the technique used by the consultant should be specified and related to a change in the mental health of the clients that would not otherwise have occurred. The latter implies using some form of control group design—for example, a matched group

294

of clients being dealt with by a matched group of consultees who do not receive the type of consultation being evaluated.

Assuming the study group shows demonstrable, and if possible measurable, changes in mental health not shown by the control group, these changes should be ascribable to the altered operations of the consultees, which should in turn be of a nature that they can be linked with the intervention of the consultant. This implies demonstrating a chain of interlocking factors—that is, consultant intervention, change in consultee perceptions and attitudes, change in consultee-client behavior, resulting in change in client behavior and performance.

Clearly, this complicated design is beyond the capacity of a consultant practitioner, who has neither the time nor sometimes the research sophistication and resources to implement such a study. As I will demonstrate later in this chapter, such a design is even beyond the capacity of a sophisticated team of research scientists at the present day. Nevertheless, the consultation practitioner must incorporate some minimal attempt to assess the differential effectiveness of his operations, and the following are some of the things that I believe do lie in his power to accomplish:

Rough Assessment of Mental Health Changes in Clients

In certain consultation situations the consultant can make a rough judgment about the mental health condition of the client population and about changes that occur in subpopulations dealt with by consultees with whom he has worked closely, as compared with subpopulations dealt with by consultees who have made little or no use of his services. He will rarely be able to make direct observations on these matters himself; although if he belongs to a clinical facility that offers direct services to the client population, such as a diagnostic and treatment center serving a school system, he may be able to monitor changes in case flow over time from schools or classes that have made differential use of his consultation services. The drawback of such figures is that they reflect attitudes and practices relating to utilization of medical care as much as, or probably more than, the incidence or prevalence of disorder in the population of schoolchildren. A lowering of referral rate among those schools or classes in which teachers have used consultation may be due to increased tolerance of the adults toward the symptomatic expression of disturbed children rather than to a reduction in the frequency of disturbance.

Evidence of such changes in the client population is usually not obtained directly by the consultant but may be elicited from key informants in the consultee system. For instance, the superintendent of schools or the school principals may be able to make a judgment, after a few years' operation of a consultation program, as to whether there are changes in the frequency of mental disorders in different parts of the school system.

In other consultee organizations, in which records of disorders of task effectiveness are routinely kept, such information should be easier to obtain and will be more reliable. For instance, in the army, statistics are kept of A.W.O.L.'s, courts-martial, and incarcerations for disciplinary infractions, that might be related to consultation services. In industry, productivity, absenteeism, and loss of materials due to errors are usually recorded. In many organizations, records of staff attrition and turnover that may reflect changes in staff morale may be used as a criterion of effectiveness of administrative consultation.

Reports by consultees about changes in the mental health picture of the clients about whom they asked for consultation may be noted but are often unreliable. They are distorted by numerous biases, including those due to the current state of the consultee-consultant relationship.

Changes in Consultee Performance

Here again the consultant is rarely able to obtain information directly but must rely on reports of informants within the consultee organization. He is usually not in a position to question his consultees systematically about their job behavior; and even if he could, or if he occasionally learns about changes in their behavior from their spontaneous comments, he might not know enough about the consultee's profession to be able to make valid judgments as to whether the new behavior is better or worse than the old. Moreover, a consultee's report to his consultant about changes in his behavior with a client must be accepted with some caution, since it will often be colored by the consultee's awareness of what he thinks the consultant would like to hear and by the complexities of the consultee-consultant relationship. A consultee may reward or punish his consultant by such a report. This is similar to the point made previously concerning consultees' reports about changes in their clients.

Vicissitudes of the relationship between the consultee organization as a whole and the consultant will also color any of the reports he receives from key informants, if their reports seem to reflect on his consultation success or failure. Nevertheless, information from a variety of informants, such as nursing supervisors, school principals, and agency executives, about improvements in the role performance of consultees, as contrasted to other staff who do not have consultation, is of some value. Particularly significant is circumstantial evidence that validates these reports, such as the expressed interest of the administrators of the organization in continuing or enlarging the consultation program, especially when this involves a budgetary decision. Although I am well aware that it may be a tribute to my personal popularity, I am usually impressed when the director of nursing or an assistant school superintendent makes a strong plea to his or her superiors to maintain or increase the budgetary allotment to my consultation program at a time of financial stringency, when many programs have to be cut back. I was equally impressed when the contract for one of our consultation programs was recently not renewed "because of shortage of funds." This led me to a careful re-examination of what we had done that might have contributed to the lowering of the budgetary priority of our service. I do not believe that "the customer is always right"; but I feel that whenever he makes a negative judgment about me, I should take it seriously as a stimulus to increased self-examination.

Changes in Consultee Perceptions and Attitudes

This is only an intermediate criterion of the effectiveness of consultation. Such changes may not, in fact, produce changes in consultee task performance; and if they do, these may not modify the mental health of the clients. But an improvement in a consultee's cognitive grasp of his client's case and in his attitudes toward him, produced by consultation, is certainly a step in the right direction; and if the consultant can validate this, he can feel reassured that he has achieved at least a preliminary goal.

The difference between this criterion of consultee improvement and those previously discussed is that data concerning it can be directly collected by the consultant himself as an integral part of his ordinary interactions with his consultee. He does not need to rely on the reports of others in the consultee system or to spend time outside the consultation setting trying to collect statistics. The consultee's verbal and nonverbal behavior, when he talks about his client, is the information from which inferences can be made about the objectivity of his perceptions and expectations of his client, about the degree of his understanding, and about his own feelings of comfort and professional commitment to the case. If a consultee begins a consultation interview tense and anxious about his task, bewildered and confused about the client's predicament, and with a narrow view of the factors involved and the options open both to the client and to himself in his helping role, and ends the interview or the series of interviews in a mood of hopefulness and relaxation but with undiminished or increased involvement and commitment, with a clear view

and increased understanding of the factors involved in his client's predicament, and an awareness of a variety of options for helping him, he has
manifested an obvious change that the consultant can reasonably ascribe
to the effects of the consultation.

To be sure, the result may be due merely to the consultee's having an
opportunity to talk freely about the case to a sympathetic listener, or to
his obtaining some nonspecific support and reassurance from the consultant, or to the latter's adding to his knowledge of mental health matters, so that he can begin to see connections among factors in the case
history that previously were obscure to him. It may also be the result of
his learning from the consultant a vocabulary or a pattern of verbal formulation that allows him to give the impression of greater competence.
In any case, it is likely that the consultee will experience some relief in
dealing with the case; and apart possibly from the last of these alternatives, it is likely that he will be in a better position to help his client than
he was before the consultation.

By watching for such changes in the consultee during the progress of
the consultation, the consultant may use them as yardsticks against
which to measure the effects of the various techniques that he uses.
Thus, if the consultant expresses support and reassurance and the consultee's tension lessens but his confusion and bewilderment do not
change, and later on if this perplexity suddenly disappears after the consultant has made a particular point in the discussion or has communicated certain information, there will be face validity to the consultant's
assumption that the change in the consultee was produced by that technique.

Such observations are often a necessary, but unfortunately not sufficient, sign of success in consultation. They must be validated in two respects. First, the inferences based upon the consultee's verbal and nonverbal behavior during the consultation interview must be confirmed by
some evidence that his increased understanding or improved attitudes
were relevant to his task and persisted sufficiently to allow him to operate more freely and competently with his client. Unfortunately, the consultant cannot observe this directly but must rely upon the consultee's
report about the situation at a subsequent or follow-up consultation session. If the problem has in fact been resolved, the consultee will have no
incentive to come back for another consultation, and the two may not
meet till weeks or months later, when the follow-up report will be subject to retrospective falsification. It would not be an economic use of the
time of consultant and consultee to make a regular practice of bringing
the consultee back for a report on how he has done after a consultation

unit has concluded. So this immediate follow-up validation is often missing.

Second, the goal of consultation is not just helping the consultee handle this current case but also increasing his capacity to handle, on his own, this type of case in the future. This goal makes it doubly clear that changes in consultee behavior from the beginning to the end of a consultation interview or series of interviews about a particular case cannot be sufficient evidence of consultation effectiveness. What is needed is information about the consultee's improved understanding, attitudes, and capacities to deal with similar task problems in the future—that is, the degree to which improvement in the current case has generalized to others or was maintained over time. Can such evidence be obtained by a consultant practitioner? I believe it can.

The essential prerequisite is that the consultant should continue to be freely available to the consultee in the future, so that the latter can have the opportunity to ask for help with his task predicaments. Under these circumstances, negative evidence is easily obtained. If the consultee repeatedly asks for consultation help with the same kind of case, the consultant can be assured that his previous consultations were not effective, however much they supported or relieved the consultee, or however pleased both were at the time by mutually acceptable reformulations of the cases.

Such negative evidence can be most valuable in guiding the development of consultation skills. For instance, in my own experience I found that the technique that we originally named "dissipating the stereotype," which was a way of influencing the consultee to give up his subjectively distorted perceptions of the client and replace them by reality-based perceptions—a technique that regularly led to a reduction of consultee tension and an improvement in his capacity to deal with the current case—was equally regularly followed by consultation requests for help with similar cases. No sooner had we helped a consultee to deal with one of these through the use of this consultation technique than he found another case of a similar type in his practice. We began to talk of the "pinball machine phenomenon"—namely, that as soon as one ball had been shot, another ball popped into place in the machine. This evidence, that the long-term results of this technique were poor, forced us to re-examine it and to contrast the lack of negative results of a similar but subtly different technique that we were also using. In this technique we accepted the consultee's perceptions of his client, however distorted, and influenced him to gain a reality-based expectation of outcome—a technique that we eventually named "theme interference reduction." Eventually, our appraisal of the presence or absence of this negative evidence in relation to the two alternative techniques led us to reformulate our concepts and to separate off the technical error of "unlinking."

The above example illustrates the value of the double negative—that is, *not* getting negative evidence about the effectiveness of dissipating the stereotyped expectation as contrasted with getting negative follow-up results of dissipating the stereotyped *initial perception.*

We are on weaker ground when we search for positive evidence—that is, when we seek data to support the assumption that a consultee is manifesting improved capacity to handle effectively the type of case in which we believe we have helped him by consultation. It may be that he does not ask for consultation help with this type of case in the future because he just has not happened to meet such a client in his case load. Or it may be that our consultation has sensitized him to such cases by focusing extra attention on that one example, so that he averts his gaze from such cases in the future and does not allow himself to get involved. It may be that he has developed a positive relationship with the consultant and does not wish to embarrass him by bringing up the same old type of problem over and over. Direct questioning by the consultant about the kinds of cases with which the consultee continues to have difficulties is unlikely to be productive, since his responses will be so much influenced by the current state of the consultee-consultant relationship.

There turns out to be one loophole in this difficult situation. Not infrequently a successful consultation is not completely so, whether it is a case of theme interference reduction or some other type of consultation such as helping the consultee overcome a lack of knowledge or skill. His handling of the current case is improved. But when he meets a similar case in the future, he again has difficulty; and if his relationship with his consultant is good and channels of communication open, he once more asks for help. If the previous consultation had been fairly effective, the consultant will observe that on the second occasion the consultee's tension is not so high and his confusion not so marked. It thus proves easier to help him, and he more rapidly improves than on the previous occasion.

After an intervening period the consultee may again return for help with a similar problem. This time the tension and confusion are still milder and the consultation still more rapidly effective.

Eventually, after a few such repetitions, each of which has diminishing intensity, the consultee will occasionally remark, in passing, while talking about another type of case for which he is invoking the consultant's help, that he recently had another problem similar to the case he discussed last time but that he had little difficulty in handling it.

Such evidence of progressively diminishing difficulty, followed eventually sometimes by evidence of increased capacity, is, I believe, the most convincing validation that a particular consultation technique has achieved its goal.

Evaluation by the Consultees

I believe that some benefit can be obtained by soliciting retrospective subjective reports from consultees about their experience of consultation at intervals throughout a program—for example, once a year as part of a general appraisal and planning procedure. Later in this chapter I will report on a systematic study of this approach, from which it emerges that with all the obvious limitations of subjective bias and memory distortion, many consultees can up to two or three years later remember and report a reasonably valid appraisal of cases in which they were helped by consultation.

In order to reduce the distorting influence of the current state of consultee-consultant relationship, I feel that such evaluation is best carried out by asking all members of the consultee population to complete simple written questionnaires that ask them to record examples of cases in which they were most and least helped by consultation, together with their assessment of what help they obtained or failed to obtain in each example.

EVALUATION THROUGH SYSTEMATIC RESEARCH

In addition to the rough-and-ready evaluation by each practitioner of consultation that has the goal of increasing his own professional understanding and capacity, we need to carry out systematic evaluative research, both to refine the generally acceptable techniques of consultation and to justify the utilization of this method in publicly supported programs.

I and my colleagues began such research * at Harvard School of Public Health in 1959 and concluded it after we transferred our program to Harvard Medical School in 1964. The following is a report of some of

* This study was financed by N.I.M.H. Grants Nos. MH3442 and MH09214. The project was directed by the author in collaboration with Louisa P. Howe, Ph.D., sociologist, and Charlotte Owens, R.N., M.P.H., public health nurse. Other staff who made significant contributions included Thomas F. A. Plaut, Ph.D., M.P.H., psychologist, Lenin A. Baler, Ph.D., Dr. P.H., psychologist, Thomas McDonald, M.S.W., social worker, Leonard Hassol, Ph.D., psychologist, Ruth Gruschka, M.S.W., social worker, and David Kaplan, Ph.D., social worker.

the relevant aspects of this project, which evaluated a three-year period of consultee-centered case consultation, organized for the public health nurses of a city health department.

The study limited itself to describing and delimiting the processes of certain types of case consultation and trying to demonstrate a relationship between different forms of consultation and changes in the knowledge, perceptions, and attitudes of the consultees. It was felt that within the context of this consultation program it would not be feasible to evaluate the accomplishments of the method in terms of changes in the performance of the nurses or in the mental health of their patients.

Introduction

The consultation program was organized in the twelve health centers of a city health department, out of which the public health nurses operated on a district basis to cover the entire city. At any particular time there were usually about seventy public health nurses and twelve supervising nurses in service. Over the three-year period of the study, staff turnover was such that a total of 112 line nurses were involved in the program. At the end of the study, 29 nurses had been in the health department less than one year; 37 had been in one to three years; 19, three to seven years; and 27 had served more than seven years. Fifty-nine nurses were under thirty and 53 were older than thirty.

A mental health consultant visited each center on a regularly scheduled basis once every one or two weeks, according to the size of the district, and offered individual consultation to any nurse who wanted to clarify a complicated, case-related mental health problem.

Eighty-six nurses made use of this consultation service. They discussed a total of 416 cases in 487 sessions. A case might need a series of one to three interview sessions to be completed. Sometimes during this series, additional cases were discussed as further examples of the current topic. Nurses requested consultation intermittently. They might see the consultant on successive visits for two or three interviews, followed by several weeks' or months' interruption. We refer to each of the consultation visit clusters as a "consultation unit." There were 331 of these consultation units during the three years.

Consultants wrote detailed process records of each interview within twenty-four hours of completing it. This was the only feasible method of recording, because the nurses expressed great opposition to having the interviews tape recorded.

At the end of the three years, the process records of the 331 consultation units were each separately examined by two members of the consultation team who had not been involved on that particular case. They were asked to assess independently whether or not the record indicated to them that the consultant had utilized the technique of "theme interference reduction."

We defined the nature of the evidence needed for a positive assessment. We specified that the record should show that the consultant had used interviewing techniques to explore, obtain, and record evidence from the consultee about the presence and specific nature of an interfering theme. The record must also have shown that the consultee had perceived her patient, or the situation surrounding the patient, as fitting into what appeared to be an emotionally sensitive category for the consultee. Then the record had to show that the consultee had coupled this initial categorization with a stereotyped expectation of a specific particularly bad kind of outcome. The judge had to find evidence in the record that the consultant had weighed the consultee's description of the patient within a given situation so that the consultant in his own mind could make a reasonable assessment of the nature of the theme which was thus indicated to be present. There had to be evidence that the consultant had then gone on to test out his own tentative ideas by eliciting material from the consultee that would strengthen or discount this tentative assessment.

Having decided that the consultant had assessed and confirmed the presence of an interfering theme, the judge had then to determine whether or not the consultant had proceeded to intervene in order to lessen, modify, or correct the consultee's overstated or distorted expectation that this would lead to a bad outcome for the patient. If the decision of the judge was that this had taken place, the judge's next step was to assess the degree of specificity with which the theme had been delineated as well as the degree to which the consultant had effectively intervened to lessen, modify, or correct the expectation of bad outcome. Examples to illustrate this are the following:

Nonspecific Theme Interference Reduction

The record shows that the consultant discovered that the consultee saw her patient as a woman who has had illicit sexual relations and that because of this the nurse expected the woman's children to be damaged. The consultant helped the consultee to understand that many promiscuous women make good mothers and that in the present case there was evidence that the client was taking proper care of her children.

Specific Theme Interference Reduction

The consultant pressed his analysis of the consultee's stereotyped perceptions and expectations a significant step further. He uncovered evidence in the consultee's story which showed that she felt that women who had frequent illicit sexual relations would damage their sexual organs, and that this in turn would lead to the birth of physically damaged children, who would become cripples or die at an early age because they had inherited their mother's degeneration. The consultant then intervened by helping the consultee see that the physical illnesses of the children in the case were not based on hereditary lesions and that it was not inevitable that promiscuity should lead to sexual damage in the absence of venereal disease, even though feelings of guilt in the promiscuous woman might often make her irrationally expect damage to herself and her offspring as a punishment for her sins.

If the judges decided that the records did not reveal that the consultant had practiced specific or nonspecific theme interference reduction, they were asked to assess whether he had used one of the following techniques:

UNLINKING. This is a specific error in consultation technique. The consultant recognizes that the consultee is distorting her perceptions of the client in a stereotyped fashion, and he discusses the case in such a way as to enable her to perceive the client more realistically. For example, the nurse talks about her patient as a "promiscuous woman" on the basis of flimsy evidence. The consultant discusses the evidence with the nurse and influences her to realize that although the woman did have extramarital intercourse on a couple of occasions, it was because she was seduced by a designing man who lowered her resistance by getting her drunk.

The effect of such a consultation technique is apparently good if the consultee has been sufficiently influenced through the strength of the consultation relationship to trust the consultant's reasoning. The unlinking result is based on faith in the consultant's reasoning, but the result may not hold in those instances in which the situation continues to be so severe that the consultee is unable to accept the consultant's reasoning on faith alone. In many instances, the consultee is helped temporarily to remove the patient from the category in which the patient had been locked by the consultee's distorted perception. The consultee is then enabled to view the patient in realistic terms and may be able to work with this patient as an exception rather than the rule in a category —that is, "If this is not in fact a promiscuous woman, I do not have to worry that she has damaged her sexual organs and that the degeneration will be handed on to her children." However, we regarded the unlinking technique to be a technical error because the nurse appeared not to be helped to weaken the underlying interfering theme; and shortly after discussing the patient who had been removed from the category, the nurse, as indicated previously in this chapter, usually discovered in her case load another patient who in turn would be perceived as a "promiscuous" woman and who would then be described in the same terms of expectation of punishment and doom.

EDUCATION. Here the consultant pays no attention to the uncovering or reducing of a theme but gives nonspecific information to the consultee concerning the psychological issues in the case—for example, about how anxiety in a mother can affect her handling of her children.

SUPPORT-REASSURANCE. The consultant uses his authority to relieve the nurse's feelings of anxiety about the case, or he supports her by expressing approval of the way she is handling it and encourages her to persevere or to lower her goals.

NOTHING. Occasionally the judge might not find evidence of any activity that could properly be called consultation. The record might show an interaction devoid of helping content—for example, the consultant may have listened to the nurse talking about the case, but there was no evidence in the record that he had either used a method of assessing the theme or had added significant content knowledge. Some of these records were of the first session of an interrupted consultation unit and, in these instances, a sound consultation relationship had not been established. In others, the patient or the family may be moved out of the nurse's district, and the nature of the problem presented was such that it did not seem profitable to continue a consultation in which the vehicle for the most appropriate intervention—namely, the patient—was no longer in the nurse's work load.

Interjudge Reliability

There were three pairs of judges working on the 331 consultation units. Judges One and Two had rated 129 consultation units produced by twenty-nine nurses. To prevent the ratings from being unduly influenced by units coming from nurses who had relatively large numbers of consultation sessions, statistical analysis was conducted only on one consultation unit drawn randomly from those involving each of the twenty-nine nurses. In this sample, the number of agreements in regard to whether theme interference reduction was used or not was 21, or 76 per cent of the total. Theme interference reduction was judged to have occurred in nine of these units and not in the rest. The Chi square test of the difference between the frequency of agreement versus disagreement yielded a value of 5.69, which, with one degree of freedom, is significant at the 0.01 level.

Judges Two and Three rated 159 consultation units from fifty nurses. The number of agreements was 34, or 68 per cent of the total. Half of these showed the presence of theme interference reduction. The Chi square test yielded a value of 6.72, again significant at the 0.01 level.

The third pair, Judges One and Three, had judged 56 consultation units derived from twenty-four nurses. They agreed on 18, or 75 per cent of the total, in which theme interference reduction was found in four instances. The Chi square test yielded a value of 3.67, which with one degree of freedom is significant at the 0.05 level.

The judgments of unlinking, education, support-reassurance, and "nothing" unfortunately did not show the above degree of agreement or reliability and Chi square tests showed that they were not statistically significant.

In all cases of disagreement, the two judges subsequently discussed their judgments and tried to come to a reconciled judgment. In a few instances they could not agree, and in these cases the director of the project was brought in to resolve the impasse.

Table 12–1 lists the final judgments, both agreed and reconciled.

Table 12–1

	Consultation Units	Nurses
Specific Theme Interference Reduction	81	46
Nonspecific Theme Interference Reduction	62	18
Total of Theme Interference Reduction	143	
Unlinking	59	34
Education	47	35
Support-Reassurance	50	31
Nothing	32	26
Total of Non-Theme Interference Reduction	188	

Evaluative Studies

The following are the main studies that we carried out to evaluate this material:

STUDY 1. *An Evaluation of the Process of Theme Interference Reduction*

This study was based upon a review of the process records dictated by the consultants. One important goal of an evaluation study is to develop ways of defining the method or technique under investigation so that its elements can be communicated and replicated, and so that it can be reliably determined whether or not the method was correctly used in specified cases. Unless this can be accomplished, further steps in an evaluation of accomplishments of the method are on shaky ground.

In the present study, this result was achieved. During the first year and a half of the study the consultants had a general idea of what they were trying to achieve by their techniques—namely, to discuss cases with the consultees in such a way that the latter would be supported in understanding the cases as realistically as possible. The concepts of theme interference, however, had not been developed nor had the important difference between unlinking and theme interference reduction been understood. In the early days of the project the technique that was called "dissipating the stereotype"—namely, influencing the consultee to perceive the client in realistic rather than in parataxically distorted terms—was thought to be an effective type of mental health consultation.

It was not until late in the second year of the consultation program that prolonged analysis of the consultants' records revealed the nature of the theme interference reduction technique and differentiated it from unlinking. This timetable has special meaning, as will be seen later, since an important part of the study has been based upon an analysis of records dictated by the consultants and is therefore open to the criticism that these records were biased by consultants, who unconsciously described improvements in the functioning of consultees with whom they had successfully utilized the method being studied. During at least the first year and a half of the consultation program the consultants had no clear idea of the essential elements of the method they were using. They had all been trained, and were being supervised, which produced a certain consistency in their approach to their consultees—for instance, the consultants definitely avoided any encroachment on the consultees' private lives and deliberately used techniques that would not uncover personal links with consultees' perceptual distortions which had been evidenced by their accounts of the patient or the patient's situation. By this means the consultants also avoided uncovering any personal issues which the consultant might have guessed to be affecting the consultee's point of view and which would have been considered to be a serious technical error. The technique used by the consultant had to conform to the consultee's use of the clients as displacement objects, both in assessment of a possible theme and in conveying messages that the consultant chose in dealing with the unwarranted expectations of the consultee in regard to the case as a displacement object. But the consultants often missed the point in their interviews, and neither they nor their supervisor was sure when or why they did so or could be certain of how this affected the consultee.

Analysis of the consultation records eventually resulted in formulating the specific sequence of technical steps in theme interference reduction and differentiating these from unlinking, support-reassurance, and education. My presentation of this material in earlier sections of this book has been based upon these results, and therefore it would be redundant to repeat them here.

STUDY 2. *Changes in Consultee Objectivity During a Consultation Unit*

This study also made use of the consultants' process records. Two social workers, who were told nothing about our methods of consultation and who were kept in ignorance about the nature of our research plans, examined the records and made independent ratings of the consultee's levels of objectivity at the beginning and end of the consultation units. They recorded the level of objectivity at the beginning of each unit on a 4-point scale—low, moderately low, moderately high, and high; and then they recorded change between this level and their rating at the end of the unit as an *increase,* a *decrease,* or *no change.* The raters were asked to make their judgments mainly on a negative basis:

> If the nurse's attitude toward the case is an objective one in the sense of showing professional distance or detachment as well as professional concern, then she is *not* emotionally over-involved with the case; she is not unconsciously trying to solve or act out her own personal problems through the case; she is not personally identified with the case nor trying to dissociate or "dis-identify" herself from the case; she does not show blocking, parataxic distortions, inconsistencies, confusion or stereotyping in the account she gives of the case.*

The raters used the consultants' records to make their ratings. They were told to focus on the reports of the nurses' behavior and verbalizations about the case and to avoid paying attention to the consultants' reports of their own activities.

* From the *Manual for Raters,* February 14, 1961, prepared by Louisa P. Howe.

Reliability agreement between the two raters was significantly high, both for the beginning ratings and for the ratings of change—reaching or exceeding the 0.001 level of probability. In cases of disagreement the raters subsequently discussed their differences and reconciled them to arrive at an agreed rating.

Table 12–2 gives the results of our investigation of changes in objectivity from the beginning to the end of consultation units in which it was judged that different types of consultation had been carried out.

The table shows a highly significant relation of percentage improvement in objectivity to the different types of consultation. If we include only those records in which the judges independently agreed on the type of theme interference reduction, the difference between this technique and the others is particularly dramatic. Even if the reconciled judgments

Table 12–2 *Changes in Objectivity Ratings for Consultation Units by Types of Consultation*

Type of Consultation	Change in Objectivity			
	Increase	No Change	Decrease	Percentage Increase
Specific Theme Interference Reduction				
Agreed *	27	1	1	93.1
Reconciled †	41	9	2	78.8
Nonspecific Theme Interference Reduction				
Agreed *	24	4	0	85.7
Reconciled †	23	9	2	67.6
Unlinking ‡	32	26	1	54.2
Education §	24	22	1	51.1
Support-Reassurance ‖	19	29	2	38.0
Nothing #	6	26	0	18.8

* **Agreed**—The two judges' independent assessments were identical.

† **Reconciled**—Consensus after judges discussed differences.

‡ **Unlinking**—A unit was placed in this category even though it might also contain evidence of education and support-reassurance.

§ **Education**—A unit was placed in this category if it did not show evidence of support-reassurance but only of education—that is, the consultant contributing specific mental health content to remedy an apparent lack in the consultee.

‖ **Support-Reassurance**—A unit was placed in this category if it showed appropriate evidence, even though it also showed education.

Nothing—This category was reserved for units in which there was no evidence of any of the previous types of consultant activity.

are included and both specific and nonspecific theme interference reduction are combined, Table 12–3 shows that there is still a major difference between theme interference reduction and other techniques taken as a group, and in turn between these and "nothing."

These results lend strong support to the assertion that theme interference reduction produced improvement in a consultee's objectivity in a significantly higher percentage than other techniques, and that all consultation techniques produce better results than "nothing" techniques. The validity of this conclusion is further demonstrated by the finding that only 18.8 per cent of cases in which no form of consultation was judged to have taken place showed an improvement in objectivity from the beginning to the end of the consultation unit.

The finding that the technique of unlinking achieved results not significantly better than education alone or support-reassurance was surpris-

Table 12–3 *Changes in Objectivity by Combinations of Types of Consultation*

Type of Consultation	Change in Objectivity		
	Increased	Not Increased	Percentage Increased
Theme Interference Reduction	115	28	80.4
Other Techniques	75	81	48.1
Nothing	6	26	18.8

ing to our consultants. Their subjective impression had been that, although this technique was unlikely to lead to a stable improvement in professional functioning, it was effective in reducing the consultee's feelings of tension and hopelessness in the current case.

A major criticism of these positive findings is that they may be the spurious result of biased recording by the consultants, upon whose reports the analysis had been made. In order to evaluate this possibility, the findings were divided into those relating to the first and second halves of the study period. In the first year and a half of the program the concept of theme interference reduction had, as indicated earlier, not yet been defined. Consultants could therefore not have known in which cases they had or had not adhered to the rules of this technique. Table 12–4 reports the relevant findings.

Table 12–4 shows that during the first period, theme interference reduction achieved significantly better results than other techniques. This improvement was more marked in the second period. During the first period, it is probable that the consultants and their supervisors were choosing a particular technique on the basis of repeating what seemed to be more effective in an unstructured manner rather than clearly spelling out a choice of method and then using this deliberately, as was done in the second period. The results of the second period, in which improvement was more marked, may indeed have been due to the consultants' biasing their records; however, it is also reasonable to assume that the consultants would have improved their technical competence as a result of delineation and elaboration of techniques and increased practice in the use of these techniques.

Table 12–4 *Change in Objectivity by Type of Consultation and Period of Study*

FIRST PERIOD			
Type of Consultation	Change in Objectivity		
	Increased	Not Increased	Percentage Increased
Theme Interference Reduction	51	15	77.3
Other Techniques	46	41	52.9
Nothing	2	9	18.2
SECOND PERIOD			
Type of Consultation	Change in Objectivity		
	Increased	Not Increased	Percentage Increased
Theme Interference Reduction	64	13	83.1
Other Techniques	29	40	42.0
Nothing	4	17	19.0

Our reliance on the uncontaminated nature of the consultation records may be supported by the fact that the variable "objectivity" was not isolated and defined until after the first year and a half of the consultation program, so that consultants could not have known before that time what criterion would be used to judge the success of their consultation efforts. Those who subsequently judged the type of consultation may, however, have been influenced to rate a unit as theme interference reduction if they also saw evidence of improvement in objectivity. Against this is the fact that the rating of change in objectivity was based on different content material than the judgment on type of consultation. As indicated previously, the objectivity ratings were made by independent judges, who were not involved in judging the type of consultation and who were kept in ignorance of the techniques being studied. We are not satisfied, however, that this source of bias has been adequately controlled. In order to do so, we would have to repeat the judgments on type of consultation, using independent judges who would be kept in ignorance that the improvements in objectivity would be used as a criterion variable. Unfortunately, a judge who was sufficiently sophisticated to be able to assess reliably the type of consultation, particularly theme interference reduction, would also be likely to realize that improvement in the consultee's objectivity would be a likely result of successful consultation, and might use evidence of this in the record to bolster his judgments on whether or not theme interference had been utilized.

Another source of error in interpreting the results of the study might conceivably lie in the relationship between the initial level of objectivity and the likelihood of improvement in that variable from the beginning to the end of the consultation unit. Table 12–5 demonstrates that this may well be a significant objection, in that the likelihood of improvement with low beginning ratings is seen to be higher, and this is significant at better than the .01 level.

Table 12–5 *Improvement in Objectivity by Low and High Beginning Ratings and by Judgment Categories*

	Improvement in Objectivity			
Beginning Ratings	Improved	Not Improved	Total	Percentage Improved
Low	141	77	218	64.2
High	55	58	113	48.7
Total	**196**	**135**	**331**	**59.2**

In the light of these findings, the question arises as to whether the improvement in objectivity in the different types of consultation is not, in fact, a manifestation of differential initial levels of objectivity rather than of differences in effectiveness. Table 12–6 shows that the initial level of objectivity in units dealt with by theme interference reduction was significantly lower than in those units dealt with by other methods.

When, however, we analyze the improvement in objectivity, keeping the initial level of objectivity constant as in Table 12–7 and Table

Table 12–6 *Initial Level of Objectivity in Relation to Type of Consultation*

	Low Units	Percent-age	High Units	Percent-age	Total Units	Percent-age
Theme Interference Reduction	108	75.52	35	24.48	143	100.00
Unlinking	45	76.27	14	23.73	59	100.00
Education	26	55.32	21	44.68	47	100.00
Support-Reassurance	21	42.00	29	58.00	50	100.00
Nothing	18	56.25	14	43.75	32	100.00

Table 12–7 *Low Beginning Ratings*

Improvement in Objectivity

Type of Consultation	Improved	Not Improved	Total	Percentage Improved
Specific Theme Reduction	55	7	62	88.7
Nonspecific Theme Reduction	38	8	46	82.6
Unlinking	23	22	45	51.1
Education	14	12	26	53.8
Support-Reassurance	7	14	21	33.3
"Nothing"	4	14	18	22.2
Total	**141**	**77**	**218**	**64.7**

12–8, we find that the general pattern of differentiated response in relation to the type of consultation is still roughly as before.

As a further test of the reliability of consultants' records, a number of consultations were tape recorded and also recorded by sound film after the termination of the evaluative study. The reports dictated by the consultants were significantly similar in their essential content to the objective data. It had not been possible to tape record the consultation interviews during the actual study because of the sensitivity of public nurses to being scrutinized. They knew the consultation program was being evaluated and approved of this; but they objected to having their interviews tape recorded lest they themselves be evaluated. In retrospect, it would appear that a much more determined effort should have been made to overcome these objections, because had the consultations been taped, a major uncertainty about the results of this study would have been avoided.

Table 12–8 *High Beginning Ratings*

| Type of Consultation | Improvement in Objectivity | | | |
	Improved	Not Improved	Total	Improved Percentage
Specific Theme Reduction	13	6	19	68.4
Nonspecific Theme Reduction	9	7	16	56.3
Unlinking	9	5	14	64.3
Education	10	11	21	47.6
Support-Reassurance	12	17	29	41.3
"Nothing"	2	12	14	14.3
Total	**55**	**58**	**113**	**48.7**

STUDY 3. *"Critical Incident" Study*

At the end of the three-year program all the nurses in the health department completed a simple questionnaire that asked them to describe in writing "an instance in which talking about a case with a consultant added to your understanding or otherwise affected your thinking about the case." They were also asked to describe an instance in which talking with the consultant "did *not* contribute to your understanding or your thinking about the case." Those nurses who had not made use of consultation were given an opportunity to explain why not, and there was space for further comments.

There were 74 responses, 61 from nurses who had participated in the program and 13 from those who had not made use of individual consultation but had attended the occasional group meetings.

In 50 of the 61 responses from those who had experienced consultation it proved possible for the research staff to identify the cases described by the nurses and to determine the consultation units in which these cases had been discussed. It was then possible to analyze the responses in relation to the type of consultation that had been carried out.

Of the 61 who had used consultation, 55 gave wholly positive responses, four said they felt consultation had sometimes been helpful and sometimes not, and two stated that it had not been helpful. One of the nurses who had not participated replied in negative terms; five were neutral or ambiguous in their answers; and seven were positive about the program and its helpfulness to other nurses, although they had not made use of consultation themselves.

In 50 instances it proved possible for us to identify the cases described by the nurse and to determine the consultation units in which these cases had been discussed. In 46 of these the nurse had found the consultation helpful, in three she had a mixed reaction, and in one not helpful.

The remaining 13 questionnaires were not detailed enough for us to be able to identify the cases about which the nurses were commenting.

Of the 46 identifiable cases designated by the nurses as helpful consultations, 29 (63 per cent) were in consultation units judged to have been theme interference reduction. This is well above the proportion (43 per cent) of theme interference reduction instances among the consultation units as a whole, the difference being significant at better than the 0.05 level.

It is necessary, however, to analyze the range of choice open to these 46 nurses. They had experienced 94 units of theme interference reduction out of a total of 195 units of consultation—the proportion of theme interference reduction being 48 per cent. Taking account of this slight bias within the sample, the choice of theme interference reduction units by 63 per cent of the nurses in their example of helpful cases is still more than would be expected by chance, at better than the 0.05 level of significance.

Further analysis shows the following: six of the 17 nurses who selected consultations other than theme interference reduction as helpful had no alternative, since their consultations did not include such experience. Among the 17 nurses, nine chose cases of unlinking and six others chose support-reassurance. When the choices available are again taken into account, the tendency of nurses in this group to single out cases of unlinking for favorable mention is significant at better than the 0.01 level.

Six nurses who chose cases in units that had been judged instances of theme interference reduction also had no choice—this was the only kind of consultation they had experienced.

If we remove the 12 nurses who had no choice, and compare the cases that the remaining 34 nurses chose as helpful from the alternatives we know were available to them, we find that 23 nurses who had experienced both theme interference reduction and other kinds of consultation chose the former. The proportion is 68 per cent, which is significantly higher (at better than 0.05 level) than the 50 per cent of theme interference reduction cases among the units available for these nurses' choice.

The relatively large number of cases of unlinking that were singled out by the nurses for favorable mention is noteworthy. Choices of unlinking and theme interference reduction combined amounted to 89 per cent for all nurses who had an alternative choice open to them, a proportion that far exceeds chance expectation. It seems that nurses, in looking back on their experience of consultation, remember as most helpful those cases in which the tension associated with the displacement of a subjective problem onto the client's predicament was lowered by the consultant's influencing them to develop either a realistic perception of the client or a realistic expectation of the possible outcome of the case—in Sullivan's terms, cases in which the consultant reduced the consultees' parataxic distortions.

STUDY 4. *"Before and After" Interview on Test Case*

A fictitious case record was constructed * which involved an account of two families, who between them suffered from virtually every sort of health-related problem that a public health nurse might be likely to find troublesome or distressing, or which might trigger some theme interference: a neglected infant, an illegitimate pregnancy, a schoolchild's emotional difficulty, a minority ethnic group, an unemployed father, alcoholism, a skin disorder, sexual perversion, marital infidelity, symptoms of senility, confinement in a mental hospital, a court record, gambling, refusal of immunization, support through Aid to Dependent Children, and distrust of social workers, public health nurses, and doctors. Nurses were asked to respond in writing to two questions about this case: "What are some of the important problems in this situation?" and "What, if anything, do you think a nurse could do in this situation?" † The nurses were then given a standardized interview covering the details of their responses.

This test and interview were given at the beginning and end of the three-year period to the 86 public health nurses who made use of consultation or, in instances in which they left the health department during the period, just before they left; to the 26 nurses in the department who did not ask for individual consultation; and to 45 comparable public health nurses from nearby city health departments in which there were no mental health consultation programs.

Table 12–9 shows that the three groups were not strictly comparable in regard to age, education, and length of service; but they were all working with similar cases in roughly similar settings.

Tape recorders were used during the development of the standardized interviews; but since some of the nurses appeared sensitive to their use,

* See Appendix to Chapter 12.
† This test was developed by Thomas A. Plaut, Ph.D.

they were later discarded and the interviewers dictated reports of their interviews immediately afterward. Interviewers knew that the nurse they were seeing was from the experimental or "control" group and whether it was a "before" or "after" interview; but they did not know what kind of consultation, if any, the nurse had experienced if she came from the experimental group. Interviewers were experienced social workers, who were engaged on a part-time basis for this task. They were kept in ignorance of the research plan. Nurses from the experimental and comparison groups were assigned randomly among them, and no interviewer saw the same nurse twice.

The two raters, who had worked on the objectivity ratings of the consultation records, were then asked to rate the same variable on the interview records. All data that might identify a record as "before" or "after," or as from experimental and control group, were deleted from the records. The raters were asked to rate on an 8-point scale the level

Table 12–9 *Characteristics of Subjects*

	86 Users	26 Non-Users	45 "Controls"
Age 40 or More	33%	50%	83%
7 or More Years of Service	21%	38%	63%
Less than Bachelor's Degree	60%	73%	83%

of objectivity of the nurse in discussing each of the two families mentioned in the case and interview records. The association of ratings on the two families turned out to be very high—exceeding the 0.001 level of probability—hence a measure was derived of "overall objectivity" for the "before" and "after" interviews on each nurse.

INTER-RATER RELIABILITY. The extent of agreement between raters was tested by asking them each to rate 50 records selected alternately from "before" and "after" interviews with different nurses. Using the Chi square test, it was found that x^2 was 45.55, which (with one degree of freedom) is considerably beyond the 0.001 level of significance.

RESULTS. Table 12–10 shows the changes in objectivity from the beginning to the end of the consultation program in the different comparison groups. This table shows no significant difference between the improvement in objectivity of the nurses in departments in which there was no consultation and those who had theme interference reduction consultation. The only statistically significant finding is that nurses in the experimental program, who made no use of the consultation offered, im-

Table 12–10 *Changes in Objectivity in Interview Responses from before to after the Consultation Program*

Nurse Group	Increase	No Change	Decrease	Total	Percentage Increase
Control Group	17	8	13	38	44.7
Nurses Who Had No Consultation	3	9	9	21	14.2
Nurses Who Had No Theme Reduction Consultation	10	9	2	21	47.6
Nurses Who Had One Theme Reduction Consultation	9	14	7	30	30.0
Nurses Who Had Two or More Theme Reduction Consultations	14	14	5	33	42.4

proved in objectivity less than any of the other groups. That they should have improved less than those who had consultation is consonant with the view that this method is efficacious; but clearly they are a deviant group within their own department, and many other factors apart from use of consultation differentiate them from their peers. If consultation were effective, it is hard to understand why the nurses in the health departments without consultation should have done as well or better than those who received consultation. Possibly, initial higher levels of objectivity among the nurses in the experimental program may have introduced a "ceiling" factor conducive to a fall in "after" scores. Table 12–11 compares the objectivity ratings in the "before" interviews of the different groups.

Table 12–11 *"Before" Interview Ratings in Objectivity in Different Groups*

Nurse Group	Low	Medium Low	Medium High	High	Total	Percentage Low
Control Group	17	13	12	3	45	37.8
Nurses Who Had No Consultation	6	5	7	3	21	28.5
Nurses Who Had Consultation	19	19	25	21	84	22.6

Low "before" ratings on objectivity were associated with improvement at better than the 0.02 level of probability.

It seems reasonable that persons who respond to a given program of intervention are those who already rank high on a scale designed to measure that program's effects. Any actual improvement that occurs must accordingly counteract the tendency characteristic of most measuring scales to show regression toward the mean when measurements are repeated at a later time. For such improvement to be registered it is also essential for the scale to provide sufficient room at the top—this may not be available for people whose initial scores were already high.

Of greater significance than this is the possibility that our measure of general objectivity was not specific enough to pick up changes in a nurse that were a consequence of theme interference reduction consultation, which is aimed at ameliorating a temporary diminution of professional effectiveness caused by a particular aspect of a certain work predicament. The analysis of the consultation records could demonstrate changes in this narrow sector, because it was focused on the specific situation that was precipitating the need for consultation. Although the fictitious case that was the basis for the interviews had many such trigger situations built into it, analysis of overall objectivity would probably be too general a measure, and changes in a particular narrow sector which is the target of our type of consultation might be obscured by alterations in other sectors which are influenced by all kinds of other personality and situational forces.

In an attempt to explore this issue, and identify a method for developing specific items which might measure changes that could be due to consultation, we analyzed the nature of the "themes" contained in the interview protocols to determine if there were changes in the different groups of nurses from the beginning to the end of the consultation program. We also ascertained whether or not the themes that were shown to have changed in the interview protocols were of a type similar to those which could be seen in the records of cases in which the nurse had experienced consultation.

Themes were categorized according to the dominant psychosocial level which they manifested and to their characteristic outcome object. This was based on a scheme worked out by Louisa P. Howe. Psychosocial levels were conceptualized as paralleling the psychosexual phases of development described in psychoanalytic writings. We postulated that each theme would manifest consistency in psychosocial level throughout an interview or a consultation protocol, and this seemed to be borne out by inspection of the data. Initial Category and Outcome Category could be rated as Type I or "oral"—that is, experiencing or responding to extreme demandingness, dependency, and helplessness, including that which accompanies physical or mental incapacity or impairment; Type II or "anal"—that is, having to do with problems of control, of power or authority, of carefulness with respect to money or other possessions, and of orderliness, or represented in their negative form by heedlessness, rebelliousness, disorderliness, and lack of control; and Type III or "phallic"—that is, having to do with conformity or nonconformity to conventional moral and customary standards—for example, in relation to sexual conduct and to "rules of the game." The outcome category was classified with respect to whether the stereotyped expectation of inevitable misfortune had to do with the self (S) or with some other person (O).

The theme could then be symbolized in the form $I.C._{I, II, \text{ or } III} \rightarrow S_{I, II, \text{ or } III}$, $O_{I, II, \text{ or } III}$. (I.C. being the Initial Category, and S and O the characteristics of the Outcome Category, each being labeled by a Roman numeral according to its level of psychosocial organization.) Take, for example, a theme in which the nurse was sensitive to a patient whose household was messy, which was seen as a sign of her lack of basic self-discipline, with the stereotyped syllogistic expectation that the woman (the self with whom the nurse appears to identify) and the woman's child (the other) will be dealt with severely by authority figures. This would be expressed as $I.C._{II} \rightarrow S_{II} O_{II}$.

If the patient had given birth to an illegitimate baby, and it was to this that the nurse was sensitive, the Initial Category would be classified as $I.C._{III}$. If the outcome expected was some form of physical defect for the child and punishment for the mother, the theme would be $I.C._{III} \rightarrow S_{II} O_{I}$.

Themes might be consistent—that is, the same level might apply to both Initial Category and Outcome Category—for example, $I.C._{I} \rightarrow S_{I} O_{I}$ or $I.C._{III} \rightarrow S_{III} O_{III}$. They might also be discrepant—for example, $I.C._{I} \rightarrow S_{II} O_{III}$ or $I.C._{II} \rightarrow S_{I}$. Themes might thus be expressed on more than one level of psychosocial functioning—for example, a mother may be seen as immoral and also uncontrolled and bad, the notation being then $I.C._{III, II}$. The outcome might be damage to her sexual organs, leading to degeneration and physical illness of her child, as well as punishment of her by powerful authorities, expressed by $S_{I, II} O_{I}$.

For administrative reasons, only one judge was available to classify the theme content of the interviews and the consultation protocols. Reliability of the categorization system was tested by comparing his ratings in twenty-four consultation units with those of two other judges. The first of these, an experienced mental health consultant, agreed in 91 per cent of cases both with the level of psychosocial functioning and the outcome categorization (S and O) that he had rated. The second judge, who was a statistical research assistant, agreed with each of the other two in 80 per cent of cases.

We also tested whether our judge was able to guess which of the interview protocols was that of a nurse who had had consultation or who had not, and whether it was a "before" or "after" interview. His guesses turned out to be no better than chance. Another rater was given the pairs of interview protocols of each nurse in the experimental and control groups, with the themes delineated and categorized, and was asked to judge whether there was any difference in the intensity of the themes expressed in each pair of interviews. Once again, tests showed that she was not able to guess better than chance whether an interview was from a nurse in the experimental or control group or whether from a "before" or "after" interview.

We then explored the relationship between theme classifications noted in the "before" and "after" interviews and themes classified from consultation unit protocols judged to have been examples of theme interference reduction consultation. If themes expressed in nurses' "before" interviews were of the same type as those subsequently dealt with in such consultation units, would these nurses be more likely than others to show improvement in the "after" interview?

In order to answer this question, the theme classifications in the "before" interviews for the 64 nurses who had had at least one consultation unit in which theme interference reduction consultation was judged to have occurred were compared with the classifications of themes in those consultation units. For 10 of the 31 nurses rated as "improved" and for eight of the 33 "not improved" the interview theme assessments were not specific enough to permit a decision to be made concerning consonance of themes in "before" interviews and consultation protocols.* These 18 nurses have accordingly been omitted from Table 12–12, which shows the consonance of theme classification of "before" interviews and themes dealt with in theme interference reduction consultation in relation to theme improvement from "before" to "after" interviews.

---

* Sometimes, interview themes could not be specifically classified, and instead statements such as the following had been made: "Many themes apparent"; "themes present, but hidden by nurses' defenses," or "intellectualized presentation makes themes hard to pick out." These nurses would be rated as showing theme improvement if, for example, the "after" interview bore a comment like "no themes apparent; objective perceptions."

Table 12–12 *Consonance of Themes Dealt with in Consultation and Those Expressed in Interviews*

Theme Type Consonance	Theme Improvement			
	Improved	Not Improved	Total	Percentage Improved
Consonant	16	10	26	61.5
Not Consonant	5	15	20	25.0
Total	**21**	**25**	**46**	**45.6**

This table shows that there is a difference which is significant at better than the 0.01 level, namely, that where the theme in the "before" interview is of the same type as that subsequently dealt with in a theme interference reduction consultation, the likelihood of theme improvement in the "after" interview is greater than when this is not the case.*

This shows that a *specific* assessment procedure *can* register changes brought about by means of a specific technique of intervention, even though *general* evaluative measures fail to indicate change.

This is also suggestive evidence that changes brought about by means of the theme interference reduction technique of consultation may persist in time—at least from the time of the consultation to the time of the "after" interview. Moreover, it seems that this technique produces an improvement that generalizes to the *class* of themes which have the same psychosocial significance as the specific idiosyncratic theme that was interfering with work functioning at the time of the consultation, which interference was reduced by the consultation intervention.

This analysis illustrates a point that in retrospect seems self-evident. Nurses who received consultation revealed certain areas of theme interference as they described the cases with which they sought help. Other areas of possibly distorted perceptions or expectations were not made manifest to the consultant, or else, in some instances, were not dealt with correctly although the opportunity to do so was present. When the areas of theme interference, opened up by the consultees and dealt with appropriately by the consultants, did not correspond to the areas of theme interference elicited by the "before" interviews, there was rela-

* Reliability was checked by having the judge carry out the same procedure twice with several weeks' interval, following which it proved impossible for her to identify cases and remember previous ratings. The second time, though, two additional nurses were excluded on the basis of insufficient information, and there were four disagreements with the earlier assessments, which represented a 91 per cent level of agreement.

tively little reason to expect that theme improvement would be shown in the "after" interviews.

By contrast, when the areas of theme interference opened up and dealt with in consultation did correspond to those expressed in the "before" interviews, improvement could be clearly discerned, as demonstrated in Table 12–12. The absence of assessed theme improvement for about half the nurses who received the theme interference reduction intervention does not necessarily mean that no improvement actually occurred. Improvement *may* have taken place in areas of theme interference which did not happen to be expressed by the nurse at the time of the "before" interview; in that case the assessment of theme improvement based on that interview would obviously not be capable of registering it.

Discussion

Study 2 demonstrates that active intervention by a consultant is associated with an improvement in professional objectivity in his consultee significantly more often than when nothing that can be labeled consultation takes place between them. It also demonstrates that improvement in professional objectivity occurs significantly more frequently when the consultant uses theme interference reduction than when he uses other techniques, such as unlinking, support-reassurance, and education.

A defect in professional objectivity is not the only factor that can interfere with a consultee's ability to work effectively with a client. This may also be due to lack of knowledge, skill, commitment, or confidence. But there is face validity to the assertion that a reduction in a defect of professional objectivity is a desirable goal of consultation, and that a method that accomplishes this is valuable. Other things being equal, it seems plausible that a consultee, such as a public health nurse, whose impaired professional objectivity is increased, is likely to behave more effectively in helping her patients achieve a mentally healthier resolution of their current problems.

Apart from the doubt cast upon our results by the fact that they are based upon records written with possible bias by the consultants, rather than upon, for example, objective tape recordings, they are also open to question because they demonstrate desirable change in the way in which consultees conceive of their clients only during the course of the consultation interviews. From our results we cannot infer that the consultee's improved way of looking at the client will persist after the consultee and consultant have parted. This applies to the client who was the object of the consultation but even more so to future clients who may manifest similar problems to which the consultee has demonstrated the kind of sensitivity that interferes with professional objectivity.

Study 4 deals with this issue. It demonstrates that theme interference reduction that is associated with an improvement in professional objectivity over the course of a sequence of consultation interviews (consultation unit) cannot be shown to be associated subsequently with an improved overall objectivity in dealing with a composite of sensitive themes, as contained in our fictitious case history. In other words, improvement in objectivity in dealing with one theme does not appear to generalize subsequently to all types of themes that may stimulate defects in objectivity.

On the other hand, the findings of this study are consonant with the expectation that improvement in objectivity on a particular case that is linked with receiving theme interference reduction consultation will indeed have a lasting effect that can be subsequently demonstrated, and that this effect generalizes beyond that case to include an improvement in objectivity in other cases that stimulate themes of a similar type.

The fact that the same study shows negative results in regard to subsequent generalization of the influence of theme reduction consultation to the composite of all these types of themes, and at the same time positive results in regard to themes of the specific type dealt with in consultation, adds considerably to our confidence in the findings.

The results of Study 3 are of interest. It would appear that the cheapest and easiest way of finding out whether consultation resulted in a lowering of tension in consultees is to ask them about it directly. This is reminiscent of the findings of Bower *et al.* in their study of emotional disturbance among schoolchildren in California.[1] Their best tests reliably identified certain children as disturbed, and this list correlated highly with the list of disturbed children drawn up by their classroom teachers, who were simply asked to rank their students in order of emotional stability. It reminds us also of the finding in World War II psychological studies that the single item that most reliably identified a disturbed group among inductees was the question, "Do you suffer from nerves?" It is significant, however, that consultees apparently cannot differentiate between unlinking and theme interference reduction, and remember both types of consultation as having been helpful, whereas both Study 2 and Study 4, as well as our clinical experience, attest to the superior results of theme interference reduction.

Of course, all our research fails to demonstrate that mental health consultation achieves more than the first step of ameliorating defective attitudes of consultees toward their clients. We were not able to study changes in consultee-client behavior or consequent improvements in client mental health. In our setting this was impossible. Will such a study ever be possible? Perhaps. I can envisage two possible designs.

First, I can conceive of a study of mental health consultation with a group of caregiving professionals who deal with a group of clients suffering from a crisis, in which we have reliable criteria that can differentiate a good from a poor mental health outcome. We may then match two groups of caregivers and clients, provide consultation to one, and compare the crisis outcomes from that group of clients with the one whose caregivers had no consultation. For instance, we could study a group of widows being dealt with by clergymen, half of whom would receive consultation. Within two or three years, research on widowhood currently in progress at our Laboratory of Community Psychiatry will provide us with the instruments with which to differentiate good and poor outcomes of this crisis.

Unfortunately, as one begins to think of planning such a study, the obstacles loom ever larger. Even though the loss of a spouse, especially in a young man or woman, significantly increases the risk of mental disorder, the actual proportion of cases with a bad outcome that can be reliably determined is quite small. So it would take quite a time to collect enough cases to make it feasible to detect significant differences between widows whose clergymen received consultation and those who did not. Second, we would have to collect a large group of widows in order to randomize other factors from our intervention that might account for possible differences in outcome. Third, the two groups of clergymen must be identical, apart from one group's receiving consultation. Fourth, clergymen do not in fact usually play a major role in crisis intervention with widows, as our current Laboratory research is demonstrating. Thus, if our consultation program to a subsample of clergymen arouses their interest in taking part in crisis intervention with widows in their congregations, any good results of such endeavors may be due to a Hawthorne effect and not to consultation—that is, to the fact that we focused their attention on this topic and aroused their motivation to intervene.

We could deal with this research difficulty by subdividing our experimental group into one subgroup that we handled educationally—that is, by means of seminars on bereavement and crisis intervention—and another subgroup to which we gave mental health consultation. It must be clear by this time that the projected study is reaching dimensions that render its feasibility highly questionable. It is hard to imagine developing the requisite channels of communication and stability of relationships with so large a group of clergymen and with their congregants and with a team of consultants and mental health educators sufficiently large to organize such a program.

Another design might be to evaluate a program of mental health consultation to teachers in a school system, by using changes in the mental health of their students as the outcome variable. It would be relatively simple to match schools and classes and to set up an experimental group, in which consultation would be given, and a number of control groups, in which the classroom teachers would receive mental health education, sensitivity group training, or no intervention at all. The problem in this design would lie in the outcome variable. What instruments would we use to differentiate the mental health changes over the period of the consultation program in the experimental and control groups of students? These changes must be of such a type that they can validly be ascribed to the influence of the classroom teachers, and not be due, for example, to extra-classroom influences, or to other factors. Randomization of such extraneous influences among the comparison groups would probably necessitate using large populations. This would raise the problem of organizing a large team of mental health consultants, which in turn would involve the difficulty of ensuring a consistent level of consultation technique and of recording, so that we could reliably determine whether or not adequate consultation had been given.

If mental health consultation to schoolteachers has real merit, it should result in a reduction in the incidence and prevalence of the kinds of mental disorders in students that plague our diagnostic and treatment facilities, so that ideally we should have no real difficulty in developing outcome criteria. For instance, would it not be sufficient to use criteria of frequency of major emotional disturbance, learning difficulties, or behavior problems like truanting or premature school dropouts? I doubt whether many mental health consultants would feel comfortable about using such outcome criteria, convinced though they might be of the merits of their methods on the basis of clinical experience. So many possible constellations of factors influence the incidence and prevalence of these gross conditions, in addition to the behavior of teachers which might be modified by consultation, that it is hard to believe that the accomplishments of this method could be reliably identified in this way.

Our fourth study indicates that we need a narrower and more precise target as a valid outcome measure. Perhaps we could combine our two hypothetical research designs and use as our criterion of accomplishment the quality of adjustment of the experimental and control groups of students to some common crisis, such as moving from elementary school to junior high school, or taking final examinations. This would imply preliminary research to describe the naturally occurring patterns of response to such a crisis, so that we could learn to differentiate the signs of good and bad outcome and develop instruments that would reliably record the gradient of adjustment response of groups of students.

These speculations make it clear that much exploration lies ahead if we wish to undertake a more ambitious evaluative study than the ones described in this chapter. This raises a final issue of a practical nature. The present system of obtaining funds for research demands the development of a grant application that is reviewed by a committee of fellow researchers, who must satisfy themselves that the proposed methods are likely to achieve the desired results. Unfortunately, such is the present state of our ignorance of evaluation technology in relation to the expectable difficulties of the task that none of us is likely to be able to write an evaluative research grant application that will be able to withstand critical scrutiny in the average research review committee of a governmental agency such as N.I.M.H. This explains why so few evaluation studies are funded. This in turn means that we are not able to explore the difficulties of the field and to make progress by grappling with them. The studies I have reported in this chapter were not funded on the basis of a specific grant application but were carried out within the framework of general program-type grants to study community mental health methods. This permitted us the latitude to develop pragmatically. Our modest success was achieved at great expense in money, time, and effort. I am convinced that these costs would not have been sanctioned and the resources granted had we been forced to specify our plans ahead of time.

On the basis of our experience, I would like, therefore, to end this chapter with a plea for some funding agency to depart from the tried-and-true approach to research support in this field and to set aside some risk capital in order to sponsor evaluative studies of mental health consultation that will be frankly exploratory and will have as one of their goals the improvement of our evaluation technology. Unless we move forward slowly by a process of progressive refinement of methodology, we will be no further advanced in this field twenty years from now than we are at the present day or than we were twenty years ago.

NOTE

1. E. M. Bower, "A Process for Early Identification of Emotionally Disturbed Children," *Bulletin of the California State Department of Education,* Sacramento, Vol. XXVII, No. 6, August 1958.

Appendix to Chapter 12

Armenez-Bianci Case History

At a staff conference Miss Kelly gives the following report on a case that she is concerned about:

She first visited the Armenez family ten weeks ago—she has been to see them four times to encourage medical supervision for an infant born at the Boston City Hospital. Mr. and Mrs. Armenez (ages twenty-seven and twenty-five) are both Puerto Rican and have only recently come to Boston. They live in a third-floor walk-up, just above the Bianci family. Mrs. Bianci (age twenty-eight) is Mr. Armenez's sister—the two women are sisters-in-law. The baby is now almost three months old and the mother has not yet taken her either to a pediatrician or to the Well-Baby Clinic. In addition to the baby there is an eight-year-old girl—Rosa—who is thin, often poorly dressed, and dirty.

The apartment is rather untidy, only sparsely furnished with some over-stuffed chairs, two kitchen tables, and two beds that usually are unmade. Mrs. Armenez, who speaks English fairly well, is a shy, quiet woman who doesn't seem to have any friends in the neighborhood. From the first visit she has been cordial and friendly to the nurse, inviting her to have coffee during her visits. The nurse has explained to her the importance of the clinic for the baby; she has also explained about immunizations—the mother has listened with interest, but as yet has not come to the clinic. The baby herself, other than exhibiting a moderate diaper rash, does not seem to be in bad health. Often when the nurse comes in the baby is crying; and when the mother brings the baby in for the nurse to see, it is obvious that the baby is very wet—sometimes also dirty, clearly not having been changed in quite a while.

Miss Kelly has seen Mr. Armenez (age twenty-seven) only once—then he was rather bleary-eyed and seemed to be suffering from a hangover. Although never an abstainer, Mr. Armenez has increased his drinking during the past two months to a considerable amount every day. Recently he was laid off from his job as a waiter at a private club. This was through no fault of his own—the club was closing down for the season. Mr. Armenez suffers from a very uncomfortable skin condition which so far has not been completely diagnosed at the Boston City Hospital Clinic. The family has very little money since Mr. Armenez has not been able to get another job. When they came to Boston they had some savings, but Mr. Armenez invested $100—without telling his wife—in some oil stock that one of the men at the private club had recommended to him. Not long ago the oil company went bankrupt and Mr. Armenez lost his $100.

Every time Miss Kelly visits Mrs. Armenez her sister-in-law, Mrs.

Bianci, is there too, usually drinking coffee. Mrs. Bianci has never been friendly to the nurse, is quite critical of nurses, social workers, etc. Mrs. Bianci belittles the importance of immunizations—saying that she never had any as a child and that she never got seriously ill. She has a healthy three-year-old boy she claims has never been examined by a doctor or a nurse. Miss Kelly saw this boy only once when he was in the Armenez's apartment playing nicely with Rosa Armenez.

Rosa has an imaginary companion—a little girl she calls Ann. She insists that a place be set for Ann at the table, takes two stuffed animals to bed, one for Ann and one for herself. Often she will hold long "conversations" with Ann, pausing to wait for Ann's "answers" to her questions. Rosa has always had a vivid imagination, but her "friend" Ann has become so important to her only in the past few months.

Mrs. Armenez doesn't know what to make of this—she finds it inconvenient to cater to Rosa's requests regarding Ann all the time and also is worried about Rosa. Mrs. B. insists that this is entirely normal for an eight-year-old girl and says that she herself had several such companions —even when she was much older. Mrs. Bianci teases her sister-in-law because she is worried about the girl. Generally, Mrs. Bianci is a very critical person. She never has a good word to say for her brother—Mr. Armenez.

Mr. Bianci was committed to Massachusetts Mental Center (Boston Psychopathic Hospital) about six months ago. He has been brought before the same judge twice on a charge of molesting young boys on the Boston Common. He had been arrested several times before this but never on a sexual charge. Because the Biancis have no other source of income and no savings, the mother is on A.D.C. When Mrs. Bianci told the A.D.C. worker that her period is three weeks late and that she is pretty sure that she is pregnant, the A.D.C. worker became quite angry at her—according to Mrs. Bianci. Mrs. Bianci has a "boy friend"—Pedro. Miss Kelly has seen him once—he is a well-dressed, rather suave young man who seems to have some money, but the nurse does not know what his job is. Mrs. Bianci apparently has had "run-ins" with this A.D.C. worker in the past. Over the years she has been on and off welfare—depending on whether or not her husband was making any money.

Mrs. Bianci's elderly father-in-law—her husband's father—lives with them. The nurse met him once on the stairs and reports that he is a very thin, weak-looking man who had considerable difficulty in managing the stairs. This old man was only recently released from Boston State Hospital where he had undergone a long series of electric shock treatments for a severe depression. He also has a heart condition and had several mild coronary attacks while he was in the hospital. Since being discharged he has had no further known attacks. The old man is a bit strange in some ways—he often mumbles to himself; once he got lost in the neighborhood. Two or three times he has wet his pants and didn't notice it until Mrs. Bianci pointed it out to him. Often he will go out for a walk without buttoning his pants. He feeds himself and generally is not irritable or "difficult."

[13]

Training in Mental
Health Consultation

INTRODUCTION

Since the Regulations of the 1963 Community Mental Health Centers Act, P.L. 88–164, specified that mental health consultation must be included among the five basic services that must be provided by all community mental health programs seeking federal funding for construction or staffing, there has been a great demand over the whole country for training programs in this method. Many otherwise well-qualified and experienced mental health clinicians have not been trained as consultants. Of course, some of them have developed consulting skills on their own; and after much experience in different settings, they may have become as proficient as those who have had the benefit of formal education.

In general, there are two settings within which training must be considered. First, formal programs provided by academic departments of psychiatry and psychology and by schools of social work, as well as by non-academic psychiatric residency or clinical psychology training establishments. Here the sequence in mental health consultation is part of a general program, and there are likely to be organized field placements with expert supervisors, as well as courses and seminars taught by specialists in mental health consultation. The second type of training is informal and is organized by a group of workers in an organization that is beginning a consultation program. It may also be organized by an *ad hoc* group of colleagues in a region where a number of agencies have become interested in developing consultation programs, but where there is no access to a training establishment, and where there may not even be anyone with previous formal training in consultation or who can claim expertise as a result of personal study. These bootstrap operations are

330

probably as numerous at present as programs organized by educational institutions. I regard them as most important in the rapid development of the field.

FORMAL TRAINING PROGRAMS

My paradigm is the program I have developed over the past fourteen years at Harvard. The program started at Harvard School of Public Health and was transferred in 1964 to the Laboratory of Community Psychiatry in the Department of Psychiatry of Harvard Medical School. It owes much to the energy, initiative, and skill of Charlotte E. Owens, R.N., M.P.H., who has been our senior supervisor and director of field training in mental health consultation since 1958. The training sequence in mental health consultation is one of the core elements of our one-year full-time educational program for community mental health specialists. Currently we have nineteen Fellows in the program, which leads to a Certificate in Community Mental Health within the framework of the Courses for Graduates of Harvard Medical School. This year's Fellows include thirteen psychiatrists, five of whom are specializing in community psychiatry during their third year of residency at Massachusetts Mental Health Center, the remainder, some of whom are quite senior, having completed their residency training; three psychologists with a minimum of three years' post-doctoral experience; a senior psychiatric social worker; a senior public health nurse with psychiatric nursing experience; and a medical sociologist.

These Fellows spend three days a week during the academic year attending lectures and seminars and two days a week on supervised field work. At the end of the academic year they have a two- to three-month full-time internship experience in a community mental health setting of their choice—usually in an administrative role at the federal or state level, although some, who are headed for careers in education or administration, choose to spend this time in a local community mental health center in order to round out their service experience.

The training in mental health consultation consists of a required seminar, which I teach, that meets once a week for one and a half hours throughout the year, and an associated supervised practicum experience that is designed to provide the Fellow with a range of consultation experience which will give him the opportunity to acquire individual and group skills in the various types of consultation. In addition, some of the Fellows—nine this year—choose as one of their elective courses a specialized case seminar, which I teach, on consultee-centered case consultation. This meets for one and a half hours once weekly for the second half of the academic year, and it has an associated supervised practicum experience in which the Fellow acts as a consultant in an agency in which he gets considerable experience with this type of consultation.

Details of the seminars, field work, and supervision follow.

General Mental Health Consultation Seminar

This seminar has two parts. For the first twelve sessions, I lecture on the theory and practice of mental health consultation, presenting in the main the contents of this book. I amplify my didactic presentations by means of seminar-type guided discussions of complicated issues of theory and technique; and I illustrate some of the points by showing movies of different types of mental health consultation that have been made by Edward A. Mason, M.D., in our Film Unit. These movies are documentaries of consultation interviews conducted by our staff and by seminar students of past years. They provide invaluable teaching material. I often interrupt a film and involve the seminar participants in a joint analysis of the meaning of the material we have so far seen, an appraisal of the problems of technique posed for the consultant, and a prediction of what will come next. It is particularly rewarding to view the film in its entirety once again after we have completed our discussion. We have transcripts of the sound track of some of the films, and I have found it sometimes useful to circulate these ahead of time, so that students can be prepared for what will appear on the screen.

During this first part of the seminar, in addition to presenting my material, I focus on two issues. First, I emphasize that mental health consultation is only one of the techniques available to the community mental health specialist, and I show how it fits into the rest of a comprehensive community program. Second, I help the seminar develop a cohesive and supportive group atmosphere as a preparation for the case presentations in the second half of the seminar.

All seminar members are expected to present cases for discussion, so they are all in the same boat; and this helps them to be tolerant and supportive of each other. But, in addition, I act as a role model, by demonstrating my indulgence toward the expectable ignorance of mental health consultants in many practice situations. I take pains, and this is not difficult, to demonstrate my own clumsiness and mistakes in technique in the case examples I present as illustrations of my lectures; so that it becomes part of the group subculture to expect that a consultant, even the most skillful, usually will be much wiser by hindsight than at the time when he is faced by an unexpected consultation predicament.

This indulgence toward the person of the consultant does not mean that we have to be fuzzy in our analytic thinking about the consultation case. In fact, I begin at the start of the seminar to lay the groundwork for logical rigor in case analysis and scientific caution in evaluating the effects of consultation intervention. My goal is that by the end of the first part of the seminar, participants will feel free to be penetratingly critical of all assumptions in case analyses; willing, nevertheless, to "stick their necks out" and develop imaginative hunches based upon minimal material; while being most sympathetic and understanding of the uncomfortable predicaments in which both competent and inexperienced consultants often find themselves, due to their never having complete information on which to base their analyses of situations and to not being able to ask the questions to elicit the needed data.

Having provided the basic content and prepared the right group atmosphere, I take up the rest of the year with discussion of illustrative case material contributed by seminar members. I emphasize at the outset that this is a didactic seminar and not group supervision—that is, our purpose is to use the case material to learn more about the theory and techniques of consultation, and not to help an individual consultant do a better job on his current case—the latter should be taken care of in his weekly supervision sessions. I warn seminar members that they may not even be able to complete their presentation of a case, because some issue in its early stages may excite my interest or that of the group, and we may spend the whole session discussing it. This is important to clarify early, because there is often a discrepancy between the needs of a presenter to obtain closure on his case problem and those of the seminar leader or members for an understanding of some important issue raised by the case. This discrepancy usually diminishes as the year progresses, once the seminar group has covered sufficient ground to be able to analyze a case as a totality.

At the start of the case presentations I ask only for vignettes illustrating some technical challenge and not for systematic and complete case descriptions. The amount of information about the agency setting, its social structure, the history of the consultation program, the experience of the presenter's predecessors, the vicissitudes of his contract negotiations, the details of his past contacts with the consultee in question, the behavior of the consultee, and the content of the consultee's communication is potentially so vast that its presentation alone could easily take up the entire hour and a half of the seminar session and leave no time for discussion. Accordingly, we have to settle for a much less than complete presentation. The way we usually deal with the problem is for the presenter to give a designedly sketchy account of what seems most salient to him and then for me and the rest of the group to draw from him, as we proceed, the added information that we feel to be relevant, always taking care not to burden him if we ask questions that he cannot answer.

My goal in fostering empathy for the presenter is not only to provide him with group support so that he may present his case with a minimum of defensiveness, and allow us vicariously to see the unfolding case freely through his eyes, but also to stimulate the seminar group to identify with him. I want all of us to put ourselves in his shoes and to have a living experience of his consultation. At crucial points I interrupt his presentation of the facts of the case, and I involve the group in trying to imagine what he must have been thinking at the time, and what decisions he must have been making about salient issues of the case and about the techniques to use. I ask the presenter not to take part in this discussion or to give us additional information, until we have come to our conclusions; and then we validate these by questioning him as to what he, in fact, did think and do in the case.

This educational method resembles the case-teaching approach developed so successfully by the Harvard Business School. In our situation, we have the advantage of not being restricted to trying to understand the case from written materials, but we have continual access to an informant who participated in the case and from whom we can draw additional information during the seminar.

Some indications of the way in which these seminar discussions progress can be obtained from my discussion of the case example in Chapter 9.

During the course of the year, the topics generally discussed by this seminar manifest an orderly progression, first because of the logical development of the interests of the participants, and second because I draw items for discussion in a systematic order from their presentations.

At the start, we are likely to spend several sessions discussing how to penetrate and appraise the social system of a consultee institution, how to negotiate sanction at different levels of its hierarchy, how to deal with initial suspicion or opposition, how to negotiate successive phases of the contract, and how to obtain information about past relationships of the consultee institution with our Laboratory and the effect of these on the current situation.

At this stage, we often spend time trying to understand the subculture of different professions and organizations and how this affects the perceptions and expectations of potential consultees, both about the mental health dimensions of their daily work and about how to deal with work difficulties in this area through the established problem-solving mechanisms of their organization and through consultation. We then move to a consideration of the problems of building and maintaining relationships with the group of potential consultees and with individuals who make contact with the consultant.

About halfway through the course, we get down to discussing actual consultation cases, first from the point of view of assessment and eventually in regard to the consultant's techniques of intervention, ending, and follow-up. We spend some time in this case-centered phase of the seminar discussing the consultation techniques, both individual and group, needed to deal with the range of situations encountered in different types of community institutions and organizations by our Fellows. As I will explicate later, we try to arrange for these experiences to be as varied as possible, so that among us in the seminar we cover most of the commonly occurring predicaments in which a community mental health worker is likely to find himself.

If I happen to be involved in a particularly exciting or unusual consultation situation during the year, I too may present a case for discussion. The atmosphere of the seminar is that we are all trying to develop and learn new concepts and techniques. I have several years' more experience in this field than the Fellows, but I am constantly reformulating and changing my ideas and practices just as they are; and certainly I do not conceive of myself as having a cut-and-dried body of information to impart to a passive receptive audience.

General Consultation Practicum

The same spirit of involving the Fellows as junior colleagues, which is a dominant note of the seminar, also obtains in their practicum experience. Years ago we conceptualized this as providing field-training placements for students, much as social work students are placed in community agencies to obtain their clinical experience. Nowadays, we have improved on this. We have changed to the model of residency training, in which the resident is treated not as a student but as a young physician, and in the later years of residency as a specialist who already has a considerable body of expert knowledge and skill and who takes a responsible role in the investigation and treatment of the patients in his department.

Our Laboratory of Community Psychiatry is constantly exploring the possibility of providing consultation services to a variety of different organizations and institutions in the Boston area. Whenever feasible, we develop a consultation contract with an appropriate institution and we organize a consultation service tailored to its needs. In all this work we involve our Fellows as junior members of our service teams, who work as colleagues alongside our senior consulting staff. Each Fellow receives an hour of individual consultation supervision each week; but his supervisor is usually not a member of the task groups on which he is doing his consultation work, so his student role is kept separate from his working role.

This system not only promotes the maximum feeling of work responsibility among our Fellows, and emphasizes that we are all constantly breaking new ground in the consultation field, but it also defines their role appropriately *vis-à-vis* the community institutions within which we are working and which are paying us for the consultation service we render to them. Our charges for our consultation services are substantially lower than they would be if all our work were being carried out by salaried staff. Also, with nineteen Fellows, each working at least half a day a week in our consultation program, we have expanded our work force and are able to offer a wider service in our community than we would if we were restricted to the efforts of our staff.

Each of our Fellows spends a minimum of four hours a week throughout the year on consultation work in the community. Most of them have two separate consultation assignments, which are selected so that they get a range of experience. Those who take the elective course on consultee-centered case consultation may have a third consultation assignment, or this practicum may be combined with one of the assignments in their general consultation course.

Of the two regular consultation assignments, one is likely to be in an established program, in which the main outlines of the contract have been worked out in previous years by the predecessors of the Fellows or by our staff. These will include, for instance, taking part in a continuing mental health consultation program in a school system, a public health nursing unit, an Episcopal diocese, or a state rehabilitation agency. In addition, each Fellow will have an assignment in which he is breaking new ground—exploring, for instance, in an antipoverty agency or a police department whether there is the need for a mental health consultation program, and then working alone or with a staff member of the Laboratory to develop relationships and negotiate a contract that will continue for future years.

The assignments in mental health consultation are integrated within the overall community field experience of the Fellows. The director of consultation fieldwork exercises overall supervision to ensure that each Fellow gets a minimum of two formally recognized consultation assignments. Apart from this, the Fellow is free to expand his consultation activities and integrate them with community organization and community development work, as well as with mental health education, within the framework of his general fieldwork experience. This totals two whole days per week throughout the year.

The Laboratory conducts a variety of programs to enhance the operations of caregiving professionals in the Boston area, and has relationships and service contracts with many state and local organizations in health, education, welfare, religion, corrections, and rehabilitation. In addition to the Fellows, the Laboratory utilizes the services of four full-time and two part-time members of staff in this program, which is coordinated within the framework of our Community Services Unit, directed by the associate director of the Laboratory.

Each Fellow is assigned to a "mini-catchment area"—namely, a relatively small geographic district in Greater Boston. He builds up working relationships with the mental health and community caregiving institutions in that district and studies the living conditions and mental health picture of the local population. He acts as the principal agent and liaison worker of the Community Services Unit in his district. Both his systematically assigned consultation work and his general community mental health practice work are mostly focused within his mini-catchment area, and so he has the opportunity of learning how to utilize relevant skills from his growing community repertoire as they are called forth by the problem situations he encounters in this population and its network of caregivers.

Our Laboratory has no legislative backing for this division of the field and for its assumption of indirect service commitments to the caregiving professionals. Boston is divided into five legislatively sanctioned catchment areas, each of which is allotted by the State Department of Mental Health to a service program linked with a local medical school or state hospital. These units are committed to providing direct psychiatric service to their population, and their activities are funded by state and federal funds. The units are also developing indirect services—mental health consultation and education—to the caregivers of their area, but naturally they are unable to cover this field completely. Their responsibilities in this connection cannot be circumscribed so that they can be held accountable, as they can, for instance, in regard to the diagnostic and treatment services to individual patients in their catchment area. Since they will never be able to cover the field of indirect services on their own, these official catchment-area programs are pleased to have us augment their efforts on a volunteer basis. Moreover, because we are not restricted to a catchment area carved out fairly artificially from the map of Boston, but are free to deal with the whole city, we are able to build relationships and deploy our staff in a system-relevant way and on a city-wide basis. Thus, we have contracts to provide in-service training and case and program consultation in mental health to the Boston School Department, the Boston Visiting Nurse Association, the Public Health Nursing Division of the Boston Health and Hospitals Department, the Episcopal Diocese that covers the Boston area, and the Boston area units of the state Rehabilitation Commission and the Youth Service Board.

Each of the official catchment-area programs deals with one segment of each of these city-wide organizations. We are able to be of value in enhancing their program because of our ongoing relationships with the central offices of the organizations and because of our system-wide contracts. We have accordingly worked out a mutually satisfactory set of agreements with the catchment-area programs, whereby we facilitate their direct and indirect services and supplement their community organization, mental health education, and consultation efforts. This setting provides an invaluable field of work for our Fellows, who are confronted not only by the problems of helping us to develop our own program but also by the challenge of doing this in such a way as also to promote the development of the other community mental health services of Boston.

A good example of this practicum is our program in the Boston School Department. We provide a service that utilizes the efforts of six staff members and six Fellows, organized in two teams. Each team deals with part of the department, and together they provide consultation or inservice training in mental health to the associate superintendents, the assistant superintendents, the principals and teachers of sample schools, the school adjustment counselors, the attendance supervisors, the teachers of classes for the emotionally disturbed and the educationally subnormal, the guidance department, and the school nurses. In addition, we help the school system develop effective relationships and channels of communication with the clinical facilities in the Boston area, so that disturbed and backward students may be diagnosed and treated with a minimum of delay.

Our contract is in its second year. Our Fellows have participated actively not only in providing case and program consultation and inservice training where indicated but also in exploring new areas for our work in various units of the school system and in developing our cumulative pool of information about its culture and social structure, upon which we base our policies for improving the mental health dimension of the school system's ways of handling its 92,000 students.

Each of the teams has a working conference every week at which tasks are allotted; and our total group meets once every five to six weeks to hear summaries of the work of each member and to pull the whole program together. This type of operation provides our Fellows with the experience of playing a responsible and independent part in a larger endeavor, and of seeing how the different parts fit together into a coordinated whole. Because of the size and complexity of the program, it is possible to assign a variety of tasks that are of graduated difficulty, so that our junior colleagues can move to increasingly demanding assignments as their consultation skills develop.

Our contract with the Boston School Department provides a good example of our way of dealing with the problem of the yearly turnover of Fellows. The Laboratory program is given continuity from year to year, and during the summers, when we have very few Fellows in residence, by the operations of our permanent staff. The contract in this and in all our community programs is between the institution and our Laboratory. The Fellows operate as members of the staff of our organization; and it is expected by our consultees that although our staff will change from time to time, the Laboratory will maintain its commitments as long as the contract is in existence. Nevertheless, whenever a Fellow or any other staff member comes or goes, there must be a renegotiation of the contract for the segment of the field in which he works, and this provides a useful learning experience for the Fellows.

The involvement of senior staff in all our consultation programs also provides us with the opportunity to grapple with a fundamental problem in the organization of an effective educational fieldwork experience for our Fellows. By and large, the best learning takes place when the student makes an error of technique, whether of commission or of omission, and then observes the negative consequences and has an opportunity to reflect on what he has done and to return to the situation in order to work out some other approach. This means that an ideal practicum must provide some kind of safety net, or assurance to the developing practitioner that his error will cause no serious damage to the program and that he will be guarded from making a mistake so atrocious that he will be thrown out of the system altogether. If this were to happen, he would not only be publicly shamed but he would also not have the opportunity to try another approach. On the other hand, if students are too closely supervised and if they are spoon fed by being presented only with safe and simple artificial training exercises, their learning will be inhibited because of lack of challenge. It is important that they be involved in doing a real job and not in "make-work"; and that they learn, particularly in consultation, to prepare for the unexpected. This means that the practicum should, as much as possible, be a segment of a real-life situation, with a minimum of ivory-tower academic preciousness.

Effective supervision provides a partial safety net by assuring the student that his supervisor will steer him away from the worst mistakes and will help him to identify others he has begun to make before he has gone too far. Unfortunately, in mental health consultation, events unfold very rapidly; and also in a program catering to a sizable group of students it is likely that a supervisor will not be able to keep up with everything that his supervisees are doing, as well as with intercurrent developments in the many complex consultee organizations in which his supervisees are working.

We try to deal with this through the active involvement of our staff in each of the consultee organizations. Their own consultation jobs demand an intimate knowledge of current events among their consultees; and they usually are sufficiently in touch with the supervisory and administrative echelons of the consultee institution so that they get immediate feedback about any change in its relationships with our Laboratory, such as might be caused by some unfortunate action on the part of one of our Fellows. Moreover, they can take remedial action, should this be necessary, and rescue the Fellow from his predicament if it appears that he would not be able to extricate himself.

The speed with which we get this feedback is sometimes most impressive. For instance, on one occasion a Fellow fell into a trap laid for him by a public health nurse consultee, who was engaged in a conflict with her supervisor about the conduct of a case. She asked the consultant for specific advice about what to do for her patient and slanted her story so that he gave her advice that ran counter to what her supervisor had told her to do. By the time the consultant had returned to our Laboratory premises an hour later, we had been informed about the incident.

The nurse had emerged from the consultation interview and triumphantly told her supervisor that the consultant had sided with her. The supervisor phoned her nursing director at head office to complain that a Laboratory consultant had deviated from our contract to restrict our intervention in such cases to increasing the nurse's understanding of the case and to leave the action plan to be worked out jointly by the nurse and her supervisor. The nursing director immediately passed the complaint on by phone to our director of consultation fieldwork, who was her liaison in regard to the administration of this consultation program. Our staff member assured the nursing director that our consultant's inadvertent *gaffe* would be immediately drawn to his attention. When the consultant got back to home base, he was told what had happened, and he at once phoned the supervisor, apologized for his error, and made an appointment to discuss the case fully with her on the occasion of his next visit.

To be sure, this bush telegraph effect depended not only on the speed of telephone communication but also on very open channels of personal communication based upon excellent relationships between the nursing organization and the Laboratory. Such ideal conditions do not always obtain, but on the whole our senior staff do maintain sufficient contact at enough levels in most of our consultee organizations that, formally or informally, we are likely to get negative feedback quite quickly. This is fostered by the experience of our consultee organizations that we welcome such information, that we do not get defensive, and that we take immediate steps to repair the damage.

Because of this feedback network we are able to say to our Fellows, "You can feel safe in making any consultation error, with two exceptions—you must never give psychotherapy to your consultee or infringe on his personal privacy."

Of course, in addition to our feedback system, our Fellows also have the safeguard that our staff knows the institutions in the Boston area so well, after working with many of them for years, that we are usually able to assign them to organizations and to tasks that will adequately challenge their current skill level and yet will not take them too far beyond the bounds of their competence. Where we still run into difficulties with Fellows who get beyond their depth is in dealing with new institutions, especially those such as the rapidly developing organizations in the antipoverty field, in which nobody knows what to expect. We feel that to allow Fellows to explore such areas may run them into hot water; but they are likely to learn so much, especially about how to deal with crisis and instability, that the risks are often worth taking. We do try to arrange that a Fellow who works in that type of pioneering setting has some safer assignments too, so that he may counterbalance a possible failure experience with the gratification of predictable successes in other phases of his fieldwork.

Supervision

A crucial element in consultation training, as in training in any skill, is the provision of adequate supervision. Until this past year we tried to give all our Fellows a comprehensive field training program that included consultee-centered case consultation. This meant that we could use only supervisors who were expert in this highly specialized field.

Since these are in short supply, we were led to a training bottleneck. Moreover, despite my own continual reiteration that consultee-centered case consultation was only one of the techniques among the many that must be acquired by a mental health consultant, we appeared to be practicing something different from what we preached. Our students felt that, since their supervisors were well known, particularly for their skill in consultee-centered case consultation, and specifically in theme interference reduction, this technique was really what we valued most. They therefore tended to focus onesidedly on cases of this type and to bring only consultee-centered cases to supervision.

This year we have modified our program in order to try to handle this difficulty. We have divided the educational program into a general sequence and a specialized consultee-centered sequence. For the former we have been able to draw from a much larger pool of supervisors, and we now have no difficulty in providing supervision for the fieldwork of the twenty-three members of our consultation seminar. (In addition to our nineteen Fellows, we have admitted four part-time members, one of whom is a new Laboratory staff worker.)

Each seminar participant has one hour per week of individual supervision of his consultation fieldwork. In past years, we have experimented with supervising students in groups of two or three—mainly in order to conserve the time of supervision, although we rationalized the procedure as providing each supervisee also with the benefit of vicariously participating in the experience of his Fellows. Despite the latter possible advantage, now that we have enough supervisors to go around, we have concluded that individual supervision is to be preferred. There is no doubt that a Fellow learns more from his own mistakes than from listening to those of his colleagues, and he also benefits from the extra time available for his supervisor to guide his efforts.

Another factor in favor of individual supervision, if there are enough supervisors available so that nobody has to deal with more than three to five supervisees, is that to keep in touch not only with the problems in technique of a supervisee but also with the social system complexities of the consultee institution is very demanding both on the attention and the memory of the supervisor. To supervise three supervisees concurrently, which means learning about a consultee institution at the most once every three weeks, and having to keep continually in one's memory the details of all of them, leads to less than optimal supervision. This problem might be eased if student consultants kept detailed process notes on their consultation interviews and on the unfolding events in their consultee institutions. We have tried this in the past, but have given it up, because it is too burdensome for the student. We prefer him to have a living memory of his consultation situations, rather than to translate this to paper and then to remember the words he has written.

Each Fellow is expected to keep whatever rough notes he needs for his personal use to remind him of what has happened and of his thinking at the time, so that he can present the case to his supervisor or to the seminar. Toward the end of the year, we ask each Fellow, as an educational exercise, to prepare a systematic report, with the guidance of his supervisor, on one consultation case. I have not been impressed by the quality of these reports, even of those prepared by Fellows whom I and the supervisors believe to have become competent consultants. Apparently, learning consultation and learning to prepare a good consultation case report are not too highly correlated. We prefer our Fellows to devote their energies to the former.

What is essential in learning consultation technique is to remember clearly what happened in the case and to spend time afterward in reflecting on the significance of what happened, as well as in planning for the next phase.

We have reason to believe that what a beginning consultant remembers and reports to his supervisor is sometimes a quite distorted account of what occurred, or of what an independent observer would have reported. With increasing supervised experience the distortions are reduced, and a competent consultant can usually present a fairly accurate picture of what transpired. We know this by comparing consultants' verbal reports with tape recordings or movie records. We have sometimes considered asking our Fellows to tape record all or most of their consultation interviews, not only to train them to remember more accurately what occurred, but also for use in supervision. We may one day use videotape to accomplish this more effectively. But in principle we have so far decided against it, mainly because we believe such recording would interfere with the spontaneity of the consultation interaction which is essential for its success. On the other hand, our occasional experience in making movies of consultations indicates that we may be exaggerating the seriousness of this interference, as psychotherapists did in the early days of tape recording interviews with psychotherapy patients.

This is something we hope in the future to explore. Meanwhile, we proceed in what we may one day come to regard as an old-fashioned conservative style of relying in supervision on spontaneous recall of interviews undisturbed by gadgets. The supervisor does not listen passively to the supervisee's report but actively draws from him additional information that appears significant. As in our consultation technique, our supervisory approach depends a great deal on the supervisor's providing support and increased understanding by asking helpful questions rather than by making expert pronouncements.

In general, the significant issues in consultation supervision resemble those of psychotherapy and casework supervision, and I will not discuss them here. Some problems, however, have particular salience in the consultation training situation.

An important aspect of the function of a supervisor is to act as a role model. The question therefore arises as to whether a consultation supervisor must be of the same profession as his consultee. Other things being equal, my answer would be in the affirmative. At Harvard, however, our most skilled consultation supervisor happens to be a public health mental health nurse, Miss Charlotte Owens. Since she is particularly expert in theme interference reduction, she is doubly in demand. Years ago we were concerned about the possibility of professional role image distortion if we used her to supervise members of other professions, and also about her acceptability as a supervisor by members of traditionally higher status professions, such as psychiatry and psychology. Perhaps these two factors cancel each other out; namely, there may be less danger of role image distortion if someone from a higher status profession is supervised by a person from a lower status profession.

In any case, we have experienced little trouble in either direction. This may be influenced by the fact that our Fellows have mainly become quite stable in their basic professional identity by the time they come to us for specialized training in community mental health; in fact, we use this stability as an important criterion in our selection process—we usually select about one candidate out of three who contact us. The other factor is that Miss Owens' personal characteristics and great skill make an immediate impression on our Fellows, and she is perceived as an expert consultant rather than as a nurse.

Another aspect of this situation is that the process of skilled communication that is the essence of consultation technique is of a generic nature; it is more or less the same, whatever the basic profession of the consultant. A psychiatrist, psychologist, social worker, or nurse who is a competent mental health consultant should use the same techniques in a given case. The style and wording of their interventions will vary from one to another, not because of professional differences but because of personality idiosyncrasies. Insofar as the content of the consultation communication is concerned, however, there may be marked differences, based upon the differential areas of interest and competence of the various professions. We do not feel the need to focus in our consultation training on the content area of professional knowledge about such issues as the personality structure and medical condition of clients, the patterns of organization of social agencies in the community, or family dynamics. We recruit only those Fellows who have already acquired competence in one or another segment of these fields as a result of prior professional training. We also rely on their having mastered the basic professional concepts and skills in handling unconscious processes in their interviewees and in themselves; and this area, too, is not a specific focus of our supervision.

Having learned from Miss Owens' supervisory experience that in her case the supervisee did not have to be of the same profession as the supervisor, we have used psychiatrists as our other supervisors, irrespective of the professional identity of the supervisees. So far, we have run into no obvious difficulties, but I must confess to some lingering concern about role identity distortion. As soon as we have a big enough pool of competent supervisors of different professions, we will try to match the discipline of the supervisor to that of the supervisee.

As a result of our supervisory experience over the years we have come to recognize a number of regularly occurring issues.

1. Apart from a few second- and third-year psychiatric residents, most of our supervisees have been mature clinicians. We have been impressed by the emotional and cognitive burden to them of having to learn a new set of techniques, especially since these are similar but subtly and importantly different from the techniques of psychotherapy or casework that by now come as second nature to them. Special support by the supervisor is needed for the supervisee to accept the student role—namely, to acknowledge that in consultation there is something new for him to learn. We have also been impressed by the finding that when an inexperienced consultant gets into difficulties in a case, he tends to regress to his basic professional style of functioning—a psychiatrist makes a psychotherapeutic interpretation, a psychologist collects data as though he were engaged in a research or testing interview, and a social worker begins to deal with the feelings of the consultee. Of these, the most dangerous is the reaction of the psychotherapist, and supervisors have constantly to be on guard against it.

We were originally somewhat reluctant to admit third-year, and especially second-year, psychiatric residents to our consultation training, feeling that students should already be competent clinicians by the time they study consultation. Empirically, we have discovered that these residents have learned consultation technique more quickly than their senior colleagues. Over the years, some of the most skillful graduates of our consultation program have been those who came to us as part of their residency training. We are not certain of the meaning of this finding. Only the brightest, most sensitive, and most highly motivated residents from the Massachusetts Mental Health Center, which probably attracts some of the best psychiatric residents of the country, gain admission to our consultation training program. Their success in learning consultation may be a reflection of their high personal caliber. On the other hand, since they are in the process of learning their other clinical skills at the time, they do not have the rigidity and the difficulty of their seniors in unlearning in the consultation setting many of their habitual psychotherapy responses.

2. A particularly difficult thing for a clinician to learn is that as he listens to a consultee talking about a client and as he asks the consultee questions about that client, he should be thinking of the problems of the consultee and not of the client. It is hard for someone who has been accustomed to diagnosing patients to inhibit his diagnostic curiosity about the client, especially if the latter is apparently suffering from a psychiatric disorder. It is also difficult for the clinician to inhibit his diagnostic curiosity about the personality structure of the consultee, and to restrict his interest to the elucidation of that segment of the consultee's functioning which is his work difficulty.

3. This leads to a fundamental problem that faces psychotherapists and caseworkers with a psychoanalytic orientation and requires special efforts by the supervisor to help them master. In their usual clinical work, these professionals have become accustomed to asking themselves the question, "Why?" They approach most behavioral manifestations in their patients or clients by trying to uncover the causative factors and sequences, both in the here-and-now and in the there-and-then. Consultants, on the other hand, ask the question, "What?" They do not have the time or the opportunity to uncover causative factors and sequences, many of which lie in the private domain of the consultee's past or present personal life; nor is this information particularly useful to them in making their consultation assessments.

Associated with this difficulty of basic mental set is the difference in speed, and therefore in the need for economy of thinking, in consultation as contrasted with most clinical interviews. A consultation supervisee needs special guidance and drill by the supervisor in order to learn how to conserve his thinking time during a consultation interview by restricting himself to those thoughts that will facilitate his consultation assessment and planning.

4. Another aspect of consultation technique that is easy to talk about

but very difficult for many people to acquire is to think concurrently on several different cognitive planes. A supervisor must help his supervisee, usually by personal demonstration in relation to case situations, to keep simultaneously in mind the manifest content of the consultee's story and behavior, the inner meaning of this in relation to the consultee's work difficulties, the relevant social system characteristics of the consultee institution, the trends in the interview in connection with evidence of the defensive picture of the consultee and the consultation relationship, the consultant's plans for assessment and intervention, and the recording in the consultant's memory of significant issues and problems for subsequent reflection or discussion with the supervisor.

5. Another issue involving an unlearning of habitual psychotherapeutic responses is that a consultant simultaneously uses a mixture of directive and nondirective approaches in his interviewing technique. He must control the interview, keep it focused on the client, and influence the consultee to talk about particular aspects of the case so that he can elicit projective material; and yet he must facilitate his consultee's associating freely, so that the maximum of unconscious data will emerge without the distortion of patterning imposed by the consultant. This implies that the consultant must be continually active in the interview and cannot afford to adopt the passive-receptive role with its free-floating attention that is characteristic of the psychoanalytic therapist. Yet the consulant must be just as alert to the unconscious significance of the productions of his consultee as the therapist is in the case of his patient.

6. Most psychoanalytically oriented clinicians are trained to focus on the depth psychological issues in their patients; and although a psychoanalyst is supposed to work from the surface down, and to deal first with the reality derivatives in his patient's productions, he does this in order to clear the way for his investigation of the unconscious material. The consultant must be helped by his supervisor to learn that the reality elements that color his consultee's perceptions and thinking are of major importance. These include, not only the current social system complications of his agency, but also the culture of his profession which makes him see work situations in certain ways and constrains him to deal with them in a patterned manner. The consultant must learn to see the consultee's problems through the latter's eyes; and for a clinically trained worker this implies, to begin with, a special effort to achieve cultural empathy that is analogous to the personal empathy he learned in his clinical training. The supervisor must also help him think concurrently on personal, cultural, and social system planes; that is, he must not

"switch off" one set of receptors as he "switches on" another, since he is dealing with a series of interpenetrating systems.

In connection with their acquisition of cultural empathy, some supervisees experience difficulty because of social class, ethnic, religious, or racial bias. For many middle-class intellectuals nowadays, this is a sensitive area and sometimes cannot be dealt with easily by direct confrontation because it would entail too great a threat to self-esteem. A skilled supervisor will find ways of helping his supervisee master such a difficulty by offering himself as an identification object, or by tactful communications that save face.

7. Finally, as in all supervision in interpersonal skill acquisition, the supervisor must pay a great deal of attention to his supervisee's personal reactions to his consultee and to the consultation predicaments in which he finds himself. In addition to the usual issues of countertransference, the supervisor must help his supervisee increase his tolerance of the discomforts of being ignorant of many essential elements in a case situation. He must help the consultant feel free to develop imaginative hunches on the basis of minimal cues and at the same time not to hang on to these if he uncovers discrepant information. The supervisee must learn how to differentiate his own subjective *gestalten* from those of his consultee and how to validate the patterns by indirect projective methods through his interview techniques.

In this connection, I would like once more to emphasize that consultation technique involves no stereotyped verbal formulae. The supervisor offers himself as a role model, but he must be careful that his supervisee identifies with his goals and approaches and not with his style and mannerisms. The latter are personally idiosyncratic, and the supervisee must develop his own spontaneous ways of achieving consultation goals.

Consultee-Centered Consultation Seminar

I am giving this seminar for the first time this year, and so I can present only my plans and not my experience. I intend to begin with a few lectures about the different types of consultee-centered consultation, and about techniques of assessment and intervention. Then I will show a series of movies, prepared in past years by Dr. Mason, which highlight problems of technique in this type of consultation. I expect that the most valuable seminar discussions will follow those movies in which the consultant made errors in technique. My approach in leading the discussions will be to keep stopping the movie and to involve myself and the seminar members in putting ourselves in the shoes of the consultant on the screen. Following our discussion and predictions of how the case will evolve, we will continue the movie and validate our expectations. We have about six good movies; and after discussing these, I intend to spend the rest of the semester in analysis of cases presented by the seminar participants.

Specialized Practicum

Each participant in the above seminar will have a fieldwork assignment that ensures him a significant number of consultee-centered consultations during the year. We have long-standing consultation relationships with public health nursing units in Boston, and with some school systems in the suburbs, for which we can predict from past experience how many consultees will request this type of consultation. The consultation contract has been well worked out; and apart from minor variations from year to year based on personnel changes or intercurrent social system upsets in generally stable institutions, a Fellow can arrive at the site and know that most of his time will be filled by a steady stream of consultees, who know their role and who mostly are requesting consultation because of theme interference. During the year, we can therefore more or less guarantee that each Fellow will average about two individual consultee-centered interviews each week, and that he will have to spend minimal time and effort in negotiating and in maintaining sanction or in dealing with social system problems. The latter are siphoned off by our senior staff, who operate as administrative consultants in these agencies and handle the problems of renegotiation of the annual contracts.

This is, of course, a highly artificial fieldwork situation; but we are not overly concerned, since each of the Fellows also has other consultation assignments in which he is confronted by situations closer to the real life experience he will have when he leaves our Laboratory and embarks on his career as a community mental health practitioner.

Specialized Supervision

Two of our supervisors provide supervision on this special practicum. Each of them also supervises the same Fellow on his general consultation practicum. The Fellow gets one hour of individual supervision on each, in order to ensure that what he brings to his supervisor is not restricted, as it used to be in the past, to consultee-centered cases. By assigning one supervisor to each Fellow to cover both types of fieldwork assignment, we hope to maximize the mutually enriching feedback from one set of techniques to another, and also to counteract the precious quality of the consultee-centered field experience.

INFORMAL TRAINING PROGRAMS

Informal training programs are harder for me to discuss because I am not so familiar with them as I am with the academic programs; but as I have traveled around this and other countries lecturing or consulting about community mental health program development, I have heard a good deal about bootstrap operations of different kinds.

The most effective informal programs appear to be those that include basic elements analogous to the three I have previously described—namely, a seminar, fieldwork, and supervision.

Since there is often no expert available to teach a seminar, the analogue is for four to six colleagues to organize themselves into a self-study group. They meet regularly, preferably on a weekly basis, so that they can keep abreast of the material. They usually begin with a literature survey, and I have been gratified to find how familiar members of such study groups are with my own writings, as well as with those of such consultants as Berlin, Coleman, and Maddux. I hope that the present book will provide a useful text for this phase of the activities of such study groups.

After the group has developed a common set of concepts about the theory and techniques of consultation, it moves into a second phase. Each member of the group carves out of his ordinary work setting some circumscribed areas analogous to practicum assignments. These should be restricted to one or two agencies or organizations in the health, welfare, or educational field, in which the professional will try to develop and maintain a consultation service in a consciously structured manner. As each group member develops his consultation settings, he shares his experience with his colleagues, who provide him with support and helpful advice.

It is important to restrict the number of consultation settings, so that the whole group can keep abreast of what is happening and so that the consultant can devote the amount of time necessary to carry out his work adequately and also to think about it.

The absence of expert supervision is a major drawback. There are two possible analogues. First, many people learning consultation on their own have made effective use of tape recorders. Despite all I have said previously about their possible interference with spontaneity, in this situation their potential benefits far outweigh their liabilities. Listening to a playback of an interview or of an exploratory conference with a group of potential consultees can be most enlightening. The record can also be played to the study group.

The second substitute for supervision is to use the group as a collective supervisor. The essential element is to present a case and for the other group members to help the presenter explore aspects of it that he previously did not regard as relevant or significant. In addition, the presentation and discussion provide the consultant with an opportunity to reflect on what he has done, explicitly to pinpoint the nature of the predicaments in which he was involved, to consider the various options that were available to him in assessing the consultation problem and in intervention, to explicate why he chose to deal with them as he did, and to evaluate the effect of his actions or thinking, as well as to imagine what would have happened had he chosen differently. The group operates primarily as a sounding board; but its members will often be able to perceive relevant issues to which the presenter was blinded by personal or cultural bias, or in which he does not have the benefit of their past experience.

Since a typical self-study group does not have the benefit of an expert consultant to act as leader, all its formulations are necessarily tentative, and this is a great advantage. It means that they have to be validated against further experience and that the results of this must be reported back to the group. Such a regular process of conceptualization leading to testing in the field, followed by reporting back and modification of the previous concepts, is a healthy basis for professional development. Most of the first-generation specialists in any field of practice, including mental health consultation, developed their own ideas and skills along these lines. The second generation, who learned under their supervision, acquired knowledge with less pain, and more easily and quickly because they did not have to explore so many blind alleys. I sometimes have the feeling that the first generation of specialists are often less rigidly attached to the principles they acquired themselves, and therefore more flexibly oriented to changing them progressively in the light of new circumstances, than those who learned from a teacher.

I do not, however, wish to romanticize the advantages of the bootstrap operation. Whenever a teacher can be found, imported, or sent away for a period of specialized study, this is a great help. At Harvard we have trained a number of consultants from overseas, who have returned home and have played leadership roles in developing consultation training for their fellow countrymen. What I do want to emphasize is that, in the absence of any of these possibilities, it is still feasible for a group to organize a satisfactory training program. This may be aided by occasionally bringing in a skilled consultant as a teacher for a three- to five-day workshop devoted to a survey of theory and techniques. I have done a fair amount of this visiting education. The most benefit from such workshops was derived when I returned on a number of occasions to talk with the same group—for instance, at yearly intervals—and when in the intervening periods the participants organized themselves into small study groups along the lines I have previously described. A short workshop or institute can be useful in helping participants learn *about* consultation; but to learn *to be* a consultant and to develop the necessary skills, some form of supervised practicum experience over a significant period is essential.

[14]

Mental Health Consultation
and Community Action

INTRODUCTION

My main concern in this final chapter is to raise questions rather than provide answers, and to show that in instances of community action the mental health specialist needs a body of theory and a set of techniques that are somewhat different from those he needs in the more traditional settings of consultation.

In the first part of this chapter, I wish to begin by describing the kinds of conflicts and confrontations which are becoming increasingly prevalent throughout our country in regard to community programs; next, to discuss the implications these confrontations have for mental health workers, the issues they raise and the problems they present; and finally, to consider several postures that mental health workers might assume in these situations.

In the second part of this chapter, I will present a specific example of a consultation involving an instance of rather turbulent community action. In the final pages, I will comment on this case and pose some questions it seems to raise in respect to developing a body of theory and a set of skills for consultation in similar instances.

THE CONSUMER REVOLT

A characteristic feature of our day is the revolt of the consumers—the potential recipients of services, such as students, patients, the poverty-stricken, the socially disadvantaged, Negroes, and other minority groups. They are expressing their dissatisfaction with the planning and implementation of community programs that are supposed to serve their interests.

This revolt is leading to recurrent militant confrontations between the consumers and the directors of community institutions. The confrontations are often turbulent, because of the build-up of past frustrations and angry disappointments, and because of the absence of a common semantic framework and a traditionally developed structure within which the two sides can communicate freely and negotiate peaceably.

The confrontations involve issues that may be psychologically disturbing but also growth promoting for participants on both sides. For instance, administrators of educational and welfare systems often are put under great emotional strain when representatives of the disadvantaged expressed their hostility against them; similarly, those who are rebelling often feel frustration when their attempts to secure their needs are thwarted. Both sides, however, may be positively affected by this experience—especially those who are rebelling against their past impotence and helpless passivity. The confrontations allow them to become active in mastering their own fate, and provide an opportunity for increased self-respect and feelings of group and personal worth. Finally, the content matter of the issues being debated may have profound significance for mental health. Often the issues involve a more adequate satisfaction of basic human needs of the consumer population, and this has clear consequences in fostering mental health and preventing mental disorder.

Although there is nothing in the training or in the mandate of mental health workers that should hold them aloof from these conflicts, many may wish to avoid such disorderly situations. The disorder is inevitable, however, since the consumer groups are rebelling precisely because they have not been able to secure their rights, at least as they perceive them, through the orderly process designed and administered by the organizers of community institutions and services. Moreover, large segments of public opinion accept the notion that disadvantaged groups perceive different needs for themselves than do the professionals and experts and that the former's perception is apt to be more authentic.

The right of the disadvantaged to the maximum feasible satisfaction of basic human needs is now beginning to be accepted as a fundamental axiom of our national life. From this, it follows that until an orderly process can be worked out for meaningful participation of consumers in the organization of services that cater to them, we must expect a transitional period of disorderly confrontation between consumers and purveyors of services.

Implications of the Consumer Revolt for Mental Health Workers

The crux of the problem for community mental health workers is that their consultation programs are carefully designed to fit inside the structure of service agencies and institutions.

The mental health consultant works hard to obtain the sanction of the successive layers of the institutional authority system for his activities, and he bases his request for sanction on his promise to accept the institution on its own terms. He promises to interfere as little as possible with the goals and ways of working which the management has chosen for its institution. In fact, he offers to help the staff achieve these very goals more effectively, while at the same time assisting them to improve the mental health dimension of their work.

This implies a basic allegiance of the consultant to the consultee institution; and in instances of militant confrontation of this institution by a dissatisfied client population, the consultant appears locked into place on one side of the conflict. And yet, from our previous discussion, the consultant might feel just as committed to the disadvantaged population, striving for satisfaction of its legitimate needs and its healthy autonomy.

Moreover, he might feel it inappropriate for him to take an advocacy role on behalf of either side. His own professional goals would best be served by an optimal resolution of the conflict so that both sides can gain what they basically want—the recipients to obtain what they know they need, and the donors to provide a service that best satisfies the needs of their clients.

Usually, however, there is no legitimated role for mental health workers as advocates for the consumer population, nor have they any status acceptable to both sides as mediators or arbitrators in trying to resolve the conflict between an institution and its clients.

It may take ten to fifteen years to work out an orderly procedure to involve recipient populations in the planning and management of service programs that cater to them, and to provide acceptable mechanisms with which to deal smoothly with the discrepancies that inevitably occur. I believe that eventually such procedures and mechanisms will be developed, just as they have been in the somewhat analogous field of labor-management conflicts.

Meanwhile, the problem will remain, and it behooves community mental health specialists to try to work out ways of dealing with the present lengthy period of transitional turmoil, and to decide what role, if any, they would like to carve out for themselves in this situation.

ALTERNATIVE ROLES FOR MENTAL HEALTH WORKERS

I expect that over the next few years community mental health workers will explore various ways of participating in this arena. Many of them are already actively trying different alternatives and are discovering the advantages and disadvantages of each.

Some of us can say, quite plausibly, "We are professionals, and in our consultation programs we have learned to deal comfortably with our fellow professionals in other community agencies. By reaching out to our colleagues beyond the walls of our own clinics and hospitals, we demonstrate our concern for the wider population which they serve. By working inside other professional agencies, we use our specialized knowledge and skills to help them become more sensitive and more receptive to the needs of their clients. If the clients are dissatisfied, we help our consultees listen with maximum sympathy to their complaints. We support our consultees while they are being confronted by militants, and we help them avoid irrational and punitive reactions to provocation, so that they keep in mind their basic goal of service to those in need."

The Consultant as an "Ally" of the Institution

The function of helping consultees manage themselves and their tasks hygienically in the face of militant confronters is a recent addition to the repertoire of mental health consultants. It represents one of several specific approaches which I will discuss. Unfortunately, the dissatisfied consumer population is likely to interpret this type of consultant operation as signifying that the mental health consultant is supporting the professional's stance on the issue in question. This is apt to alienate the consumers from mental health workers and their programs—an undesirable consequence for their future relations.

Moreover, there is some truth in the militants' accusations. In a conflict situation, it is almost impossible not to identify with those whom one is helping, since one tends to get information about the situation which is biased by their partisan point of view. This puts the mental health consultant in a particularly uncomfortable position, not only as he analyzes his behavior in the conflict situation, but also as he responds to the criticism of colleagues who accuse him of siding with the "establishment" against the disadvantaged. This can be particularly hard to bear if the consultant has a population orientation and is committed to the mission of serving the needs of populations at special risk. This is the main reason why he left the comfort of his clinic to begin with and why he organized his consultation program in the community institution.

The Consultant as an "Ally" of the Consumer

Some mental health professionals take the other side in these confrontations and offer their expert help to the dissatisfied consumers. In fact, they help them to organize, and they act as "advocacy planners" in helping them prepare their case against the community caregiving network and in proposing radical solutions to their problems. They help to lead rent strikes and sit-ins in public buildings. Their goal is to provide the disadvantaged with a countervalent force in their struggle against the might of the organized institutions.

Unfortunately, since the mental health professional usually derives his resources and his sanction from public authorities, these insurrectional activities introduce strain in his home base. If he proves successful as an advocate or agitator, this is not likely to improve his relationships with professionals in the community institutions which he is helping to attack. Since there is probably some feeling of solidarity among most professionals in the education, health, and welfare network, the bad reputation derived from such social action activities may significantly interfere with other projects that the mental health worker may wish to carry out in the community which require professional collaboration.

Perhaps of more importance than these drawbacks is the realization of mental health workers themselves that they have become partisan opponents of institutions and staffs that are fundamentally committed to the service of the needy, however shortsighted and inefficient their programs have turned out to be.

It is hard to enter an adversary situation without coming to regard your opponent as an "enemy." Mental health workers are not trained to be professional advocates like lawyers, nor are their professional colleagues in the beleaguered community institutions. Both sides are likely to take the conflict personally; and unlike lawyers or boxers who can remain the best of friends after the bout is over, mental health and community agency professionals are prone to continue to hate each other. This is hardly conducive to the optimal interdigitation of professionals in the community.

Mental Health Workers as Consultants for Both the Institution and the Consumer

Some mental health programs have attempted to overcome these obstacles by trying to legitimate a new role for their staffs, similar to the advocacy role of lawyers. This kind of program seeks to provide workers to both sides of the conflict and to inform both parties that it is doing so. The idea is for each set of workers to help its side and to provide it with professional advocacy support, so that in the eventual confrontation, each party can present its case most effectively and with a minimum of emotionally based cognitive distortion.

It is too early to assess the feasibility of this approach. It has obvious merit. Unfortunately, we know much more about building consultation relationships inside a circumscribed institution manned by professionals than we do about gaining acceptance in a loosely knit group of militant disadvantaged, with rapidly changing composition and leadership, and with a possible basic distrust for the contribution of professionals, who are its traditional opponents.

These difficulties are exacerbated if the dissidents are poverty-stricken blacks and the mental health workers are affluent whites. It is hard for a professional to fit into the culture of anti-establishment dissidents, and harder still for him to maintain leverage on the situation during the moments of escalating tension at the height of a confrontation.

Also there is the problem of colleagues within an agency maintaining good relationships when some are on one side of a polarized conflict and some are on the other. The question of preserving confidentiality to one's own side is particularly vexing, as is the difficulty in convincing one's friends that there has been no information leakage to the "enemy" or his agents.

The Mental Health Worker as a Mediator

A logical alternative is for mental health workers to operate as mediators, owing primary allegiance to neither side but trusted by both to safeguard their interests to the maximum possible degree and to assist each to clarify the priorities of its demands and then to negotiate an agreement by mutual trade-offs. This might be the ideal role for a community mental health worker, assuming that he could develop the requisite skills, which are probably not identical to any that he traditionally possesses.

The trouble with this idea is that at present there is no legitimated framework in community life for such mediation, as there is, for example, in labor disputes. Moreover, except in a few instances, mental health specialists are not regarded with equal trust by both sides, and so would have difficulty being accepted as nonpartisan and "above the fray."

Nevertheless, I feel that community mental health programs should persevere in this direction, at least to the extent that we discover whether we can become effective mediators and, if so, how this affects other aspects of our programs.

As an illustration of some of the problems encountered in this fascinating field, I present the following example of how one group of community mental health specialists carried their explorations beyond the boundaries of a traditional mental health consultation approach.

CASE EXAMPLE

A community mental health center in a city of 300,000 had just initiated a contract with the school department to help them develop a program to deal with their psychologically disturbed students. As part of this program, the mental health center had placed members of its staff as case consultants in several of the city schools, which they visited on a regular half-day-a-week basis.

A psychiatric consultant in one school, which was housed in a dilapidated building in the middle of the city's Negro ghetto (population about 40,000), reported to the center director that racial tensions seemed to be mounting between the local population and the school's predominantly white personnel. During a recent consultation visit, the psychiatrist had been talking to the principal about a disturbed student when a deputation of black parents forced their way unannounced into the principal's office.

They told the principal that they were not satisfied with the way in which the school was being run, and they complained aggressively about the quality of education their children were getting, as well as about the deplorable conditions of the school building, with its broken windows, inadequate heating, peeling paint work, and unsanitary toilet facilities. They said they had been complaining individually about these things for years without result. Now they had banded together into a committee and were demanding immediate action.

The principal, a rather shy middle-aged white man, was shaken by this sudden confrontation. The consultant supported him during the ensuing discussion; and after the parents had temporarily withdrawn into the outer office, he helped him review their demands and work out a reasonable reaction. The principal discussed the problem over the telephone with his district superintendent. He then called the deputation back into his office and informed them that their grievances would be brought to the attention of the school administration and that something concrete would be done about the matter.

The parents asked for a report in two weeks' time and set up a meeting for this purpose, to be attended by parents and teachers.

After the deputation left, the consultant continued to support the principal and to help him accept the legitimacy of some of the parents' demands, despite the hostile manner in which they were voicing them. He offered to come to the proposed parent-teacher meeting as a resource person for the principal. This offer was gratefully accepted.

When the consultant discussed this experience with the center director, they recognized that his offer to attend the community meeting was a departure from usual consultation policy. It involved the psychiatrist, at least potentially, in a more collaborative participant role in the school activities than as a "pure" consultant; it implied that the consultant felt the principal might not be able to handle the problem on his own; and it brought the psychiatrist into the view of the community as a member of the school staff, aligned with, and to some extent responsible for, school policies that were a bone of contention.

Nevertheless, the psychiatrist and his director both felt that the principal was in need of support, that the immediate offer of help in time of need would consolidate the consultation relationship, and that with care the various dangers to relationships in the school and the community might be minimized. Also, the center was interested in learning more about racial tensions in the community, and this situation provided a good opportunity for privileged observation of an unfolding incident.

It was decided that the psychiatrist should avoid, if possible, an active role at the meeting of parents and teachers and should make observations on what transpired that he could use in a post-meeting consultation discussion with the principal.

At the meeting, the consultant adhered closely to this planned role. He sat near the principal but was not called upon to make a public statement and was not separately introduced to the parents.

The meeting—the first opportunity in many years in that school for an open discussion between parents and teachers—was well attended by both sides. It turned out, however, to be something of a fiasco. The principal announced that he had relayed the parents' demands to the administrative authorities of the school department, that some of the repairs to the building had already been ordered and would be carried out in due course, and that other demands involved additional budgetary provisions which would have to be taken up with the city board of education.

This provoked an angry outburst from several parents, who said they had waited too long already and that they wanted immediate action, not promises of meetings at the board of education. The principal began to explain why this was necessary.

At this stage, a new element was added to the meeting. Two men in the audience, who were not parents but black community militants, became active in the discussion. They spoke in a hostile and insulting way to the principal and school staff, calling the latter a "pack of white-assed bitches" and stirring up the rest of the audience to join in their attacks, which became increasingly more ugly. The principal and a couple of teachers attempted to defend themselves and engage in rational discussion, but they were shouted down and the meeting broke up in disorder.

The principal emerged pale and shaken. The consultant spent the next two hours with him and some of the teachers, trying to help them regain their poise and understand what had happened. The psychiatrist pointed out that the local issue of dealing with the legitimate requests of the parents was being overridden by the more generalized tensions in the community. It seemed as though Black Power activists were exploiting the situation as an opportunity to bring a basic black-white conflict into the open. He suggested that, since the situation was beginning to extend beyond the jurisdiction of that school, it might be a good idea to refer the matter to the higher authorities of the school system, and he offered the help of the mental health center as a specialized resource in dealing with the larger community issues.

On the consultant's return to the center, the director concurred with his position and offered to attend a meeting with the district superintendent and perhaps to try to bring in some of the local black leaders for a behind-the-scenes discussion. The consultant phoned the principal and conveyed the director's offer, and the principal said he would discuss the matter with his district superintendent.

The following week, the principal reported to the consultant that the district superintendent did not wish to open up this matter in the manner suggested by the center and that while he appreciated their offer, he would not accept it at this time. If he felt the need for the center's help, he would get in touch with the director.

This response was rather disappointing to the center staff. It seemed to indicate that their relationship with the school system was still precarious, and that the district superintendent, with whom they had had little previous contact, possibly feared the loss of face that might be involved in publicly admitting that he could not handle the affairs of his own district and needed to bring in a group of outside experts to bail him out.

At a meeting at the center the staff discussed whether the director should make personal contact with the district superintendent or even with the superintendent of schools himself, but they decided that this would be inadvisable from the viewpoint of relationship building, since there had been a clear message implying, "Keep out. Don't call us, we will call you!"

The consensus at the staff meeting was that the center should maintain a "watching brief," continue to consult with the principal about case problems and whenever he requested it also about relationships with the parents and the community, and hold itself in readiness to offer further help when the school people were more motivated to ask for it. They also decided that further contact with the district superintendent should be delayed for a while and should be initiated in connection with some other school or issue. It was hoped that in due course the school people would feel more trust and respect for the center as a result of further opportunities for interaction and relationship building.

Over the next few months there were sporadic incidents reflecting community unrest at the ghetto school. The principal kept the consultant informed about these happenings and continued to discuss the problems he was having with the parents, but he did not invite the psychiatrist to attend any of the meetings he was holding with members of the parents' committee. The main topics of consultation sessions reverted to discussions of individual problem children and their classroom management.

Toward the end of the school year the center staff member who was coordinating the consultation program in the school system had a routine meeting with the district superintendent to evaluate the year's work. The superintendent did not raise the issue of racial tension in his district but kept the discussion focused on problems of helping teachers deal with emotionally disturbed and educationally backward students. The center worker followed suit, feeling that the superintendent's defenses should be respected. No other legitimate opportunity occurred for further contact with the district superintendent.

During the summer vacation period, contact with the school department was in abeyance. A week after the new school year started, a series of dramatic incidents occurred. The center staff read in the local press that there had been trouble at the ghetto school. A new principal had been appointed and had apparently been approached by the parents' committee with the request that he come to an evening meeting with the total group of parents at their community headquarters. He had refused and had told them he would interview parents only by appointment in his office during school hours.

On the first day of school, there had been some disorder in the school yard, sparked by black community leaders and parents who had come unannounced to confront the principal and who were apparently not seen by him. The police had been called to remove "unauthorized persons" from the school building. The following day, a group of community organizers descended on the school and marched most of the students, together with some of their teachers, to a nearby community recreational building, where they set up a "Freedom School." The sponsors of this overt act of rebellion were the parents' committee, aided by a number of black community militant organizations.

That day, five professional community workers from the ghetto called on the center director. They gave him a more detailed story of what was happening, and they emphasized the dangers of a serious community conflagration if the impasse were not quickly resolved. They felt that the main problem revolved around the school authorities' refusal to meet with the parents and to discuss their legitimate demands; and they placed particular blame on the new school principal, who was making matters worse by his highhanded authoritarian approach to the parents. They said that the parents' committee represented the moderate leadership of the ghetto community, which wanted to resolve the conflict peaceably and were interested only in improving a very bad school. They also said that the black community contained a group of extremist militant leaders who intended to use this situation to wrest power from the moderates and to provoke a bloody confrontation with white authorities, particularly the police, whose brutality they wished to expose publicly. Press, radio, and television reporters were continually on the scene, and the stage was set for a major battle.

The group of community professionals, which included both white and black workers, said they had come to ask the center staff to intervene in this situation because the center's consultation contract with the school system gave it direct access to the superintendent. The center must use its influence to persuade him of the absolute necessity of reinstituting communication with the black parents so that the problems might be handled quietly and rationally. Otherwise, they would become a cause of racial strife, in which people would be injured and possibly killed and property would be damaged.

One of the visitors, a black community organization worker from one of the ghetto settlement houses, asked the center director what his staff had already done in this matter. The director gave a brief report on their consultation activities in the school and said that they had not yet begun their program for the new school year. The visitor asked somewhat aggressively, "How can you justify this passivity and slow routinized style of operations, when people's lives are at stake?"

The director replied with some heat that he saw no need for them to justify their style of consultation on these grounds; their program with the school system was in its early stages and the beginning relationships had to be developed gently lest the school staff feel that the center was infringing on their internal domain. It was center policy that no moves should be made into new problem areas until the school staff asked the mental health workers to help them. This meant that inevitably the consultation program would develop slowly and at a rate dictated by the consultee institution. The alternative could easily be the disintegration of the center program and their ejection from the school system—a fate that had befallen many other mental health workers in the past, who had come in with missionary zeal to reform that institution.

The community organizer was not convinced. He apologized for his vehemence but said he was concerned about the immediate dangers to his community and to the school system. He accused the center of "fiddling while Rome burned." He admitted that the center approach to its consultation program was in keeping with the latest and best theories of mental health consultation, but he asked whether the center had no concern for basic issues of community life that had clear implications for the mental health of wide sections of the population. He urged that such concern should convince the director to set aside, at least temporarily and as an emergency measure, his slow, deliberate professionalized style of operations. He also questioned the wisdom of the center's decision several months earlier to retire from the community action approach in the ghetto school.

The center director was impressed by these arguments and promised that despite the risks to his consultation program he would try to intervene immediately with the superintendent of schools in order to promote communication with the black parents.

The next day the center director and some of his staff had an emergency meeting at school headquarters with the deputy superintendent and the district superintendent. The director described his discussion with the community workers and offered his help in resolving the communication impasse with the parents of the ghetto school.

At first the superintendents were rather surprised to discover the center's interest in this matter. The deputy superintendent said he could not see what this administrative issue had to do with problems of emotionally disturbed or subnormal children, which he thought was the center's area of interest.

The director replied that his center was concerned with all community issues that might affect the sense of well-being of children and their families and that might be conducive to mental health or mental disorder. He felt that racial tensions and lack of consonance between parents and educators must inevitably affect the feelings of security of many families, and might have a deleterious effect on the emotional stability of school-children. Moreover, problems of communication between individuals and groups were a topic of special interest to mental health specialists and one in which they had developed some expert knowledge.

He also told the superintendents that his visitors had predicted a more dangerous community upheaval if the local problem between the ghetto school and the parents' group was not quickly resolved. He said that the center staff, like all citizens, had a fundamental interest in preserving public order and preventing damage to property and lives, such as had recently occurred in other cities as a consequence of similar racial conflicts in the schools.

The superintendents' immediate response was very positive. They freely admitted to being at their wit's end and warmly welcomed this offer of help. They then gave a detailed account of their problems in dealing with the parents of the ghetto school. The parents were making a series of outrageous demands, most of which could not be dealt with in practical terms. For example, they wanted complete community control over the school, with power to hire and fire its personnel. They demanded a black principal. They wanted several of their number to be put on the school payroll as "guardians of discipline" in the school.

The district superintendent said that he was more than eager to talk to the parents, but all his efforts to involve them in rational discussion had been unavailing. Three weeks before the start of the school year he had gone to an evening meeting with the parents and community leaders at their neighborhood center. He had tried to explain to them that he was most anxious to do all in his power to improve the school but that some of their demands would require state legislation for implementation and other requests should be submitted to the board of education and not to the administrators of the school department.

He said the meeting went on till midnight, and he had never been so uncomfortable or so frightened. They had shouted and screamed at him. They had insulted him with vile language, and they had poured out onto him a torrent of hatred and abuse against white people, the like of which he had never imagined. He had felt that if he stood there and accepted their insults without flinching, they might eventually quiet down and allow some rational discussion; but by midnight this had not happened, and he gave up and left the meeting.

When the new principal informed him that he had been invited to meet the parents in that same place, the district superintendent told him what had happened to him. He was not surprised when the principal told him he had refused to go and had requested the parents to come by appointment and talk in his office.

The district superintendent said that he was very willing to talk to the parents individually or collectively and had told them he would see them at any time in his district office. They had refused to come, saying that if he were really interested in listening to them, he should visit them "on their turf."

Both superintendents felt that the disruption of the school and the organization of the Freedom School were the work of "outside agitators." They reported that the board of education was preparing to institute criminal charges against the ringleaders. The district superintendent was being pressed to call in his truant officers to take coercive action, through the courts if necessary, in regard to parents of students who were absenting themselves from school and were attending the unauthorized Freedom School. He was trying to delay such action because of the numbers involved and because he did not wish to exacerbate an already inflamed situation.

In response to the director's questions, the superintendents said that they would welcome help from any quarter in building a communication bridge with the parents of the students. Unfortunately, nobody so far had proposed anything sensible.

The superintendents also complained about all the current publicity. Whenever they and the parents got near each other, radio and television equipment would obtrude, and they felt that the behavior of the black community leaders was as much a bid for public notice as a sincere attempt to deal with the real issues.

The center staff offered two types of assistance. First, they promised to consult with the district superintendent, whenever he felt the need, about the day-to-day tactical problems of managing the crisis. He accepted this offer with alacrity and set up the first consultation appointment for that afternoon. Second, they offered to make informal contacts with leaders of the black community to explore how and where the two sides could be got together for a behind-the-scenes discussion outside the orbit of the public media.

In that connection, the center director asked the superintendents whether they would approve his searching for a suitable community leader whose prestige would place him above the fray, who would be acceptable to both sides, and who would convene a closed meeting between them and the parents at some neutral site. The superintendents welcomed this suggestion with enthusiasm.

As the meeting was breaking up in a spirit of warm comradeship, the center director felt sufficiently confident about his relationship with the district superintendent to express his regrets that they had not commenced this collaboration several months earlier, when the problems at the ghetto school first came into the open and their psychiatric consultant in that school had offered to convene a community meeting.

The district superintendent reacted with surprise. He said he knew nothing about the offer. He knew the psychiatrist was offering consultation to that school, but he had never been informed that the consultant had been involved in the principal's confrontations with the parents, and he certainly did not know of the center's interest in convening a joint meeting with black leaders. Had he heard of the offer at that time, he would have been as keen to accept it as he was to avail himself of the help they were offering this day.

The district superintendent's reaction was open and sincere, and the center director quickly closed the incident with some light remark about how, if difficulties of communication arose even within and between professional organizations, they should not be surprised at blocked communications between white professionals and black laymen.

When this incident was subsequently discussed at a staff meeting at the mental health center, the consensus was that either the school principal must have been too insecure to pass the center's offer on to his district superintendent or he must have so distorted the message that the busy superintendent had not understood him. In any case, by hindsight it was now clear that the center's decision not to raise the matter directly with the district superintendent had been wrong, and that the criticism of the community organizer from the ghetto settlement house had been valid.

The center director and his staff learned from this an important lesson: Never rely on messages being sent and received undistorted within another organization, especially in times of insecurity and tension. A valid judgment about the attitudes of higher authorities in a system can be made only on the basis of direct interaction with them.

The center director then proceeded to try to arrange for a mutually acceptable community leader to convene a private meeting of the parents and the school authorities. He first phoned one of the militant black ghetto leaders with whom he had a long-standing friendly relationship and asked his advice. The leader readily agreed to talk with the parents' committee to see if they would be willing to attend a meeting behind the scenes with the school authorities, if somebody they trusted were to convene it. A few hours later he reported back that they were eager for such a meeting, and he proposed a list of names of acceptable conveners. The center director discussed this list over the phone with the superintendent of schools, who rejected some of the names and proposed alternatives.

The center staff then contacted some of these dignitaries informally to elicit their interest in assuming the role of convener, but all expressed reluctance to act on their own initiative. They said, however, that if somebody in an official position, such as the mayor, were to invite them, they would be pleased to act.

The center director then went to see the mayor. The latter was obviously keeping in close touch with the situation but at first said that school business was outside his jurisdiction, being the domain of an independent elected board of education. The center director informed him of the impending threat of a race riot if the impasse was not broken, and the mayor replied that he already knew this from his police chief. He asked the director what additional specialized services he and his mental health colleagues had to offer. The director replied that they could act as an informal liaison between the conflicting parties and develop a list of mutually acceptable people from whom the mayor might choose an individual or group who might convene a meeting. He presented his list of names, and the mayor said he knew them all and he did not believe that they would be truly acceptable to both sides but would think about it and discuss the matter with his advisors.

The center director left the interview in some perplexity. Subsequent inquiries among his friends who had expert knowledge of current city politics threw possible light on the mayor's apparent reluctance to act. The mayor had recently been elected by a narrow majority over an opponent who had appealed to the anti-Negro sentiment of the sizable lower-middle-class white population of the city. Since his election, he had come under heavy attack for allegedly attempting to build an image of fairness and impartiality on racial issues by preserving his friendship with the black community, while assuring the white backlash sentiment that he was not a weakling who would give in to mob violence. The center director's request that he take an active role in the present conflict endangered his political "tightrope act."

Nevertheless, it appeared that the mayor was the only one who had the leverage power in this situation. After repeated phone calls over a two-day period produced no action, the center director and his friend, the black leader, decided to make a more determined attempt. They went together to see the mayor and gave him a new list of names to consider.

On this occasion the mayor appeared more receptive, partly because of the presence of the black leader, for whom he obviously had considerable respect, and partly because it had now become clear that a major public disorder was imminent. The mass media were reporting new inflammatory incidents by the hour, and editorials were calling for the mayor to intervene to avert a calamity.

That evening the mayor announced that he had appointed a blue ribbon committee to carry out a fundamental inquiry into the school conflict. Unfortunately, he had carefully included on the rather large committee representatives of both the pro-Negro and the anti-Negro political factions of the city, which would ensure that the committee would not be able to take quick and definite action (and would be unlikely to embarrass the mayor in regard to his relations with either side); and he announced in a radio and television interview that he would not convene the committee until all the children had returned to the ghetto school and order had been restored.

At this point, it became abundantly clear to the center staff that not only was the conflict between the ghetto school and the parents being used by black militants as grist for their mill in advancing their own political ambitions, but that other political units in the city, such as the mayor's office, were unable to deal effectively with the apparently simple issue of convening a meeting of the two sides because it catalyzed a complicated tangle of forces in their own political situation. Everyone involved seemed unable to take a step because of the web of issues in which he was already caught up.

Frustration at this realization emboldened the center director to take the matter into his own hands. He phoned the superintendent of schools and the black politician and simply invited representatives of both sides to an informal meeting in his office that evening. The invitations were promptly accepted.

The meeting took place according to plan. The deputy superintendent and the district superintendent represented the school department. The chairman and three of the four other members of the parents' committee, as well as the black leader, represented the parents of the ghetto school. The center director acted as chairman.

The meeting proceeded in an amicable atmosphere and both sides discovered that they could communicate easily with each other. The parents talked in detail about the obvious shortcomings of the school and presented a series of reasonable requests for improvements. The school administrators expressed their interest in working with the parents to improve the school plant and the curriculum. Mutual respect developed, as each side began to see the matter from the point of view of the other.

But when the center director tried to close the meeting, the chairman of the parents' committee drew from his pocket a written statement that he said had been prepared by a group of the parents, and started to read it. The statement was written in intemperate language and called for complete local control of the school by the parents and the ghetto community.

The amicable atmosphere immediately gave way to tense hostility. The school administrators showed signs of barely suppressed anger, and the parents began to speak provocatively and with raised voices. The center director broke into this discussion and pointed out that the meeting had been progressing well until the inflammatory words "local control" had been used. He felt that such "fighting words" should be ruled out of order, because they probably meant completely different things to each side and because they were more like battle cries than attempts to convey information. He called on all participants to return to the spirit of cooperation which had brought them together.

The center director's appeal was successful, and the final few minutes of the discussion reverted to friendly rationality. Both sides were obviously grateful for the psychiatrist's intervention that had prevented an outbreak of hostilities. They asked him to reconvene a further meeting a few days later, and a date was fixed.

The second meeting followed more or less the same pattern as the first, except that only two of the parents' committee attended, and rather more time was taken up at its end in irrational and provocative arguments about community control and the demands of the parents for a black principal. This was partially initiated by the parents and partially provoked by one of the superintendents, who questioned the connection between the parents' committee and the Freedom School.

Again the center director attempted to bring the meeting back to a rational discussion. This time he did not succeed, and it broke up in an atmosphere of mutual frustration, the parents obviously feeling that in his pleas for "rationality" he was acting as the agent of the school system. On the other hand, some of the center staff who had an hour-long post-meeting discussion with the parents on the sidewalk outside the director's office reported that the parents were most upset that they had wrecked the meeting with their vociferous behavior. They felt this had been a reaction to the provocativeness of the superintendent, who had attacked their connection with the Freedom School. They also quietly admitted that they were "putting on" the superintendents when they demanded the appointment of a black principal. They would certainly settle for a white principal if he were competent and if he respected the parents of his black students.

At the request of the chairman of the parents' committee, a third meeting was convened at the center the following week. This time he was the sole representative of the parents, and the meeting was conducted entirely in a businesslike rational manner. He presented a list of requests and the superintendents discussed each, telling him which they could deal with and which were outside their jurisdiction.

It became clear that part of the difficulty in communication was caused by the parents' oversimplified view of the school system. They had not understood the complication of its internal layers of authority and of the jurisdictional boundaries within which it operated. They expected the school spokesman to be able to fulfill any or all of their requests; and if he did not, they were apt to feel that he was being hostile and depriving rather than that he did not have the jurisdictional power.

The center director drew this point to the attention of both sides and emphasized the necessity, in order to ensure meaningful communication, of their learning the cognitive framework that each was using. He then said that he believed his role as a convener of informal meetings was at an end. The need now was for formal negotiation and no longer for the two sides to get to know and respect each other. The latter had to some extent already occurred.

He offered, as an aid to effective negotiation, to attach some of his staff to the parents' committee to help them formulate their demands so that these would be understandable and not irritating to the school department. He also pointed out what had already been recognized by the parents—that other center staff were acting in a similar role as consultants to the superintendents. In addition, he offered personally to accept the role of mediator to move between the two sides and try to help them come to the best possible agreement in their negotiation, if the parties would invite him to do so.

Both his offers fell on deaf ears! The chairman of the parents' committee completely ignored them. He obviously by now perceived the center director to be an agent of the school department, and after this third meeting he and his group initiated no further contacts with the center. Over the next four weeks, however, now that the ice was broken, the parents' committee had a series of formal negotiating meetings in the offices of the district superintendent and the superintendent and eventually concluded a mutually satisfactory agreement. The Freedom School was disbanded, and all the children were brought back to the ghetto school.

The three "secret meetings" at the mental health center were never reported in the mass media. However, during that period, there was frequent mention in the press, and on one occasion in a court case associated with the school conflict, that behind-the-scenes informal contacts between the parents and the school authorities were taking place and that this hopeful development was counteracting community tensions and preventing an open violent confrontation.

The staff of the mental health center were satisfied with the results of their limited intervention. They felt that they had helped to cool an inflammatory situation and to allow both sides to overcome the obstacles to communication that for a while had completely impeded their wish to negotiate a settlement of the problems of the ghetto school. As this negotiation got under way, the participants became able to focus effectively on their real problems and to prevent outsiders from exploiting them for the satisfaction of their own political needs. As soon as the militant black leaders saw that the ghetto school issue appeared to be on the way to a peaceful resolution, they transferred their focus to a conflict in another school with a black student body, which promised a better opportunity for violent racial confrontation.

Meanwhile, the ongoing consultation relationship between the center and the school department did not appear to have suffered. In fact, there had been a growth of personal trust and respect between center staff and the two school superintendents who had collaborated with them on a day-to-day basis.

It was not clear how the affair had affected the center's relationships with the black community. The parents were apparently grateful for the center's help in the crucial phases of arranging the negotiations, but they perceived the center as part of the services of the school department and not as an acceptable advocate for their side. It was difficult to determine how the black community had perceived the center before its intervention in this conflict, and how this image had been affected, if at all, by this operation.

COMMENTS ON THE CASE EXAMPLE

The incidents and the pattern of unfolding of events in this case are typical of episodes occurring with increasing frequency in racially mixed United States cities. Characteristically, there are periods of frustration and mounting tension as the two sides to a conflict get locked into position because of mutual suspicions, provocations, and defensive maneuvers and because they lack a common semantic framework and cognitive map to form a basis for communication.

Frequently, the formal governmental network proves inadequate in resolving the conflict in its early stages, for reasons similar to those portrayed in this case. Often there is no indication for involving the formal legal services; but sometimes the dispute escalates and leads to major disorder and bloodshed, following which the courts and governmental authorities do manage to effect a resolution.

Sometimes, this exacerbation is avoided by the intervention of third parties similar to the center director. Usually, these are not psychiatrists but other citizens with recognized status in the community and some measure of acceptability to both the disputing parties. Examples have included clergymen, attorneys, judges, bankers, civic leaders or senior staff of community service coordinating bodies, such as the local community chest and council or the chamber of commerce, or of professional organizations, such as the state bar association.

In the present case, it is questionable whether the mental health center director's contribution to resolving the community conflict was intrinsically different from what any individual on the above list could have contributed. His skills as a psychiatrist may have stood him in good stead in handling the acute deterioration in rapport between the antagonists at the end of the first meeting. I doubt, however, that he accomplished more than what would be expected from an experienced chairman drawn from any of the other professions. My analysis of the case persuades me that his effectiveness in the whole episode derived from his friendship with the black leader, who was inside the camp of the ghetto school parents, and from his access to the superintendents, made possible by the center's ongoing relationship with the school department. His success was probably not based on specialized community mental health knowledge and skill.

The prime mover in the case was probably the community organizer of the ghetto settlement house. He realized the need for a go-between who was free of political entanglements. He chose the center director and stimulated him to take action. He might just as well have chosen some other public-spirited citizen with appropriate status and contacts.

There does not, therefore, appear to be specificity in the professional knowledge and skills demanded of a person who acts as a third party in convening an informal meeting of disputants, on neutral territory and in an atmosphere that allows them to sidestep the tangle of defenses they have each erected against attack, which also prevent them from communicating rationally with each other.

I do feel, however, that the community mental health worker behaved appropriately in this case. He was certainly acting in line with his professional mission in the community, and more so than if he had maintained his previous conservative posture as a mental health consultant inside the framework of the school system. He happened to be in the right place at the right time; and I feel that it might have been professionally justifiable but not meritorious, from the point of view of his ultimate goals in reducing psychological suffering in his community, had he said, "I have my program to consider. Please go and ask somebody else to do the job." In fact, he made a feeble attempt to do this, but he was sufficiently open-minded and flexible to assume personal responsibility for taking action to convene the necessary meeting.

What of the psychiatrist's main reason for hesitation? The case report does not state it explicitly, but clearly this was a question of sanction. Other community leaders who were approached by the center staff to act as conveners said that they would be willing if some competent authority invited them. In the interchange between the psychiatrist and the mayor, the mayor was clearly questioning the center director's right to take the initiative in this matter. He had his own good political reasons for trying to fend off his unwelcome visitor, but the question he asked was nevertheless meaningful in its own right: "What specialized contribution are you able to make?" The implication is that if a mental health worker has a unique set of concepts and skills, this would validate a professionalized role for him in such a situation and would constitute a legitimate claim for public sanction. Otherwise, the psychiatrist is just one more citizen among the many who at that moment are concerned about impending civil unrest.

What I find attractive about the operations of the psychiatrist in this case is his willingness to explore a novel role for himself in response to his awareness of an unmet community need. Community psychiatrists in many places are treading similar ground, and perhaps we shall soon develop a body of specialized concepts and skills that will give us a particular claim for a sanctioned role in this area, similar to that which we have developed in consultation. In that field, too, we are only one among many professions that have worked out a technology which provides a basis for public recognition of expertise.

Pending this generally accepted legitimation, it is of interest in the present case to observe that although the mayor did not accord active sanction to the psychiatrist, but only dealt with him as he would with any high-status citizen, the parents' committee and the school superintendents did sanction his operating as an intermediary. In each case, however, the center director had to take specific steps to secure the sanction. He could not assume that he had it even from the school department, because his contract limited his operations to intrasystem consultation focused on emotionally disturbed and educationally backward students.

It will be remembered that the deputy superintendent expressed surprise to find that the center director viewed his area of professional interest as extending to tensions between the school and the community of parents. It was important that the director clearly enunciated to the superintendents his professional rationale for this extension of his domain. When he had done so, the superintendents were able to make an explicit choice to enlist his help in this area. From then on, he had their sanction. He would have been on uncertain ground had he bypassed this important step.

From the point of view of technique, the situation was less clear in the securing of sanction from the parents. It seems that this developed gradually during the director's search for a convener, as the parents were kept appraised of his activities by the black leader, who had personally vouched for the psychiatrist's *bona fides*. Nevertheless, the case report documents that the psychiatrist was continually preoccupied with the need to obtain the parents' sanction for his activities, and he did not presume to take any step on their behalf without first asking for their permission through their mutual contact. The parents gave their sanction until the center director asked them to accept one of his staff as an advocate and to accept him as a mediator. At this point the parents withheld permission, and this signaled the psychiatrist's withdrawal from active participation in the case. A less skilled community psychiatrist might not have explicitly negotiated for widened sanction in that third interview and might have continued his activity, only to be politely or rudely ejected a little later in the case.

Whether or not community psychiatrists eventually develop a technology on which to base a claim for expert status as conveners and mediators, I do believe that cases such as this emphasize an urgent community need. Those of us who are concerned about developing mechanisms to improve human relations among community groups should get together to organize some form of community mediation machinery. This should be outside the political system, so that it does not get caught up in entanglements like those that inhibited the mayor in our case example. This machinery should be available whenever community groups are involved in a dispute that does not fall within the legal framework, and whenever there is a need for a third party to convene a meeting or for a mediator to facilitate a task-oriented negotiation that is in danger of being obstructed by emotionally toned issues or communication blocks. It might well have a small, or part-time, core staff and be able to call on the *ad hoc* services of a variety of professionals, including judges, city planners, community organizers, attorneys, educators, labor leaders, clergymen, and mental health specialists. These conveners and mediators should be carefully chosen, as are labor mediators, so that they develop and maintain a reputation as impartial community agents.

I believe that an appropriate mission for a community mental health specialist would be to work collaboratively with like-minded people from other professions in developing such community mediation machinery. I feel that our background of knowledge and skills in mental health consultation and community processes should be a great help in our accomplishing this and in developing our own special brand of mediation skills.

This structured community framework would have a built-in sanction to intervene that was so obviously missing in our case example. Such a mediation unit would prevent many conflicts from escalating to dangerous proportions and would facilitate the rational negotiation of solutions to disputes that would ensure that both parties got maximum feasible satisfaction of their basic goals.

Before concluding this discussion, I wish to refer to certain details of the case example that have relevance for the sorts of problems that will confront community psychiatrists who move into the mediation field.

I am impressed by the change of atmosphere in the later stages of the first two meetings between the parents and the superintendents. At the beginning of each meeting, the interaction was rational. Each side was behaving in a mature and reasonable way, and the verbal behavior had the goal of exchanging information. Toward the end of each meeting, the parents began to behave irrationally, and their words expressed hostile feeling rather than communicating information. They used "fighting words," and the parents admitted later that they had "put on" the superintendents by demanding a black principal.

This behavior, although of lesser intensity, was similar to that of the parents' group during their public meetings with the first principal and with the district superintendent. The provocative lists of demands, including the "guardians of discipline," seem to have been similar "put-ons" —that is, ostensibly logical requests that are so outrageous that they lead to the discomfiture of the opponent. The opinion of the school administrators that such behavior seemed to be exacerbated by the presence of reporters and television equipment adds further weight to my belief that a significant causative factor of the irrational behavior may be that the orientation of the spokesman in that phase is more toward his own constituency than toward his ostensible listeners.

My hunch is that the shift from secondary process thinking and the verbal communication of information to primary process thinking and the verbal expression of feeling is occasioned by a shift in orientation from a focus on the opponents, with whom one must empathize in order to communicate, to a focus on the speaker's own reference group, whose needs he must satisfy. This shift in orientation occurs naturally as a meeting draws to its close and the representative begins to think about reporting what has transpired to his constituents. If the latter are physically present, as in a public meeting, or potentially present, as in front of the television camera, this focus is almost completely obtrusive and blots out the antagonist altogether as someone with whom one must empathize. It changes him into a relatively depersonalized and stereotyped target for the hostile feelings of one's in-group.

In this regard, it was significant that the switch to expressive behavior in the first meeting was signaled by the chairman of the parents' committee reading the manifesto that had been prepared by the whole parents' group. It is also significant that in the third meeting, when the chairman of the parents' committee came on his own, there was no switch to primary process thinking and acting. He was operating throughout with an orientation to his current listeners, and his constituency apparently did not obtrude on his consciousness because he got too caught up in his excitement at the start of productive negotiations.

My view on this sequence is buttressed by some observations I recently made during a confrontation between representatives of a group of welfare recipients and a state official. The welfare recipients were staging a sit-in at a public building to protest inequities in their winter-clothing allowance. At the invitation of the state official, I was present while he received a deputation of the leaders of the demonstration. Three ladies came somewhat shyly into his office and, controlling their anxiety, delivered a lucid and factual message about their grievances. Some of this information was quite new to the official and threw valuable light on a complicated administrative problem. He expressed his appreciation and then began to talk quite positively to the deputation about possible ways of handling the issue. He promised to convene a meeting of regional administrators of the welfare program in order to arrive at uniform criteria and distribution practices in the state welfare offices.

Unfortunately, both his language and the content of his discussion of administrative planning were incomprehensible to the deputation, and they showed signs of increasing tension and frustration. One of them got up and tried to leave the room, muttering something about "a lot of words—why doesn't he talk plain?" She was turned back at the door by one of the community advisors who had accompanied the deputation, and who told her that the man was trying to be helpful.

Then one of the other women said to her friends, "All he is offering is a meeting. What will they say out there when we tell them that? They ain't going to like that at all!" At this point there was a dramatic shift in the behavior of the deputation. They began talking loudly, and one of them got up and started pacing restlessly about the office, demanding immediate action in response to their demands. She talked angrily about all they had to put up with and accused the official of hardheartedness. Then she pounded on the desk and said they would not leave the building until they had all been given winter coats and shoes.

The official began to explain that this was impossible. She shouted him down and said she knew there was a store of clothing in the building because when one of her neighbors had been burned out one night, she had been given emergency clothing before morning. She threatened that her group would stay in the corridor all night, if necessary, until they were given their rightful allowance of clothing on the spot. The official became increasingly upset at this verbal onslaught and left the room.

Here, too, I discern a similar biphasic pattern of behavior. On this occasion, the switch to loud, angry, expressive behavior and the "put-on" of an impossible demand was clearly signaled by the question, "What will they say out there?" The deputation then began to express to the official the feelings of anguish, frustration, and anger of the group they were representing; but they did this in an irrational and relatively uncontrolled way, which might soon have got out of hand had the official not applied appropriate constraints. He chose to deal with it by leaving the room.

I believe that a crucial factor in this shift to irrationality is the insecure relationship of such deputations to the people for whom they are speaking, which mirrors the lack of organization of the deprived group and the precariousness and instability of its leadership structure. Leaders rise and fall quite rapidly, and there is little sense of allegiance among the followers. They are quick to repudiate a spokesman who does not give continual evidence of identifying with their feelings of anger and rebellion. Successful agitators, such as Saul Alinsky, go to great lengths to train both leaders and followers to channel this aggression and control its direction onto suitable personalized targets. In the absence of such training, the hostility remains free-floating and is apt to focus on their own leaders if the concrete demands are frustrated. A good example is the Biblical story of the murmurings and rebellions of the Children of Israel against Moses in the wilderness.

In the case of the welfare confrontation, I believe that the deputation was most secure about its support by the outside group just after they had received their mandate to act as its spokesmen. This emotional support was evident when they came into the official's office, and it undoubtedly helped them overcome their initial diffidence in confronting the important man in his impressive and awe-inspiring setting. They therefore were able to think and talk in a controlled and task-oriented way and to communicate the informational message of their constituents.

As time passed in the interview, the effect of this initial feeling of solidarity and ego-extension began to diminish. They also began to feel confused when they could not understand the abstract issues involved in the official's response. Their impulse was to retreat back to the support of their constituency in the outside corridor. Then they began to worry about how they would be received outside. At this point, they started to portray the angry feelings of their people and to represent and abreact their hostility against the authorities, rather than to negotiate on behalf of their people as would be appropriate for leaders and representatives, part of whose organizational role must be to control and channel the destructive feelings and irrational ideas of the mob.

This situation reminds me of Fritz Redl's recent discussion of the characteristic behavior of adolescents during individual psychotherapy sessions. Redl in his usual picturesque language talks about the "gang under the couch." [1] By this he denotes that the adolescent patient is constantly aware of what his fellows would be feeling about the therapist as a representative of the hostile adult world. Although the patient is alone with the therapist, he behaves as though his whole gang were invisibly present, and he takes care not to say or do anything of which they would not approve. This usually means stereotyping the therapist as an enemy and behaving toward him with the full force of the gang's rebellious hostility.

QUESTIONS CONCERNING THE ROLE OF MEDIATOR

If this analysis of the situation has merit, it raises some interesting questions for the mediator. How can he help the representative of the community agency, in this case the state official, pay attention to the possibly important information conveyed in the first phase, without being distracted by the provocative and emotionally burdensome effects of the second phase, so as to increase his opportunity for collecting information directly from the deputation? As in our case example, some of this information is likely to be new to the official, despite the most adequate communication system inside his department.

Can the second phase be altogether prevented? It is doubtful that anything the official can do during the interview could accomplish that, because it is linked with the leader-follower relationships of the complaining group, over which he has no immediate control. How should the official react to and deal with the provocative behavior of the second phase? Grass-roots workers are exposed at the local level to frequent confrontations with spokesmen for underprivileged receivers of care. How can they be supported by their supervisors so that they may register the information communicated during phase one and not overreact to the provocativeness of phase two?

In addition to offering help to the official, the mediator also has the task of helping the leaders of the underprivileged. How can he help them understand the administrative structure of the community agency, so that they develop a cognitive map that allows them to make sense of what the official says in response to their demands? How can the discontented group improve its level of organization and its allegiance to its leaders so that the latter do not feel so insecure that they regress rapidly to phase two? How can the leaders be trained to exercise appropriate control over the hostile feelings of their followers so that they are given a mandate in the confrontation that allows them the freedom to negotiate effectively? This presupposes, of course, that effective negotiation implies rational communication between the confronters and the agency representatives—namely, that the consumer group must learn the language of the caregivers and negotiate within the logical framework of their system. Is this inevitable?

What if, as expressed clearly by some of the national leaders of the revolt against welfare programs, the goal of the various confrontations is not to gain minor benefits, such as extra winter clothing, but to destroy the welfare system itself? This means that the prime movers will not be satisfied by local agreements but intend to achieve a rising tide of tension by provoking a succession of frustrating and increasingly violent and disruptive confrontations. The Black Power agitators in the ghetto school appear to have had similar ambitions. As soon as the conflict in that school began to be resolved by peaceful negotiation, they moved on to intervene in another school where there was a communication block and the likelihood of a violent upheaval.

What role should community mental health workers play in regard to this approach? Must we inevitably be on the side of conflict resolution by facilitating rational communication between the parties to local disputes, or is there also a role for us in aiding the revolutionary forces that seek the destruction of systems in order to produce a fundamental improvement in the lot of the underprivileged population? When I describe the behavior of the deputations in phase two as "irrational," is this not an expression of my biased identification with the system that prescribed the rules and seeks to force the recipients of care to communicate in a mode that inevitably gives the caregiving official the whip hand? In behaving violently and intemperately and in expressing the hostile feelings of their constituents, are the leaders not acting most sensibly, and should we be trying to cool them off? If we succeed, are we not helping to perpetuate the bad system, apart from a few minor changes?

These questions point to some of many avenues in philosophy and technique that present themselves for exploration. They also emphasize the kind of contribution that mental health specialists may be able to make in this field by using their clinical, social-psychological, and community mental health concepts and skills. I believe that the next decade may see advances in this area as significant as those we have achieved in the past decade toward developing the theory and practice of mental health consultation.

NOTE

1. F. Redl, "Adolescents—Just How Do They React?" In G. Caplan and S. Lebovici (eds.), *Adolescence: Psychosocial Perspectives* (New York: Basic Books, 1969), pp. 79–99.

Bibliography

Abramovitz, A. B. "Methods and Techniques of Consultation." *American Journal of Orthopsychiatry, 28,* 126–133, 1958.

Adams, Robert and Howard Weinick. "Consultation: An In-Service Training Program for the School." *Journal of the American Academy of Child Psychiatry, 5 (3),* 479–489, 1966.

Adult Education Association of the United States of America. *Supervision and Consultation.* Chicago: Adult Education Association, 1956.

Allerton, W. S. and D. B. Peterson. "Preventive Psychiatry: The Army's Mental Hygiene Consultation Service (MHCS) Program with Statistical Evaluation." *American Journal of Psychiatry, 113,* 788–794, 1957.

Altrocchi, J., C. Spielberger, and C. Eisdorfer. "Mental Health Consultation with Groups." *Community Mental Health Journal, 1,* 127–134, 1965.

Anderson, Florence and B. Shangold. "Role of the Consultant in Adult Education." *Adult Education Bulletin, 14,* 14–20, 1950.

Argyris, C. "Explorations in Consulting-Client Relationships." *Human Organization, 20,* 121–133, 1961.

Babcock, C. "Some Observations in Consultative Experience." *Social Service Review, 23,* 347–357, 1949.

Baker, Gladys. *The County Agent.* Chicago: University of Chicago Press, 1939.

Balinsky, Benjamin. "Outside Consultants to Industry: Strength, Problems, and Pitfalls (a symposium) II." *Personnel Psychology, 2,* 107–114.

Barker, W. J. "The Psychiatric Consultation." *U. S. Armed Forces Medical Journal, 3,* 243, 1952.

Barrett, Richard. "Outside Consultants to Industry: Strength, Problems and Pitfalls (a symposium) I." *Personnel Psychology, 17(2),* 128–133, 1964.

Bartemeier, L. H. "The Psychiatric Consultation." *American Journal of Orthopsychiatry, 111,* 364–365, 1954.

Bartlett, Harriett M. "Consultation Regarding the Medical Social Program in a Hospital" (conference). *American Association of Medical Social Workers* (New Orleans), 11, May 1942.

Beaumont, J. A. *et al.* "Consultant Service Report as a Function of Administration." *National Business Education Quarterly, 21,* 15–21, May 1953.

Beckhard, R. "Helping a Group with Planned Change; a Case Study." *Journal of Social Issues, 15* (2), 14–19, 1959.

Benjamin, Charles M. "Consultee Receptivity to Consultation as a Function of Crisis." *Dissertation Abstracts* (University of Texas), *28* (*5-A*), 1698–1699, 1967.

Benne, K. D. "Some Ethical Problems in Group and Organizational Consultation." *Journal of Social Issues, 15,* 60–67, 1959.

Bennis, W., K. Benne, and R. Chin. *The Planning of Change: Readings in the Applied Behavioral Sciences.* New York: Holt, 1961.

Berlin, I. N. "Learning Mental Health Consultation: History and Problems." *Mental Hygiene, 48,* 257–266, 1964.

———. "Mental Health Consultation in Schools as a Means of Communicating Mental Health Principles." *Journal of the American Academy of Child Psychiatry,* October 1962.

———. "Mental Health Consultation in the Schools: Who Can Do It and Why?" *Community Mental Health Journal, 1,* Spring 1965.

———. "Mental Health Consultation with a Juvenile Probation Department." *Crime and Delinquency,* January 1964.

———. "Preventive Aspects of Mental Health Consultations to Schools." *Mental Hygiene,* January 1967.

———. "Some Learning Experiences as Psychiatric Consultant in the Schools." *Mental Hygiene, 40,* 215–236, 1956.

———. "The Theme in Mental Health Consultation Sessions." *American Journal of Orthopsychiatry, 30,* 4, 827–828, 1960.

Bernard, Viola W. "Psychiatric Consultation in the Social Agency." *Child Welfare,* 1954.

Bettelheim, B. "Psychiatric Consultation in Residential Treatment; the Director's View." *American Journal of Orthopsychiatry, 28,* 256–265, 1958.

Bindman, Arthur J. "Mental Health Consultation: Theory and Practice." *Journal of Consulting Psychology, 23,* 473–482, 1959.

———. "The Psychologist as a Mental Health Consultant." *Journal of Psychiatric Nursing,* July–August 1964.

Bindman, A. J. and L. H. Klebanoff. "Administrative Problems in Establishing a Community Mental Health Program." *American Journal of Orthopsychiatry, 30,* 696–711, 1960.

Blaha, M. J. "When and How a Consultant Can Be Used Most Effectively." *Educational Leadership, 10,* 96–100, 1952.

Blain, D. and R. F. Gayle. "Distribution, Form and Extent and Psychiatric Consultation." *J.A.M.A., 154,* 1266–1270, 1954.

Blumberg, A. "The Consulting Function of Leadership." *Adult Leadership, 8,* 265–266, 1960.

———. "A Nurse Consultant's Responsibility and Problems." *American Journal of Nursing, 56,* 606–608, 1956.

———. "A Selected Annotated Bibliography on the Consultant Relationship with Groups." *Journal of Social Issues, 15,* 68–74, 1959.

Boehm, W. "The Professional Relationship between Consultant and Consultee." *American Journal of Orthopsychiatry, 26,* 241–248, 1956.

Boguslaw, F. and G. R. Bach. " 'Work Culture Management' in Industry: A Role for the Social Science Consultant." *Group Psychotherapy, 12,* 134–142, 1959.

Bonkowski, R. J. "Mental Health Consultation and Operation Head-Start." *American Psychologist, 23,* 769–773, October 1968.

Bordin, E. S., *et al.* "Effective Consultation." *Adult Leadership, 3,* 13–26, 1955.

Boverman, H. and R. S. Mendelsohn. "Pediatric Consultation in a Public Mental Hospital." *Pediatrics, 39,* 929–931, June 1967.

Bowman, P. H. "The Role of the Consultant as a Motivator of Action." *Mental Hygiene, 43,* 105–110, 1959.

Bradford, L. P. "The Use of Psychodrama for Group Consultants." *Group Psychotherapy,* 192–197, June 1947.

Bragg, R. and W. Freeman. "Principles of Mental Health Consultation to a School System." *American Journal of Orthopsychiatry* (46th Annual Meeting), 1969, *39* (*2*), March 1959. Digest of Papers.

Brockbank, Reid. "Aspects of Mental Health Consultation." *Archives of General Psychiatry, 18* (*3*), 267–275, 1968.

Brook, A. "An Experiment in General Practitioner-Psychiatrist Co-operation." *Journal of College of General Practitioners, 13,* 127–131, January 1967.

Brown, Jonathan W. "Pragmatic Notes on Community Consultation with Agencies." *Community Mental Health Journal, 3* (*4*), 399–405, 1967.

Brown, T. H. "The Business Consultant." *Harvard Business Review, 21,* 183–189, 1942–1943.

Buckle, D. F. "The Relationship between Psychiatrist and Pediatrician." *Clinical Proceedings of the Children's Hospital DC, 24,* 24–33, January 1968.

Bushard, B. L. "The U. S. Army's Mental Health Consultation Service." *Symposium on Preventive and Social Psychiatry.* Walter Reed Army Institute of Research, April 1957. Washington, D.C.: U.S. Government Printing Office, 1958.

Bureau of Labor Standards. "The Consultative Approach to Safety." *Safety in Industry Bulletin 223.*

Cady, Louise L. "The Tuberculosis Nursing Consultant." *Public Health Nursing, 38,* 394–398, 1946.

Canter, S. and Bud Fedor. "Psychological Consultation in Head Start Programs." *American Psychologist, 23* (*8*), 590–592, 1968.

Caplan, Gerald. "An Approach to the Education of Community Mental Health Specialists." *Mental Hygiene, 43,* 268–280, 1959.

———. *Concepts of Mental Health and Consultation.* Washington, D.C.: U.S. Children's Bureau, 1959.

———. *Manual for Psychiatrists Participating in the Peace Corps Program.* Washington, D.C.: Peace Corps, Medical Program Division, n.d.

———. *Mental Health Aspects of Social Work in Public Health.* Washington, D.C.: U.S. Children's Bureau, 1956.

———. "Mental Health Consultation in Schools." *The Elements of a Community Mental Health Program.* New York: Milbank Memorial Fund, 1956, 77–85.

————. *Principles of Preventive Psychiatry*. New York: Basic Books, 1964.

————. "A Public Health Approach to Child Psychiatry." *Mental Hygiene*, April 1951.

————. "Recent Trends in Preventive Child Psychiatry." In Gerald Caplan (ed.), *Emotional Problems of Early Childhood*. New York: 1955, 153–163.

————. "The Role of the Social Worker in Preventive Psychiatry." *Medical Social Work, 4*, 144–159, 1955.

Caplan, Gerald, Lee B. Macht and Arlene Wolf. *Manual for Mental Health Professionals Participating in the Job Corps Program*. Washington, D.C.: Office of Economic Opportunity, May 1969, Document #JCH 330-A.

Cartwright, D. and A. Zander. *Group Dynamics: Research and Theory*. Evanston, Ill.: Row, Peterson and Sons, 1960.

Charters, W. W., Jr. "Stresses in Consultation." *Adult Leadership*, 1955, *3(10)*, 21–22, 1955.

Cocking, W. D. "Role of the Educational Consultant." *School Executive, 75*, 7, 1956.

Cohnstaedt, M. L. and T. K. Phillipson. "The Urban Extension Agent." *Adult Leadership, 10*, 2, 1962.

Coleman, J. V. "The Contributions of the Psychiatrist to the Social Worker and to the Client." *Mental Hygiene, 37*, 249–258, 1953.

————. "Mental Health Consultation to Agencies Protecting Family Life." *The Elements of a Community Mental Health Program*. New York: Milbank Memorial Fund, 1956, 69–76.

————. "Psychiatric Consultation in Casework Agencies." *American Journal of Orthopsychiatry, 27*, 533–539, 1947.

Covner, B. J. "Principles of Psychological Consulting with Client Organizations." *Journal of Consulting Psychology, 11*, 227–244, 1947.

Croley, H. T. "The Consultative Process." *The Voluntary Health Agency Meeting Needs*. Continuing Education Monograph No. 1. San Francisco: Western Regional Office, A. P. H. A., 1961, 39–45.

Curtis, H. A. "Improving Consultant Services." *Educational Administration and Supervision, 39*, 279–292, 1953.

Custer, G. E. "A Look at the Personnel Consulting Business." *Personnel Administration, 22* (5), 24–31, 1959.

Davis, Alice T. "Consultation: A Function in Public Welfare Administration." *Social Casework, 37*, 113–119, 1956.

Davis, W. E. "Psychiatric Consultation—the Agency Viewpoint." *Child Welfare, 36(9)*, 1957.

Decker, J. H. and F. Itzin. "An Experience in Consultation in Public Assistance." *Social Casework. 37*, 327–334, 1956.

Dement, J. C. "Field Consultation in a State Health Department." *California Health, 12*, 57–60, 1954.

Drake, R. "The Use of Consultants in a State Agency." *Public Welfare, 4*, 88, 1946.

Eisenberg, L. "An Evaluation of Psychiatric Consultation Service for a Public Agency." *American Journal of Public Health, 48*, 742–749, 1958.

Elkins, A. M. and G. O. Papanek. "Consultation with the Police: An Example of Community Psychiatry Practice." *American Journal of Psychiatry, 123,* 531–535, November 1966.

Erikson, E. G. "An American Consultant Faces a Foreign Social Environment." *Journal of Educational Sociology, 29,* 184–190, 1955.

Faust, Verne. *The Counselor-Consultant in the Elementary School.* Boston: Houghton-Mifflin, 1968.

Feldman, F. "The Tripartite Session: A New Approach in Psychiatric Social Work Consultation." *Psychiatric Quarterly,* 42:48–61, 1968.

Ferguson, Charles K. "Concerning the Nature of Human Systems and the Consultants' Role." *Journal of Applied Behavioral Science, 4,* 179–194, April–June 1968.

Ferneau, E. F. "Which Consultant?" *Administrator's Notebook, 2 (8),* April 1954.

Forstenzer, H. M. "Consultation and Mental Health Programs." *American Journal of Public Health, 51,* 1280, 1961.

Foster, E. "Planning for Community Development through its People." *Human Organization, 12 (2),* 5–9, 1953.

Foster, J. T. and Jane Hartmann. "A Project in Voluntary Consultation for Hospitals." *Public Health Reports, 74,* 607–614, 1959.

Fulcher, E. and F. Beasley. "Consultant Nurses Can Help Staff Nurses." *Nursing Outlook, 1,* 208–212, 1953.

"Functions, Standards and Qualifications for Practice of Consultants." *American Journal of Nursing, 58,* 1281–1282, 1958.

Garrett, Annette. "Psychiatric Consultation." *American Journal of Orthopsychiatry, 26,* 234–240, 1956.

Gibb, J. R. and R. Lippitt (eds.). "Consulting with Groups and Organizations." *Journal of Social Issues, 15,* 1–74, 1959 (whole issue).

Gibson, R. "The Psychiatric Consultant and the Juvenile Court." *Mental Hygiene,* 1954.

Gilbert, Ruth. "Functions of the Consultant." *Teachers College Record, 61,* 177–187, 1960.

Gilbertson, E. C. and E. M. Williamson. "Consultation Process in Public Health Nursing." *Public Health Nursing, 44,* 146–147, 1952.

Glidewell, J. C. "The Entry Problem in Consultation." *Journal of Social Issues, 15(2),* 51–59, 1959.

Gluck, M. R. "School Organization and the Mental Health Consultation Process." *Psychological Reports, 12,* 1963.

Goldin, Gurstin D. "The Psychiatrist as Court Consultant: A Challenge to Community Psychiatry." *Community Mental Health Journal, 3 (4),* 396–398, 1967.

Gordon, Dorothy E. "The Functions of the Consultant." *Nursing Outlook, 1,* 575–577, 1953.

————. "A Study of the Functions of Consultants." *Nursing Research, 1,* 41, 1952.

Green, J. W. "Success and Failure in Technical Assistance: A Case Study." *Human Organization, 20(1),* 2–10, 1961.

Greenberg, H. A. "Psychiatric Consultation in Residential Treatment." *American Journal of Orthopsychiatry, 28,* 256–290, 1958.

Group for the Advancement of Psychiatry. *The Consultant Psychiatrist in a Family Service Agency*. New York: GAP, 1956, Report No. 34.

Hader, M. "The Psychiatrist as Consultant to the Social Worker in a Home for the Aged." *Journal of American Geriatric Society, 14,* 407–413, April 1966.

Hallowitz, D., A. V. Cutter and Katharine Pitkin. "Helping Disturbed Children through Parent Consultation." *Children, 8,* 22–27, 1961.

Harris, M. R. "Community Mental Health and Mental Health Consultation." *Psychosomatics, 8,* 255–258, September–October 1967.

Hasty, W. A. "What the Hospital Consultant Does." *American Journal of Nursing,* March 1948.

Haylett, C. H. and L. Rappaport. "Mental Health Consultation." In L. Bellak, (ed.), *Handbook of Community Psychiatry and Community Mental Health*. New York: Grune and Stratton, 1963.

Henry, Charlotte S. "Criteria for Determining Readiness of Staff to Function without Supervision." *Administration, Supervision and Consultation,* New York: Family Service Association of America, 1955.

Hicks, W. and R. S. Daniels. "The Dying Patient, His Physician and the Psychiatric Consultant." *Psychosomatics, 9,* 47–52, January–February 1968.

Hirschowitz, R. "Psychiatric Consultation in the Schools: Sociocultural Perspectives." *Mental Hygiene,* April 1966.

Hoiberg, O. G. "Problems of the Consultant in Small Communities." *Journal of Educational Sociology, 29,* 164–172, 1955.

Hollister, W. G. "Some Administrative Aspects of Consultation." *American Journal of Orthopsychiatry, 32,* 224–225, 1962.

Holt, M. "The Existential Conflicts between Psychiatrists and Ministers." *Mental Hygiene,* April 1966.

Houghton, L. "Interprofessional Communications for Improved Patient Care." *Quarterly National Dental Association, 25,* 8–11, July 1967.

Howell, R. W. "Mental Health Consultation to Public Health Nurses." *The Elements of a Community Mental Health Program*. New York: Milbank Memorial Fund, 1956, 57–68. Papers presented at the 1955 Conference.

Hull, J. H. "Value of Continuing Professional Consultant Service." *School Executive, 71,* 44, 1952.

Insley, Virginia. "Program Consultation." G. Caplan, *Concepts of Mental Health and Consultation*. Washington, D.C.: U.S. Children's Bureau, 235–246, 1959.

———. "Social Work Consultation in Public Health." *Concepts of Mental Health and Consultation*. Washington, D.C.: U.S. Children's Bureau, 215–232, 1959.

Jacobson, S. R. "The Psychiatric Social Worker as Visiting Case Consultant to Community Social Agencies." *Journal of Psychiatric Social Work, 22,* 98–104, 1953.

Jaques, E. *The Changing Culture of a Factory*. New York: Dryden, 1952.

———. "Social Therapy: Technocracy or Collaboration." *Journal of Social Issues, 3(2),* 59–66, 1947.

Jarvis, Paul E. and Sherman E. Nelson. "Familiarization: A Vital Step in

Mental Health Consultation." *Community Mental Health Journal, 3*
(*4*), 343–348, 1967.

Kampmeier, R. H. "The Psychiatric Consultation in the General Hospital."
Southern Medical Journal, 59, 979–980, August 1966.

Karp, H. Neil and James M. Karls. "Combining Crisis Therapy and Mental
Health Consultation." *Archives of General Psychiatry, 14(5)*, 536–
542, 1966.

Katrit, Ron. "The School Psychologist and Mental Hygiene." *Mental Hygiene,* July 1968.

Kauffman, I. "The Role of the Psychiatric Consultant." *American Journal
of Orthopsychiatry, 26,* 223–234, 1956.

Kaufman, P. "Consultation Services." *International Psychiatric Clinics, 3,*
123–139, Fall 1966.

Kazanjian, V., Sherry Stein and W. L. Weinberg. "An Introduction to
Mental Health Consultation." *Public Health Monographs, 69,* 1962.

Kearney, T. R. "Psychiatric Consultations in a General Hospital." *British
Journal of Psychiatry, 112,* 1237–1240, December 1966.

Kendall, K. "Commitment, Communication and Co-operation: The Essence
of School-Agency Relations." *Social Casework,* January 1967.

Kevin, D. "Use of Group Method in Consultation." In L. Rapoport (ed.),
Consultation in Social Work Practice. New York: National Association
of Social Workers, 1963, 69–84.

Kidneigh, J. "The Philosophy of Administrative Process and the Role of
the Consultant." *Public Health Nursing, 43,* 474–478, 1951.

Kimball, S. T., Marion Pearsall, and Jane A. Bliss. "Consultants and Citizens: A Research Relationship." *Human Organization, 13(1)*, 5–8,
1954.

Klaes, M. M. "Consultant Service for School Nurses." *Public Health Nursing, 40,* 195–198, 1948.

Klein, D. C. "The Prevention of Mental Illness." *Mental Hygiene, 45,* 101–
109, 1961.

Klessman, E. "Pediatrician and Consultation in Education." *Prax Kinder-
psychol., 15,* 60–62, February–March 1966.

Kline, M. V. and R. Cummings. "A Study of the Learning Characteristics
of Public Health Nurses in Relation to Mental Health Education and
Consultation." *Journal of Social Psychology, 42,* 43–60, 1955.

Kuhn, R. "Surgeon and Psychiatrist." *Praxis, 56,* 381–384, March 1967.

Kysar, J. E. "The Community Psychiatrist and Large Organizations." *Mental
Hygiene, 52,* 210–217, April 1968.

Langley, Grace E. "Community Development—Republic of India." *Community Development Review, 6,* 6–23, 1957.

Laski, H. "The Limitations of the Expert." *Harpers, 162,* December 1930.

Lawler, Marcella R. *Curriculum Consultants at Work.* New York: Teachers
College, Columbia University, 1958.

———. "Raising the Level of Consultant Service." *Educational Leadership,
5,* 445–450, 1948.

———. "Role of the Consultant in Curriculum Improvement." *Educational
Leadership, 8,* 219–225. 1951.

Leader, A. L. "Social Work Consultation to Psychiatry." *Social Casework,* *38,* 22–28, 1957.

Leon, R. "A Participant-Directed Experience as a Method of Psychiatric Teaching and Consultation." *Mental Hygiene, 44,* 375–381, 1960.

Libo, Lester M. "Multiple Functions for Psychologists in Community Consultation." *American Psychologist, 21(6),* 530–531, 1966.

Libo, Lester M. and Charles Griffith. "Developing Mental Health Programs in Areas Lacking Professional Facilities: The Community Consultant Approach in New Mexico." *Community Mental Health Journal, 2 (2),* 163–169, 1966.

Lippitt, G. L. "Consulting with a National Organization: A Case Study." *Journal of Social Issues, 15,* 20–27, 1959.

———. "A Study of the Consultation Process." *Journal of Social Issues, 15,* 43–50, 1959.

Lippitt, R. "Dimensions of the Consultant's Job." *Journal of Social Issues, 15 (2),* 5–12, 1959.

Lippitt, R., Jeanne Watson and B. Westley. *The Dynamics of Planned Change: A Comparative Study of Principles and Techniques.* New York: Harcourt, Brace & Co., 1958.

Little, W. "Making the Consultant's Service Serve." *Educational Administration and Supervision, 38,* 480–485, 1952.

Lockhead, A. V. S. "Administrative Coordination in Community Development Programs." *Community Development Review, 4,* 55–61, 1957.

Loeb, M. B. "Concerns and Methods of Mental Health Consultation." *Hospital and Community Psychiatry, 19,* 111–113, April 1968.

Losty, M., H. M. Wallace, and H. Abramson. "What the Hospital Nursing Consultant Does." *American Journal of Nursing, 48,* 158–160, 1948.

Lovatt-Dolan, J. "The Law and the Consultant." *Irish Journal of Medical Science, 6,* 515–521, November 1967.

Lundstedt, S. "The Interpersonal Dimension in International Technical Assistance." *Community Development Review, 7 (1),* 75–90, 1962.

MacDonald, E. "The Super-Consultant System." *Lancet, 1,* 470–471, March 1968.

McGarry, Louis A., William J. Curran and Donald P. Kenefick. "Problems of Public Consultation in Medico-Legal Matters: A Symposium." *American Journal of Psychiatry, 125 (1),* 42–59, 1968.

McGehearty, Joyce. "The Case for Consultation." *Elementary School Guidance and Counseling, 47 (3),* 257, November 1968.

———. "Consultation and Counseling." *Elementary School Guidance and Counseling, 3 (3),* 155, March 1969.

McGregor, D. "The Staff Function in Human Relations." *Journal of Social Issues, 4 (3),* 5–22, 1948.

McGregor, D., I. Knickerbocker, M. Haire, and A. Bavelas. "The Consultant Role and Organizational Leadership: Improving Human Relations in Industry." *Journal of Social Issues, 3,* 3–54, 1948.

Macht, L. B., D. J. Scherl and J. T. English. "Psychiatric Consultation: the Job Corps Experience." *American Journal of Psychiatry, 124,* 1092–1100, February 1968.

Macht, L. B. "Education and Mental Health: New Directions for Interaction." *Elementary School Guidance and Counseling* (855) *47*, 9, May 1969.

Macht, L. B. and D. J. Scherl. *Job Corps Mental Health Consultation.* Washington, D.C.: U.S. Government Printing Office, 1967.

McIver, Pearl. "Survey of Consultant Nurses in Health Agencies." *Public Health Reports, 68,* 519–526, 1953.

Mackey, R. A. and F. R. Hassler. "Group Consultation with School Personnel." *Mental Hygiene, 50,* 416–420, July 1966.

Maddison, D. "The Changing Responsibility of the Psychiatrist." *Medical Journal of Australia, 2,* 302–306, August 1966.

———. "Psychiatric Consultation in a Public Welfare Agency." *American Journal of Orthopsychiatry, 20,* 754–764, 1950.

———. "Psychiatric Consultation in a Rural Setting." *American Journal of Orthopsychiatry, 23,* 775–784, 1953.

Maddux, J. F. "Consultation in Public Health." *American Journal of Public Health, 45,* 1424–1430, 1955.

Malez, Roger F. and David Levine. "Differences between Guidance Counsellors Who Accept and Reject Psychological Consultation." *Psychological Abstracts, 22* (*1*), 332, 1967.

Mannino, F. V. "Developing Consultation Relationships with Community Agents." *Mental Hygiene, 48* (*3*), 356–362, 1964.

Meehan, M. "Administrative Staff Consultant as a Service to the School Administration for the Improvement of Interpersonal Relations." *American Journal of Orthopsychiatry, 39* (*2*), 286, March 1969.

Mercer, M. E. "Mental Health Consultation to Child Health Protecting Agencies." *The Elements of a Community Mental Health Program.* New York: Milbank Memorial Fund, 1956, 47–56.

Miel, Alice. *Changing the Curriculum: A Social Process.* New York: Appleton-Century, 1946.

———. "How to Use Experts and Consultants." In K. D. Benne and B. Muntyan (eds.), *Human Relations in Curriculum Change.* New York: Dryden, 1951, 208–210.

Milbank Memorial Fund. *The Elements of a Community Mental Health Program.* New York: M.M.F., 1956.

Millar, T. P. "Psychiatric Consultation with Classroom Teachers." *Journal of the American Academy of Child Psychiatry, 5,* 134–144, January 1966.

Moe, E. O. "Consulting with a Community System: A Case Study." *Journal of Social Issues, 14,* 28–35, 1969.

Morphet, E. L. "What Is a Consultant?" *School Executive, 72,* 9, 1952.

Morrow, A. J. and J. R. P. French. "Changing a Stereotype in Industry." *Journal of Social Issues, 1* (*3*), 1945.

Mouw, M. "Mental Health Consultation in a Public Health Nursing Service." *American Journal of Nursing, 67,* 1447–1450, July 1967.

Mukerji, B. *Community Development in India.* Bombay: Orient Longmans, 1961.

National Institute of Mental Health. *Essential Services of the Community*

Mental Health Center: Consultation and Education. Bethesda, Maryland: N.I.M.H., 1966, 4–5.

National Training Laboratory in Group Development. "Consultation as a Training Function." *Explorations in Human Relations Training.* Washington, D.C.: National Education Association, 1953, Chap. 5.

Neuman, F. "The Use of Psychiatric Consultation by a Casework Agency." *Journal of Social Casework, 26,* 1945.

Newman, Ruth G. *Psychological Consultation in the Schools.* New York: Basic Books, 1967.

Norman, E. C. "Role of the Mental Health Consultee." *Mental Hygiene,* April 1968.

National Organization for Public Health Nursing Mental Hygiene Committee. "The Nurse Mental Health Consultant." *Public Health Nursing, 42,* 507–509, 1950.

"Nurse Mental Health Consultant: Functions and Qualifications." *Public Health Nursing, 42,* 507, 1950.

O'Connor W. J., and D. W. Morgan. "Multidisciplinary Treatment of Alcoholism, a Consultation Program for Team Coordination." *Quarterly Journal of Studies on Alcohol, 29,* 903–908, December 1968.

Oettinger, K. B. "Why a Nurse Mental Health Consultant in Public Health." *Journal of Psychiatric Social Work, 19,* 162–168, 1950.

Orton, H. "The Non-treating Consultant." *British Dental Journal, 124,* 56, January 1968.

Papanek, G. O. "Dynamics of Community Consultation." *Archives of General Psychiatry, 19,* 189–196, August 1968.

Parker, Beulah. "Psychiatric Consultation for Nonpsychiatric Professional Workers," *Public Health Monographs,* (53), 1958.

———. "Some Observations on Psychiatric Consultation with Nursery School Teachers." *Mental Hygiene, 46,* 559–566, 1962.

———. "The Value of Supervision in Training Psychiatrists for Mental Health Consultation." *Mental Hygiene, 45,* 94–100, 1961.

Perkins, G. L. "Psychiatric Consultation in Residential Treatment: The Consultant's View." *American Journal of Orthopsychiatry, 28,* 256–290, 1958.

Perkins, K. J. "Consultation Services to Public Schools by a Mental Health Team." *Mental Hygiene, 37,* 585–595, 1953.

Phillips, L. M. "What a Consultant Hopes to Accomplish." *Instructor, 66,* 19–20, March 1957.

Porter, W. H. "The Specialized Public Health Nursing Consultant in State Health Departments." *American Journal of Public Health, 41,* 13–19, 1951.

Querido, A. "The shaping of Community Mental Health Care." *British Journal of Psychiatry, 114,* 293–302, March 1968.

Quittmeyer, C. L. "Management Looks at Consultants." *Management Review, 50* (*3*), 4–10, 1961.

Reaves, W. C. "The Place of the Consultant: The School Administrator Needs the Expert for Special Problems." *Nations Schools, 41,* 24–25, 1948.

Rehage, K. J. and S. J. Heywood. "Consultant Services to Administrators." *Elementary School Journal, 53,* 131–133, November 1952.

Rice, A. K. *Productivity and Social Organization: The Ahmedabad Experiment.* London: Tavistock Publications, 1958.

Rieman, D. W. "Group Mental Health Consultation with Nurses." In L. Rapaport (ed.), *Consultation in Social Work Practice.* New York: National Association of Social Workers, 1963, 85–98.

Robbins, Paul R. and Esther C. Spencer. "A Study of the Consultation Process." *Psychiatry, 31,* 362–368, 1968.

Robbins, Paul R., Esther C. Spencer and Daniel A. Frank. *A Casebook of Consultations.* Berkeley, Calif.: California State Department of Public Health, 1969.

Rosenfeld, J. M. and G. Caplan. "Techniques of Staff Consultation in an Immigrant Children's Organization in Israel." *American Journal of Orthopsychiatry, 24,* 42–62, 1954.

Ross, M. G. *Community Organization.* New York: Harper, 1955.

Rumrill, Mary S. "The Supervisor and the Consultant." *Nursing Outlook, 5,* 164–165, 1957.

Satin, D. G. "Allocation of Mental Health Resources in a Military Setting: A Community Mental Health Approach." *Military Medicine, 132,* 698–703, September 1967.

Schowalter, John and Albert Solnit. "Child Psychiatry Consultation in a General Hospital Emergency Room." *Journal of the American Academy of Child Psychiatry, 5* (*3*), 534–551, 1966.

Schultz, Richard. "The Organization Advisor." *Personnel Journal, 48*(*2*), 139–140, February 1969.

Schumacher, H. C. "Nature of Mental Health Programs in Health and Educational Agencies under the Mental Health Act: Role of the Consultant." *American Journal of Public Health, 40,* 13–19, 1951.

Schwab, John J. *Handbook of Psychiatric Consultation.* New York: Appleton-Century-Crofts, 1968.

Schwab, J. J. and R. S. Clemmons. "Psychiatric Consultations, the Interface between Psychiatry and General Medicine." *Archives of General Psychiatry, 14,* 504–508, May 1966.

Seashore, C. and E. Van Egmond. "The Consultant-Trainer Role in Working Directly with a Total Staff." *Journal of Social Issues, 15,* 36–42, 1959.

Seney, Wilson. "Effective Use of Business Consultants." *Financial Executive,* 1963.

Shapiro, David, *et al. The Mental Health Counselor in the Community: Training of Physicians and Ministers.* Springfield: Charles C. Thomas, 1968.

Siegel, D. "Consultation: Some Guiding Principles." *Administration, Supervision and Consultation.* New York: Family Service Association of America, 1955, 98–114.

Silverio, J. S. "Learning through Consultation Abroad." *International Social Work, 3*(*4*), 23–27, 1960.

Simon, Elizabeth. "Medical Consultation in a County Welfare Department." *Public Welfare, 24,* 274–277, October 1966.

Simon, W. "Should Faculty Members Do Psychotherapy with Their Students? The Problem of Conflict of Interest." *Mental Hygiene,* January 1967.

Sofer, C. and G. Hutton. *New Ways in Management Training.* London: Tavistock Publications, 1958.

Stanley, C. M. *The Consulting Engineer.* New York: Wiley, 1961.

Stewart, L. "The State Hospital Consultant Team as an Education Instrument." *Current Psychiatric Therapies, 3,* 264–271, 1963.

Stokes, J. H. "What is a Consultant?" *Public Health Nursing, 39,* 239–245, 1947.

Stringer, Lorene. "Consultation: Some Expectations, Principles, and Skills." *Social Work, 6,* 1961.

Symposium on Preventive and Social Psychiatry. Washington, D.C.: Walter Reed Army Institute of Research, 1958.

Tanenbaum, D. E. "Establishing Psychiatric Consultation for Agency Program." *Social Casework, 32,* 196–202, 1951.

Tilles, S. "Understanding the Consultant's Role." *Harvard Business Review, 39 (6),* 87–99, 1961.

Valenstein, A. F. "Some Principles of Psychiatric Consultation." *Social Casework, 36,* 253–256, 1955.

Wagner, F. "The Psychiatrist and the Dying Hospital Patient." *Mental Hygiene,* October 1967.

Warriner, A. "The Psychiatric Social Worker as a Consultant." *Public Health Nursing, 41,* 392–397, 1949.

Webb, J. "The Specialist Consultant in a Public Health Agency." *Canadian Journal of Public Health. 59,* 155–158, April 1968.

Weld, C. (ed.). *Experiences of 202 Companies with Management Consultants.* Chicago: Dartnell, 1965.

White, Gillian. *Use of Experts by International Tribunals.* Syracuse: Syracuse University Press, 1965.

Williams, Claire T. (New York University). "The Effectiveness of Psychological Counseling with Pupils and Psychological Consultation to Teachers in Producing Changes in Pupils' Attitudes towards Authority." *Dissertation Abstracts, 28(12-A),* 4919, 1968.

Wodinsky, A. "Psychiatric Consultation with Nurses on a Leukemia Service." *Mental Hygiene, 48,* 282–287, 1964.

Wolberg, A. and E. P. Lawson. "The Training of Mental Health Consultants at the Post-Graduate Center for Psychotherapy." *International Mental Health Research Newsletter, 4,* 3, 1962.

Wolf, M. (ed.). "The Role of the Community Consultant." *Educational Sociology, 29,* 1955.

Woodward, L. E. and W. W. Arrington. "Consultation in the Planning and Expansion of Clinics." *American Journal of Orthopsychiatry, 24,* 153–164, 1954.

Wylie, H. C. and M. Sills. "Psychodynamically Oriented Procedures in School Consultation." In M. G. Gottsegen and G. B. Gottsegen (eds.), *Professional School Psychology.* New York: Grune and Stratton, 1960, 148–161.

Yamamoto, Kazuo. "Mental Health Consultation Method and the Issues in Japanese Culture." *Journal of Mental Health, 15,* 59–68, 1967.

Young, Charles, *Consultancy in Overseas Development.* London: Overseas Development Institute, 1968.

Zwick, P. A. "Special Problems in the Consultation Function of Child Guidance Clinics." *American Journal of Orthopsychiatry, 28,* 123–125, 1958.

Index

Action for Mental Health, viii
administrative consultation
  (*see* consultee-centered administrative consultation; program-centered administrative consultation)
agencies, mental health: distribution of efforts among, 47; framework, conceptual, developing a, 38–39; mission of, 35–38; philosophy of, basic 35–38; program, development of, 35–47
Armenez-Bianci case history, 328–329

Baler, Lenin A., 301 fn.
Beck, Aaron T., 186–188
Berlin, Irving, 17
Bruner, J. S., 186

Caplan, Gerald, background of, 8–17
case consultation (*see* client-centered case consultation; consultee-centered case consultation)
certificate, community mental health, 331
client-centered case consultation, 32, 109–124; assessment of problems, 112–118; follow-up, 122–124; introduction to, 109–111; process of, steps in, 111–124; recommendations of consultant, implementation of, 121–122; report on, 118–121; request for, 111–112
Coleman, Jules, 17
collaboration: differentiated from consultation, 26–28; ground rules for, 61
Commonwealth Fund, 14
communication: channels of, building, 51–53; obstacles to, 53–56
community, explorations of, 43–44

community action, mental health consultation and, 353–381
Community Mental Health Centers Act (1963), viii, ix, 4, 330
confidentiality, 94–96
consultant, mental health: as "ally" of the consumer, 357; as "ally" of the institution, 356–357; as role model, 92–93; building relationships with consultee institutions, 48–79; building relationships with consultees, 80–108; confidentiality, maintainence of, 94–96; consultees anxiety about, dealing with, 90–92; defined, 19; distortions of the, 59–61; evaluation by, 294–301; initial session, ending the, 106–108; methodological issues encountered by, 67–79; status problems, dealing with, 68–69. *See also* specialists, mental health; workers, mental health
consultation: defined, 19; differentiation from other specialized methods, 21–28; educational aspect of, 20; goals of, 29; resistance to, on part of consultees, 69. *See also* client-centered case consultation; consultee-centered administrative consultation; consultee-centered case consultation; mental health consultation; program-centered administrative consultation
consultation contract (*see* contract, consultation)
consultee-centered administrative consultation, 33–34, 265–293; building relationships with consultees, 271–274; choice of consultees, 267–269; consultant intervention, 282–292; follow-up, 292–293; initial contacts,

consultee-centered consultation (*cont'd*) 269; introduction to, 265–267; negotiations, 269; operations of the consultant, 267–293; studying the social system of the consultee institution, 274

consultee-centered case consultation, 32–33, 125–150; example of, 191–222; introduction to, 125–127; theme interference reduction techniques, 151–190; types of, 127–150

consultee-centered consultation seminar, 348–349

consultees: defined, 19; anxiety of, dealing with, 88–92; building relationships with, 80–108; changes in objectivity during a consultation unit, 308–314; characterological distortions of perception and behavior by, 142–144; confidentiality of material communicated, 94; direct personal involvement with client, 132–136; getting to know, 82–84; identification with client, 137–138; professional culture of, problems relating to, 70–79; resistance to consultation as sign of professional inadequacy, 69; self-respect of, fostering, 87–88; theme interference and, 144–150; transference and, 138–142; undue dependency among, avoidance of, 70

consumer revolt, 353–355; implications of, for mental health workers, 355

contract, consultation, 63–67; adequate communication of, to consultees, 67–68; clarification of, 94; content of, 65–66; negotiating the, 236

"critical incident" study, 314–316

Deutsch, Felix, 168, 211

education, differentiated from consultation, 23–24

evaluation, 294–329; by the practitioner, 294–301; through systematic research, 301–327

Ewalt, Jack, 16

expectation, distortions of, 54–58

feasibility, of goals, 41–43

formal training programs, 331–349

general consultation practicum, 335–341

general mental health consultation seminar, 332–335

goals, 29; feasibility of, 41–43; salience of, 40–41

Gruschka, Ruth, 301 fn.

Harvard Medical School, 12, 17, 301, 331

Harvard School of Public Health, 12, 14, 17, 301, 331

Harvey, O. J., 186

Hassol, Leonard, 301 fn.

Health Amendments Act (1955), viii

Howe, Louisa P., 301 fn.

Hutcheson, Bellenden R., 16

informal training programs, 350–352

institutions: choosing, for a consultation program, 44–45; consultee, building relationships with, 48–79

Job Corps, 17

Joint Commission on Mental Illness and Health, viii, ix, 40, 41

Kaplan, David, 301 fn.

Kennedy, John F., 4, 40, 41

Laboratory of Community Psychiatry (Harvard Medical School), 17, 331, 335, 337, 339–341

Lasker Mental Hygiene and Child Guidance Center of Hadassah (Jerusalem), 8–11

language, common, development of, 61

Lindemann, Erich, 12, 14, 15, 16

Maddux, James, 17

Mason, Edward A., 332, 348

McDonald, Thomas, 301 fn.

mediators, mental health workers as, 358–381

Mental Health Act (1946), vii

mental health agencies (*see* agencies, mental health)

Mental Health Centers Act (*see* Community Mental Health Centers Act)

mental health consultation: characteristics of, 28–30; choosing institutions for program of, 44–45; community action and, 353–381; defined, 20, 28; distribution of efforts among agencies, 47; initial contacts, promoting, 45–46; initial session, ending the, 106–108; policy statement, 78–79; program development, 35–47; training in, 330–352; types of, 30–34. *See also* client-centered case consultation; consultation; consultee-centered administrative consultation; consultee-centered case consultation; program-centered administrative consultation

Mental Hygiene Division, Massachusetts Department of Mental Health, 16–17

mission, of mental health agency, 35–38

mother-child relationship, 10–11, 13

Murray, H. A., 145

National Institute of Mental Health, vii, viii, 4, 14, 301 fn.

nurses, public health, 14–16; characteristics of units of, 71–79

Owens, Charlotte, 301 fn., 331

perception, distortions of, 54–58

philosophy, basic, of mental health agency, 35–38

Plaut, Thomas F. A., 301 fn.

Postman, L., 186

practicum: general consultation, 335–341; specialized, 349

program, mental health agency, development of, 35–47

program-centered administrative consultation, 33, 223–264; consultant's recommendations, 247–259; consultation report, 259–263; continuing contact with the director, 254–255; fact finding, 240–247; follow-up, 263–264; initial agreement, negotiating the, 231–233; introduction to, 223–224; preliminary contacts, 231; preparation for the consultation visit, 234–236; procedure, 231–264

psychotherapy: avoidance of, 97–106; differentiated from consultation, 24–26

Rapaport, D., 186

Redl, Fritz, 379

reduction, theme interference (*see* theme interference reduction)

relationships, building: between consultant and consultee institution, 48–79; between consultant and consultees, 80–108; fundamental issues in, 84–108

research, systematic, evaluation through, 301–327

Rogers, Carl, 12

salience, of goals, 40–41

Sarbin, T. R., 186

seminar: consultee-centered consultation, 348–349; general mental health consultation, 332–335

specialists, mental health: contacts with other caregiving persons, 5–7, 14–15, 20–21, 30; role of, successive stages in, 62–63; shortage of, 3, 4. *See also* consultant, mental health; workers, mental health

status problems, dealing with, 68–69

supervision: differentiated from consultation, 22; training and, 340, 341–348, 349

Thematic Apperception Test, 145

"theme interference," 15, 144–150

theme interference reduction, 16; evaluation of process of, 307–308; in a group, 184–186; nonspecific, 303; rationale of, 186–190; specific, 304; techniques of, 151–190

Thom, Douglas, 16

training, 330–352; formal programs, 331–349; informal programs, 350–352; supervision and, 340, 341–348, 349

"unlinking," 10, 13, 304–305

Vaughan, Warren, 16

Wellesley Human Relations Service, 12–13

Whittier Street Family Guidance Center (Boston), 14

Whittier Street Health Center (Boston), 14–16

workers, mental health: alternative roles for, 356–380; as consultants for both the institution and the consumer, 358; as mediators, 358–381. *See also* consultant, mental health; specialists, mental health

Yolles, Stanley F., vii

Youth Aliyah organization, 8–11, 13, 14